TOPICS IN

African Diaspora

HISTORY

Edited by JIM C. HARPER II | CHARLES D. JOHNSON | TONY A. FRAZIER | JARVIS L. HARGROVE

North Carolina Central University

Kendall Hunt
publishing company

Cover image courtesy of Thomas Massey

www.kendallhunt.com
Send all inquiries to:
4050 Westmark Drive
Dubuque, IA 52004-1840

CONTENTS

FOREWORD

One of the great rewards for a professor is to have had students who not only have been influenced by him, but to witness their collaboration in preparation of an important publication such as this one. The credit in this case is all theirs, as they extend the continuum to the next level of study.

Several things distinguish and commend this volume. First, the field it represents, the African Diaspora, is still in its academic infancy. It emerged at a time in the 1950s and 1960s when neither African nor African American studies existed as a field of study recognized in the U.S. colleges or universities. While a few African American colleges offered a course or two about African Americans, Professor William Leo Hansberry established several courses in African studies at Howard in 1922, convened a Pan-African symposium on Africa there in 1925, and continued the program until the formal establishment of the university's African Studies Program in 1954. Hansberry's long-range objective envisioned a "Varia Africana" program that would challenge the deeply ingrained misconceptions about Africa, Africans, and people of African ancestry generally.

In 1954, the Ford Foundation awarded grants to Howard, Boston, and Northwestern Universities to establish programs in African Studies. While none of these programs included African American courses, Hansberry continued to promote a Pan-African perspective in the study of Africans and communities of African descent abroad. The simultaneous development of the Black Studies Movement in the United States and the Caribbean enhanced that appeal among blacks in particular and thus generated greater pressure for the inclusion of African and African American studies in the academy.

In 1965, United Nations Educational, Scientific and Cultural Organization (UNESCO) and Tanzania hosted the First Congress of African Historians that was designed to reinterpret African history and to establish it as a legitimate academic field of study. One of the consequences that emerged from that Congress was the presentation of a panel entitled, the "Africans Abroad or the African Diaspora." After considerable debate, UNESCO approved the African Diaspora as a legitimate theme in the reinterpretation of African history. That decision linked Africa and its Diaspora in the subsequent publication of the eight-volume *General History of Africa* that appeared in Arabic, English, French, Spanish, and Portuguese as well as in condensed versions in a number of African languages. In 2013, UNESCO convened a planning committee to revise and update those earlier volumes, and to prepare a separate volume on the African Diaspora.

The confluence of those early developments had a great impact on this historian who organized the First African Diaspora Studies Institute in 1979 that convened over a hundred delegates from Africa, Europe, the United States, and the Caribbean at Howard University. The Second African Diaspora Studies Institute convened in 1981 at the University of Nairobi in Kenya with nearly a hundred delegates from Africa, the United States, and Brazil. The agenda for both of those Institutes was to encourage the promotion of research and teaching of African Diaspora studies and the development of repositories as well as academic and public programs in educational institutions. Subsequent communication confirmed that new and expanded courses on the African Diaspora were developed in a number of countries.

Although earlier movements to promote research and teaching African Diaspora studies in the United States generally are better known, less well-known but significant developments occurred in South America where Abdias Nascimento (Brazil), Manuel Zapata Olivella (Colombia), and others organized several seminars on blacks in that region. Especially noteworthy was the International Seminar: Research and Teaching in Afro-South American Studies that met in Colombia in 1986. And in 2005, Brazil hosted the Association for the Study of the Worldwide African Diaspora. Finally, The African Diaspora in Asia (TADIA) convened in Goa, India, in 2009.

These initiatives and the introduction of courses and programs across disciplines clearly demonstrate the emergence of the concept and application of the global African Diaspora perspective. They also affirm a consciousness of identity that requires a new orientation in the study of Africans, their extensions and impact abroad.

Thus, *Topics in African Diaspora History* is timely and takes its place as a milestone in the study of Africa and communities of African descent worldwide.

Professor of History Emeritus
Howard University
July 2016

PREFACE

Topics in African Diaspora History is a diverse body of various themes in the study of the African Diaspora. These themes include African Nationalism, Resistance, Pan-Africanism, Spirituality, Black Power and Transnationalism and they cover a broad spectrum of the Diaspora experience that spans across the globe. In writing this text, our goal is to provide more perspectives of the stories of the economic, political, religious, and social impact of Africans and people of African descent around the world from an African-centered perspective. Hence, this volume was motivated by the desire to further strengthen the study of the African Diaspora through historical methodology, theory and research. This is more than a book about the African Diaspora; it is a collection of essays that depict the stories of a people who transcended the physical, mental and emotional realities of very brutal environments in which they survived. For purposes of this text, we are defining the African Diaspora as the dispersal of people of African descent to a location around the world (involuntary or voluntary) where they developed diasporic identities in their new locations and their eventual return or connection to their homeland of Africa.

This edited volume came to fruition as the result of a conversation that I had with my colleagues, Charles Johnson, Jarvis Hargrove and Tony Frazier, regarding the connections in our research and the study of the African Diaspora. We acknowledged that our research was inspired by the work of our former professors/mentors: Dr. Joseph E. Harris, Dr. Sylvia M. Jacobs and Dr. Aziz Batran. Their research in African and African Diaspora history has greatly opened the field for further research and we are grateful for the opportunity to have had the opportunity to learn from such a group of outstanding scholars and educators. For that we are eternally thankful. The legacies of our professors in the field of African Diaspora prepared and provided us with the framework that led us to bring together a group of African Diaspora scholars to compile the articles in this book.

I would like to acknowledge the contributors for their research, which culminates in this text that seeks to broaden the scope and perspectives of the African Diaspora experience. Their research for this text is fundamental to studying the African Diaspora from a global perspective. Those contributors are: Sheila Walker (Executive Director, Afrodiaspora, Inc.), Jarvis Hargrove (North Carolina Central University), Takeia Anthony (Edward Waters College), Yaba Blay (Dan Blue Endowed Professor, North Carolina Central University), Charles Johnson (North Carolina Central University), Azaria Mbughuni (Lane College), Tony Frazier (North Carolina Central University), Iyelli Ichille (Florida A&M University), Quito Swan (Howard University), Msomi Moor (University of the District of Columbia), Pedro Rivera (Savannah State University), Jim C. Harper, II (North Carolina Central University), Neo Lekgotla laga Ramoupli (Council on Higher Education), Nina Smith (North Carolina Central University), and Milagros Denis (Hunter College, CUNY).

The photography on the cover and the interior of this text is the statue of a man with a chain around his neck which depicts the imagery of an enslaved person. In taking a closer look you will see that there is a broken link in the chain. As you know, during the colonial period millions of Africans were brought to various parts of the world in chains. The stories within this text illuminate the resistance, struggles and triumphs of a people of African descent who are breaking every chain through social, economic, spiritual and cultural cohesion. They are creating spaces where their voices can be heard, where they have positive identities, and where they are safe despite all of the forces of imperialism. The chains are breaking.

INTRODUCTION

A HISTORICAL AND THEORETICAL OVERVIEW OF THE AFRICAN DIASPORA

Charles D. Johnson

GLOBAL AFRICAN DIASPORA

It might come as a surprise to some that the presence of peoples of African ancestry is essentially global. Scholars refer to this global presence of communities of peoples of African descent as the Global African Diaspora. Through a series of essays, this book introduces readers to different aspects of the African Diaspora. Over the past two decades a lot has been written about the African Diaspora, and the expression itself has become commonplace.[1] This was not always the case. The study of the African Diaspora emerged from the study of African history, which remains the essential cornerstone of the field. Howard University has played a leading role in promoting the study of the African Diaspora. This is due in no small part to the pioneering research and work of Joseph E. Harris, Distinguished Professor Emeritus of History at Howard University and "Dean of African Diaspora Studies". Certainly, Harris was not alone in pioneering the field, but he was on the forefront of the push to establish the African Diaspora as a legitimate field of scholarly inquiry within the academy. At Howard University, he taught his students that Africa was the most important part of the African Diaspora. This volume is written in recognition of his contribution and serves to honor his legacy.

This introductory essay gives a theoretical and historical overview of the African Diaspora, which as an academic pursuit should be utilized as a tool for understanding how peoples of African descent are connected through ties of blood, culture, and experience. In its simplest interpretation, a diaspora is a community, and there are numerous types of diasporas. The African Diaspora is our subject and unless otherwise stated references to diaspora are referring to the African Diaspora. The African Diaspora conveys the idea of movement because African people are a people on the move, whether in the form of migration, travel, dance, or cultural

---

[1] Since it was examined by Shepperson and Harris at the International Conference of African Historians in Dar es Salaam, Tanzania in 1965 during the session, *Emerging Themes in African History*, there have been several subsequent conferences that have discussed the Global African Diaspora and contributed to its development as a concept. Harris organized two conferences on the diaspora, FADSI I and FADSII, whose papers were ultimately published in *Global Dimensions of the African Diaspora*, 1982; a second edition, 1993, with papers from the second conference was also published. There are numerous themes and sub-themes relevant to the Global African Diaspora.

exchange. When viewed along the routes of passage and lines of communication that connect one diaspora to another, the global dimensions of the African Diaspora emerge. People of African descent can be found on every habitable continent. It is necessary to emphasize this point because it is not widely known. Diasporas start with movement, the voluntary or involuntary migration of a segment of a people from their homeland to what Joseph E. Harris referred to as a new hostland. A hostland is a general term used to describe the landing places of Africans as they migrated from Africa. Once in those new hostlands, they went through a period of cultural adaption that transformed their self-conception from one rooted in Africa to one blended with many cultures. Culture is the collective expression of our values, beliefs, worldview, language, sense of time, the food we eat, how we prepare our food, and even our forms of entertainment.

ORIGIN OF THE ACADEMIC USAGE OF THE CONCEPT

Elliott Skinner traces the origin of the expression diaspora to the dispersal of the Jews during their periods of captivity.[2] George Shepperson suggests that there are references to the concept of diaspora in the Holy Bible similar to those of the Jews.[3] However, he is uncertain whether the biblical concept informed the academic usage of the expression diaspora with regard to the voluntary and involuntary migration of Africans. Clearly, though there are similarities between the exile experiences of the Jews at the hands of various aggressors and the experiences of people of African descent during the slave trade, enslavement, and colonialism. Shepperson ultimately traces the origin of the African Diaspora to the nineteenth century as a political response to white supremacy. "It is to this period that the origin of the African Diaspora, with its emphasis on the positive contribution of black men and women to world history, may be traced."[4]

By all indications, the development of the African Diaspora concept is part of the larger movement by black scholars to "vindicate" or legitimize African history as a preparatory step in the overall process of challenging western-hegemonic ideology that recognized Blacks only as inferiors and held them to be less than human. The concept also derived from the need for Blacks to explain the creation and development of communities of Africans outside of the

---

[2] Elliott Skinner, "The Dialects between Diaspora and Homelands," in Global Dimensions of the African Diaspora, 2nd ed., ed. Joseph E. Harris (Washington, DC: Howard University Press, 1993), 11–12. References to the dispersal of the Jews are found throughout the Holy Bible. See for instances, II Kings Chapters 25:1–5, which chronicles the coming of Nebuchadnezzar and the Dispersal the inhabitants of Jerusalem. Also see, I Chronicles 6:15: "And Jehozadak went tino capacity, when the Lord carried away Judah and Jerusalem by the hand of Nebuchadnezzar."

[3] George Shepperson, "African Diaspora: Concept and Context," in *Global Dimensions in the African Diaspora*, 2d ed., ed. Joseph E. Harris (Washington, DC: Howard University Press, 1993), 41. Shepperson refers to biblical quotes such as Psalms 68:31, "Ethiopia shall soon stretch out her hands unto God" before mentioning a few works from the 19th century, such as, Robert B. Lewis, *Light and Truth: Collected from the Bible and Ancient and Modern History, Containing the Universal History of the Colored and Indian Race, from the Creation of the World to the Present Time* (1844), that discussed Africans in a diaspora context without making specific reference to the term.

[4] Ibid., 43. Shepperson points to William Wells Barnett's, *The Rising Son; or the Antecedents and Advancement of the Colored Race*; and an address by Edward Blyden entitled, "Ethiopia Stretching Out Her Hands unto God; or, Africa's Service to the World," as examples of early manifestations of the origin of the African Diaspora.

continent of Africa and their relationship to one another. Thus, the African Diaspora is both a physical reality formed out of willful and coerced migrations of African people off the continent of Africa, and it is an intellectual concept that helps us to interpret and comprehend history and experiences of the global presence of people of African descent.

Shepperson opined that it was during the period when continental Africans and Diaspora Africans were cooperating to combat colonialism and racial discrimination that the academic usage of the expression "African Diaspora" came into use. He specifically, points to the period between the founding of the Society of African Culture (SAC) in 1956 and the International Congress of African Historians in 1965. During the Congress of African Historians held in Dar es Salaam, Tanzania, the expression appeared twice during the session *Emerging Themes in African History*: in Shepperson's, "The African Abroad or the African Diaspora" and in Joseph E. Harris', "Introduction to the African Diaspora".[5]

In the 1950s, African nations began to win independence from European colonial powers. The emergence of these new states in a world then divided along a West/East Axis posed challenges to Western elites concerning where these emerging states would enter the global arena: on the West with the United States and its allies or on the East with the Soviet Union and the communist bloc countries. A desire to have a better handle on how these new African nations might be brought into the capitalist fold was a driving influence among western scholars in the development of the serious academic study of Africa and its history. Prior to that time, Africa was studied as an extension of European empires, e.g., the British Colonial Africa and French West Africa, etc.

Shortly thereafter, western academicians began posing questions about communities of peoples of African descent living outside of the continent of Africa. Serious implications informed their initial questions because peoples of African descent formed large segments of societies in the West. How might these descendants of Africans relate to those that were emerging from colonialism? Such questions proved particularly vexing because in the United States, for example, African Americans were still struggling to overturn Jim Crow, the United States' peculiar brand of domestic colonialism.

In 1965, at the International Congress of African Historians in Dar es Salaam, Tanzania, George Shepperson presented a paper entitled, "Africans Abroad or the African Diaspora." He was perhaps the first scholar to apply diaspora to the experiences of peoples of African descent in an academic context. Shepperson was not the first scholar to raise such questions about Africans living in communities geographically separated from Africa. W.E.B. DuBois, Carter G. Woodson, William Leo Hansberry, and Melville Herskovits amongst other researchers had previously done so.[6]

Shepperson presented "Africans Abroad or the African Diaspora" and Harris, who was just starting his career as a historian, gave comments. Shepperson was already a seasoned

---

[5] Shepperson, "African Diaspora: Concept and Context," 41.

[6] Herskovits was an anthropologist by training and performed decades of field research on African peoples both on the continent of Africa and in the Diaspora. Herskovits trained at Columbia University before accepting a position at Howard University in 1925. He would finish his career at Northwestern University, where he established both the Anthropology Department and the Program of African Studies. Joseph E. Harris, a graduate of Howard University, would later earn his doctorate at Northwestern.

professional. In 1958, he had published *Independent African: John Chilembwe, the Origin, Setting, Significance of the Nyasaland Native Uprising of 1915* which told the story of a Christian-educated African who had received his education for the ministry at Virginia Theological Seminary and College (VTSC). Chilembwe adopted the rebellious spirit of his African American counterparts at VTSC. He returned to his native land and started a blood revolution for liberation from German colonialism fashioned in a similar form as John Brown's heroic effort to liberate enslaved African Americans. "Africa for the Africans" was the battle cry of Chilembwe's revolutionists, a philosophy Joseph Booth, a radical white Baptist missionary and former confident, had earlier taught him. In the wake of the African independence movements, Shepperson pondered what Chilembwe learned from African Americans that set him on a revolutionary trajectory. Such questions fall between African history and African American history because they are relevant to both. The study of the African Diaspora fills that gap. Students of African Diaspora history are interested in connections between Diasporas and homelands as well as the cultural continuities and differences from the homeland that have developed among Africans living in a new hostland, such as Brazil or Panama, for example. Diaspora researchers are curious about how Africans in their new communities adapt to their new environment.

GLOBAL AFRICAN DIASPORA AS CONCEPT: DISPERSAL, SETTLEMENT, AND RETURN

There are numerous definitions of African Diaspora. We have already learned that as an academic pursuit it is a tool for understanding how people of African descent are related in terms of blood, culture, and experience. Joseph E. Harris defined the African Diaspora as "a triadic relationship linking a dispersed group of people to the homeland, Africa, and to their host or adopted countries."[7] Harris also says that diasporas share certain characteristics, including collective memories and myths about Africa as a place of origin, a common socio-economic condition, a transnational network (formal and informal) that links the diasporic communities, a sustained resistance to their presence abroad by other groups and an affirmation of their human rights.[8] Harris maintains that the Global African Diaspora comprises three essential and interdependent phases. The first phase is dispersal or voluntary and involuntary migration of Africans from Africa to a new hostland. The next phase is settlement, whereby Africans adapt to their new communities removed from Africa, and the final phase is the process by which Africans in the diaspora reconnect with the continent of Africa either on an emotional/spiritual level or literally in making a physical return to Africa.

Dispersal: Voluntary and Involuntary Migrations

So then, how is it that peoples of African descent have come to be scattered deliberately across great geographical distances? The answer is found in the voluntary and involuntary migrations of Africans to every habitable continent around the world. It may be well at this

---

[7] Joseph E. Harris, "Introduction to the African Diaspora" in *Global Dimension of the African Diaspora*, (Washington, DC: Howard University Press, 1993).

[8] Ibid.

point to remind readers that humanity was born on the continent of Africa, that these first Homo Sapiens looked phenotypically African, and that these early humans populated the rest of the world starting from their home in the Great Lakes region of Africa. These outward migrations of humans from Africa started approximately 100,000 years ago and continue on to the present date.[9]

African Diaspora scholarship emphasizes involuntary migrations over voluntary migrations because of the magnitude, contemporaneity, and far-reaching consequences of the Atlantic Slave Trade or European Dominated Trade in African Peoples. However, as noted above, the outward-voluntary migration of African people is thousands of years old. Africans were in what became the Americas long before Christopher Columbus. In 1922, Leo Wiener, a Harvard University Professor of Slavic Languages and Literature, penned a three-volume set of histories entitled, *Africa and the Discovery of America*. In them, Wiener assessed the presence of American tobacco, cotton, and shell-money in Africa prior to 1492 or, as he states, "previous to the *so-called* discovery of America by Columbus."[10]

Wiener's pioneering exposition was popularized most recently by Ivan van Sertima, a Guyana-born anthropologist and author of several works on the pre-Columbian presence of Africans in the America's. *They Came Before Columbus: The African Presence in Ancient America* is perhaps the most widely read book on the subject. Not without it detractors, *They Came Before Columbus* challenges the idea that Africans arrived in the Americas only as a result of European agency. Van Sertima expands the focus of his evidence from crops and money to include ship building, navigation, cultural analogies, diaries and letters from the European explorers in the Americas, recorded tales from the griots to the court of the kings of Mali, and archeological findings in the Americas. He argues that Africans made at least two significant periods of contact with peoples in the Americas before the coming of Columbus. Perhaps his most compelling piece of evidence is the stone heads associated with the Olmec culture and located in Tres Zapotes. The features of the huge stone sculpture exemplify strong African features including pronounced lips, full eyes, and strong cheek bones. The seven-braided hairstyle depicted on the back of the heads of the sculptures is common among certain West African groups and is foreign to Native Americans. Van Sertima points to the Olmec culture as being distinctly African and the oldest culture in the Americas. Other parts of the world follow a similar pattern of early African occupation.

---

[9] Cheikh Anta Diop, combating racist anthropology from the previous century, proposed that thousands 40,000 years ago, the first Homo Sapiens Sapiens, a black skinned humanoid he labeled Grimaldi Man, migrated from Africa to the other continents and was thus the progenitor of the other races. See Diop, *Civilization to Barbarism: An Authentic Anthropology* (Brooklyn, NY: Lawrence Hill Books, 1991). Raymond Dart and other anthropologists proposed that humans originated in Africa. See *Africa's Place in the Emergence of Civilization* (Johannesburg: South African Broadcasting Corporation, 1959) or Louis S. B. Leakey, *The Progress and Evolution of Man in Africa* (London: Oxford University Press, 1961). Leakey also found one of the earliest recorded hominid skeleton in East Africa. He named his find Lucy. See, Donald C. Johanson and Maitland A. Edey, *Lucy, the Beginnings of Humankind* (New York, NY: Warner Books, 1981).

[10] Wiener intimates that his work on this subject was not well received by anthropologists. See, Leo Wiener, *Africa and the Discovery of America* ([NP]: Innes & Sons, 1922; reprint, New York: A & B Books Publishers, 1992), unnumbered forward by Wiener.

In Asia, people with African ancestry known as Negrito can be found in Thailand, Malaysia, the Andaman Islands, and the Philippines. The Pacific realm including Melanesia, Australia, New Zealand, Tasmania, and Hawaii also have or have had in their past populations of people with African ancestry. Quito Swan's research in Melanesia, for instance, reveals that African descendants in Vanuatu self-identify as having an African origin. So, voluntary migrations by Africans to other areas of the world are themselves ancient.[11]

THE SLAVE TRADE TO THE ORIENT (EAST)

Tragically, the most significant migrations out of Africa in the last 500 years have been involuntary, in the form of the occidental and Oriental slave trades. Although considerable emphasis has been given to the westward migration, the involuntary movement of Africans towards the East is much older. In 1971, in a ground-breaking work entitled *The African Presence in Asia: Consequences of the East African Slave Trade*, Joseph E. Harris found that Arab and later Islamic slave traders carried Africans from the Horn of Africa to work in what is today the Middle East. He also located communities of people of African ancestry in the southern Arabian Peninsula, in southern India, where they worked as pearl divers, and in Turkey. Patrick Manning established that although men, women, and children were taken into the Oriental Trade, young women represented the largest number of captives. These women were deposited among the harems of the wealthy Islamic leaders in the Arabian Peninsula, where they were forced into concubinage or prostitution. African boys were frequently captured and castrated in order to make eunuchs who were responsible for tending to the needs of the harems. Having been deprived of their male anatomy, they were incapable of impregnating the women in the harem though still capable of being intimate with them. Some eunuchs rose to levels of influence because of their position as mediators between the harem and the Islamic ruler who owned the harem.[12]

THE ATLANTIC SLAVE TRADE

The trade of African men and women to the occident or West got a later start than did the Oriental trade, but the magnitude of the trade and the consequent effects of transporting large numbers of Africans out of one set of societies and forcing them into another had a significant impact on both sides of the Atlantic. African societies were frequently raided of the flower of

---

[11] See Ivan van Sertima, *They Came Before Columbus: The African Presence in Ancient America* (New York: Random House, 1976). For an oppositional perspective see, Kenneth Feder, *Frauds, Myths, and Mysteries: Science and Pseudoscience in Archeology* (Mountain View, CA: Mayfield Publishing Company, 1990). Feder and others challenge Van Sertima on the grounds that his work was biased because he made a diffusionist argument, claiming knowledge flowed from a "more advanced" African societies to less advanced Native American societies. Quito Swan, "Melanesia's Way: Black Interationalism in the South Pacific", lecture at the Sonya Hayes Stone Center at the University of North Carolina at Chapel Hill, February 4, 2016.

[12] A seminal work on Africans in Asia is Joseph E. Harris, *The African Presence in Asia: Consequences of the East African Slave Trade* (Evanston: Northwestern University Press, 1971). Patrick Manning, *Slavery and African Life: Occidental, Oriental, and African Slavery* (Cambridge: Cambridge University Press, 1990).

their youth, many of whom were sent to labor in the Americas, Europe, and even other parts of Africa. Once in their new environments, Africans were forced to make the necessary adjustments to survive. This multilayered process of adaptation and acculturation revealed temporal and spatial differences because of a multitude of influences, such as the racial demographics of the communities into which the captives were being taken as well as the types of labor in which the enslaved people were engaged. Nevertheless, it was during this process that people of African descent begin to create new identities based in part on wedding the memory of their ancestral home with the realities of their day-to-day lives. Differences in culture among enslaved Africans regardless of time, geographical location, or their relative proximity to one another was never so great that they could not communicate with one another. Perhaps complex expressions were difficult but basic forms of communication could be ascertained from gestures or even facial expressions. Even where aspects of their respective cultures were at variance, enslavement provided the sinew that bound people with distinct ethnicities into a single group of peoples we refer to today as African.

Scholars differ over the origin of the Atlantic slave trade.[13] Certainly, the desire to obtain species and gold from the East set the Europeans on a course of exploration, adventure, and rapine that would last for 500 years. Wars in Europe and the Christian Crusades had depleted the supply of gold in Europe. Christian warriors returned from conflicts in the Holy Lands with precious goods from India and China. Were it not for the empire of the Ottoman Turks, one could question whether a sea route to the Indies would have been as eagerly sought after in Europe as it in fact was. That the Muslim-Turkish Empire sat firmly and defiantly in the lands between Christian Europe and the East all but assured that Europeans would have to find a sea route to the markets that they sought.

Columbus' voyage under the flag of the Spanish crowns of Aragon and Castile in 1492 was monumental for many reasons, not the least of which being that it confirmed for the Europeans that there was land to the west across the Atlantic Ocean that they had neither charted nor claimed. Spain was stunned when Portugal made a claim to Columbus' "discovery."[14] Controversy over the division of foreign lands would become a re-occurring theme in the annals of European and African history. In 1493, Spain and Portugal agreed to arbitration by the Pope, who in a series of papal bulls conveniently divided the "new world" along an East/West axis: Spain's rights were to lands in the West, while Portugal's were to those in the

---

[13] See, Walter Rodney, *A History of the Upper Guinea Coast, 1945–1800* (Oxford: Oxford University Press, 1980). Rodney argues that the Portuguese were able to establish a trading monopoly in the region that they maintained with items that were difficult for Africans to obtain elsewhere and with superior force of arms. He places the blame for the origin of the trade on the Europeans. See also, John Thornton, *Africa and Africans in the Making of the Atlantic World, 1400–1800* 2nd (Cambridge: Cambridge University Press, 1990). Thornton disagrees. Thornton contends that initially the Portuguese did not establish trading monopolies because they did not have the military capability to do so. He further argues that Africans had direct access to many of the items that the Portuguese were hoping to exchange. In effect, he argues that Africans played a more eager and active participatory role in the Atlantic Slave Trade than scholars have previously considered. Scholars have also argued that Bishop Bartholomew De Las Casas was a principle cause of Africans being brought as substitutes for the Native Americans who were dying in large numbers. Today, all things considered, his suggestion seems to be more inevitability than a causative idea.

[14] Williams, 3. Portugal claimed ownership of Columbus' "discovery" based on a papul bull of 1455 that authorized her to compel infidel peoples into servitude.

East. Portugal was not satisfied with this distribution and importuned until the two countries agreed on the Treaty of Tordesillas, which gave the Portuguese rights to the lucrative territory of Brazil where they could grow their lucrative sugarcane. Of course, when it came to the division of potentially profitable lands, papal bulls had little currency among the other European powers, and it was only a matter of time before Columbus' "discovery" set the stage for a global competition between rival European countries over the control of land and valuable natural resources that would last the better part of five hundred years, 1490s–2000s.[15]

Portuguese sailors began taking Africans from the Guinea coast as early as the 15th century. In June 1466, the Portuguese crown granted a charter to Portuguese settlers in Cape Verde that "gave them absolute rights over Africans, and granting them exclusive license to trade on the adjacent mainland."[16] By the sixteenth century, the Portuguese were taking Africans from a region they referred to as "the Guinea of Cape Verde," the area between the Gambia and Cape Mount.[17] Initially, captives were taken to the islands of Cape Verde and the Iberian Peninsula, while Madeira and the Canary Islands were secondary markets. Columbus' "discoveries" shifted the epicenter of Iberian interest from the Mediterranean and the islands of the mid-Atlantic to Hispaniola and South and Central America.[18] Over the course of the next four centuries, the Atlantic slave trade grew in magnitude as well as European participation. All of the great nations of Europe during that period would come to have some bearing on the trade. Although the early years of the trade were dominated by Portugal and Spain, the French, the Dutch, the English, and even the United States would eventually participate in the trade.

In 1510, King Ferdinand of Spain authorized fifty Africans to be taken to Hispaniola to replace the indigenous laborers who were dying from European diseases as well as from the exacting demands of avaricious Spanish settlers. Africans were immune to many European diseases and endured the hardships better than the Indians. Therefore, in 1518 the King of Spain authorized transporting 4,000 African captives to the new Spanish colonies in the Americas.[19]

Portuguese contacts with Africans in the "Guinea of Cape Verde" exposed them to the possibility of using Africans as laborers in their new colonies. With what must have seemed to the Portuguese and Spanish of that day like an unlimited source of farmland and precious stones, the source of labor was the only question remaining to be answered. That it would be coerced labor, servants or slaves, was fait accompli. To the early slave traders and imperialists, the proximity of Africans to the colonies in the Americas, their familiarity with the types of

---

[15] Henry VIII of England separated from the Catholic Church and formed the Church of England because the Pope refused to grant him a divorce. He placed himself at the head of the Church of England. England therefore did not follow the papul bulls as an authority for the division of new lands. In 1580, the English government established the concept of "effective occupation." It required that to be sovereign over an area, the European country who laid claim to that land had to actually occupy and use it. The sovereignty of Autochthons could be challenged on the grounds that they were infidels.

[16] Rodney, 74.

[17] Ibid.

[18] Ibid, 95.

[19] A good examination of the Spanish occupation of the Indies can be found in Bishop Bartolomew de las Casas, *A Brief Account of the Destruction of the Indies Or, a faithful NARRATIVE OF THE Horrid and Unexampled Massacres, Butcheries, and all manner of Cruelties, that Hell and Malice could invent, committed by the Popish Spanish Party on the inhabitants of West-India, TOGETHER With the Devastations of several Kingdoms in America by Fire and Sword, for the space of Forty and Two Years, from the time of its first Discovery by them.*

crops that the Europeans wanted to harvest, their presumed immunity to tropical diseases, and their obvious physical differences set Africans apart from the Native Americans and Europeans as the best possible answer to satisfy their insatiable appetite for inexpensive labor. European slave traders or slavers shipped Africans as cargo to the Americas. This Kafkaesque journey is known as The Middle Passage.

THE MIDDLE PASSAGE

The Middle Passage is inextricably interwoven with the African Diaspora.[20] It is a part of the collective conscious of Africans in the Americas who have a fascination with it as the conveyance that tore their ancestors from their homelands and hurled them unapologetically onto America's unfriendly shores. When taken together with their cruel experience in slavery, its meaning is magnified, part of a permanent and hard-hearted symbol of their collective suffering that signifies the horrible consequences of humanities' inhumanity run amuck.

The Middle Passage often began in the African interior, where slave raiders kidnapped unsuspecting victims who they overpowered and forced through violence to submit. Africans did not merely acquiesce. They fought back with courage and resolve, and where that failed they attempted to run away. Africans did not volunteer for the Atlantic slave trade because it lay at the deepest and hottest depths of Dante Alighieri's *Inferno*. The most common method of becoming enslaved was to be taken as a prisoner of war and then sold into the slave trade. As the trade expanded, more elaborate means were created to produce captives for the trade. For instance, in Dahomey, court rulings could be handed down that bound the guilty to be sold into the slave trade. Thus, as punishment for certain severe crimes such as rape, murder, or adultery, a person could end up enslaved. Not paying taxes, not paying tribute, or not paying off debts were also used as justifications for enslaving people.[21]

Africans were captured or collected in different areas. Michael Gomez divides the slave trading areas of densest concentration on the West African coast into six zones: Senegambia, Sierra Leone (Pepper Coast), Gold Coast, Bight of Benin (Slave Coast), Bight of Biafra, and West Central Africa. Europeans named some of the coastal zones by the principal items of trade in that region.[22] The region that supplied the largest percentage of Africans to the Americas was West Central Africa, and the majority of those Africans went to Brazil. Brazil received the largest number of Africans out of the total volume of the trade and remains today the nation with the largest population of people with African ancestry in the western hemisphere. The Islands of the West Indies received the second largest number of Africans relative to the total

---

[20] Charles Johnson, *Middle Passage* (New York: Simon & Schuster, 1998). Johnson's historical fiction chronicles the experiences of Rutherford Calhoun, an African American stowaway on the slave ship *Republic*. It is an imaginative exploration of western avarice, African American identity, and African resistance. Robert Harms used the private journal of First Lieutenant Robert Durand to re-create that actual voyage of the French slaver *The Diligent*. See, Harms, *The Diligent: A Voyage Through the Worlds of the Slave Trade* (New York: Basic Books, 2002).
[21] Orlando Patterson, *Slavery and Social Death: A Comparative Study* (Cambridge, MA: Harvard University Press, 1982), 105.
[22] The regional divisions can be found in Michael Gomez, *Exchanging Our Country Marks: The Transformation of African Identities in the Colonial and Antebellum South* (Chapel Hill, NC: University of North Carolina Press, 1998), 27–29.

volume. West Central Africa, the coastal zone south of Cameroon that extends to the northern tip of Namibia and includes Angola and Congo, supplied 26.1 percent of the trade. The Bight of Biafra, which is located in southeastern Nigeria, supplied 24.4 percent of the trade. The Ibo ethnic group made up the largest number of Africans taken from that region. Sierra Leone, Senegambia, and the Gold Coast supplied 15.8 percent, 14.5 percent, and 13.1 percent of the trade respectively. The Bight of Benin was the smallest contributor to the trade, supplying only 4.3 percent. Over the course of the history of the trade different regions were more active than others at different times. The largest number of Africans were brought to the United States between 1721 and 1820. However, the United States received only 5 percent of the approximately 12 million Africans imported into the "New World". To put that percentage in perspective, the United States received roughly the same number of captives as the island of Barbados.[23]

Africans who were captured in the interior were chained individually and then bound at the neck by a coffle to prevent them from escaping or attempting to kill their captors. Slave trading was dangerous business, and captives had to be bound and watched at all times. Once confined, the slave traders forced them to march to a designated location along the coast. This entire process varied with time and location, as did most of the processes associated with slavery. The journey to the coast may have taken a few weeks or it may have taken several months. Distances increased over time such that by the late 18th century, for example, captives taken from Angola may have had to march 500 miles or more.[24] If waterways were accessible then the captives would travel in dugout canoes or on barges. At the coast, the captives were held in the dungeons of the European forts on the coast such as Cape Coast Castle or in make-shift wooded pins. Conditions inside the dungeons were hellish. Both men and women were stripped of their clothes, which made them feel exposed and vulnerable. Their heads were shaved to limit infections from parasites. Inside the dungeons, the tropical heat pushed temperatures above 100 degrees. Often the dungeons were filled to capacity such that captives were almost always inadvertently touching other captives. In the high heat, the smell of human waste, vomit, open sores, and secretions mixed with the effluvium of the dead to make an odor so noxious that the air was transformed into an almost unbreathable poison. The dead lay in place until handlers removed them, which could be hours or even days. For the Africans trapped in this dismal circumstance, the misery of the dungeons was amplified by the anticipation of what cruelty lay ahead.[25]

Branded as property in the dungeon, their wait ended when the captives were transferred to the slave ship via small boats. Conditions did not improve once the Africans were on board the slave ship. The misery of the dungeon was transferred to the hold of the ship where the confinement was even worse. Captives represented a significant financial investment for the slave traders and the companies that owned the rights to the Africans as property. Therefore,

---

[23] Gomez, *Exchanging our Country Marks*, 29.

[24] Patrick Manning, *Slavery and African Life: Occidental, Oriental, and African Slave Trades* (New York: Cambridge University Press, 1990 reprinted 1993), 64–80. Manning gives estimates for the distances that captives had to travel based on region and time period.

[25] C.L.R. James, *The Black Jacobins: Toussaint L'Ouverture and the San Domingo Revolution*, 2nd Edition (New York: Vintage Books, 1963, reprinted 1989), 7–8.

each day they were brought on deck for exercise and to be fed if the weather was permissible and the crew felt sure of its ability to control their human cargo. If the captives refused to eat, a Speculum Oris was used to pry open their mouths so that food could be forced down. Their hands being bound meant that Africans could not self-regurgitate food they did not want in hopes of starving themselves to death. Nets were extended over the sides of the ship to catch any captive who attempted to commit suicide by jumping overboard. Any attempt to escape the slave ship was met with fiendish violence. One slave ship captain punished a captive who had attempted to leap overboard to commit suicide by having the crew kill him and cut him into pieces. The pieces were fed to the remaining captives as a deterrent. Mortality depended upon a combination of unpredictable variables. The normal length of the trip from West Africa to the Americas was six to eight weeks, depending on the point of origin and the destination and if the winds were favorable. If the winds were not favorable, the trip could last much longer. In such cases, food and other supplies had to be rationed, which meant less to eat for the Africans. In the worse cases, the captives starved to death or were thrown overboard. Many of the cargoes of captives were insured against loss. Entire collateral economies developed in support of the trade. If the seas were rough then Africans were kept below deck, which meant they did not get to exercise or eat. Captives often had open wounds caused by the abrasion of the shackles against their skin. Being chained in the hold of the ship in a physically weakened state with open sores also increased the likelihood of them acquiring diseases such as smallpox or the bloody flux and dying. Smallpox is a highly contagious virus that causes a rash which covers much of the sufferers' body. Food contaminated with the Shigella bacteria caused the bloody flux or flux, which was a type of bloody dysentery or diarrhea. As slave traders came to better understand the causes of the diseases, vinegar was used to clean the area where the Africans were held to help lower the chance of disease. For the traders, such measures were smart business practices and not momentary expressions of humanity amid the insanity of the slave ship. Deaths during the crossing might be as high as 15 to 20 percent. Slave ships often carried 500 captives, some considerably more. Slave traders used different means to offset their losses including "tight packing" which meant overloading the ship with captives.[26]

Africans who survived the Middle Passage came out on the other end of the journey as close as siblings. Fictive kinships formed between them and often these relationships remained strong for the remainder of their lives. They referred to one another affectionately as shipmates. Their circumstance as co-sufferers and the love needed to help each other sustain themselves for the duration of the trip forged tight bonds that transcended ethnic differences and former rivalries. The forces that thrust Africans together without regard to their ethnic identities also created the environment wherein new social relations were formed based upon the experiences the Africans shared during the Middle Passage. Africans taken captive were not always mixed across lines of ethnicity, which was a view historians held for a long time. The rationale put forth for doing so was that it would prevent Africans from communicating and thus make coordinating revolts more difficult. Gwendolen Midlo Hall has demonstrated that in fact Europeans frequently collected and transported Africans of the same ethnicity to the Americas because they

---

[26] Gomez, *Exchanging Our Country Marks*, 163.

may have possessed a specific skill set that the planters or mine owners needed in the particular area where the captives would be taken. Still, the Middle Passage and the forces that attempted to mold them into slaves or pliable workers often created among them a feeling of common loyalty. From the vantage point of the Africans, the Middle Passage was also a rite of passage from the familiar to the unfamiliar, from freedom to captivity, and from an ethnic identity based in homegrown and age-old cultural traditions to a new composite and alien identity made up of their old traditions and those the slave owners forced upon them. Africans in the Americas did not become distinctly African Americans or Jamaican or Afro-Brazilian or Afro-Mexican upon first arriving in the Americas. This occurred over a long period of time during a process Harris describes as settlement.

SETTLEMENT

Most of the African captives were brought to South America and the islands of the Caribbean. A smaller number were brought to the colonies and later states that would comprise the United States. Depending on the ethnicity of the Africans and where they were taken determined a great deal about the communities that they established and the culture they retained overtime as well as the culture they fashioned in the Americas. The amount of control that whites could exert over the Africans was hugely important in determining cultural retentions and the trajectory of cultural development. Where racial demographics favored whites, as it did in much of the United States, European values and culture largely came to replace the former African values and culture. In South America, Central America, and the Caribbean where Africans were a numeric majority, African values and culture often survived enslavement. In remote regions of those areas, African culture mirrored culture back in the areas from where the Africans had been taken. For instance, the Yoruba spoken in parts of northeast Brazil retains the purity of form that it had back in western Nigeria where many Yoruba resided. Implicit in what has been stated is that there was a prodigious struggle between slaveholders and Africans over whose values, beliefs, and culture Africans would possess.[27]

The terrain of racial slavery in the United States varied with time and location. Moreover, human personality, which is filled with contradiction and discontinuities of thought and action, was a major influence on the system. Consider the vicissitudes that made possible the contradictory human personalities of the pliant Sambo and the defiant Nat Turner or the slaveholder John Calhoun and the slave liberator John Brown.

What requires explanation is how these complimentary and contradictory forces helped to construct an African American identity out of the African identities that were settled in the Americas. Africans who arrived in the Americas directly from Africa were still conscious of their ethnicity with their language and culture intact. This was true, for instance, of those who were imported into the South Carolina low country and Louisiana during the colonial period. Others took a more circuitous route arriving after having already been settled in the West Indies, as was the case of some captives brought to New England and North Carolina in the

---

[27] Sterling Stuckey, *Going Through the Storm*; Gomez, *Exchanging Our Country Marks*, are sources that deal with the development of culture among persons of African descent in the Americas.

eighteenth century. Thus, one could find among captive laborers in the Americas Asante, Ewe, Fon, Yoruba, Ibo, and Angolans.

Spatial relations of power often determined the extent to which Africans could retain their ethnic African identity and culture over long periods of time. In the Chesapeake or North Carolina, for instance, in labor communities that Ira Berlin called "Societies with Slaves", because enslaved labor was not central to the productive process, those slave owners could exert more direct power over their workers than say in Haiti in the West Indies where a single plantation might have 2,000 captive laborers with perhaps as few as 40 whites, making it virtually impossible for an overseer and the small number of white handlers to have direct control over the captive Africans. "Slave Societies" was the name Berlin gave to communities where enslaved labor was central to the productive process. Yet, even where the racial demographics were not tilted in favor of the Africans, captive workers still retained much of their culture including their language well into the nineteenth century.[28]

In situations where captive Africans did not work under the constant gaze of the slave owner or overseer, it is not difficult to imagine that those African workers would be able to continue to practice their culture, i.e., their spiritual beliefs, language, food preparation, and modes of entertainment. Under those circumstances, away from the moderating power of whites, captive laborers would have had the necessary social space to adapt their culture based on their environment and memory of their old traditions. Lorenzo Dow Turner's and Joseph Holloway's work on the Gullah, descendants of African peoples who reside on the sea islands off the coasts of South Carolina and Georgia confirms this.[29]

Religion and language practices were the most important aspects of culture in shaping the identity of Africans in the Americas during and after slavery. In the Circum-Caribbean and Brazil African religious systems have retained their vital essence in slightly modified forms. For example, Vodun in Haiti and Santeria in Venezuela have been adapted to their new environments in the Americas but remain recognizable in their structure and form to their African counterparts. Slaveholders forbade Africans from practicing their religious beliefs, but in Brazil and the Circum-Caribbean, this did not stop them from carrying on their spiritual traditions. Africans adapted by practicing their religions secretly. Santeria is a Yoruba religious system adapted to the circumstance of Africans in the Americas.[30] Its practitioners maintained its form with small modifications to hide its existence from Europeans. Olodumare remained God and beneath him were the Orishas or lesser deities, who influence over specific aspects of life. In the Spanish

---

[28] See for instance, Eugene Genovese, *Roll Jordan Roll: The World the Slaves Made* (New York, 1974) and Ira Berlin, *Many Thousands Gone: The First Two Centuries of Slavery in North America* (Cambridge, MA: Harvard University Press, 1998), 142–143.

[29] See Lorenzo Dow Turner, *Africanisms in the Gullah Dialect* (Chicago, IL: University of Chicago Press, 1949). Turner's work emphasizes lingual similarities between the Gulllah Dialect or creole and African languages. Also see, Joseph Holloway, ed., *Africanisms in American Culture*, 2nd ed. (Bloomington, IN: Indiana University Press, 2005) and William Pollitzer, *The Gullah People and their African Heritage* (Athens, GA: University of Georgia Press, 1999).

[30] See, John S. Mbiti, *Introduction to African Religion, 2nd edition* (Portsmouth, NH: Heinemann, 1991, originally published 1975). Mbiti explains that there is no word in any African language that directly translates to religion as it is commonly understood in Europe or the West because African beliefs and their philosophy of life were interwoven into everything they did. For the sake of comprehension in this short summary I have elected to use the word religion in a similar manner as Mbiti in the title of his book.

colonies of Cuba and the Viceroyalty of New Granada (Colombia, Ecuador, Panama, and Venezuela), Africans created pairings between Catholic Saints and Orishas based on function, and then substituted the names of the Orishas with the names of Catholic Saints. Syncretism is the general name given for the blending of cultural traditions, in this case religious systems, Yoruba Ile Ifa and Catholicism. Santeria and Lucumi (the name given to the adapted Yoruba religion in Cuba), Candomble in Brazil, and Vodun in Haiti are still vitally important cultural traditions today with many devote followers.

Christian Europeans have demonized African traditional religions down to the present day. Hollywood films have depicted Vodun in such a negative light that in American Culture Voodoo, a western corruption of Vodun, has become an accepted reference for evil cults and witchcraft. Slaveholders understood the importance and the power of African religions to sustain African identities and in uniting its adherents behind a common, but alien, ideology. Thus, they condemned the worship of African deities and the practice of African religious rituals. In their place, the Europeans attempted with varying success to convert the Africans to Christianity.

In the United States, after the Great Awakening in the 1760s, many slave owners attempted to introduce Christianity to their captive laborers as a way of socializing them to European or western values and ideas. Spurred on by evangelical preachers, such as Jonathan Edwards and George Whitefield, The First Great Awakening was a period in United States history where large numbers of whites sought individual salvation from their sins. According to Gomez, they imitated the emotionalism they witnessed among African worshippers.[31] In a twist of irony, this emotionalism, which blacks refer to as "getting happy" or "catching the spirit", was essentially a manifestation of traditional African religious expression. Even descriptors, such as "catching the spirit" can be explained in the context of African religious tradition. In Santeria, for instance, for the purpose of divination, worshippers hoped to be "mounted" by a particular Orisha or in essence to "catch the spirit" which would reveal to them the specific answers to their life questions.

Captive laborers participated in the revivals of the Great Awakening and many became converts. Christianity had a medicinal quality that with its forward gazing promise of eternal peace in the next life was a wellspring of hope for many captive workers. If happiness is at least partly having something to look forward to then Christian salvation opened the door to the possibility of unending halcyon days, but not without a steep price. Africans had first to renounce their former African beliefs. Such a step took them further along the road from an African identity to a creole identity that was part African and part European.[32]

After religion, language is the most important cultural element in shaping the identity of Africans in the Americas. Language is how we interpret and define our environment. It is the medium through which we connect to the world and communicate ourselves to the world. Slaveholders from Europe and Christian missionaries working in Africa and the Diaspora encouraged and even coerced people of African descent to speak in their language, be it English, Spanish, French, Portuguese, or Dutch. South African educator and writer, Njabola Ndebele has stated that the spread of the English language is inextricably tied to the spread of English

---

[31] Gomez, *Exchanging Our Country Marks*, 253. See also, Robert Farris Thompson, *Flash of the Spirit: African & Afro-American Art & Philosophy* (New York: Vintage, 1984).

[32] Ibid.

and American colonialism.[33] This is so because language is fundamental to who we are and the shortest route to controlling a conquered population is to have them to begin thinking and acting like their conquers. Fluency in the language of the conquers was therefore an essential ingredient of colonial conquest.

Montesquieu, a French political philosopher of the Enlightenment period, claimed that "As long as a conquered people has not lost its language, it can have hope." The hope to which he refers is the hope of maintaining ones' ethnic and cultural identity. I would venture a guess that most African Americans never question the fact that their first language is English. In fact, it would be hard for most to imagine it being anything other than English because if it were a language other than English they would no longer be American. Wherever they met them in a colonial context, Europeans forced Africans to learn to speak their languages. This was true of the British in Tasmania and India, just as it was true of the Dutch in Surinam and the French in Haiti. Culturally speaking, on a global scale then people of African descent have been lingually colonized. They describe the world and themselves using the language of their former colonizers. Language is more than just the obvious message carried in a made statement or sentence read; it is also pregnant with the perceptions, attitudes, and goals of the originating society. When considered in this way, it becomes clear why captive laborers in the Americas fought so hard to maintain their African languages, and why European slave owners worked so hard to force them to speak their language.

Naming is a function of language and power, and it helps to establish a person's identity as a member of a specific group. Under slavery and colonialism, Africans were forced to accept new names that aligned them with whites or Europeans and alienated them from themselves and their African relations. In the original made-for-television film Roots, based on the book by the same name, which chronicles the family history of the author Alex Haley, there is a powerful scene where the proud young African Kunta Kente is flogged because he refuses to accept the name Toby given to him by the slave owner. Kunta Kente fought to retain his African name because it connected him to his people and his past. His new name, Toby, had a new history that was associated with white authority, enslavement, and white society. An ongoing saga of the black experience is the contestation over the control of one's identity. Africans in the Diaspora with European names are an indication of their subjugation by Europeans.

Today, naming resistance, taking back the power and authority to name, often takes the form of a "made up" forename or given name. For instance, some might recall the fictitious female character "Sheneneh Jenkins" from the television show Martin. The character Sheneneh callously mocks the tragic social circumstance of African Americans trapped in enduring economic and educational poverty, a poverty that is a byproduct of slavery, Jim Crow segregation, and ongoing white supremacy. The skits about Sheneneh would be funny if those persons and whole communities of people of African descent being mocked had the know-how and power to collectively remediate their condition, but they don't.

For them their circumstance is like being trapped at the bottom of a well. Above them is the small and distant opening of the well that allows in just enough light for them to get glimpses

---

[33] Njabulo Ndebele, "The English Language and Social Change in South Africa," in Ndebele, *The Rediscovery of the Ordinary: Essays on South African Literature and Culture* (Durban, South Africa: University of KwaZulu-Natal Press, 1991), 104.

of people actually living as opposed to struggling to stay alive. Looking up in glances, they struggle perpetually in spasmodic fits of dog paddling to keep from drowning. Like the proverbial crabs in a barrel they pull down on one another in individual attempts to stay afloat. They claw the cold slick walls of the well in vain hope of gaining traction in order to escape their Sisyphean existence. Many succumb to exhaustion and sink into the belly of the well. From below, the faces at the bottom of the well cannot fully see the world, but above them looking down at them are people who look like them, people who only recently, perhaps a generation removed, have themselves emerged from the well. But instead of lowering the rope of succor, they peer back into the well to make fun of and laugh at the condition of those who remain trapped at the bottom of the well.

These black "elites" do not help because they no longer identify with those blacks trapped in stasis at the bottom of the well who look like them. At the top of the well, the black "elites" take pride in speaking European languages, have European names, and practice European beliefs that connect them, loosely and precariously, to societies Europeans created for themselves. The well metaphor helps us to see broadly how adaption under the duress of colonialism can lead the descendants of Africans to different identities. The extent to which Africans embraced or resisted the indoctrination to white supremacist ideas and European culture determines in large measure their relative place in white societies.

"Sheneneh", which was intended to insult blacks, particularly poor blacks, is in fact, a classic, albeit unintended, example of naming resistance. With no past and no prior connection to any people, it is a name without a history, which opens the possibility of starting a new history that for the parents who created or "made up" the name is an attempt to at least partially disassociate their child from the white society and white supremacy that oppresses them and then mocks their condition.[34] Naming resistance also includes the use of names associated with Africa or its Diaspora, such as the popular girl's name Ashanti, which is taken from the powerful and historic African empire of central Ghana. Whenever someone calls out "Ashanti" an ideological allusion to the attributes of the empire, e.g., beauty, strength, and power, becomes manifest in the conscious of all those who are familiar with the old empire.

Language and personal names are a major component of a person's identity and serve as an organizing principle. Within democratic societies in the west, names, language, and even religious beliefs, delimit the contours of membership in those societies and access to political and economic power within those societies. Africans in the Americas for instance have historically had a qualified membership in societies in the west and have wage protracted struggles for recognition as full citizens with rights equal to their white counterparts. A basic qualification of membership in those societies is fluency in the former colonizer's language and having a name that identifies you as a member of the group. Religious affiliation too is important in spite of official proclamations and public pronouncements of religious freedom and religious tolerance that are so common in western societies.

Cultures grow out of particular environments. Within the socially prescribed limits of the societies in which they lived, blacks in the diaspora have fashioned their culture out of the

[34] The derivation of Jenkins was found at "Last name: Jenkins," *The Surname Database*, accessed July 5, 2016, http://www.surnamedb.com/Surname/Jenkins.

fragments of their ethnic African cultures and the cultures of the people with whom they were in enduring contact. Samba in Brazil, for example, is a beautiful and festive form of music and dance that originated in Angola and Congo but that its practitioners have adapted to Brazil. Originally Samba musicians used string and percussion instruments, but today brass instruments such as the trumpet and trombone are often played in accompaniment. Although it originated with the Africans brought to Brazil as captive laborers, today people of all races participate and enjoy Samba.

The Garinagu in Belize and Honduras are the descendants of Africans taken from the Bight of Biafra in 1635 who were shipwrecked on the Island of St. Vincent in the Caribbean. On St. Vincent they married with the Caribe Indians, a local indigenous people, and together formed their own distinct community. After two major wars with the British in the 18th century, the Black Caribs were exiled to Roatan and Honduras. Many of the Black Caribs died enroute to Roatan. Today, the Garinagu people have developed a thriving culture in Belize. A favorite cultural celebration among them is the Jankunu Dance or John Canoe. Male dancers put on masks resembling white men while male drummers string together dulcet rhythms. The dance commemorates the Garifuna struggle for freedom from enslavement and mocks their former British colonizers.

Readers are probably already familiar with many aspects of African American culture. Black spirituals, Blues music, Jazz, Rap music, Hip-Hop Culture, Soul Food, and popular dances like the Twist, the Freak, and the Nae Nae. People of all persuasions participate in black culture in the United States. Where at one time African American culture was a subculture of the predominate white culture, today aspects of black culture are in the mainstream of American life. African American slang and expressions like "What's up" or "What's happening" are so widely used as to be indistinguishable from mainstream greetings. Hip-Hop Culture has brought about a centripetal effect among the younger generations of all races in the United States and globally. It has become a unifying platform for people of different races, genders, classes, and religions. Such points of identification have historically helped to weave together the many threads that make up the global presence of people of African descent.

Harris believed that the identification of communities of people of African descent was a function of their consciousness of their African ancestry and their desire in some way to reconnect to their African heritage. He called this idea of reconnecting to the source Return, the third phase of the African Diaspora.

RETURN: PHYSICAL AND IDEOLOGICAL EFFORTS TO RECONNECT WITH AFRICA

Physical return is pretty straight forward and easy to conceptualize as it is the literally return of Diaspora Africans to the continent of Africa. By ideological return we mean to return in ways that are not physical, such as making a healthy emotional reconnection to Africa or somehow reconnecting via our thoughts or ideas. Sheila Walker, anthropologist and former Chair of the Department of African Studies at the University of Texas at Austin, has used the Osirian legend as a powerful metaphor for aiding our comprehension of the

African Diaspora. Understanding the key points of the legend helps us conceptualize its relationship to the experiences of people of African ancestry in the context of the African Diaspora.

A broad outline of the Osirian legend is that Osiris was once a man who became the god-king of Kemet or ancient Egypt. He taught his people agriculture, how to worship the gods, and gave them laws. Osiris married his sister Isis. Osiris' brother Seth became jealous of Osiris and he coveted his wife Isis. Seth plotted with 72 conspirators and murdered his brother Osiris. Isis was able to find her husband whose body had been placed in a coffin and set afloat on the Nile River. Seth found out and attacked Osiris' body, cutting it into 14 pieces. Isis again with patience and cunning searched for and found all of the pieces save one. Using magic, she was able to reanimate her husband long enough to be impregnated with their son Horus who avenged his father by defeating Seth and regaining the throne of Kemet. Horus regaining the throne symbolically represents the re-establishment of order and peace over the kingdom.[35]

From this metaphor, the relationships between the Osirian legend and the historic experiences of African peoples emerge. Walker draws an analogy between Africans who were taken into the Atlantic Slave Trade and other coerced migrations of African peoples to the body of Osiris, which Seth cut into 14 pieces. By this analogy, Seth could represent European, Arab, or even African slave traders. Isis embodies a consciousness of Africa as the motherland or source of people of African ancestry. She also symbolizes efforts to reunite African people. Her son Horus could not be born until first she reassembled her deceased husband and brought him back to life. This is instructive as an allusion to the condition of people of African ancestry. Horus represents the protest ideologies and the individuals who have campaigned and fought against the cruel forces that have scattered and exploited the sons and daughters of Africa. Africa must be made whole and healed before its descendants can have true peace and prosperity. Osiris, Isis, and Seth were siblings who collectively represent humanity and the conflicts that often arise between members of the human family.

In the Osirian analogy above, Joseph E. Harris' concept of Return, the third phase of his triadic model, represents the work of Isis and her son Horus to piece together the Africans scattered into communities around the world. Before this can take place, Africans in the diaspora must first have a consciousness of Africa. Without that consciousness, Diaspora Africans will not embrace Africa as a real or a symbolic homeland, which is why our opening definition of the African Diaspora is that it is a tool for understanding how people of African descent are related by ties of blood, culture, and experience. Harris maintains that Diaspora communities have collective memories and myths about Africa as a place of origin. These memories and myths have informed repatriation efforts as well as the elaboration of protest ideologies aimed at the liberation of African people from enslavement and colonialism, which serve as the historic backdrop of our discussion.

---

[35] For a good discussion of the Osirian legend see, Tony Browder, *Nile Valley Contributions to Civilizations* (Washington, DC: Inst of Karmic Guidance, 1992) or Tony Browder, *From the Browder File* (Washington, DC: Inst of Karmic Guidance, 1989).

Physical Return: Emigration Efforts

There have been numerous emigration projects directed at repatriating the sons and daughters of Africa. Some of these projects were small but noble endeavors while others were more ambitious. Most often, regardless of their size, they were attempts by disfranchised and disaffected groups of blacks to improve their quality of life in a new, or sometimes old, land. There efforts met with varying degrees of success and failure. Relative to the total population of Africans living in the Americas, only a small number of them every actually emigrated though many more certainly sympathized with those who did. Some of the blacks who have led emigration efforts include Paul Cuffee, Martin Delany, Edward Blyden, and Henry McNeil Turner.

In 1816, Captain Paul Cuffee returned 38 free people of color to the British colony of Sierra Leone in West Africa. By the 18th century, Great Britain emerged as one of the leading transporters of captive Africans in the European Dominated Trade in African People. An early effort to return free people of color in the Americas back to Africa therefore was the colony of Sierra Leone established by British anti-slavery advocates in 1792. From the vantage point of whites, free people of color were not desirable either in the United States or in continental Europe. In the United States, slaveholders viewed free people of color as a threat to the institution of slavery because they were often actively opposed to slavery and aided captive laborers to escape. Whites both in the United States and Europe generally viewed them as an innately inferior irritant with whom they had unnecessarily to compete with for jobs and work. At the conclusion of the American Revolution, Britain temporarily settled blacks liberated during the war in Halifax, Nova Scotia. In 1792, the British abolitionist John Clarkson led the 1,100 blacks who had been settled in Nova Scotia to Sierra Leone.[36]

Captain Paul Cuffee was the son of an Asante father and a Wampanoag Indian mother. He was born Paul Slocum in 1759 in Massachusetts. His father Cuffee Slocum had been the property of a Quaker named John Solcum who reconciled the conflict between his economic aspirations and his Quaker beliefs by liberating Cuffee Slocum. Paul Slocum's mother, Ruth Moses, and his father had nine children; Paul was the seventh. He grew up on his parent's large farm in Dartmouth, Massachusetts. Slocum was the name that linked his family to the institution of slavery, so in an act that was a common practice among former captive workers, Paul convinced his siblings to change their names. Sometimes this is done by simply changing the spelling of the last name to distinguish it from the name of the former slaveholder. Paul however elected to make his father's first name, Cuffee, the family name. In this way, he became Paul Cuffee. Paul's father's people, the Asante, have specific given names for sons and daughters based on the day of the week that they were born. Kofi is the name given to a boy born on a Friday. By taking his father's African given name as the family name, Paul was reconnecting the family to its roots.

---

[36] Cuffee's account can be found in, Paul Cuffee, *A Brief Account of the Settlement and Present Situation of the Colony of Sierra Leone, in Africa* (New York: Printed by Samuel Wood, 1812). See also, Paul Cuffee, *Narrative of the Life and Adventures of Paul Cuffe A Pequot Indian: During Thirty Years Spent At Sea, And In Travelling In Foreign Lands* (New York, 1839).

Captain Cuffee was a skilled business man who had tremendous success in the shipping industry, and he used that success to lend support to black people. He built a large fleet of cargo ships, the largest ship, "Alpha", weighed 268 tons. Being a business man of color, Captain Cuffee appreciated the racial difficulties that faced people of African descent. He had dealt with them many times. Some racial bars he was able to pass over or around, but others he found immovable. With the establishment of Sierra Leone as a possible landing spot and the push by abolitionists and slaveholders, Captain Cuffee thought that emigration might be the best way for people of color to be free of racial prejudice and to reach their God-given potential. Captain Cuffee made his first vist to Sierra Leone in 1811, on the eve of the War of 1812. British import tariffs made his goods too expensive for resale, but he was able at least to meet with some of the black business leaders in the colony to learn from them their needs and the needs of the people. Together they drafted a letter requesting that settlers be able to participate in the whaling industry, as farmers, and merchants. The War brought about a U.S. embargo in British goods, which frustrated Cuffee's plans and ensnared his ship *Traveller*.

U.S. Customs officials confiscated his ship, forcing him to make pleas to the government that eventually reached President James Madison. President Madison invited the wealthy Cuffee to the White House to hear his entreaty concerning *Traveller* and became convinced that Cuffee's ship and its merchandise should be returned to him. Captain Cuffee regained his ship, but he still had to contend with the financial problems brought on by the War. The U.S. embargo meant that his ships could no longer trade goods to British controlled ports. Cuffee decided to turn his attention to organizing and publicizing the resettlement project along towns on the Eastern Seaboard of the United States by making speeches and distributing pamphlets advocating for colonization.

The War ended in 1814, and a year later Cuffee set sail for Sierra Leone, arriving in Freetown in early February 1816. He financed the voyage and resettlement effort out of his own money and a donation of $1,000 from a citizen of New Bedford. His out of pocket expense was more than $8,000; at the time, a hefty sum for anyone, but especially a free person of color. Cuffee died in 1817, only a year after his successful expedition to reconnect Diaspora Africans to Africa. Cuffee's dream of returning blacks to Africa was not fully realized, but his example lives on in figures like Martin R. Delany, Marcus Mosiah Garvey, and even Captain Harry Dean.

Martin Robison Delany also believed that emigration was the only practical way for African Americans to be truly independent and self-determining. By the 1850s, the United States had long outlawed the European overseas trade in African people, but the institution of slavery in the U.S. had found new life in the Deep South where coerced labor was the engine driving the cotton economy. With the international trade in Africans limited by British slave patrols, southern slave traders or speculators, as they were commonly known, began importing captive laborers from the northern and mid-Atlantic states of the United States. According to Edward Baptist, in the seventy-year period beginning in 1790 and ending in 1860, over a million captive laborers were sold into the Deep South. The Cotton Kingdom was an infernal machine that grew stronger and more efficient throughout the first six decades of the 19th century. Overseers and drivers used a whip that produced a sonic boom and was capable of ripping deep gashes into the flesh of its victim. It created a new level of terror among the black men and women who saw it used or were unfortunate enough to be beaten with it. Avoiding the whip, drove cotton pickers to new levels of efficiency, and they improved as pickers each decade from the turn of the 19th century to the first shots fired on Fort Sumter. Thus, the expanding slave system along with The Fugitive Slave Act, the Kansas-Nebraska Act, the Dred Scott Decision, and efforts among some whites to re-open the slave trade convinced Martin Delany to develop a program to assist blacks to emigrate.[37]

Delany was an educated man and abolitionist, who would later become a Major in the Union Army. Born in Charles Town, Virginia (now West Virginia) in 1812, he worked for Frederick Douglas on the North Star Newspaper and took courses in medicine at Harvard Medical School before racist whites forced his separation from the institution. Delany was a Black Nationalist, someone who promoted black political and economic self-determination. He recognized how deeply entrenched slavery was in the United States and began advocating for blacks to emigrate. He and his wife had emigrated to Chatham-Kent in present day Ontario, Canada where he continued to practice medicine. Chatham-Kent was a promised land for coerced laborers fleeing the slaveholding states of the United States. Many free people of color also settled there to escape the harsh racism of the U.S. John Brown recruited followers there for his 1859 plan to overthrow slavery in the United States and form a new nonracial government. At Brown's personal request, Delany had helped organize one of Brown's final recruitment meetings in Chatham-Kent, where according to Delany plans were laid for an assault on Kansas. Of course, the real target turned out to be Harper's Ferry in Virginia (now West Virginia).[38]

In 1854, Delany had participated in the National Emigration Convention of the Colored People on the United States held in Cleveland, Ohio. He set forth his views on emigration in the form of a justification he entitled, "Report on the Political Destiny of the Colored Race on the American Continent." Believing that blacks had no future in the United States, Delany proposed that a commission be formed that would travel to Africa and survey the Niger Valley as a possible location for the repatriation of African Americans. In 1859, Delany and his retinue traveled to West Africa aboard the ship *Mendi*, which was owned by African merchants, and carried out a study, which he published as the "Official Report of the Niger Valley Exploring Party." They landed in Liberia before going on to what is today Nigeria. Having reached Nigeria, they traveled into the interior of the continent to the town of Abeokuta, which is approximately 40 miles north of present day Lagos. At Abeokuta, Delany made a treaty with four local chiefs that granted the commissioners the right to settle members of the African race in America among the Egba people.[39]

---

[37] Edward Baptist, *The Half Has Never Been Told: Slavery and the Making of American Capitalism* (New York, NY: Basic Books, 2014). Baptist contend that it was the Southwest whip that drove the captive laborers to become more efficient cotton pickers.

[38] Delany's political motives can be found in Robert Kahn, "The Political Ideology of Martin Delany," *Journal of Black* Studies, 14, no. 4 (June 1984): 416–417. Frank A. Rollin, *The Life and Public Service of Martin R. Delany* (Boston, MA: Lee and Shepard, 1883), 87–90. Delany apparently told Rollin that Brown was recruiting men to attack Kansas, but this is contradicted by later reports.

[39] Martin R. Delany, *Official Report of the Niger Valley Exploring Party* (N.P., 1861).

The Civil War ultimately derailed Delany's plans to re-settle African Americans in the Niger Valley. John Brown's bold sacrifice along with the election of Abraham Lincoln as president toppled the final dominos leading to the secession of the South and civil war, not to make men free, but to save the Union. Nevertheless, blacks and their white allies saw in the war an opportunity to push for emancipation, understanding as Lincoln himself had openly stated, that the nation could not survive half slave and half free. Delany put all of his effort in fighting for freedom. It is a fact of that conflict that different men fought that war for different reasons. The victory of the north and the 13th amendment obviated discussion of large-scale black emigration for at least a half century.

Edward Blyden was born in St. Thomas in 1832; he went to New York in 1847 and then to Liberia in 1850, three years after it declared independence. Blyden, like Delany, was proud of his African heritage and was quick to correct blacks who put too much faith in "European travelers' accounts" of Africa. He became a "pioneer theorist of the 'African personality'", and in 1890, he published *The African Problem and other Discourses*. Blyden did not repatriate Africans to the continent but his own travels serve as an example of how Diaspora Africans with a consciousness of Africa often return to Africa.[40]

Henry McNeil Turner was a state politician in Georgia during Reconstruction (1865–1877) and a self-taught preacher of considerable rhetorical ability. After joining the African Methodist Episcopal Church (AMEC), his aptitude for his work propelled him to the Bishopric. Bishop Turner was also a proponent of emigration, but he believed that emigration was only for blacks who had the proper mindset. He made multiple trips to South Africa in the 1890s and arranged for black South African students to go to college in the United States. Behind Turner's leadership, the AMEC merged with the Ethiopian Church in South Africa.

Ideological Return: The Emergence of Black Nationalism and Pan Africanism

Black Nationalism is a political ideology that black political thinkers elaborated in response to the impact of enslavement and colonialism. Black Nationalism emphasizes black self-determination and the need for blacks to have their own nations. Pan Africanism holds that since all people of African descent are family who share a common ancestry, a common history, a common circumstance, and a common destiny, then, as family, they must work together in their collective best interest. Both political philosophies relate to the idea of Return because like Horus they attempt to protect the natural rights of African people and to restore order and peace in their communities and lives. The ethos of anti-colonialism within the Pan African movement, which gained full expression after 1945, was that movement's most identifiable attribute because it elicited a centripetal response that brought together Africans throughout the continent of Africa and the Diaspora across wide chasms of distance, ethnicity, and religion. This solidarity in the face of European imperialism did not cause the dissolution of ethnicity, or wipe away traditional rivalries. It simply reflected a heightened sensitivity to a shared circumstance among people of African descent globally and encouraged them, where possible, to

---

[40] Information on Blyden can be found in Sterling Stuckey, "Black Americans and African Consciousness" in *Going Through the Storm: The Influence of African American Art in History* (New York, NY: Oxford University Press, 1994), 130.

coordinate resistance to their oppression. African Americans were in the van of the Pan African Movement because of educational opportunities and the opportunity to build institutions, such as churches, where they could organize independent of whites. Prior to the twentieth century, Africans on the continent had far fewer opportunities for higher education then did their U.S. born brothers and sisters.[41]

It was during the second quarter of the nineteenth century that manifestations of Black Nationalism began to take form. It was even later for Pan Africanism and even later still before they became part of the protest vernacular of Africans and other Blacks living under western hegemony. It was the dialectic interplay of a multiplicity of contradictory forces, destructive and creative, that best articulates why and how these ideologies of protest came into being in the United States. Certainly, efforts to shore up slavery in the second quarter of the nineteenth century provided an incentive for actuating blacks to respond in a manner pregnant with qualities indicative of nationalism.

In a similar manner, the final half of the nineteenth century was a convulsive period for Africans at home and abroad. In the United States at mid-century, harsh legislation, like the Fugitive Slave Act, challenged the freedom of "free" blacks in the north in a manner not existent since the revolutionary period. The Civil War came and went with little meaningful change in the lives of most blacks while concomitantly Europeans carved up Africa preparatory to imposing colonial domination across the continent and around the world. These forces combined to produce a corporate identification out of which Diaspora Africans fashioned the ideology of Pan Africanism.[42]

BLACK NATIONALISM

The American Revolution (1775–1788) and the Haitian Revolution (1791–1802) contributed to an increasing desire for liberation among captive laborers and free blacks in the United States, but even more they stimulated an aspiration to be independent from ubiquitous racial hostilities. This desire is evident in the migration efforts of Paul Cuffee and in the independent church movement led by Richard Allen, father of the African Methodism. There is a large measure of certainty in the belief that the equalitarian ideas promulgated at the birth of the United States also provided a fertile field for cultivating Black Nationalist sentiment. This seems even more obvious when one considers that no blacks were able to enjoy the benefits of the nation's new "democratic" freedom. As Sterling Stuckey points out, "it was precisely in such ironic soil that an ideology of Black Nationalism eventually took root."[43]

Before the collapse of slavery in the northern and mid-Atlantic states, the growth of nationalism in the United States was geographically paradoxical. In the South, especially

---

[41] Sterling Stuckey, "Classical Black Naitonalist Thought," in *Going Through the Storm: The Influence of African American Art in History* (New York, NY: Oxford University Press, 1994), 83–84.

[42] Reconstruction was a period of renewed hope and development for some African Americans in the South, but it was a fleeting peace and prosperity that was followed by a reign of terror and labor arrangements that were slave like. See, Rayford Logan, *Betrayal of the Negro from Rutherford B. Hayes to Woodrow Wilson*.

[43] Sterling Stuckey, "Classical Black Naitonalist Thought," in *Going Through the Storm: The Influence of African American Art in History*, 85.

in the Sea Islands off the coast of South Carolina and Georgia as well as in the Louisiana territory where the racial demographics were advantageous for blacks, captive laborers did have opportunities to development nationalistic ideas. Yet, in the North, where a larger proportion of the black population was "free" and, presumably literate, there were more such opportunities to ponder about nationalism. In spite of this fact, the captive laborers in the south were more likely to be potential nationalists. Stuckey suggests that this paradox, where "free" blacks developed the ideology of nationalism while southern captive workers acted it out, was due to the infusion of Africans directly from Africa or the West Indies into the slave states of the south.[44] Africans coming straight from Africa and Africans who were transshipped through the West Indies before coming to the United States had lived free and were inherently nationalistic. They had not been broken or fully acculturated to slave life. Many of the earliest black nationalists often railed against the evils of slavery and their thoughts are captured in what they said and wrote.

The nineteenth century personalities who fashioned Black Nationalism shared a worldview that included an awareness of a common experience of racial oppression, a cognizance and appreciation of the persistence of group traits, a universal recognition of connections and responsibilities between all people of African ancestry, and a fervent belief that Africans in America and globally living under varying forms of racial oppression must take responsibility for liberating themselves.[45]

Two of the earliest proponents of this line of thinking were Robert Alexander Young and David Walker. Historians have had more to say about Walker than Young, but several months before Walker released his *Appeal to the Coloured Citizens of the World, but in Particular, and Very Expressly, to those of the United States of America*, Young published his *Ethiopian Manifesto*. In it, Young portends the coming of a black messiah who will lead the liberation of black people. Young's decision to use Ethiopian also suggests that he identified with the country of Ethiopia and perhaps all of Africa since at that time people often referred to Africa by the name Ethiopia. Yet, it was Walker's *Appeal* that was the strongest statement of Black Nationalism in the nineteenth century. Walker who was born in Wilmington, North Carolina presumably in the 1790s, openly attacked the hypocrisy of American Christianity and democratic freedom while calling for captive laborers to take their liberty. His "loud and proud" denunciation of white supremacy in the *Appeal* foreshadowed the protest rhetoric of nineteenth century black radicals such as Henry Highland Garnett and Martin R. Delany as well as twentieth century black radicals such as Marcus Garvey, Cyril Briggs, Elijah Muhammad, Malcolm X, and Kwame Ture. Walker was appealing to blacks everywhere though his principle audience were blacks in the United States.[46]

Garnett was another early champion of Black nationalism. In 1843, in his *Address to the Slaves*, given before the Negro Convention at Buffalo, Garnett called for the overthrow of American slavery and insisted that all blacks should be willing to support them in their

---

[44] Ibid., 86.

[45] Ibid.

[46] Ibid., 88–91. Also see, David Walker, *Appeal to the Coloured Citizens of the World, but in particular, and very expressly, to those of the United States of America*, 3rd Edition (David Walker, 1830 reprinted Baltimore, MD: Black Classic Press, 1993).

efforts. He was convinced that blacks should determine their own destiny and by the middle of the nineteenth century even began to support emigration as a viable option for blacks.[47]

PAN AFRICANISM

The origin of Pan Africanism is closely associated with W.E.B. DuBois and Henry Sylvester Williams. In 1897, at a meeting of the American Negro Academy, W.E.B. DuBois presented a paper entitled, "The Conservation of the Races," wherein he posited that if African Americans were going to assume a position of leadership in the movement of "Pan-Negroism," as he clearly felt they should. He urged that, if so, then they must retain their racial identity and reject absorption by white America.[48] DuBois recognized Williams, a Trinidadian lawyer, as the originator of the expression Pan African. Williams called a Pan African conference in 1900. It preceded a series of Pan African Congresses starting with the Paris congress of 1919 that emphasized anti-racism and anti-colonialism. This conference set in motion the Pan African movement. Paradoxically, Pan Africanism was practiced before it was reified into an intellectual concept. "Pan Africanism was born in a definite sequence of events which went from practice to concept to the term to the movement."[49]

Marcus Garvey emerged as a Pan African leader in the first quarter of the twentieth century. His "Back to Africa" movement, which advocated for both the physical return and the ideological return to Africa, gained momentum behind the adverse social conditions that dogged blacks in the United States between 1880 and 1930. During this period, convict leasing, the peonage system, and white vigilantism made life for blacks in the southern states of the United States extremely difficult. Blacks began to leave the south for the north in search of "The Warmth of Other Suns" and ushering in the period of the great migration, which lasted from the turn of the century to the early 1970s. Garveyism arrived in the United States during this rising tide of diminished black hope.[50]

Garvey is arguably the best exemplar of Pan Africanism. In 1913, he established the United Negro Improvement Association (UNIA) and African Communities League. After short but important stays in London and his home country of Jamaica, Garvey moved to the United States to promote black uplift, self-determination, and economic empowerment. He established the UNIA in New York City, a crossroads of black internationalism that was also a landing point for disfranchise and frustrated blacks who were fleeing the south. His movement took root in Harlem and spread around the world. Garvey's aims were to establish ties between all people of African ancestry, to promote race pride, to give assistance

---

[47] Sterling Stuckey, "Classical Black Naitonalist Thought," in *Going Through the Storm: The Influence of African American Art in History*, 95.

[48] See St. Clair Drake, "Diaspora Studies and Pan-Africanism," in Global Dimensions of the African Diaspora, Joseph E. Harris, ed., 451–514 (Washington, DC: Howard University Press, 1993), 462–463 and also see, Ronald Walters, *Pan Africanism in the African Diaspora: An Analysis of Modern Afrocentric Political Movements* (Detroit, MI: Wayne State University Press, 1993), 38.

[49] Walters, *Pan Africanism in the African Diaspora*, 52.

[50] For a discussion of Convict Leasing and the Peonage System see, Douglas Blackmon, *Slavey By Another Name*. Isabella Wilkerson discusses the great migration in, *The Warmth of Other Suns: The Epic Story of America's Great Migration* (New York, NY: Vintage Books, 2010).

to continental Africans and those in the diaspora, and to develop independent black nations.[51] Garvey's motives, like those of Cuffee and Delany before him, were clearly based at least in part on the idea of African redemption. Garvey conceived of redemption in an economic context. Garvey believed that black economic self-determination and economic power would effectively neutralize white supremacy. For Africans both on the continent and in the African Diaspora this must remain an important goal.

This section on physical and ideological Return reveals that each of these black leaders identified with people of African heritage in their mutual struggles against racial oppression. Like Isis, who reassembled the body of her murdered husband, they attempted to reconnect Africans across the global African Diaspora to Africa and to each other. In addition, they these leaders sought independence from the influence of whites. Return therefore must be acknowledged as the reification of a Global African Diaspora political consciousness that emerged out of the struggle against European world domination. Emigration came to be synonymous with the idea of black independence of white authority and control. Its success, which was limited, was a function of the personal perception of Diaspora Africans and the extent to which many of them had come to identify with their hostlands. The ideology of opposition to enslavement, colonialism, and other forms of racial oppression created by these early Black Nationalists and Pan Africanists became the foundation upon which later groups of black radicals built their efforts for political and economic freedom.

CONCLUSION

We have learned that there were voluntary and involuntary migrations of Africans around the world. These migrations led to the rise of communities of people of African ancestry on every habitable continent including the islands of the Pacific. Once in their new domiciles or hostlands, these Africans had to adapt to their new environment. For those Africans transported to the Americas as part of the European Dominated Trade in African Peoples the societies that they entered needed them for specific purposes. Slaveholders attempted to mold them into property or pliable slaves with varying degrees of success.

Thus, Africans in the Diaspora are a "constructed", made-up people, the "cooked Savages" Charles Johnson refers to in "Middle Passage" inhabiting a mythical world veiled in reality. Filled with the values of societies who do not value them as human beings, these Africans suffer alienation, mental anguish, and psychological dysfunctions. Many are driven mad by their attempt to be themselves devoid of what society tells them they ought to be. Many others go through life never knowing who they are or that they are somebody, that they matter and have value as they are. This volume aims to affirm the dignity and value of African people. With an understanding of the forces that have created the modern African personality, we are more confident in ourselves and better equipped to contribute to society.

---

[51] Robert Trent Vinson, *The Americans Are Coming!: Dreams of Liberation in Segregationist South Africa* (Ohio: Ohio University Press, 2012).

KEY TERMS

African Diaspora
Pan Africanism
Middle Passage
Naming Resistance
Society with Slaves
Syncretism
Joseph E. Harris
George Shepperson
Ivan van Sertima
Martin R. Delany
Slave Society
Garinagu
Black Nationalism
Leo Wiener
Paul Cuffee
Henry McNeil Turner
Santeria
Samba

PART I

SANKOFA: REMEMBERING THE SOURCE BUT MOVING FORWARD

CHAPTER 1

THE IMPORTANCE OF STUDYING THE SCHOLARSHIP OF AFRICAN HISTORY WITHIN THE HISTORICAL CONTEXT OF THE AFRICAN DIASPORA

Jarvis L. Hargrove

> I found Africa not only where I was not taught to expect to find it, but even where I was specifically taught not to expect it to be. ... My later experiences in Africa and the African Diaspora ... enabled me ... to understand what I had been seeing, hearing, saying even tasting—and to percieve clues leading to explanations, interpretations, and various levels of meaning.
>
> Dr. Sheila S. Walker, *African Roots/American Cultures: Africa in the Creation of the Americas*

The study of African History has gone through several different paradigm shifts over two centuries since Europeans decided to invade Egypt in a series of waves beginning with France in 1798. Once discredited by the vast majority of academia outside a few select universities and scholars, African History has now become the foundation for numerous fields of historical studies that include Egyptology, works in Antiquity, and today the more popular area of the African Diaspora. Nevertheless, as the historical field of African Diaspora has become the more widespread area of research today across several continents and the most well-known and recognized univerisities, its foundation continues to remain in the study of African History. As such, studies on people of African descent throughout the diaspora, show that all have their linkages to the continent of Africa and this should to be. Moreover, the transition of African History following independence also reveals numerous answers about the birth and study of the African Diaspora.

In the years following independence, a series of works were published which attempted to rewrite and refute the traditional scholarship about the continent. Furthermore, several of these early publications discussed the sources of African History and the current trends, which also included a series of problems associated with the subject. Albeit, these works not only listed the problems associated with African History following independence due to traditional scholarship, but they also set out to answer the questions associated with this list. One of the many works to follow this pattern, published in 1968, included Robert O. Collins' edited work *Problems in African History*, which in the preface discussing the term "Problems" he writes, "This appellation refers not only to those topics which at present invoke controversy and conflicting interpretations, but also to those subjects which lend themselves to discussion and inquiry."[1] Nonetheless, works

---

[1] Robert O. Collins, ed., *Problems in African History* (Englewood Cliffs, NJ: Prentice Hall, 1968), v–vi.

which highlighted the problems associated with African History also included a synopsis of the African Diaspora.

Although these problems and answers have changed since the publication of Collins work, today, this language has been replaced by the seemingly more accepted term "Topics." While the popularity of African History among scholars increased after independence, the acceptance African Diaspora Studies sometimes referred to as Global Black Studies, across academia gained substantial momentum as a search of the topic renders an abundance of resources from numerous universities domestically and globally. This has also resulted in a growth of scholars also defining themselves as specialists of the African Diaspora.[2] Together the two fields, African History and African Diaspora, overlap substantially in several fields which can also include: Latin American Studies, religious studies, colonial studies and analyses of world economic systems.[3] As such, a work titled *Topics of the African Diaspora* must and should include a discussion on African History and its place in the field, but most importantly highlight its past and current trends.

Furthermore, the African Diaspora placed within the context of world history has taken on numerous studies that have included works on language patterns, cultures, customs, religious practices, and peoples stretching across many generations, centuries, and self-created color barriers. Professor Joseph E. Harris, one of the most recognized historians in the field who also has a background in African History, wrote about this link between Africa and the African Diaspora. He stated, "The African Diaspora is a triadic relationship linking a dispersed group of people to the homeland, Africa, and to their host or adopted countries. ... Diasporas ... reinforce images and ideas about themselves and their original homelands. ... Diasporas are therefore significant factors in national and international relations."[4] Although his statement refers to the linkages of people across the African Diaspora, this relationship also speaks about the connections that should be viewed within the historical lens of both fields of study. Therefore, those who study the African Diaspora should be able to make the necessary connections to the continent of Africa and its diverse array of people and states across numerous regional zones. The basis and foundation of these connections are tied firmly to African historiography, written, oral, past, and present.

While many historians can agree, individuals must have a grasp of African History, we do not acknowledge the necessary scholarship they should familiarize themselves with across the discipline. How can one understand the Trans-Saharan or Atlantic Slave Trades without first studying aspects of captivity within Africa and its numerous states? How can one study the cultures and customs of peoples in Jamaica or Colombia without acknowledging the linkages to the Ghana (Gold Coast)? How can one study the languages and speech patterns of the Gullah of South Carolina and Georgia without knowing the connections to the Caribbean

---

[2] Colin Palmer, "Defining and Studying the Modern African Diaspora," *Perspectives on History: The Newsmagazine of the American Historical Association*, (September, 1998): Accessed, July 7, 2016. https://www.historians.org/publications-and-directories/perspectives-on-history/september-1998/defining-and-studying-the-modern-african-diaspora

[3] Patrick Manning, "Africa and the African Diaspora: New Directions of the Study," *Journal of African History*, Vol. 44 (2003), 488.

[4] Joseph E. Harris, "The Dynamics of the Global African Diaspora," in *The Africa Diaspora*, eds. Alusine Jalloh and Stephen E. Maizlish (College Station, TX: Texas A&M University Press, 1996), 7.

and Senegambia region of West Africa? How can one understand the various religions and spiritual ceremonies practiced around the world without a grasp of common religous concepts and practices in Africa? To understand these influences and relationships, one must study the continent of Africa before they can fully understand the different levels of meaning across the broad range of topics in African Diaspora, which suggest students must have a firm grasp of the scholarly works.

Today, the popularity of the African Diaspora is very much evident among a young and enthusiatic generation of students choosing to enter into the field of history. Nevertheless, these same students often overlook the scholarship of African History, instead giving the vast majority of their attention to learning only about the location of which those people of African descent are whom they are choosing to research. This results in a lack of understanding about Africa, the historigraphy concerning the subject matter and its connection to the foundational basis for the study of the African Diaspora, which are a part of the triadic relationship mentioned in the publications of Joseph E. Harris. This unitentional or intentional decision to leave out African historiography leaves us with several glaring questions as follows: (1) Should one have a solid foundation first in African History in order to learn about the African Diaspora? (2) Where should Africa be placed when conceptualizing the study of the African Diaspora on a broader scale? (3) Which works should one consider as a major component of the African historiography? This chapter is a focus on African History and how one should approach this topic and its historiography before preceding on to any analysis of the African Diaspora.

THE BIRTH OF AFRICAN HISTORY: THE CHALLENGES AND ACCEPTANCE FROM THE ACADEMY

The introduction of African History into academia has gone through several different stages since the eighteenth century. These stages of both teaching and written scholarship have more often than not coincided with the exploration, conquest, the start of colonial rule, and later the independence movement across Africa. Furthermore, until the mass publication and acceptance of revisionist history, the academy did not include scholarship produced by historians of color throughout the African Diaspora, whom often argued for the acceptance of oral interpretations of the numerous states across the continent and Africa's place in history. As a result, the work and research produced by some of the most well-known scholars in the early half of the twentieth century were often dismissed by the European-dominated academy and its historical organizations, which itself crossed numerous language, country, and continental barriers. Albeit, these numerous historians continued to publish works and created their own organizations to find acceptance within the academy and to refute the claims of those whose works were most widely acknowledged by the masses.

Nevertheless, four of the most important watershed years in African History to those whom argued the African continent and its people had no value to the world include: Napoleon Bonaparte's 1798 attack on Egypt, the publication of Charles Darwin's 1871 work the *Descent of Man*, the 1882 British occupation of Egypt, and finally the Berlin Conference of 1884–1885.

Furthermore, these numerous events left the continent and its history in the hands of those with no connection, ancestral or otherwise, in charge of the information and knowledge presented, which distorted the way its past was offered to the public.

Through the late eighteenth and first half of the twentieth century, the widely accepted scholarship about Africa came from missionaries, explorers, and colonial officials or those well outside the realm of academia. The many attempts by individuals to discredit Africa's place in the historical scholarship began with George Hegel whom famously stated is his indifference for Africa, "Africa is not a historical continent . . ."[5] which was followed by Hugh Trevor-Roper whom wrote, "Perhaps in the future, there will be some African History to teach … darkness is not a subject of history."[6] Furthermore, those trained as historians viewed Africa as a subject that they need not worry with as A. P. Newton famously argued in 1923, "History only begins when men take to writing, primitive custom … was the concern of archaeologists, linguists and anthropologists."[7] Nevertheless, being shortsighted due to issues of race during their day, these scholars overlooked the significant contributions of Africa and Africans. These arguments also overlook the significance of major empires, their oral history, the introduction of Arabic writing as well neglect *The Histories* (440 BC) written by Herodotus or the significance of the work, *Muqaddimah: An Introduction to History* (1377) by Ibn Khaldun.

Herodotus' work, *The Histories*, is divided into several books about the numerous peoples and states throughout Africa including, the Egyptians, Libyans, and the Ethiopians. In book 2, he highlights the importance of the Egyptians to the development of the calendar, which is a significant contribution to not only history but to the everyday life of people. Herodotus in his work states:

> The Egyptians, they said, were the first to discover the solar year, and to portion out its course into twelve parts. They obtained this knowledge from the stars. (To my mind they contrive their year much more cleverly than the Greeks, for these last every other year intercalate a whole month, but the Egyptians, dividing the year into twelve months of thirty days each, add every year a space of five days besides, whereby the circuit of the seasons is made to return with uniformity.) The Egyptians, they went on to affirm … the names of the twelve gods, which the Greeks adopted … and first erected altars, images, and temples to the gods; and also first engraved upon stone the figures of animals. In most of these cases they proved to me that what they said was true.[8]

This is just one of the many contributions scholars routinely overlooked or often used to give credit to the wrong group, diminishing the importance of Africa and Egypt to the world. Several

---

[5] George Hegel, *Philosophy of History*, in J. Ki-Zerbo, "The Development of African Historiography," in *General History of Africa: Methodology and African Prehistory*, Abridged Edition Vol. 1, ed. J. Ki-Zerbo (Berkley, CA: University of California Press, 1990), 12.

[6] Hugh Trevor-Roper, "The Past and Present: History and Sociology," *Past and Present*, Vol. 42, (1969) in J. Ki-Zerbo, "The Development of African Historiography," in *General History of Africa: Methodology and African Prehistory*, Abridged Edition Vol. 1, ed. J. Ki-Zerbo (Berkley, CA: University of California Press, 1990), 12.

[7] A. P. Newton, Rhodes Professor of Imperial History Kings College, 1923 in *General History of Africa: Methodology and African Prehistory*, Abridged Edition Vol. 1, ed. J. Ki-Zerbo (Berkley, CA: University of California Press, 1990), 12.

[8] Herodotus, *The Histories, Book 2*, trans. George Rawlinson (Massachusetts Institute of Technology, 2009), Accessed February 5, 2016, http://classics.mit.edu/Herodotus/history.2.ii.html.

notable scholars later attributed this lack of connection to Africa as a sign of race being a factor for this reason. Although this continuous determination to overlook the contributions of African states carried over well into the latter half of the twentieth century, this began much earlier according Herodotus and whose theory regarding the subject is later supported by the likes of Islamic scholar Ibn Khaldun. Khaldun writes, "The inhabitants of the north are not called by their colour, because the people who established this conventional meaning of words were themselves white. Thus, whiteness was something usual and common to them, and they did not see anything sufficiently remarkable in it to cause them to use a specific term."[9] The decision not to use a key term or identifier crosses numerous generations and centuries. Furthermore, because no key identifier was used, Egypt through scholarship is often removed from Africa or the only credible or accepted work comes from those associated with the field of Egyptology. Moreover, scholarship from those within the accepted academy became critical for both Herodotus and Ibn Khaldun whom both credited the people of Africa and the Nile Valley as being the apart of the earliest civilizations in the world.

Nevertheless, this was the prevailing attitude of an overwhelming number of scholars inside the accepted intuitions with a small minority whom disagreed with this argument. The most well-known being, Melville J. Herskovits, a Jewish anthropologist whom was studying Africa and those of African descent in the United States and Caribbean islands. In 1941, Herskovits wrote, "The myth of the Negro past is one of the principal supports of race prejudice in this country ... it rationalizes discrimination in everyday contact. ... To give the Negro an appreciation of his past is to endow him with the confidence in his own position in ... the world."[10] Herskovits work should not be undervalued in any way as he often criticized the idea of racial and cultural hierarchy in his research.[11] Nevertheless, as Herskovits work gained traction with some in the academy, others publishing similar works, before his studies, were continuously overlooked.

As some institutions began to transition from their previous attitudes after independence, the earlier theories about African History remained well into the start of the 1960s. In 1963, Robert Rotberg said, "African history is a relatively recent addition to university curriculums ... and is taught as subject in its own right, rather than as an aspect of European expansion. ... There is no standard approach to the teaching of African history."[12] This statement follows the European model for the writing and teaching of African History and does not consider work being done by several notable scholars in the United States and the various areas of the African Diaspora whom were already actively teaching these courses and had done so for nearly forty years.

---

[9] Ibn Khaldun, *The Muqaddimah: An Introduction to History*, Abridged Edition, trans. Franz Rosenthal (Princeton, NJ: Princeton University Press, 2005), 60–61.

[10] Melville J. Herskovits, *The Myth of the Negro Past* (New York: Harper & Brothers Publishers, 1941), 1–32.

[11] Jerry Gershenhorn, *Melville J. Herskovits and the Racial Politics of Knowledge* (Lincoln, NE: University of Nebraska Press, 2004), 4.

[12] Robert I. Rotberg, "The Teaching of African History," *The American Historical Review* 69, no. 1, (1963): 47. Rotberg's work relies heavily on the works published scholars of European ancestry and does not mention the scholarship of those of African ancestry which was long being taught and discussed at numerous colleges and universities.

While some in the academy continued to argue scholarly research on Africa was limited, numerous individuals suggested otherwise and did so across several disciplines and platforms. Several of the most notable scholars whom were often overlooked included Martin Delany (1812–1885), George Washington Williams (1849–1891), W. E. B. DuBois (1868–1963), Arturo Alfonso Schomburg (1874–1938), Carter G. Woodson (1875–1950), William Leo Hansberry (1894–1965), and J. A. Rogers (1880–1966). These individuals ultimately gave way to the likes of Chancellor Williams (1893–1992), John G. Jackson (1907–1993), Frank Snowden (1911–2007), Joseph E. Harris (b.1929), John Henrik Clarke (1915–1998), Cheik Anta Diop (1923–1986), George G. M. James (d. 1956), Yosef Ben-Jochannan (1918–2015), Ivan Van Sertima (1935–2009), and Walter Rodney (1942–1980).

Each scholar played an extremely critical role in the promotion and preservation of African History, publishing works for the masses as well as the academy along with developing a curriculum to be used at each level of education. Martin Delany, as early as 1852, published works on the condition of Africans and African Americans and *The Origin of Race and Color* (1879), which challenged many of the racial prejudices associated with people of African descent and the idea that the only the history associated with Africa was that of Europeans. George Washington Williams' *The History of the Negro Race in America, 1619–1880* (1882), published before the Berlin Conference of 1884–1885, gives a detailed account of African Americans in world history and the role of Africa. His work also led to the creation of one of the first African Studies associations in the United States which greatly contributed to the preservation of history.

W. E. B. DuBois is known for many works, but his study, *The World and Africa: An Inquiry into the Part Which Africa Has Played in World History* (1947), outlines Africa in a number of capacities including the peopling of the world, its role in Europe and Asia and finally the rape of the continent by outsiders. Carter G. Woodson, *The Mis-Education of the Negro* (1933), begins his study with a criticism of the people of African descent whom in his view shunned Africa and chose not teach its history. He was so committed to the education of the masses, he published numerous historical pieces in black-owned newspapers throughout the United States and established the Association for the Study of Negro Life and History, today the Association for the Study of African American Life and History as well as the *Journal of Negro History* today the *Journal of African American History*. J. A. Rogers, *World's Great Men of Color* (1946) also joined this conversation by discussing the role of Africa, African people and civilizations, and their influence on the rest of the world outlining numerous well-known states and peoples.

Arturo Schomburg, took different steps to spread knowledge about Africa to the rest of the world, coming to notoriety in New York City in the 1890s as someone who actively promoted the liberation movements in Cuba and Puerto Rico. Schomburg, later played a pivotal role in helping to create the American Negro Academy as well as serving as the principal founder of the Negro Society for Historical Research. These two organizations contributed greatly to the academy and gave black scholars throughout the African Diaspora opportunities to spread knowledge about Africa and people of African descent in the various corners of the world. A known bibliophile, or collector of books and artifacts, Schomburg in 1925 stated, "The American Negro must remake his past in order to make his future."[13] Today, the Schomburg

---

[13] Arturo Alfonso Schomburg, "The Negro Digs Up His Past," *Survey Graphic*, (1925), 670–673.

Center for Research in Black Culture in Harlem, NY, along with the Moorland–Spingarn Research Center[14] at Howard University remains two of the most visited centers in the United States. Moorland–Spingarn Research Center began with a collection of works and documents from Jesse Moorland and Arthur B. Spingarn, both collectors themselves and continued to grow under the guidance Dorothy Porter Wesley whom was trained as a scholar and librarian. Both centers routinely attract scholars from throughout the African Diaspora researching and writing about people of African descent.

One of the notable scholars of this generation and perhaps the most respected among his peers was William Leo Hansberry, whose contributions cannot be underestimated as his work helped usher in a new generation of scholars. Although Hansberry was very undecided about publishing his work, Joseph E. Harris' collection published in two volumes of his personal lectures and notes, *William Leo Hansberry: Pillars in Ethiopian History, Vol. 1* and *William Leo Hansberry: Africa & Africans as Seen by Classical Writers, Vol. 2* (1981). Both of these volumes published after his death, outline the career and contributions of this great scholar to African History. One of the greatest contributions of Hansberry according to Harris' work is the creation of several classes in African History while teaching at Howard University despite facing criticism from colleagues.

Harris writes that only two years after arriving at Howard University, Hansberry had created three courses in African History with an enrollment of more than 800 students. This included courses titled: Negro Peoples in the Cultures and Civilization of Prehistoric and Proto-Historic Times, The Ancient Civilizations of Ethiopia, and The Civilization of West Africa in Medieval and Early Modern Times. This series of classes discussed Pre-Dynastic Africa, Ancient Egypt and its relationship with Eastern and Western Asia as well as the Mediterranean, Ethiopia, and West Africa before and after the arrival of European nations.[15] By the 1950s, through student response and desire for more African History, Hansberry expanded his course listing by five, adding the following: Peoples and Cultures of Africa in Stone Age Times, Culture and Political History of Nilotic Lands in Historical Antiquity, Cultural and Political History of Kushite or Ethiopian Lands in the Middle Ages, Cultural and Political History of the Kingdoms and Empires of the Western Sahara and the Western Sudan, and Archaeological Methods and Materials.[16]

Hansberry's work ultimately proves the previously mentioned George Hegel, Hugh Trevor-Roper, A. P. Newton, and Robert Rotberg all to be incorrect. William Leo Hansberry is also credited with starting a tradition of African History/Studies being taught at Howard University that has witnessed some of the most recognized names in both fields as educators and students. Furthermore, Hansberry should be viewed as the father of African History/Studies as his series of classes was replicated at other universities first by his students and then those whom followed

---

[14] Moorland–Spingarn Research Center at Howard University in Washington, DC, has over the years grown into one of the largest and most recognized research centers in America for the study of people of African descent dispersed throughout the world.

[15] Joseph E. Harris, *William Leo Hansberry: Pillars in Ethiopian History, Vol. 1* (Washington, DC: Howard University Press, 1981), 6–7. Also see: Joseph E. Harris, *William Leo Hansberry: Africa & Africans As Seen By Classical Writers, Vol. 2*, (Washington, DC: Howard University Press, 1981).

[16] Ibid, 18.

this legacy at Howard University. Not only has his impact been felt here in the United States and throughout the African Diaspora, but also in Africa as well, by African students he helped bring to the university, which included Nnamide Azikiwe. Azikiwe, whom later became president of Nigeria encouraged the University of Nigeria to create the Hansberry Institute of African Studies and invited Hansberry to serve as Distinguished Visiting Professor of History for a year in 1963.[17]

Moreover in 2008, the African Studies Department at Howard University in Washington, DC, with its foundation based on the work of William Leo Hansberry celebrated its sixtieth anniversary. Although not a part of the discussion to create the department as it was done in his period of absence from the university, it was Hansberry's early work that was undoubtedly critical to the decision by the university and colleagues to move forward with such an area, when he faced criticism from these two groups only a few years earlier.[18] Nevertheless, the contributions of Hansberry to the study of African History were not overlooked in this anniversary as guest presenter Howard Dodson, Director of Moorland–Spingarn Research Center, acknowledged the role of this great historian. Dodson notes that it was Hansberry's 1925 conference at Howard University on the cultures and civilizations of Negro peoples in Africa which featured twenty-eight of his former students and their scholarly research on the topic as a turning point for African History in academia. Dodson also respectfully refers to Hansberry as the father of African studies in the United States.[19]

Each of these individuals whom greatly contributed to the early study of African History had their works built upon by numerous scholars who followed in the coming years. Chancellor Williams whom studied at Howard University under William Leo Hansberry, published, *The Rebirth of African Civilization* (1961) and *The Destruction of African Civilization: Great Issues of Race 4500BC to 2000AD* (1971). These two studies along with John G. Jackson's numerous works on Africa and religion with the most notable being *Introduction to African Civilizations* (1937), built upon the foundations laid by their predecessors in their scholarship. Similar works also include those by George G. M. James, *Stolen Legacy: The Egyptian Origins of Western Philosophy* (1954), whose work argues for the African contributions to the world being credited to Greeks and Romans.

Cheik Anta Diop building upon this scholarship in his works, *The African Origin of Civilization: Myth or Reality* (1967) and *Civilization or Barbarism: An Authentic Anthropology* (1991), also supports the theories of an African contribution to the development of the world. Two of his most important chapters in the *African Origin of Civilization* titled, "Birth of the Negro Myth" and "Modern Falsification of History," are in fact direct challenges to the most accepted members of the academy during the day proving their studies wrong. Diop argues the conquering of Egypt began the process by which the place of Africans in the region was displaced and provides a series of images proving their place in the establishment and creation

---

[17] Ibid.

[18] Ibid, 17.

[19] African Studies at Howard University, "Celebrating 60 Years: African Studies at Howard University," (November 8, 2013), Library of Congress, 149 minutes, http://www.loc.gov/today/cyberlc/feature_wdesc. php?rec=6226.

of the state. In the latter mentioned book, Diop in his chapter titled, "Modern Falsification of History," is critical of Egyptologists and the created field, as he states:

> Egyptologists were dumbfounded with admiration for the past grandeur and perfection then discovered. They gradually recognized it as the most ancient civilization that had engendered all other. But, imperialism being what it is, it became increasingly "inadmissible" to continue to accept the theory—evident until then—of a Negro Egypt. The birth of Egyptology was thus marked by the need to destroy the memory of a Negro Egypt at any cost in all minds. … Almost all Egyptologists stress its falsity as a manner of course. … Unable to detect any contradiction in the formal statements of the Ancients after an objective confrontation with total Egyptian reality, and consequently. … They express regret that people as normal as the ancient Egyptians could have made so grievous and error as thus create so many difficulties and delicate problems for modern specialists. Next they try in vain to find a White origin for Egyptian civilization. They finally become mired down in their own contradictions. … They then repeat the initial dogma, judging that they have demonstrated to all honorable folk the White origin of Egyptian civilization.[20]

Not only does Diop challenge the field of history and dominant academy but also Egyptology a field only widely accepted at a few universities around the world. Cheik Anta Diop's scholarship calls for an acceptance of Africa's place in history and lends greatly to the preservation and acceptance of African History across broad circles.

Similarly, Frank Snowden, *Blacks in Antiquity* (1970), *Before Color Prejudice: The Ancient View of Blacks* (1980), Yosef Ben-Jochannan, *Africa: Mother of Western Civilization* (1971), and finally Ivan Van Sertima *They Came Before Columbus: The African Presence in America* (1976) continued to build upon this tradition and research of the previously mentioned scholars and Diop one their contemporaries. Each followed the legacy, arguing African civilizations and states should be viewed as the earliest in the world; they greatly impacted states found in Western Asia, the Mediterranean, the Americas, and those found in Europe challenging the ideas of racial prejudice found in historical research.

According to Snowden, "Scholars differ in their views as to the proper … classification of the African blacks known to the ancient world … further complicated by changing modern usage … to which dark and black-skinned peoples have been described at different times as colored, Negro or black. The ancients … however … have provided perhaps the best picture of the physical characteristics of African blacks."[21] Following the argument of Snowden, one should realize the color prejudices of the day in fact impacted the objectivity of many of the most widely accepted scholars of the day and those recognized by the academy as experts on Africa and its place in history. Moreover, this argument made by Snowden is still emphasized by current scholars of the African Diaspora such as Michael A. Gomez, whom states, "Our understanding of Ancient Egypt is complicated by our own conversations about race. … A contemporary preoccupation, race was of scant significance in Ancient Egypt, if the concept even existed."[22]

---

[20] Cheikh Anta Diop, *The African Origin of Civilization: Myth or Reality* (Chicago, IL: Lawrence Hills Books, 1974), 45.

[21] Frank Snowden, *Before Color Prejudice: The Ancient View of Blacks*, (Cambridge, MA: Harvard University Press, 1983), 5.

[22] Michael A. Gomez, *Reversing the Sail: A History of the African Diaspora*, (New York: Cambridge University Press, 2005), 9.

This scholarship on Africa was continued by Joseph E. Harris, *Africans and Their History* (1972), whose work begins with a discussion on the derogatory terms used throughout the writing of African History. Such a chapter is monumental because this was the first time specific stereotypes were taken beyond the physical interaction among people and placed in written scholarship within the humanities. Harris wrote in this work, "Perhaps the best approach to an understanding ... should begin with an examination of some of the early characterizations of Africans ... in order to see how the roots of racial prejudice became interwoven in Western culture, which internationalized the concept of black inferiority and colonized Africa's history."[23] Thereafter, each of Harris' publications challenged black inferiority and promoted both African History and the African Diaspora.

Moreover, one of Harris' most lasting contributions to the scholarship, both written and teaching is the study of the African Diaspora across historical academic studies. Similar to William Leo Hansberry, Harris continued the groundbreaking research coming out of Howard University one of the leading institutions to study African History and with his efforts, now the African Diaspora. Harris, in 1979, with First African Diaspora Studies Institute (FADSI) brought together scholars from around the world to acknowledge the contributions of people of African descent in the Americas, Europe, and Asia.[24] Thereafter, Harris' edited volume *Global Dimensions in the African Diaspora* (1982) provided the foundation for later studies of the African Diaspora as it brought together the research underway around the world. Although later conferences convened to study the African Diaspora, FADSI remained the standard for which others were compared in the years that followed.

Walter Rodney's work, *How Europe Underdeveloped Africa* (1982), and John Henrik Clarke, who was also a pupil of Hansberry, published *African People in World History* (1993). Each of these scholars contributed to the revisionist period of African History by discussing the continent itself, its numerous peoples and languages, the roll of Europe in colonizing the continent, and what this contributed to its problems following the start of the independence movement.

RECENT TRENDS IN AFRICAN HISTORIOGRAPHY

Today, African History has continued to develop across several different studies to include more revisionist history on culture, religion, language, local histories of people and states, independence movements, and economies. Like the history of any group of people or place, it continuously evolves and recent African historiography continues to prove this point. This has led to the publication of numerous works by scholars from around the world as well as textbooks designed to match the courses have been designed and those which are continuously being developed.

In 1964, the United Nations Educational Scientific and Cultural Organization (UNESCO) began compiling together an eight volume series on the history of Africa. This series known as the *General History of Africa* covered a wide array of topics ranging from the methodology

---

[23] Joseph E. Harris, *Africans and Their History*, Revised Edition (New York: Meridian Books, 1972), 2.
[24] Emmanuel Akyeampong, "Africans in the Diaspora: The Diaspora and Africa," *African Affairs* 99, no. 395, (2000): 184.

of African History, ancient civilizations, spread of religions, migration of people, the various states of the north, west, east, and south, arrival of Europeans, the start of colonialism, involvement in international conflicts, independence movements, and the future outlook for the continent. These volumes brought together then the world's most recognized historians on African History whom each brought their own expertise to the subject matter. This ultimately has led to scholars meeting, in 2014, to consider adding a ninth volume to series which discusses Africa since the end of decolonization and apartheid.[25]

These changes in the theory of African historiography continued to experience a paradigm shift only a year after UNESCO began to take the steps to compile its eight-volume series. The independence movement sweeping across Africa in the 1960s also brought along with it a series of conferences and from that published scholarship which was widely accepted following the start of decolonization. In October 1965, at the Proceedings of the International Congress of African Historians in Dar Es Salaam, historians from around the world ushered in the widespread acceptance of African History. In the published works from this conference, the overall themes of the African History were being formulated but greater emphasis was placed on the historiography across regions, languages, and periods itself.

This emphasis on the historiography begins with the opening statements from Julius K. Nyerere, who was the newly elected President of an independent Tanzania. Julius K. Nyerere stated, "The new consciousness that we have a history, and the amount of study which it needs and deserves, is not confined to Africa ... the rest of the world feels a need to understand this continent ... which was unnecessary when we were simply colonial subjects."[26] Nyerere's statement points to the idea that Africa's history was no longer that of Europeans in the continent but now one of its own people, states, languages and religions.

R. Cornevin in his chapter "The Problems and Character of African History," outlines the evolution and transition of African History beginning in nineteenth century through the mid-twentieth century pointing to the important classical sources; oral, written, and art. Moreover, he also connects the history of Africa to the history of the world, writing, "The precolonial history of Africa ... belongs ... to the general history of the world."[27] This is a theory long promoted by many scholars previously mentioned in this chapter, but was beginning to be viewed as acceptable following the start of decolonization.

Nonetheless, numerous textbooks have been published to make the study of African History even more relevant to students. Today, Kevin Shillington's *A History of Africa*, Christopher Ehret's *Civilizations of Africa to 1800*, and Molefi Kete Asante's *The History of Africa: The Quest for Eternal Harmony* have become the most widely used textbooks across university classrooms. This has also led to the publication of regional texts which have included works such

---

[25] The *General History of Africa, Vol. 1–8*, became some of the first published works to bring together scholars of African History from around the world to establish revisionist history trends when approaching the study of Africa.

[26] Julius K. Nyerere, "Opening Speech," in *Emerging Themes of African History: Proceedings of the International Congress of African Historians, Dar Es Salaam October 1965*, ed. T. O. Ranger (Nairobi, Kenya: East African Publishing House, 1968), 2–3.

[27] R. Cornevin, "The Problems and Character of African History," in *Emerging Themes of African History: Proceedings of the International Congress of African Historians, Dar Es Salaam October 1965*, ed. T. O. Ranger (Nairobi, Kenya: East African Publishing House, 1968), 77.

as: Emmanuel Akyeampong's *Themes in West Africa's History*, Phillip Naylor's *North Africa: A History from Antiquity to Present*, Robert A. Maxon's *East Africa: An Introductory History*, David Birmingham and Phyllis Martin's *A History of Central Africa: The Contemporary Years Since 1960*, and Kevin Shillington's *A History of Southern Africa*.

These works have also given way to works published on empires, states, culture, and religion across the entire continent. Published works on religion include: Elizabeth Isichei's *A History of Christianity in Africa: From Antiquity to the Present* and David Robinson's *Muslim Societies in Africa*. Both works discuss in detail Africa's influence on the start of these major religions as well as their eventual spread to other areas of the world in the centuries which followed. Today, these works being produced also challenge the traditional scholarship which negated Africa's role in the development, transition, and expansion of religion.

Writing African History has continued to evolve with the expansion of digital sources found on the internet and new innovative ways to present information to a younger generation. Trevor Getz and Liz Clarke's *Abina and the Important Men: A Graphic History* (2012) and Liz Clarke's second work, *Inhuman Traffick: The International Struggle Against the Transatlantic Slave Trade—A Graphic History* (2014), follows in the line of J. A. Rogers work *Your History: From Beginning of Time to the Present* (1940). These graphic novels present history in easier form for younger audiences to follow and become interested. Numerous museums, like the Smithsonian, the Louvre, British Museum of History, and organizations such as UNESCO have all created important online sources for African History. This should also include the Slave Voyages Database, which has also become an instrumental tool for those whom research the slave trade.

CONCLUSION: AFRICAN HISTORY AND ITS CONNECTIONS TO STUDYING AFRICAN DIASPORA

The study of the African Diaspora is one branch of the study of African History and should always be viewed as such. Historian Colin Palmer in his article titled, "Defining and Studying the Modern African Diaspora," wrote about the following about Africa within the context of studying the African Diaspora:

> Methodologically ... the study of the modern African diaspora should ... begin with the study of Africa. The African continent ... must be central to any informed analysis and understanding of the dispersal of its peoples. Not only must the programs that are designed promote an understanding of the history and nature of the variegated African cultures, but it must be recognized that the peoples who left Africa and their ethnic group, coerced or otherwise, brought their cultures, ideas, and worldviews with them as well. Africa ... remained very much alive in the receiving societies as the various ethnic groups created new cultures and recreated their old ways as circumstances allowed. Consequently, the study of the modern African diaspora, particularly the aspect of it that is associated with the Atlantic slave trade, cannot be justifiably separated from the study of the home continent.[28]

---

[28] Colin Palmer, "Defining and Studying the Modern African Diaspora," *The Journal of Negro History* 85, nos. 1–2 (2000): 30.

Such an argument should prove that in order to understand the cultures and customs found throughout the African Diaspora one should have a firm grasp of African History first.

Studying the many works on African History will give readers an understanding of the stages, the promotion, and preservation, the subject has crossed in the last century of scholarship. Moreover, it is very important that before and after analyzing any topic across the wide realm of the African Diaspora, one should look for any possible connections to the continent of Africa and its long history of culture, customs, and languages.

KEY TERMS

Moorland–Spingarn Research Center
Martin Robinson Delany
William Edward Burghardt DuBois
George Washington Williams
Carter G. Woodson
William Leo Hansberry
Joel Augustus Rogers
Arturo Alfonso Schomburg
Schomburg Center for Research in Black Culture

CHAPTER 2

THE INVISIBLE WOMAN: A HISTORIOGRAPHY OF AFRICAN DIASPORIC SCHOLARSHIP

TaKeia N. Anthony

Black women were largely omitted from African Diaspora scholarship until the 1980s. This essay demonstrates how scholars, throughout pivotal moments in history, have focused or highlighted black women in African Diaspora scholarship as a means to address their invisibility. According to Paula Giddings' monograph, *When and Where I Enter: The Impact of Black Women on Race and Sex in America*, black women's histories were invisible until the 1980s. She notes, "In that time period, the voice of black women, the living narrative of our experience, not only emerged but began to define the literature, arts, and scholarship that were informed by it." Specifically, in 1983, the movement crystallized with the founding of the Association of Black Women Historians (ABWH). ABWH organized a conference entitled, "Women in the African Diaspora: An Interdisciplinary Perspective," at Howard University with the purpose to "address the issues of feminism in history and its relevance for the reconstruction of the African Diaspora."[1]

Rosalyn Terborg-Penn provides an overview of the conference in her article, "Women in the African Diaspora: An Overview of an Interdisciplinary Research Conference." She highlights the three themes of the conference: Developing a Theoretical Framework for the study of Women in the African Diaspora, Cosmology or World View; Women in the African Diaspora; and African Women in the Culture of New World Societies: Past and Present; and emphasized four important reasons for the study of women in the African Diaspora. First she explains, the "common nature of their struggles," second, "the similar ways black women deal with the problems and the joys in their lives," third, "how women of African Descent view themselves," and finally, how they "provide their own cultural parameters."[2]

---

[1] Paula Giddings, *When and Where I Enter: The Impact of Black Women on Race and Sex in America*, (New York: Harpers Collins Publishers), 5; Joseph E. Harris, *Women in Africa and the African Diaspora*, (Washington D.C.: Howard University Press), viii.

[2] Rosalyn Terborg-Penn, "Overview- Women in the African Diaspora: An Overview of an Interdisciplinary Research Conference," in *Women in Africa and the African Diaspora*, edited by Rosalyn Terborg-Penn, Sharon Harley, and Andrea Benton Rushing (Washington, DC: Howard University Press), xi–xxi.

LITERATURE REVIEW

In "African Feminism: A Theoretical Approach to the History of Women in the African Diaspora," Terborg-Penn discusses the methodological approach to studying women in the African Diaspora. She argues, to traditional historians, African Diaspora Women's history is seen as unorthodox because it requires a nontraditional methodological approach. Historical analysis and data have dealt with black women in the Diaspora in one of the following three ways: it failed to include the female presence entirely, it only included the female presence in passing, or it has lumped the black women's struggles with blacks or with women. Terborg-Penn notes that the nontraditional approach is the foundation of African Diaspora Women's history and suggests scholars reexamine some of the old documents and secondary sources to find the female perspective, include traditionally neglected sources such as oral histories, and the field must involve interdisciplinary sources.[3]

Filomina Chioma Steady defines and advocates the urgency for a theory of African Feminism in her article, "African Feminism: A Worldwide Perspective." She states African feminism "combines racial, sexual, class, and cultural dimensions of oppression to produce a more inclusive brand of feminism" that humanizes women instead of viewing them as sexual beings. It can be defined as an ideology which "encompasses freedom from oppression based on the political, economic, social, and cultural manifestations of racial, cultural, sexual, and class biases." Moreover, she argues because black women are seen at the bottom of race, class, and gender. Therefore, "African feminism . . . encompasses freedom from the complex configurations created by multiple oppressions is necessary and urgent."[4]

Terborg-Penn agreed that Steady's African feminist theory should be the approach to the study of women in the African Diaspora according to her article, "Through an African Feminist Theoretical Lens: Viewing Caribbean Women's History Cross-culturally." Terborg-Penn argues the way to view the cross-cultural analysis is through an African feminist lens, "because the view achieved is all inclusive; African feminists concern themselves with race, gender, class, religion, age, and ethnicity." These are all factors in the cultural survival of the people.[5]

Women have always been activist against international oppression. Steady affirms in her article, "Women of Africa and the African Diaspora: Linkages and Influences," the two most dominant values in African Feminist theory are encouraging self-reliance through female networks and developing survival strategies. The following examples of literature on black women in the African Diaspora contain one or more form of the abovementioned methodologies.

---

[3] Rosalyn Terborg-Penn, "African Feminism: A Theoretical Approach to the History of Women in the African Diaspora" in *Women in Africa and the African Diaspora*, edited by Rosalyn Terborg-Penn, Sharon Harley, and Andrea Benton Rushing, (Washington, DC: Howard University Press),43–63.

[4] Filomina Chioma Steady, "African Feminism: A Worldwide Perspective," in *Women in Africa and the African Diaspora*, edited by Rosalyn Terborg-Penn, Sharon Harley, and Andrea Benton Rushing, (Washington, DC: Howard University Press),Pg.4

[5] Rosalyn Terborg-Penn, "Through an African Feminist Theoretical Lens: Viewing Caribbean Women's History Cross-culturally," in *Engendering History: Caribbean Women in Historical Perspective*, edited by Verene Shepherd, Bridget Brereton, and Barbara Bailey (New York: St. Martin's Press),Pg.4

Black women in the African Diaspora were moved to the center of slavery scholarship with Deborah Gray White's monograph *Ar'n't I a Woman?: Female Slaves in the Plantation South*. White examines slave women in the United States South primarily during the antebellum period, 1830–1860. She argues that black female slaves were not submissive and highlights the nature and life cycle of female slavery as well as the female slave network.[6]

In the British Caribbean, Barbara Bush addresses the invisibility of black women in slave literature in her monograph, *Slave Women in Caribbean Society, 1650–1838*. Bush explains it was not until 1990 that academic literature began to "single out for special attention" slave women in the West Indies as an "individual whose experience and reactions to slavery were somehow intrinsically different from those of the male slave." The reason black women were not being included in slavery literature, she explains, was a result of how historians have approached the study of slavery and their interpretation of original source material. According to Bush, scholars' approach to slavery was based on inherent racism; they portrayed the slave as a passive figure and emphasized inferior racial traits. Therefore, they underplayed the extent of resistance.[7]

Bush examines black women as political activist during slavery as she noted, "The historical invisibility of women in descriptions of slave revolts may be merely a result of the cultural conditioning of the authors." She explained that women participated in slave revolts physically and culturally. Discussing the Maroon leader Nanny from Jamaica, Bush notes that Obeah was a common cultural form that women used to resist slavery throughout the Caribbean. Obeah is a spiritual practice most common among the Igbo of West Africa.[8]

Rebel Women in the British West Indies During Slavery moved slave women to the center of resistance scholarship. Lucille Mathurin Mair discusses how women in the British West Indies resisted the institution of slavery by demonstrating examples of negative resistance such as pretending to be ill and avoiding work and positive resistance such as armed rebellion. Mair also discusses female leaders and connects their roles to African cultural survivals in the New World.[9]

Alvin O. Thompson addresses black women and slave resistance in his monograph *Flight to Freedom: African Runaways and Maroons in the Americas*. He illustrates that the flight of slaves was a direct attack to end the institution of slavery and argues pregnant women's flight was a clear indication of the refusal to bring up their children under slavery. Moreover, he notes that more pregnant women in the Caribbean and Brazil took flight compared to pregnant women in the United States. Thompson also highlighted a female maroon leader in Jamaica, Nanny. He describes her leadership skills as being similar to those of other female African leaders. For example, he notes her knowledge of the spiritual practice Obeah as a cultural means to galvanize maroons to stage revolts.[10]

---

[6] Deborah Gray White, *Ar'n't I a Woman?: Female Slaves in the Plantation South* (New York: W. W. Norton and Company), 1999.

[7] Barbara Bush, *Slave Women in Caribbean Society, 1650–1838* (Bloomington: Indiana University Press),Pg 1.

[8] Barbara Bush, *Slave Women in Caribbean Society, 1650–1838* (Bloomington: Indiana University Press), 67.

[9] Lucille M. Mair, *Rebel Women in the British West Indies During Slavery* (Kingston: Institute of Jamaica Publications), 1995.

[10] Alvin o. Thompson, *Flight to Freedom: African Runaways and Maroons in the Americas* (Jamaica: University of the West Indies Press), 2006.

Michael Gomez centers black women's spiritual practices as a form of slave resistance in his monograph *Reversing Sail: A History of the African Diaspora* Gomez examines their infanticide practices in the Americas and the Caribbean and argues that the knowledge of African abortion procedures, particularly through, which involved the use of "herbs, shrubs, plant roots, tree bark, lime, mango, papaya, yam, manioc, frangipani, and sharp sticks and stalks" were being used by slave women to deny the plantocracy, ruling planter class, the labor it needed to maintain the institution of slavery.[11]

Reproduction was a major form of women's resistance during slavery. Jennifer L. Morgan examines African slave women's reproduction in the British West Indies and on the North American mainland in *Laboring Women: Reproduction and Gender in New World Slavery*. She argues that African women's labor was at the heart of monoculture export economies in both the Caribbean and the American South, and their reproductive lives were at the heart of the entire venture of racial slavery. Centering women as slave resisters, Morgan argued that some women in the Caribbean and in the American South refused to bear children as means to dissemble the institution of slavery. She notes that enslaved West African women brought with them to the New World the knowledge of contraception, methods of birth control, and abortifacients (an agent that induces abortion), specifically, in Suriname, women used seeds from plants to abort their children. Other African abortifacients to the Caribbean were okra, aloe, snake roots, and cotton roots. In another example, Morgan explains in the American South, enslaved women used vaginal suppositories and infusions of gum, camphor, and rue to abort a pregnancy.[12]

Specifically examining Jamaica, Mair argues that slave women exercised effective control over their reproduction as a means to dismantle slavery in her article, "Women Field Workers in Jamaica during Slavery." She conveyed that slave women were the mainstay of the economy in Jamaica by the late eighteenth century and in an effort to frustrate the plantocracy's hopes for a self-reproducing labor force, slave women practiced abortions, prolongs lactation, and drew exclusively on the midwives knowledge of birth processes in order to depress their fertility deliberately. Mair also notes that motherhood became the catalyst for much of women's subversive and aggressive strategies directed against the might of the plantation. Slave women withheld their labor and that of their children from the dominant socioeconomic system.[13]

Bernard Moitt addresses the invisibility of black women in slavery literature in the French Caribbean in, *Women and Slavery in the French Antilles, 1635–1848*. Moitt explains the invisibility of women in the literature is a result of inadequate sources on slavery in the French Caribbean, minus those of Saint-Domingue. Concentrating primarily on the islands of Saint-Domingue, Guadeloupe, Martinique, and French Guiana, Moitt argues, "Women resisted to slavery in the same ways men did," however, "the allocation of tasks based on gender, conditioned women's

---

[11] Michael Gomez, *Reversing Sail: A History of the African Diaspora* (Cambridge: Cambridge University Press), 2005.

[12] Jennifer L. Morgan, *Laboring Women: Reproduction and Gender in New World Slavery* (Philadelphia: University of Pennsylvania Press), 2004.

[13] Mair, "Women Field Workers in Jamaica during Slavery," in *Slavery, Freedom and Gender: The Dynamics of Caribbean Society*, edited by Brian L. Moore, B. W. Higman, Carl Campbell, and Patrick Bryan (Barbados: University of the West Indies Press, 183–198.

responses to slavery." Women's resistance to slavery ranged from armed revolt, to flight, to maroonage, and poisoning. He highlights the women's roles in the Saint-Domingue and Guadeloupe wars, noting women participated in armed revolt alongside the men and took refuge in the mountains. Women were more likely to run away due to the low status of washerwomen, compared to seamstresses and domestic servants. Moreover, he adds maroonage was a very important dimension of female resistance, and poisoning was one of the most common and earliest forms of resistance for women.[14]

C. L. R. James highlights the women's role in the Haitian Revolution in, *Black Jacobins: Toussaint L'Ouverture and the San Domingo Revolution.* He notes the women's spirituality rituals and ceremonies coupled with the male African warrior nature were the two major components for victory in the revolution. He provides examples of women's rituals of dance, song, praise, and chanting to the ancestors and spirits for protection and victory.[15]

Rhoda E. Reddock centers black women during slavery in, *Women, Labor, and Politics in Trinidad and Tobago.* Reddock, acknowledging the invisibility of black women in literature, asserts that black women, particularly Black Third World Women, had to tell their own story for the importance of establishing a tradition of black women's struggle. Reddock's study covers black women's activism in Trinidad and Tobago from slavery until the 1956 General Elections. She highlights gender, race, class, and culture as comprising factors in the feminist struggle in Trinidad and Tobago.[16]

Benjamin Quarles addresses the invisibility of black women as political activists in abolitionist literature in, *Black Abolitionists.* He argues that black abolitionists were in the vanguard of the antislavery movement; however, this narrative has largely been ignored. He affirms that the white media (newspapers), following the Southern press, had to ignore the black abolitionist because if "otherwise it would unhinge the cardinal tenet of the Southern faith, the concept of the contented slave and the impassive Black." Highlighting black women, Quarles notes, "Negro women abolitionists sensed the pivotal role of politics, particularly its relationship to slavery." Women's rights, specifically suffrage, were the major tasks for the black women abolitionists, some of the women Quarles discussed were Sojourner Truth, Frances Ellen Watkins, and Charlotte Forten.[17]

Sharon Harley centered black women in labor history scholarship in her article, "Northern Black Female Workers: Jacksonian Era." Focusing on the Jacksonian Era, 1815–1848, Harley explores the view of Andrew Jackson as the champion of the working class by examining the work experience of free black female workers in the northern urban centers. She explains that black women were restricted to domestic work because racism did not permit them to enter into the factories. Harley concludes that African American female workers gained no significant benefits from the rise of the "common man" and labored under strenuous circumstances during

---

[14] Bernard Moitt, *Women and Slavery in the French Antilles* (Bloomington: Indiana University Press), xv.

[15] C.L.R. James, *Black Jacobins: Toussaint L'Ouverture and the San Domingo Revolution* (New York: Vintage Books), 1989.

[16] Rhoda E. Reddock, *Women, Labor, and Politics in Trinidad and Tobago: A History* (New Jersey: Zed Books), 1994.

[17] Benjamin Quarles, *Black Abolitionists* (Oxford: Oxford University Press), Ix, 178.

this time period. President Jackson and many of his followers praised the industrious, simple, hardworking man but women or blacks were not included in this rhetoric.[18]

Terborg-Penn's work, *African American Women in the Struggle for the Vote, 1850–1920* is a study of the first three generations of African American women suffragists and their fight for equality in the realms of triple jeopardy (race, class, and gender). Before Terborg-Penn's monograph, scholars omitted the involvement of black women in the history of women's suffrage; nonetheless, Terborg-Penn centers black women in the suffrage movement with her Black Nationalist Feminism methodology. This methodology views the women's struggle from "inside the black communities rather than looking from the outside through a white filter."[19]

Black Professional women moved from the margin to the center of scholarship with Stephanie Shaw's monograph *What a Woman Ought to Be and Do: Black Professional Women Workers During Jim Crow Era*. Shaw's two-part study highlights the triple jeopardy of race, class, and gender that black professional women faced from the 1880s to the 1950s. She focuses on the upbringing of the women in the first section; examining education, family, and the tradition of womanhood. The second section explores the work of black women in the private and public sectors and personal public work done to achieve full professional status. Shaw highlights that even though these women are seen as professional black women they were underpaid in both the private and public sectors and still faced discrimination because of race, class, and gender.[20]

Living in, Living Out: African American Domestics and the Great Migration by Elizabeth Clark-Lewis, centers women in the Great migration and labor history scholarships. Clark-Lewis uses oral interviews to tell the stories of ninety-seven women who were part of the Great migration from the rural south to Washington, DC, in the first three decades of the twentieth century. She illustrates how black women sought to transform a master-servant relationship into an employer-employee relationship. She highlights the family networks that supported the migrations and the strategies of black women workers who sought to determine their own work lives by "living outside of these relationships."[21]

Sylvia M. Jacobs centered African American female missionaries' work in Diasporic scholarship in her article, "Afro-American Women Missionaries Confront the African Way of Life." Jacobs highlights ten African American women missionaries who served in Africa from 1882 to 1951, which was the peak of missionary fervor. She establishes that black American women went to Africa as second-class missionaries, however, they viewed Africans with similar prejudices that white American missionaries held. Jacobs argues that black American female missionaries' concern for African women, their second-class status as missionaries, and their experiences on the continent transformed their preconceived Western notions about the "dark continent."

---

[18] Sharon Harley, "Northern Black Female Workers: Jacksonian Era," In *The Afro-American Woman: Struggles and Images*, edited by Sharon Harley and Rosalyn Terborg-Penn (Baltimore: Black Classic Press), 5–16.

[19] Rosalyn Terborg-Penn, *African American Women in the Struggle to Vote 1850-1920* (Bloomington: Indiana University Press), 1998.

[20] Stephanie J. Shaw, *What a Woman Ought to Be and to Do: Black Professional Women Workers During the Jim Crow Era* (Chicago: The University of Chicago Press), 1996.

[21] Elizabeth Clark-Lewis, *Living In, Living Out: African American Domestics and the Great Migration* (New York: Kodansha International), 1996.

As a result, African women and black American female missionaries formed networks to assist African women and their children.[22]

Anna Julia Cooper focuses on black women in their fight for equality in the United States with her work *A Voice from the South*. Cooper argues that the status of black women is the only true measure of collective racial progress because black women are most likely responsible for the nurturing of families; and therefore, she represents the entire race. Cooper criticizes black men for securing higher education for themselves and denying women access to those same opportunities. She was equally critical of white women throughout her essays. She asserts that black womanhood is the vital agency for social and political change in America.[23]

Sharon Harley's article, "Anna J. Cooper: A Voice for Black Women," discusses Cooper's intellectual activist scholarship. She argues that Cooper advanced the idea that black women need to speak up for themselves and not allow black men to always speak for them. Moreover, Cooper believed that black women should be in the forefront for the fight for black rights.[24]

Deborah Gray White's monograph, Too *Heavy a Load: Black Women in Defense of Themselves 1894–1994*, highlights black women organizations in the fight for equality. This study begins with club organizing in the 1890s and ends with a black woman's conference held in 1994. White examines five national black women's organizations and shows how black women persistently spoke on their own behalf on issues of race leadership, negative stereotypes, woman's suffrage, women's rights, civil rights, and civil liberties. White illustrates the differences these black women's associations had in the approach to racial and gender equality, highlighting that black women are not a monolithic group.[25]

Focusing on college-educated black women, Paula Giddings discusses black sorority activism, with *In Search of Sisterhood: Delta Sigma Theta and the Challenge of the Black Sorority Movement*. Giddings illustrates the increasing involvement of black women in the political, social, and economic affairs of America by examining the work of the largest black woman's sorority, Delta Sigma Theta Sorority, Inc. Giddings' three-part study explores the foundation of the organization, its activism throughout the years highlighting leadership and initiatives, and the new directions of the organization.[26]

Cynthia Neverdon-Morton centers women in the struggle for equality in the United States South in her article, "The Woman's Struggle for Equality in the South, 1895–1925." Neverdon-Morton argues that black women were a positive force for change and worked to improve the conditions of the race. She highlights the role of educated black women, mentioning affluent black female educators and activists such as Mary Church Terrell, Lugenia Burns Hope,

---

[22] Sylvia M. Jacobs, "Afro-American Women Missionaries Confront the African Way of Life" in *Women in Africa and the African Diaspora*, edited by Rosalyn Terborg-Penn, Sharon Harley, and Andrea Benton Rushing (Washington, DC: Howard University Press), 121–132.

[23] Anna J. Cooper, *A Voice from the South* (New York: Oxford University Press), 1988.

[24] Sharon Harley, "Anna J. Cooper: A Voice for Black Women" in *The Afro-American Woman: Struggles and Images*, edited by Sharon Harley and Rosalyn Terborg-Penn (Baltimore: Black Classic Press), 87–96.

[25] Deborah Gray White, *Too Heavy a Load: Black Women in Defense of Themselves, 1894–1994* (New York: W. W. Norton and Company), 1999.

[26] Paula Giddings, In Search of Sisterhood: Delta Sigma Theta and the Challenge of the Black Sorority Movement (New York: William Morrow and Company, Inc.), 1988.

Rosetta Douglass Sprague, and Charlotte Hawkins Brown. The issues these women fought for were education, suffrage, and antilynching.[27]

Frank Andre Guridy addresses the invisibility of Afro-Cuban women by highlighting them in *Forging Diaspora: Afro-Cubans and African-Americans in a World of Empire and Jim Crow*. Guridy discusses the works of the leading Afro-Cuban women's organization of the 1930s, the Asociacion Cultural Femenina (AFC) (Women's Cultural Association). Noting the similarities of the AFC and National Council of Negro Women in the United States, Guridy highlights the AFC's main objectives were racial uplift and the civil and cultural involvement of women. The difference in this organization opposed to other Afro-Cuban women's organizations was the AFC emphasized on Afro-Cuban's civic involvement that mobilized women voters. Women gained suffrage rights in 1934. Guridy also highlights Afro-Cuban feminist and educator, Ana Echegoyen de Canizares, who was the major force behind the AFC.[28]

George Reid Andrews highlights black women's activism for labor rights in, *Blackness in the White Nation: A History of Afro-Uruguay*. In the 1930s–1940s Afro-Uruguayans were influenced by Booker T. Washington's industrial education ideology and used it to campaign for better jobs, however, black women in the labor market faced social and economic disadvantages. Andrews highlights the activism of the 1936 Women's Congress in Montevideo where women advocated for full labor rights for domestic workers; including the right to unionize, workplace protection, pensions, and other benefits. Moreover, in a 1940 major case study, Andrews explores a group of black women domestic workers who sought to organize a mutual aid society and support legislation that was recently introduced in Uruguay's General Assembly that extended labor rights to domestic servants. Andrews argues that the work of the Afro-Uruguay women was a fight against restricting black women to the lowest jobs and living in the poorest classes of society.[29]

Ula Taylor and Tony Martin center black women's activism in the Pan-African movement by focusing on the involvement of Amy Jacques Garvey and Amy Ashwood Garvey. Taylor's biography, *The Veiled Garvey: The Life and Times of Amy Jacques Garvey*, examines the life of the black female radical and second wife of Marcus Garvey, Amy Jacques Garvey. Taylor discusses that Jacques Garvey, after attending the fifth Pan-African Congress in Manchester, England, committed her life's work to the Pan-African Movement. As one of few women, Taylor explains that Jacques Garvey participated in the Pan-African movement mostly through literature as she wrote political columns for two diasporic, Pan-African newspapers, *The African: The Journal of African Affairs* and *West African Pilot*.[30]

Martin's biography, *Amy Ashwood Garvey: Pan-Africanist, Feminist and Mrs. Marcus Garvey No. 1 Or, A Tale of Two Amies*, explores the black female radical and first wife of Marcus Garvey,

---

[27] Cynthia Neverdon-Morton, "The Black Woman's Struggle for Equality in the South, 1895-1925," in *The Afro-American Woman: Struggles and Images*, edited by Sharon Harley and Rosalyn Terborg-Penn, (Baltimore: Black Classic Press), 43–57.

[28] Frank Andre Guridy, *Forging Diaspora: Afro Cubans and African Americans in a World of Empire and Jim Crow* (Chapel Hill: The University of North Carolina), 2010.

[29] George Reid Andrews, *Afro-Latin America, 1800–2000* (New York: Oxford University Press), 2004.

[30] Ula Taylor, *The Veiled Garvey: The Life and Times of Amy Jacques Garvey* (Chapel Hill: University of North Carolina Press), 2002.

Amy Ashwood Garvey. Martin discusses Ashwood Garvey's early involvement and marriage to Pan-Africanist, Marcus Garvey; he noted how her ideas and passion as a Pan-Africanist were reflective in the Garvey Movement. He continues to discuss her Pan-African activism in London and then in Africa with well-known activists such as George Padmore, W. E. B. Dubois, Ras Makonnen, and Kwame Nkrumah to name a few. Ashwood Garvey's involvement with numerous organizations and influential meetings with Pan-Africanist leaders and heads of state throughout the Diaspora situates her as an active and vital Pan-Africanist.[31]

Black women were vital to Nigeria's Independence Movement. Cheryl Johnson-Odim and Nina Emma Mba focused on activist Funmilayo Ransome-Kuti in their biography, *For Women and the Nation, Funmilayo Ransome-Kuti*. The authors discuss the early and political life of activist Ransome-Kuti by centering her as a civil rights advocate who played a pivotal role in the women's suffrage movement, was involved in a successful campaign against the women's tax, also was a supporter of the Nigerian Youth Movement and Nigerian Union of Teachers, and mother of the world renowned musician Fela Kuti. The authors emphasized the racial, cultural/ethnic, gender, and class discriminations as they occurred throughout Ransome-Kuti's activism.[32]

Carole Boyce Davies seeks to recover the radical Claudia Jones and situate her as a radical black Caribbean female intellectual activist in the African Diaspora, left history, and black feminist scholarship with, "Left of Karl Marx: The Political Life of Black Communist Claudia Jones." Davies highlights Jones' battle with triple jeopardy and anti-imperialism with the race question at the forefront of all arguments. As an advocate for racial equality, Davies illustrates how Jones' activism was left of Karl Marx, as the communist party did little to address the racial and women's question.[33]

Sojourning for Freedom: Black Women, American Communism, and the Making of Black Left Feminism is another monograph that centers black women's activism on the left. Eric McDuffie reveals the ways a small group of black women defiantly rejected the middle-class political agendas and cultural sensibilities of traditional black protest groups and looked to Communism as a fulcrum for radical change and transnational political solidarity. He argues that when most black women make an appearance in existing scholarly literature, these accounts focus on the Depression or the post-World War II period, overlooking how black women's radicalism evolved over an extended period of time. Nonetheless, McDuffie shows how black left feminists were part of a community of black women radicals whose collective history spanned more than fifty years. The women that McDuffie focuses on were Claudia Jones, Grace P. Campbell, Louise Thompson Patterson, and Ester Cooper Jackson.[34]

---

[31] Tony Marin, *Amy Ashwood Garvey: Pan-Africanist, Feminist and Mrs. Marcus Garvey No. 1 Or, A Tale of Two Amies* (Dover: The Majority Press), 2007.

[32] Cheryl Johnson-Odim and Nina Emma Mba, *For Women and the Nation: Funmilayo Ransome-Kuti of Nigeria* (Urbana: University of Illinois Press), 1997.

[33] Carole Boyce Davies, *Left of Karl Marx: The Political Life of Black Communist Claudia Jones* (Durham: Duke University Press), 2007.

[34] Erik S. McDuffie, *Sojourning for Freedom: Black Women, American Communism, and the Making of Black Left Feminism* (Durham: Duke University Press), 2011.

Steven D. Gish addresses black women's political activism during antiapartheid movement by highlighting Maddie Hall Xuma in, *Alfred B. Xuma: African, American, South African*. Gish intertwines the activism of Maddie Hall Xuma, Alfred B. Xuma's second wife, into the Biography of Xuma's political work as the president of the African National Congress (ANC), 1941–1949. Gish explains, Hall a native of Winston-Salem, North Carolina, married Xuma and relocated to South Africa, and As the first lady of the ANC, she started the ANC women's league that advocated triple jeopardy equality and encouraged African women to fight for suffrage, and she advocated for issues such as fair housing, equality in schools, and police brutality against African women during Apartheid. Moreover, the ANC women's league also fought for gender equality as some women were not allowed schooling and were held in subservient positions to their husbands and fathers.[35]

Women's activism during the antiapartheid and Civil Rights Movements was centered in Pamela E. Brooks' *Boycotts, Buses, and Passes: Black Women's Resistance in the U.S. South and South Africa*. Her comparative study on women's activism in Montgomery, Alabama, and Johannesburg, South Africa, demonstrates how the working and middle-class black women were in the vanguard of these two movements: in the United States, fighting for racial equality against the Jim Crow system, and in South Africa fighting for racial equality against the system of Apartheid and gender equality with their husbands. Both women conducted boycotts against the bus system and in Johannesburg women fought against carrying passes.[36]

Our Separate Ways: Women and the Black Freedom Movement in Durham, North Carolina, by Christina Greene centers black women's activism in Durham, North Carolina, during the Civil Rights Movement. Greene addresses the invisibility of black women in the scholarship by maintaining, "too often the women that participated in these struggles have remained invisible, elusive, or unappreciated" . . . and "their participation has received little scholarly attention until recently." She focuses on women's activism because she believed, ". . . women's activism suggests new ways of understanding protest, leadership, and racial politics. The inclusion of women, especially African-American women, in this history demands an entire rethinking of a movement that changed forever a region and a nation."[37]

Examining twenty years, the 1940s through the late 1960s, Greene argues that black women's activism was more militant, better organized, and more numerous than their male counterparts. Despite organizing to fight for racial equality against Jim Crow, black women also galvanized according to class status to advocate for equality in housing and jobs. Greene discusses how low-income black women were the major organizers and protestors during the movement, which highlights the importance of grassroots activism.

At the Dark End of the Street: Black Women, Rape, and Resistance–a New History of the Civil Rights Movement from Rosa Parks to the Rise of Black Power, centers black women's sexual abuse as the cause of the Civil Rights Movement, and centers Rosa Parks as the leading activist for

---

[35] Steven D. Gish, *Alfred B. Zuma: African, American, South African* (London: MacMillian Press), 2000.

[36] Pamela E. Brooks, *Boycotts, Buses, and Passes: Black Women's Resistance in the U.S. South and South Africa* (Amherst: University of Massachusetts Press), 2008.

[37] Christina Greene, *Our Separate Ways: Women in the Black Freedom Movement in Durham, North Carolina* (Chapel Hill: University of North Carolina Press), Pg. 5.

women's rights before the movement. Danielle McGuire argues the rise of the Civil Rights Movement was a result of sexual abuse against black women in the South. Absent from most Civil Rights literature, McGuire dedicates the first part of her study to explaining the history of and struggle against black women's sexual abuse in Washington; Tallahassee, Florida; Montgomery and Selma Alabama; Raleigh, North Carolina; and Hattiesburg, Mississippi to name a few. These rape cases galvanized communities across the South, making women's sexual abuse a catalyst for the Civil Rights Movement.

The primary investigator of these rape cases was Rosa Parks, the secretary of the National Association for the Advancement of Colored People (NAACP). The second part of McGuire's monograph sought to reimage Rosa Parks as a lifelong activist who advocated for racial and gender equality, and not a tired old women who remained seated on a bus similar to other portrayals of her in literature. McGuire discusses Parks as a militant race woman, sharp detective, and an antirape activist long before she was involved in the bus boycott.[38]

Biographies have been the vital way to move black women's history from the margin to center of African Diasporic scholarship. Barbara Ransby explores the personal, political, and intellectual life of Ella Baker and centers her as an activist in Diasporic movements but particularly the Civil Rights Movement in the United States in *Ella Baker and the Black Freedom Movement: A Radical Democratic Vision*. Ransby highlights Baker's Diasporic work as an antiapartheid and antiracist student at Columbia University and the University of Michigan in the 1980s, an advocate against the war in Vietnam, a supporter of Puerto Rican independence, and an activist against political repression, prison conditions, poverty, unequal education, and sexism. Similar to McGuire's mission with Parks, Ransby informs readers that Baker's activist career was ubiquitous before the Civil Rights Movement. It spanned from 1930 to 1980 and touched thousands of lives and contributed to over a dozen organizations.[39]

Elizabeth Higginbotham addresses the invisibility of black women in integration literature in the United States in *Too Much to Ask: Black Women in the Era of Integration*. Higginbotham affirms, "Scholars now recognize that race is both a social construction and a key feature of the stratification system in the United States"; however, scholars have not yet explored the contributions of black women, "thus insights from scholarship on Black women now have a more profound impact on the state of general knowledge." Higginbotham's study examines the race, social class, and gender constraints of fifty-six black women who graduated from predominantly white colleges in the late 1960s. She emphasizes that these women did the actual desegregation of higher learning white institutions in the United States.[40]

In Canada, black women were invisible in integration scholarship until Historian Karen Flynn's monograph *Moving Beyond Borders: A History of Black Canadian and Caribbean Women in the Diaspora*. Flynn focuses on black Canadian and Caribbean nurses in her work and noted they were invisible in Canadian literature as the only literature that discussed black women

---

[38] Danielle L. McGuire, *At the Dark End of the Street: Black Women, Rape, and Resistance—a New History of the Civil Rights Movement from Rosa Parks to the Rise of Black Power* (New York: Alfred A. Knopf), 2010.

[39] Barbara Ransby, *Ella Baker and the Black Freedom Movement: A Radical Democratic Vision*. (Chapel Hill: The University of North Carolina Press), 2003.

[40] Elizabeth Higginbotham, *Too Much to Ask: Black Women in the Era of Integration* (Chapel Hill: University of North Carolina Press), 2001.

pertained to domestic workers. From a diasporic perspective, she notes that Canada was not heavily discussed in literature; therefore, she sought to add the Canadian black women's integration narrative. Flynn, similar to Higginbotham, discusses how black Canadian and Caribbean women were pioneers in the integration of nursing schools and as nurses in hospitals in Canada in the 1940s.[41]

The invisibility of black women in the Black Panther Party is addressed through the autobiographies of the women in the party. Activist Elaine Brown tells her life story in *A Taste of Power: A Black Woman's Story*. Highlighting the triple jeopardy disparities, Brown paints a portrait of her life. She discusses her childhood environment with racial and economic disparities and her involvement and leadership with the Black Panther Party in Oakland, California. As the first female chairperson of the party, Brown discusses her experiences with sexism within the party. She also highlights her political and educational involvement by working political campaigns and starting the Panther Liberation School.[42]

Assata Shakur tells her life story and involvement with the Black Power Movement in *Assata*. Beginning with her childhood, Shakur explores the racism that permeated her life and provides a clear understanding of the systematic racism of the United States and the global world. She offers an African American female perspective of the fight for self-determination and development.[43]

The War Before: The True Life Story of Becoming a Black Panther, Keeping the Faith in Prison and Fighting for Those Left Behind is a collection of essays by Safiya Bukhari, who was an active member of the Black Panther Party, Republic of New Africa, and Black Liberation Army. Her work reflects her experiences and attitude on becoming a Black Panther, keeping the faith in prison, and fighting for other political prisoners. Sexism was a major issue Bukhari discusses. She explains that she was brought up on charges in the Black Panther Party because she would not become sexually involved with one of the men in the Party. She credits the behavior of the men in the party to the conditions of the black ghettos. Bukhari emphasizes that the Black Panther Party was a bottom-up organization, made up of the masses of the people from the ghettos; therefore, the sexist mentality stemmed from the ghetto environment. As a result of the sexist attitudes, the women of the Black Panther Party were able to bring these issues to the forefront. Bukhari notes that no other organizations were highlighting sexist issues.[44]

In sum, this chapter examines the invisibility and centering of black women's histories throughout African Diaspora scholarship. Starting with the conference held by the ABWH in 1983, a theoretical framework on how to study women in the African Diaspora was established. As sources show, most invisibility of black women in the literature is a result of gender and race as most scholars have not acknowledged the contributions of black women. For the past thirty years, the literature has centered black women in major "moments" in political or cultural

---

[41] Karen Flynn, *Moving Beyond Borders: A Hisbtory of Black Canadian and Caribbean Women in the Diaspora* (Toronto: University of Toronto Press), 2011.
[42] Elaine Brown, *A Taste of Power: A Black Woman's Story* (New York: Pantheon Books), 1992.
[43] Assata Shakur, *Assata: An Auto Biography* (Chicago: Lawrence Hill Books), 1987.
[44] Safiya Bukhari *The War Before: The True Life Story of Becoming a Black Panther, Keeping the Faith in Prison and Fighting for Those Left Behind* (New York: The Feminist Press), 2010.

activity. Some studies examine women as individuals, in networks across the Diaspora, or in organizations; all in all black women's histories must continue to be uncovered and moved from the margin to center of African Diasporic scholarship.

KEY TERMS

Abortifacients
Contemporary White Media
Monoculture
Obeah
Plantocracy

CHAPTER 3

GLOBAL WHITE SUPREMACY, SKIN BLEACHING, AND THE COMMODIFICATION OF WHITENESS

Yaba Blay

If you do not understand White Supremacy—what it is, and how it works—everything else that you understand, will only confuse you.

—Fuller (1969)

INTRODUCTION

The cosmetic use of chemical agents to lighten the complexion of one's skin, also referred to as skin whitening, skin lightening, and/or skin bleaching, is currently a widespread global phenomenon. While the history of skin bleaching can be traced to the Elizabethan age of powder and paint (Blay 2009b; Peiss 1998; Williams 1957), in its current manifestations, skin bleaching is practiced disproportionately within communities "of color." Among these populations, colorism[1] constructs a spectrum upon which individuals attempt to circumnavigate the parameters of the white/nonwhite binary racial hierarchy by instead assigning and assuming color privilege based upon proximity to whiteness. In this context, the white ideal (Kardiner and Ovesey 1951)—pale skin, long, straight hair, and aquiline features—exacts prevailing and enduring influences on societal assessments of human value. Skin bleaching then represents one attempt to approximate the white ideal and consequently gain access to both the humanity and social status historically reserved for whites.

Beyond impacting communities "of color," in general, the skin bleaching phenomenon has long affected African communities in particular (Blay 2009b). Paradoxically, situated within the first wave of the African independence movements, skin bleaching surfaced as an increasingly popular cosmetic practice as early as the late 1950s (Blay 2009a; de Souza 2008); and is currently widespread. Seventy-five percent of traders in Lagos, Nigeria (Adebajo 2002; Oyo 2001); 52% of the population in Dakar, Senegal; 35% in Pretoria, South Africa (Gbenga 2004); and 50% of the female population in Bamako, Mali (Baxter 2000) all use skin bleaching products. In

---

[1] I define colorism as a system of hierarchical perceptions of value and discriminatory treatment based upon skin tone. Alice Walker first coined the term "colorism" in her essay, "If the Present Looks Like the Past, What Does the Future Look Like?" (1983). In her discussion of the relationships between what she refers to as "black black women" and "light-skinned black women," she states that "unless the question of Colorism—in my definition, prejudicial or preferential treatment of same-race people based solely on their color—is addressed in our communities and definitely in our black 'sisterhoods' we cannot, as a people, progress. For colorism, like colonialism, sexism, and racism, impedes us" (290–291).

Cote d'Ivoire, it is estimated that "eight out of every [ten] seemingly fair-complexioned women use skin-lightening products on a regular basis" ("Gender Bulletin," 1998). Among Zambian women ages 30–39, as many as 60% reportedly use skin bleaching agents (Pitche, Kombate, and Tchangai-Walla 2005). In Ghana, dermatologists estimate that upwards of 30% of the population, primarily women, use bleaching creams regularly (Delle 2001; McKinley 2001). It seems that in many parts of the continent, skin bleaching is nothing less than a way of life.

While it is true that skin bleaching represents a multifaceted phenomenon, with a complexity of historical, cultural, sociopolitical, and psychological forces motivating the practice (Blay 2007; Charles 2009), the large majority of scholars who examine skin bleaching at the very least acknowledge the institutions of colonialism and enslavement historically, and global white supremacy contemporarily, as dominant and culpable instigators of the penchant for skin bleaching (Blay 2007, 2009a, b; Charles 2003, 2009; de Souza 2008; Glenn 2008; Lewis et al. 2010; Mire 2001; Thomas 2008; Wallace 2009). How exactly has this come to be? The reality is that for many of us, colonialism and global white supremacy exist as taken for granted realities, and although we understand their basic premises, few of us are familiar with their historical development or understand them as continually generated processes. As such, we have limited insight into the particular ways in which they continue to impact perceptions of and attitudes about skin color and subsequently contribute to the decision to bleach one's skin.

The purpose of this paper is to critically examine the symbolic significance of whiteness, particularly for and among African people, by outlining the history of global white supremacy, both politically and ideologically, discussing its subsequent promulgation, and further investigating its relationship to the historical and contemporary skin bleaching phenomenon.

WHITE SUPREMACY DEFINED

Here, I define global white supremacy as an historically based, institutionally perpetuated system of exploitation and oppression of continents, nations, and people classified as "nonwhite" by continents, nations, and people who, by virtue of their white (light) skin pigmentation and/ or ancestral origin from Europe, classify themselves as "white." Although history illuminates the fabrication, changeability, and contingencies of whiteness (e.g., the case of Irish and Italians once being denied entry into the white "race"), it is important to note that this global power system is structured and maintained not for the purpose of legitimizing racial categories as much as it is for the purpose of maintaining and defending a system of wealth, power, and privilege.[2]

---

[2] Two definitions of white supremacy have been useful in my development of this particular definition. The Challenging White Supremacy Workshop (CWS) organizers (http://www.cwsworkshop.org) define white supremacy as "an historically-based, institutionally-perpetuated system of exploitation and oppression of continents, nations, and peoples of color by white peoples and nations of the European continent for the purpose of maintaining and defending a system of wealth, power, and privilege." African American behavioral scientist and psychiatrist, Dr. Frances Cress Welsing (1991, 2) defines racism/white supremacy as "the local and global power system and dynamic, structured and maintained by persons who classify themselves as white, whether consciously or subconsciously determined, which consists of patterns of perception, logic, symbol formation, thought, speech, action and emotional response, as conducted simultaneously in all areas of people activity (economics, education, entertainment, labor, law, politics, religion, sex and war), for the ultimate purpose of white genetic survival and to prevent white genetic annihilation on planet Earth—a planet upon which the vast majority of people are classified as nonwhite (black, brown, red and yellow) by white skinned people, and all of the nonwhite people are genetically dominant (in terms of skin coloration) compared to the genetic recessive white skin people."

Thus, it has been whites who have constructed racial categories based on the economic, political, and social aspirations of whites, for the benefits of whites (Ross 1995). In this way, whites define who is white; a definition that has changed and will likely continue to change based upon the particular economic, political, and social conditions of the moment (e.g., the case of Egyptians now being classified as white when they were once classified as Arab, and previously as Black). It is clear then that white supremacy is based less on racial whiteness (as evidenced by skin color) than it is on ideological whiteness—the exclusive value assigned that involves "a series of immunities, privileges, rights, and assumptions . . . This [value is] not inherent, natural, or biologically determined. Rather [it reflects] artificial beliefs created by social, economic, and political conditions" (Ross 1995).

As an historical process and global power structure, white supremacy stands on the shoulders of European nationalism and white nationalism and now operates in tandem with American nationalism. Whereas European and white nationalism reflected imperialist agendas, white supremacy materialized as a system of maintenance. In the US context, the fact that contemporary usage of the term "white Supremacist" often conjures images of the Ku Klux Klan or members of the Aryan nation illustrates the extent to which white supremacy as a political system has been well maintained insofar as the terminology is largely connected with extremist and not mainstream thought. In this way, white supremacy as the political ideology of practice remains largely invisible to the majority of the American public notwithstanding the reality that white supremacist beliefs lie at the core of the American experience (Ross 1995). Its invisibility further masks its reliance upon violence for its maintenance. From the egomaniacal standpoint of white supremacy, given the self-assigned superiority of whiteness, white people have the moral right to exact brute force whenever white interests are threatened, while those classified as "nonwhite" have no equivalent moral right to defend themselves against white aggression, especially when such aggression is enacted in the name of "democracy" (Ross 1995).

Given the historical fact that white supremacy has been constructed by whites for the benefit of whites, white supremacy is routinely interpreted as a code word for white people. However, white supremacy is more than a collection of white people. As a system, many people participate in it, and as an ideology, many people think, feel, behave, and operate according to it, and in many ways defend and uphold it—white and "nonwhite" alike. The institution of colorism exemplifies how "nonwhites" serve to uphold white supremacy. For example, while most individuals who bleach their skin vehemently reject accusations that they desire to be white, and in fact are aware that no amount of chemical intervention will actually render them white nor will whites, the gatekeepers to whiteness, ever grant them access to the racial or social category, as they seek to gain access to the privilege that has historically been afforded to lighter skin as an approximation of whiteness, they endorse the constructed superiority of whiteness and thus white supremacy. As such, any true understanding of white supremacy must transcend focus on white people and physical white power alone. It must address white supremacy as an ideology and confront the psychological power of whiteness.

As a means through which to understand some of the methods through which white supremacy has come to infiltrate the minds of Africans/Blacks in particular, in the next section, I examine the interdependence of Christianity and European nationalism, because as Michael Gomez (2005, 18) notes, "the Bible has affected the lives of Africans and their descendants in the Diaspora possibly more than any other document in human history."

BIRTH OF A NATION: CHRISTIANITY, THE WHITE IDEAL, AND THE RISE OF WHITE NATIONALISM

Integral to the capitalist mode of production advanced through colonization and enslavement was the rise of European nationalism[3] as a pervasive and deeply ingrained principle in European thought. Christianity, a religion whose spiritual ideals provide the ideological tool(s) through which Europeans have understood and subsequently controlled the material world, is requisite to the historical development of European nationalism. Positioned as the universal doctrine to which all of humanity should subscribe, Christianity not only informs many of the fundamentals of Western (European) culture, but as the handmaiden of colonization and enslavement, it also undergirds the construction of a hegemonic white identity (Dyer 1997) which then further substantiates a consciousness of nationalism. Although it developed initially as a misappropriation of more ancient African religious traditions, namely Memphite theology and Gnosticism (Ashby 2002), Christianity has been thought and felt in distinctly white ways for most of its history due explicitly to doctrinal persistence of the Manichean dualism of white versus black and the subsequent whitening of religious imagery, particularly that of Christ (Akbar 1996; Dyer 1997). In this context, particularly during the period of expansionism and colonialism, whiteness came to be projected and furthermore perceived in a manner consistent with both Manichean and Christian ideologies such that whiteness—godliness, "the light," moral, good—represents everything that blackness—darkness, damnation, immoral, and evil—is not (Blay 2009b). Thus, the Manichaeism inherent to Christianity has been instrumental in the defining of what I will now refer to as white nationalism—"an expression of European nationalism which identifies caucasian [sic] racial characteristics with superiority and African racial characteristics with inferiority" (Ani 1994, xxvi).

In his discussions of the psychology of the oppressed/colonized, Fanon (1963, 1967) used the term "Manichean" to describe the world of the oppressed/colonized. Of or relating to Manichaeism, "a doctrine based on the ideas of the Persian philosopher Manes, which saw the world as polarized between forces of absolute good and evil, symbolized in the oppositions of light and darkness, black and white" (Dyer 1997, 225), a Manichean view is one that not only divides the world into dualities, but sees those dualities as irreconcilable oppositions:

> Its logic is a categorical *either/or*, in which one of the terms is considered superfluous and unacceptable. Yet in reality, this duality of opposites in the Manichean outlook are interdependent. Each is defined in terms of its opposite and each derives its identity in opposition to the other. Yet in such a perspective, it is necessary to keep the line of demarcation quite clear or else the Manichean [world] collapses. (*Emphasis his*, Bulhan 1985, 140)

In this way, the Manicheans conceived of darkness, or black, and things associated with it as evil, while light, or white, symbolized those things that were good.

---

[3] I take this definition of European nationalism from African-centered cultural scientist Marimba Ani. In her groundbreaking text, *Yurugu: An African-centered Critique of European Cultural Thought and Behavior* (1994), she defines nationalism as an "ideological commitment to the perpetual advancement, and defense of a cultural, political, racial entity and a way of life" (xxvi). She further defines European nationalism as "all forms of thought and behavior which promote European Hegemony/global white supremacy" (xxvi).

While the Church formally denounced Manichaeism heresy because of its Babylonian (read: pagan) roots ("Manichaeism" n.d.), "it has provided a moral framework, and not least a powerfully simple symbolism, that has profoundly marked Christian/[European] thought" (Dyer 1997, 225). "The conflict between Christ and Satan, the spiritual and the carnal, good and evil came finally to be expressed by the conflict between white and black, which underlines and synthesizes all others" (Bastide 1968). Thus, within Christianity, the Manichean order manifests in identical conceptualizations of good versus evil, pure versus diabolical, light versus dark, as well as the diametrically opposed God/Satan, man/woman, Christian (believer)/heathen (nonbeliever), Christianity/paganism, and heaven/hell. Christianity's analogous conceptual split between mind and body ("flesh"), having the latter as the more inferior and evil compartment, seemingly influenced what would later come to be known as dualism, a time-honored and highly influential philosophical position exemplified by the works of Hume, Kant, Heidegger, and Descartes ("Dualism" n.d.). Christianity, by way of this Manichean worldview, also influenced semantics, "the study of the way in which language expresses meaning" (Harrell 1999, 15). While some of the literal definitions of "white" include "the achromatic color of maximum lightness; unsullied; pure; and snowy," and "black" "without light; soiled, as from soot; dirty; evil; wicked; depressing; gloomy; angry; sullen; morbid; and absence of light" (The American Heritage Dictionary 2001), these definitions are best understood in the context of their moral symbolic meanings—white dove of peace, White Christmas, white collar, and white lie as opposed to Black Death, blackball, blackmail, Black Market, and black eye.

While the impact of both Manichaeism and Christianity on European thought has been profound, the most powerful implications of this dualistic and hegemonic ordering has been on the construction of identities—that of a superior white (European) identity as well as that of an inferior black (African) identity. "The [European] Christian structure of feeling"—whiteness associated with "the light," or salvation, godliness, and morality/blackness associated with darkness, or damnation, devilish, and immorality—"are realised [sic] in concrete images and stories . . . [centered] on embodiment" and further mapped onto skin color difference (Dyer 1997). Even though Christianity developed out of African religious precursors, once it became a tool of both European and White nationalism, Christ, the iconic measure of perfection, is (re)interpreted, (re)imagined, and (re)presented as not just white skinned, but extremely white; so white as to illuminate. Additionally, Christ is depicted with blonde hair and blue-eyes, eerily reflective of the proclaimed racial superiority of the Nordic race. "It was necessary that this man, the incarnation of God, be as far removed as possible from everything that could suggest darkness or blackness, even indirectly" (Bastide 1968, 37).

If, Christ, the Son of God, is portrayed as white, the logical assumption is that God too is white. And if, as according to Christian doctrine, God made man in His image and gave him authority over all other creatures,[4] approximations of this whiteness when embodied by "man on earth" communicate not only a greater nearness to God, but humanity itself. In the Manichean sense, then, whiteness, embodied by humanity, communicates moral and physical superiority.

---

[4] Genesis 1:26–27 "And God said, Let us make man in our image, after our likeness: and let them have dominion over the fish of the sea, and over the fowl of the air, and over the cattle, and over all the earth, and over every creeping thing that creepeth upon the earth. So God created man in his own image . . ." (The Holy Bible, King James Version).

Conversely, blackness, the absence of whiteness, communicates inhumanity, immorality, and physical inferiority, *divinely* subjected to the dominance of God and/or His earthly counterpart—man (read: white man). In fact, the Christianity of the colonial order characterizes black skin not only as punishment from God via the "curse of Ham,"[5] but divine justification for the enslavement of Africans (Akbar 1996; Bastide 1968; Gomez 2005). Here, we witness the Manichaeism inherent to Christianity materialize as one of the ideological antecedents of hierarchical racial demarcations that not only hold whiteness as superior and inherently good, and blackness as inferior and inherently evil, but *necessitate* the domination of those who embody blackness by those who embody whiteness. It is this Manichean/Christian worldview that would not only substantiate and proliferate global white nationalism, but also further validate European colonialism and the enslavement of African people.

As noted by Bulhan (1985, 142), "the Manichean psychology is hard to counteract once it takes root in people, the environment, and the culture. Those who live it rely on it for their individual and collective identity." However, since the Manichean order situates the duality of opposites as interdependent, yet irreconcilable forces, the construction and humanization of individual and collective white (European) identities is dependent upon the destruction and dehumanization of individual and collective black (African) identities. Thus, it is conceivable that the enslavement and colonization of Africa and African people served not only functional, capitalistic needs, but those required for the maintenance of dominant individual and collective European (white) identities, or better stated, European/white nationalism. Just as Europeans would become materially dependent upon Africa for raw materials and Africans for physical labor, so too would they remain ideologically dependent upon Africa and Africans for their superior sense of self.

According to Mudimbe (1988, *Emphasis his*, 2), colonization, characterized by "the domination of physical space, the reformation of *natives'* minds, and the integration of local economic histories into the Western perspective," organized and transformed Africa into a fundamentally European construct. Given the ideological foundations of European/white nationalism, of which colonialism was a necessary outcome, this "transformation" was predicated on Manichean imaginings of the religious, social, economic, and political ordering of the world. Three key figures in this nationalist project were the explorer (soon to be dubbed the anthropologist), the soldier (colonist),[6] and the missionary (Mudimbe 1988), all of whose seemingly distinct agendas were in fact perceptibly interdependent, and furthermore instrumental in the justification and espousal of European dominance.

One of the first steps in advancing the notion of European superiority in the minds of both Europeans and Africans was the explorer's metaphorical construction of Africa as the "Dark

---

[5] The "curse of Ham" refers to the curse that Noah placed upon his youngest son, Ham after he saw Noah naked because of drunkenness in his tent. "And Noah awoke from his wine, and knew what his younger son had done unto him. And he said, Cursed be Canaan; a servant of servants shall he be unto his brethren" (*The Holy Bible*, King James Version, Genesis 9: 24–25). Although Caanan is the son of Ham, this "curse" has come to be known as the "curse of Ham"; and while the Bible makes no reference to skin color, given this Manichean context, blackness as a curse is "logical."

[6] Though both agents of the colonial agenda, Mudimbe (1988) makes a distinction between the colonist (those settling a region) and the colonialists (those exploiting a territory by dominating a local majority), a contrast important to note in this context.

Continent." Described as an impenetrable and hostile environment whose balmy heat and rampant disease "invited mental prostration and physical debility" (Jarosz 1992, 106), Africa represented everything that the "Enlightened" West (Europe) was not. Thus, "logically," any people able to survive in what was later termed the "White Man's Grave" represented everything that Europeans were not—barbaric, unintelligent, and powerless. With such oppositional characterizations in place, the explorer's accounts of his travels and the "natives" he encountered provided the soldier with information that assisted in his ability to physically colonize and socially "civilize" the land and its people (Mudimbe 1998). The missionary, relying on the accounts of both the explorer and the soldier, counterposed the Manichean/Christian metaphor of darkness as sin and ignorance with the "light" of Christian doctrine and epistemology (Jarosz 1992). Because his whiteness positioned him nearer to God, the missionary considered himself the embodiment of supreme good; and because of his blackness, the missionary portrayed the African as the incarnation of evil (Bulhan 1985). He thus embarked on the divinely ordained mission to "save the natives' souls" (Jaroz 1992; Mudimbe 1998).

Each of these figures' accounts of their experiences with Africa and her people constituted a type of knowledge and discourse about Africa and her people (Mudimbe 1988). Moreover, each of these figures' knowledge and discourse constituted a type of *power over*[7] the objects of which they were knowledgeable (Mudimbe 1988). In this way, those who had gained power by way of their embodiment of God and acquisition of knowledge—Europeans—had a *divine responsibility* to choose for those who were ungodly and ignorant—Africans—thus legitimatizing, precipitating, and further maintaining the colonization of Africa by Europe and the enslavement of Africans by Europeans. Colonization and enslavement thus served to an actualize European nationalism and came to symbolize and solidify a unity in European consciousness (Mudimbe 1988) that would influence the contact and interaction of cultures (read: races) for centuries to come.

Most important to note about the history of white nationalism is that insofar as it espoused the "natural" and *divine* superiority of whites, and ultimately constructed a system of black exploitation for the purposes of maintaining and defending a system of white wealth, power, and privilege, it provided the *ideological* justification for the systematic and systemic racial subjugation that would come to be known as global white supremacy. In this regard then, we should neither take our definitional nor conceptual understanding of the term "ideology" for granted. Beyond "a system of beliefs or theories . . . held by an individual or a group" (American Heritage Dictionary New Dictionary of Cultural Literacy 2005),

> ideology is how the existing ensemble of social relations represents itself to individuals; *it is the image a society gives of itself in order to perpetuate itself.* These representations serve to constrain us (necessarily); they establish fixed places for us to occupy that work to guarantee coherent social actions over time. Ideology uses the fabrication of images and the processes of representation *to persuade us that how things are is how they ought to be and that the place provided for us in the place we ought to have* (*Emphasis mine*, Nichols 1981, 1).

---

[7] Weber's definition of power is instructive to understanding the European/white nationalist agenda. Weber defines power as "the probability that one actor within a social relationship will be in a position to carry out his will despite resistance, regardless of the basis on which this probability rests" (Einsenstadt 1968, 15).

Thus, as an ideology, global white supremacy is exceptionally potent, particularly as it attempts to create an "image of itself in order to perpetuate itself." Insofar as the superior European/white identity was constructed on Manichean grounds, Europeans/whites would be continually dependent not only upon the "construction" of Africans/blacks as inferior (Blay 2009b), but furthermore, in the projection of corroborating imagery. As the next section examines, not only did Europeans create images to substantiate their falsified and inflated sense of self, but in form true to their capitalistically exploitative nature, they "dressed-up" commodities with these images, thus profiting from their marketing and sale.

COMMODITY RACISM: MARKETING AND SELLING THE WHITE IDEAL

At the same time that European colonialists were creating and instituting color hierarchies vis-à-vis Manicheanism/Christianity, they were also taking additional measures to assert the power "inherent" to whiteness. Commodities, with their ability to produce forms of knowledge, subjectivity, identity, and consciousness (Burke 1996), represented vehicles through which the colonial order was able to not only gain capital, but also advance both its white nationalist agenda and its "civilizing mission." Through commodities, namely soap, Europeans positioned and furthermore advertised whiteness as the color of civilization.

In 17th century Europe,

> baths were only taken as a cure for gout, rheumatism, and "to amend . . . cold legs against the winter." . . . The idea of regularly washing . . . the body even in a basin or hip-bath in the home was alien to these years. Instead [Europeans] rubbed themselves down with a coarse cloth, with a daubing of rose water (Williams 1957, 13).

This aversion to bathing, a characteristically European proclivity, continued through the Elizabethan era. If Queen Elizabeth I was *distinguished* as bathing "regularly every month whether she needed it or not" (McClintock 1995, 210), the regularity with which the general public bathed was assuredly even less frequent. Thus, soaps were the cheapest of all toiletries sold at the time (Williams 1957). However, with the rise of colonialism (imperialism) and the spread of European/white nationalism, European culture became obsessed with cleanliness. Given the centrality, if not inescapability, of African (black) representation to the construction of white identity, particularly in the context of European/white nationalism, the cleanliness associated with whiteness relied upon the projection of dirtiness as inherent to blackness. Despite the fact that according to many early accounts of European explorations into Africa,[8] its inhabitants were very concerned with cleanliness in everyday personal hygiene, using "native soaps" to clean the body and palm oil, lard, or shea butter "to anoint" it, *at least* twice *daily* (Daniell 1856); or that oddly enough, in its whiteness, it is white (not black) skin that makes the presence of dirt unmistakably apparent, countless European writers have associated Africans (blacks) with dirt—namely

---

[8] See Marees's Description and Historical Account of the Gold Kingdom of Guinea (1602), Romer's A Reliable Account of the Coast of Guinea (1760), and Daniell's (1856) On the Ethnography of Akkrah and Adampe, Gold Coast, Western Africa.

with the dirt that comes out of the body (the racist perception that they smell) (Dyer 1997). Lest they themselves be associated with blackness, and all of the connotations it assumed, Europeans became invested in the process of cleansing the skin, thus furthering anchoring the projected superiority of whiteness. In this way, soap became an agent of the colonial agenda itself. It is not surprising then that by the end of the nineteenth century, soap, once the cheapest of all European toiletries, had soon become one of the most highly valued commodities of the time.

What the colonialists found in soap was the consummate logo for the colonial agenda—the projected European (white) values of Christian virtue ("being *washed* in the blood of the lamb") and *divine responsibility* for the "uncivilized" ("*washing* and clothing the savage")—"could [both] be marvelously embodied in a single household commodity" (McClintock 1995, 208). Arguably, however, Europeans' use of soap as a mechanism through which to "civilize the natives" obscured their actual intent, which was to profit from its trade and sale. European colonialists began to import soap into its colonies in record numbers. Despite popular belief, Africans did not readily welcome colonization, "civilization" nor European commodities. In fact, the history of African European trade includes a long history of African resistance to European attempts to under-value their economies by transporting useless goods into the colonies in exchange for much more valuable goods like gold, palm oil (necessary for the production of soap), and ivory. Rather than agreeably trade with Europeans, Africans reportedly either discarded their goods, walked away with them, refused trade altogether, or demanded that Europeans present cargo that was of equal or higher value (McClintock 1995). As would be expected, colonialists often took Africans' refusal "to show due respect" to their goods as contempt and responded with violence, often killing African carriers for their derision (McClintock 1995). Thus, it was through violence that Europeans impressed the value of their goods upon Africans. Soap, a commodity that was once of little value in Europe, when inscribed as a marker of civilization and a commodity worth killing over, became a highly valued commodity in both Europe and its colonies.

McClintock (1995, 33) notes that this newfound European reliance on commodities to address the "condition" and "needs" of the "natives" represents a shift from scientific racism to what she terms "commodity racism." Whereas in the name of science, Europeans relied on studies of skin color, facial structure, and genitalia to construct classifications of human types, provide prescriptions for human behavior and subsequently establish social hierarchies based upon degree of humanity, by the end of the nineteenth century, this narrative of European superiority was converted into "mass produced *consumer spectacles*" (*Emphasis hers*, McClintock 1995, 33). The civilization and progress that was once specific to middle class Europeans, would now be available through the purchase and use of commodities.

No place is the shift from scientific racism to commodity racism more apparent than in the advertising of commodities. Advertisers expressed the European/white nationalist ideology of cultural and racial superiority thorough the display of commodities. Commodities were not just things to be bought and sold, but with the persuasive imagery used to market them, they further represented ideas and attitudes to be consumed as well. In its mission to *domesticate* the "uncivilized," the colonial order began plastering intimate scenes of domesticity (children bathing, men shaving, etc.) in public arenas, thus giving consumers access to the most private of spaces—the Victorian bathroom—the space within which soap's "magical, fetish powers" would come to life (McClintock 1995, 207).

Pears Transparent Soap's nineteenth century advertising campaign best exemplifies the extent to which soap, as an agent of the colonial mission, was literally commissioned to carry out Europe's civilizing duties. In its advertisements, consumers bared witness to soap's "magical, fetish powers"—the power to not only keep the European (colonial) body pure, but to wash black skin white. In 1899, the same year that Rudyard Kipling's poem "The White Man's Burden" first appeared in *McClure's Magazine* (Merriam 1978), so too did a Pears soap advertisement linking "The White Man's Burden" to cleanliness (McClintock 1995). Through an enlarged window, the viewer is privileged to watch a distinguished-looking British captain, with a head full of white hair and a white moustache, dressed in an impeccably white uniform, wash his hands. Surrounding the window's view, the viewer is introduced to the "bigger picture." At the top of the advertisement, on both the left and right, we see images of sailing ships, one of which is presumably the captain's ship. At the bottom of the advertisement to the left is an image of a ship docked at port, surrounded by large containers of Pears soap. To the right, we see a seemingly grateful dark skinned "native" kneeling down to receive his ration of soap in the same way that an "obedient" worshipper might kneel before a priest, or a domesticated animal might kneel before its master.

The advertisement's caption reads:

> The first step towards lightening The White Man's Burden is through teaching the virtues of cleanliness. Pear's Soap is a potent factor in brightening the dark corners of the earth as civilization advances, while amongst the cultured of all nations it holds the highest place—it is the ideal toilet soap.

Through its imagery, wording, and connection to Kipling's poem, the advertisement implies that not only does using Pears soap purify and protect the white man's body while in contact with the black (read: dirty) natives, but as he shares the soap with the natives, it further "lightens" his burden and thus helps him to "[brighten] the dark corners of the earth" and advance civilization.

In an 1875 advertisement for Pears soap, the juxtaposition of "light" (civilized) and "dark" ("uncivilized") is more blatant, making the presumed "magical powers" of soap more readily comprehensible. Amid the wording of an endorsement "**I have found PEAR'S SOAP matchless for the Hands and Complexion,**" the viewer is again given access into the private, Victorian bathroom. In the left frame (which represents the "before"), a little black boy sits in the bath, gazing at the water with a look of shear amazement on his face, which suggests that bathing is a new experience for him. A little white boy, wearing a white apron, which suggests that he was preparing to engage in "dirty work," extends his magic tool—a bar of Pears soap. The manner in which the white boy shows the soap to the black boy again suggests that this is the black child's introduction to bathing. In the right frame (which represents the "after"), as the black boy stands up, the white boy shows him his "new" image in the mirror, which, by the smile and look on his face, is very much pleasing to the black child. Magically, the black boy's body has become white, but his face remains black. The message? As the part of the body that more often than not carries the immutable signs of phenotypical/racial categorization, one's face (read: race) cannot be changed, not even with the magic of Pears soap. All in all still, the viewer realizes that it is through the white boy, a smaller and younger version of the white man, that the black boy becomes "domesticated," thus reinforcing whites' position as active agents toward civilization while blacks remain passive recipients of their "kindness" and "goodwill."

Identical to the dependence of inflated white identities on maligned black identities, the projection of white skin as immaculately clean depended upon imaginings of black skin as filthily dirty. Moreover, in the case of soap, the product's supreme cleansing abilities would only be realized in its capacity to wash the dirtiest of dirt—black skin—clean. In the simplicity of the messages, commodity racism, unlike its ideological predecessor scientific racism, extended its reach beyond the privileged and educated. Whereas one needed to either be literate, if not highly educated in order to "benefit" from and further advance scientific racism, one need only have sight to understand and further endorse the messages being marketed by commodity racism. In linking racist imagery with everyday domestic commodities, products that most everyone wanted, needed, or used, white nationalist motifs made their way into homes all over the world. Seemingly unassuming and passive when compared to the scientific racism of the Enlightenment, commodity racism was in many ways more accessible and thus more persuasive than scientific racism. Through the historically repetitive portrayal of social power relations via "popular" imagery, ideas about the superiority of whites and the inferiority of blacks eventually become seen as simple, taken-for-granted truths, among Europeans and Africans alike.

SKIN BLEACHING AND COMMODIFIED WHITENESS: THE LEGACY CONTINUES

As we begin to connect the dots, so to speak, and link the legacy of global white supremacy vis-à-vis European/white nationalism and commodity racism to the contemporary skin bleaching phenomenon, it is important to note that the history of skin bleaching via the use of whitening commodities began with Europeans themselves. Christianity, as it helped to construct the ideological blueprint through which inflated European (white) identities were constructed and furthermore enacted, likewise informed the notion of *true* whiteness (Godliness) as unattainable. Christ is "what one should aspire to be like and yet also what one can never be. This sets up a dynamic of aspiration, of striving to be" (Dyer 1997, 17). Undoubtedly, the intended implications of "striving to be" are Christian morals and values and Christ-like behavior, however, the manifested ideological implications are efforts to make white skin appear whiter than it is naturally. Consequently, much of the history of European aesthetic practices is a history of whitening the skin.

Whiteness, when considered in the context of European/white nationalism, contributed to a conceptualization of power as the ability to act or do from a position of advantage and thus designated those who embodied whiteness as those who had access to power (Blay 2009b). When this particular reality was gendered, European women, in their physical capacity to produce future generations, represented the "bearers of whiteness" (Dyer 1997, 74); and historically, their whiteness communicated their ability to continue and maintain the purity of the race. European women who exhibited the whitest of skins thus represented the most desirable mates and as such, they stood to benefit from the display of an exceedingly white appearance more so than European men. It is not surprising then that those aesthetic practices related to the whiteness of skin were employed primarily by European women. As not only the explicit ideal, but the feminine aesthetic ideal, whiteness impacted nineteenth century women in ways similar to how it continues to impact women of all races and culture; and so began cosmetic efforts to whiten the skin.

Though there are reports of English women using wheat powder, also referred to as blaunchet, to blanch their faces and Italian women using "a great variety of beautifying waters, paints, and plasters for their faces" (Williams 1957, 2), it was not until Queen Elizabeth I's reign that cosmetics and whitening commodities gained popularity among European women (Gunn 1973). As the personification of the ideal of beauty characteristic of the time period, "no single individual has ever exerted such an influence on the fashions and beauty of a period" (Gunn 1973, 73). Elizabeth's "toilet"[9] included an entire series of preparations, the base of which was white powder. As a contrast to her remarkably pale skin and to further simulate a youthfully translucent complexion, Elizabeth reportedly painted artificial veins on her forehead (Brownmiller 1984; Gunn 1973). Her pale complexion was the inspiration for what would come to be known as the Elizabethan ideal of beauty. It is not surprising then that during the Elizabethan era, a large majority of European women coated their skins with whitening products (powders, paints, whitening lotions/creams) containing such toxic compounds as ceruse, lye, and ammonia (Peiss 1998; Williams 1957). American women later "inherited" this European tradition of whitening. Brought to the colonies by English immigrants, many of the formulas and recipes employed by European women found immense popularity among American women (Peiss 1998). In fact, skin whiteners remained the most popular cosmetic throughout the nineteenth and first half of the twentieth centuries (Peiss 1998; Thomas 2008). American women, irrespective of class or age, used a variety of products known generically as "lily white, white wash and white cosmetic" in efforts to achieve the "ideal face," which in the American context not only "asserted bourgeois refinement" but also racial privilege (Peiss 1998, 40). And similar to the commoditization of soap in Europe and its colonies, with the increased popularity of skin whitening commodities came increased profitability.

But with presumed benefits came substantial risks. In Europe, the most "successful" whitening formulas contained ceruse, or white lead, which not only allowed for the appearance of matte white skin but further had a toxic effect on its wearers, including shortness of breath, dizziness, blindness, and even paralysis (Dyer 1997; Gunn 1973; Peiss 1998; Williams 1957). In America, by the end of the Civil war, medical case records of women applying dangerous lead-based whitening lotions surfaced (Peiss 1998). Lead (ceruse) was not the only dangerous cosmetic to be employed by European and American women. Eating arsenic wafers, which by virtue of their toxicity produced the pale appearance so desired, was also popular (Brownmiller 1984). Most of the cosmetics sold on the American market contained not only lead and arsenic, but also mercury (Peiss 1998).

Although the whitened face was in line with the projected ideal of the times, women's use of "artifices" was met with much public disdain. Invoking the biblical motifs of Eve and Jezebel,[10] early Christian moralists, European and American alike, likened painting to idolatry and thus

---

[9] Defined during the period as "the act or process of dressing or grooming oneself" (*The Random House Unabridged Dictionary*, 2006).

[10] Eve—who when presented to Adam by God was "adorned with jewellery [sic] and plaited hair" (Tseelon 1995), and Jezebel—who was notorious for painting her face and dressing her hair with ornaments (Williams 1957), both represented the dangerous power of women to engage in trickery, seduction, and the arousal of sexual desire.

urged women to avoid all forms of artifice in service of virtue, purity, sexual chastity, and natural beauty (Peiss 1998). Popular perceptions of the time assumed that the "painted woman," as she was called, was a harlot or prostitute "who brazenly advertised her immoral profession" as a way to attract customers (Peiss 1998, 27). Furthermore, public criticism of men who whitened their skin was particularly scathing, regarding them effeminate and accusing them of falling to the vanity endemic to women (Gunn 1973; Tseelon 1995). Consequently, as much as they were able to, those who whitened concealed their practice for fear of public ridicule. The great lengths to which many Europeans went to conceal their use of whitening cosmetics often thwarted attempts at medical treatment.

This discussion of the white ideal bears interesting parallel to the contemporary skin bleaching phenomenon. From research conducted in Africa in particular, we learn that skin bleaching is practiced disproportionately among female populations (Baxter 2000; Blay 2007, 2009a, b; Delle 2001; Lewis et al. 2010; Pitche, Kombate, and Tchangai-Walla 2005; Thomas 2008). In their exploration of skin bleaching among Tanzanian women, Lewis et al. (2010) discovered six primary reasons motivating the practice: (1) to remove pimples, rashes, and skin disease; (2) to have soft skin; (3) to be white, "beautiful," and more European looking; (4) to remove the adverse effects of extending skin bleaching use on the body; (5) to satisfy ones partner and/or attract mates of the opposite sex; (6) to satisfy/impress peers; and (7) feel clean and fresh. According to the investigators, these skin bleaching motivation themes speak directly to participants' desire to obtain the approval of others and to be seen as beautiful, with their conceptualizations and standards for beauty reflecting "Eurocentric beauty ideals" (Lewis et al. 2010). In an extensive study of skin bleaching in Ghana, Blay (2007) found that Ghanaian women engage in the practice for a variety of reasons, the most prominent of which were: (1) to counteract the effects of the sun; (2) to appear clean; (3) to be and appear beautiful; (4) to attract attention and/or potential mates; (5) to appear sophisticated and/or modern; and (6) to gain and/or maintain capital, both economic and social. Furthermore, in a similar study investigating the relationship between gender, skin bleaching, light skin, and beauty among Ghanaian women who bleach, Blay (2009a) found that light (relatively white) skin as gained through skin bleaching serves many functions: it (1) allows access to particular social networks; (2) facilitates the performance of particular social identities; (3) enables the performance of "modernity;" (4) attracts attention; (5) ignites heterosexual (male) desire; and (6) boosts marriageability/"husband maintenance." In this context, the act of skin bleaching allows participants access to social capital (Blay 2009a). In both studies, Blay argues that it is the symbolism and consequent functionality of light skin that motivates the practice insofar as it approximates, emulates, and/or reflects white/whiteness and its assigned/presumed value. When examined in comparison with the historical practice of skin whitening among European and early American women, we see that in choosing to bleach the skin, both African and European/American seem to have responded not only to the projected white ideals of beauty and femininity, but in as much as the use of whitening products conferred upon them desirability among men, and thus potentially increased their marriageability, they seem to have responded to societal gender roles and expectations—that women *should* become wives and mothers.

Similar to the European outcry against the use of "artifice," skin bleaching in Africa engenders public disdain. As was the case in nineteenth century Europe, in Africa, skin bleaching is popularly regarded the practice of prostitutes (Dorkenoo 1990; Odoi 1991). In and by the media, women who bleach are often portrayed as naïve, irrational, and gullible, and have been chastised and ridiculed. They have been "diagnosed" with low self-esteem, self-hate, and colonial mentalities (Bancroft-Hinchey 2001; Fuller-Dappah 2004; Chisholm 2001; Lewis 2002; Odoi 1991; Tuma 2010; White 2004). Their engagement in skin bleaching has been said to be reflective of their moral character and inner strength (Dzide 1997). One Ghanaian journalist decried skin bleaching "an insult to the dignity of the Black race in general and the African in particular," and thus accused women who bleach of betraying their culture ("Skin Bleaching" 1999). As was the case among Elizabethan European women, although they are willing to suffer pain, risk physical damage to their skin and further compromise their general health, rather than endure public ridicule and/or have their characters questioned, many African women attempt to conceal their practices. And in the same ways that European and American men who bleached were regarded effeminate, African men who bleach are also seen as effeminate and often assumed homosexual (Blay 2007). It seems then that in addition to notions of whiteness as ideal and whiteness as feminine ideal, European aesthetic/cosmetic practices and popular perceptions about those practices were among the ideas and values that were introduced to Africa via colonialism.

Having discussed the similarities between the skin bleaching phenomena in Europe, America, and Africa, one critical dissimilarity deserves mention and that is the manner in which the sale of whitening chemicals has been regulated in Europe, America, and Africa. During the Elizabethan era, once it became clear that many of the active agents used to whiten the skin were indeed toxic and life threatening, measures were employed to attempt prohibition. As early as 1724, an English Act provided for the inspection of all drugs, medicines, and preparations sold within a 7-mile radius of London (Williams 1957). The act authorized officials to "enter any shop, inspect goods and order those which did not come up to their standards to be destroyed. Although cosmetics were not specifically mentioned in the Act, many of the ingredients used in their preparation most certainly came within its terms" (Williams 1957, 1968). Fast forward 277 years to January 2001 and hydroquinone, one of the primary active agents found in contemporary skin bleaching products, is banned from over-the-counter cosmetics in the European Union (Kooyers and Westerhof 2006). Currently in the United States, hydroquinone cannot be obtained in percentages above 2% without a prescription; and by prescription, the highest percentage legally available is 4% (Engasser and Maibach 1981). It should be noted that in 2006, the US Food and Drug Administration (FDA) began debating a ban similar to that enacted in Europe (Stoppler 2006). To date, however, no such ban is in effect. Conversely, although several African countries have legislated bans against the manufacture, import, and sale of certain bleaching agents/products, South Africa, Tanzania, Zambia, the Gambia, and Ghana to name a few, the issue is one of enforcement as skin bleaching products are readily available throughout the continent. Worse still is that the manufactured skin bleaches found in Africa contain potentially lethal doses of substances like hydroquinone (between 4% and 25%), corticosteroids,[11] mercury iodide,[12] and various additional caustic agents (Mahe et al.

---

[11] Hormones used dermatologically to thin the skin (Machet et al. 1996), for example in the treatment of keloids.
[12] A highly toxic substance that functions to inactivate and further inhibit the proper function of tyrosine, the protein responsible for the synthesis of melanin (Engasser and Maibach 1981).

2003). Manufactured primarily in European and Asian countries, places where many of the active bleaching agents are banned from sale, Africa has thus become a proverbial dumping ground yet a thriving market for products deemed dangerous if not lethal. Many companies manufacture bleaching products almost exclusively for African populations.

Mire (2001) notes that the perception of skin bleaching as an exclusively black problem had informed the intervention, or lack thereof, of the global medical community, which in her eyes constitutes "racialized medicine." According to Mire, while previous research found that even in percentages of 2%, prolonged absorption of hydroquinone caused extreme skin damage among dark-skinned Africans, because no complications from hydroquinone use had been reported among white populations, who, according to two of the world's leading dermatologists, Findlay and DeBeer, were the biggest users of skin bleaching agents at the time (1980s), the medical, pharmaceutical, and cosmetic industries saw no justifiable need to ban the product (Mire 2001). For Mire, the global medical community thus asserted the corporeal superiority of whites. It should be noted that the impetus to finally legislate the ban on hydroquinone in the European Union was precipitated by results of animal studies linking hydroquinone to cancer (Kooyers and Westerhof 2006). Despite the fact that the life-threatening effects of even small amounts of hydroquinone have been reported among African populations, since as early as 1980, it took animal testing to convince Europeans that hydroquinone is in fact a dangerous substance. Indeed, the global medical community operates in tandem with global white supremacy—white bodies have value and require protection, black bodies are of no value and are not deserving of defense. Reminiscent of colonization and enslavement, so long as the potential to amass white wealth exists, black bodies are worthy of exploit, even if ultimately, it leads to death.

Commodity Racism in Africa: The Case of Ghana

Another manner in which the European/white nationalist legacy continues to impact African realities is in the transmission of commodity racism. Although the colonial regime may have physically left African soil, their legacy of colonial hegemonic ideologies remained. Through commodity racism, Europeans continued to assert the power "inherent" to whiteness. First attempting to instill within the psyche of its colonized subjects notions about their inherent inferiority as evidenced by their blackness (read: dirtiness), the colonial order then attempted to exploit the very psyche it created, as well as the markets it sought to dominate, by importing and further promoting commodities (soap, laundry detergent, powder, cosmetics, and skin bleaching agents) that promised miraculous transformations—from dirty to clean, from dark to light. Commodities "were by their very nature about the transformation of the 'traditional' African self into something the advertisers argued would be more commensurate with 'modern' society" (Burke 1996, 159).

In preindependent Ghana (1955–57), *The Sunday Mirror* featured countless advertisements for various cleansing agents, namely bathing soaps, laundry detergents, and toothpaste. Nearly all of the advertisements referred to whiteness in their claims about the product's ability to make things (clothes and teeth) and people clean. With the tagline reading, **"Buy Lux Toilet Soap today—the white soap with the lovely perfume,"** one advertisement for Lux Toilet Soap not only highlights that the soap itself is white, but further plays into European perceptions of

African bodily odor by purporting that the soap will garner a more attractive smell. Another advertisement for Surf laundry detergent actually provides its viewers pictorial instructions on how to use the product to wash clothes. And given that the viewers are assumed to not have any experience in clothes washing, evidence of their inherent "uncivilization," the advertisers maximize on this presumed ignorance by announcing that their product is "magical" as the headline reads **"It's New! It's Magic! Surf washes clothes with Magic Power!"** The advertisement further instructs that Surf can be used safely on both whites and coloreds. It is no wonder then that in the 1950s, many Ghanaians reportedly used laundry detergent as bathing soap as it was an often cheaper alternative to many of the available imported soaps.[13]

In newly independent Ghana (1957–70), "modernity" became the new code for "civilization" and advertisements begin to feature key figures as seemingly engaged in modern activities. Now ads for Lux soap feature African subjects, both male and female, with straightened hair bathing in bathtubs. One advertisement for Pepsodent toothpaste depicts a dark-skinned African as a Western-dressed businessman talking on a telephone, a device that was not yet readily accessible in newly independent Ghana. The tagline **"Progressive people everywhere use Pepsodent because it is the modern way of keeping teeth clean and white"** makes the underlying message even clearer. These ads communicated that Africans could, or rather should, change their less civilized ways. Modernity, and perhaps even whiteness, could be accessed through the purchase and use of commodities.

Years later, we begin to see advertisements for cosmetics, namely white face powder and skin bleaching creams. In an advertisement for Snowfire Cosmetics, we see the key figure, a relatively light-skinned African woman, through a Victorian-style mirror. With a large headline, **"Be modern with Snowfire Luxury Cosmetics,"** the advertisement informs its viewer **"The modern girl uses Snowfire."** Snowfire promotes itself as an affordable "luxury" that provides "magic beauty," somehow implying that in the absence of the powder, the viewer is neither "modern" nor "beautiful." Although it claims to be "specially blended to fit every complexion," Snowfire, like many other cosmetics of the time, came only in shades suitable for European and/or very "fair" complexions. Thus, African women using Snowfire would have to wear relatively white faces in order to fit into this conceptualization of "beauty."

The first skin bleaching advertisement to appear in *The Sunday Mirror* on September 3, 1967 was for a product called Colibri Snow Cream. Between the years 1967 and 1971, ads for nine different types of bleaching creams were displayed on the newspaper's pages. Early ads described the products as cleansers that had the ability to unclog pores, reduce and prevent bumps while also removing "discolorations." As time went on, and bleaching creams gained popularity, we see no association with cleansing or acne prevention/treatment as the ads blatantly boast "smoother," "lighter," "softer," "lovelier" skin. An advertisement for Venus, **"The ideal Skin Lightening Cream for Extra Beauty,"** depicts a white statue of the Greek goddess juxtaposed to the key figure, an African woman who has relatively light skin, presumably due to her use of the cream. Through a 1971 advertisement for Satina, we see the reemergence of the "before and after" motif. Here, we witness the transformation of an African woman, from dark-skinned to relatively light-skinned, right before our eyes through a progression of images,

---

[13] Personal communication with Mr. Reginald Sam, historian and Assistant Librarian at the University of Ghana, Legon's Africana Holdings, July 25, 2005.

the lightest of which appears at the forefront. The caption encourages the potential customer to **"Buy Satina today. Then watch the miracle of light skin beauty unfold."** Though these ads may appear unashamedly blatant by today's standards, combined with the long history of associating commodified whiteness with civilization, modernity, femininity, and beauty, at the time they were not perceived as any more direct than the any of the other ads for soaps, laundry detergents, and cosmetics.[14]

Unfortunately, little has changed in the projected connection between whiteness and female beauty in Ghana, or Africa for that matter, nor has the manner of advertising skin bleaching products. One magazine, *Amina*, written in French, published in Paris, and marketed throughout West Africa, promotes itself as "Le Magazine de la Femme Africaine" (The African Woman's Magazine). At first glance, given the aesthetic qualities of the cover models, namely their relatively dark skin, one might assume that *Amina* supports a different ideal of female beauty than do other popular "women's magazines." Surprisingly, however, content analysis of the December 2006 edition reveals that out of a total of 77 advertisements featured in the magazine, 41% ($n = 18$) are for skin bleaching products. As was the case with ads of the colonial past, one need not be literate, or in this case fluent in French, to understand the messages being sent to the readers of *Amina*. If light skin signifies beauty, and products symbolize the means through which to attain beauty, ads coupling relatively lighter skinned, if not seemingly bi-racial and/or non-African descended women with products, send the message that it is through the featured products that the key figures attained their beauty; and if the viewer desires the kind of beauty the key figures represent, then they too should use the featured products.

In addition to magazine advertisements, in contemporary Africa, advertisements are aired on local television and radio stations and are also strategically positioned throughout urban areas and along major thoroughfares in the form of 60 ft billboards. In Ghana, most of the bill boarding advertisements depict a woman baring most of her skin, positioned next to a series of products with captioning that generally indicates that her "nice" skin was gained through the use of the products. Two particular advertisements, one for Plubel (" . . . **and he only has eyes for her**"), and the other for G & G (**"Let your Skin do the Talking"**), connect the sexual desirability associated with light skin to the effectiveness of the products. In the early 2000s, hand painted advertising for a plethora skin lightening agents decorated the wall surrounding the National Cultural Center in Kumasi. One must indeed question the predominant message being sent to both Ghanaians as well as outside visitors when the entrance to the National Cultural Center displays such imagery with the wording **"Our Cultural Heritage"** as the heading.

As its functionary, commodity racism promoted the ideology of white nationalism—the "natural," if not *divine* superiority of the white race. In their equation of whiteness with all things "civilized," "clean," "modern," "luxurious," "beautiful," "feminine," and "desirable," advertisements reinforced well-established notions of whiteness as a symbol of respectability and social power, only now, through consumerism, Africans would be able to change their circumstances and seemingly gain access to varying degrees of that respect and power. We see here that much of European manufacturer's success in marketing and consequently selling their products to Africans was predicated upon European (colonial) promotion of idealized whiteness.

---

[14] Personal communication with Mr. Reginald Sam, July 25, 2005.

CONCLUSION

Skin bleaching is a widespread global phenomenon. Within the context of global white supremacy, skin color communicates one's position to and within the dominant power structure. Given this reality, many people, namely those historically subjected to white domination, colonization, and enslavement, have internalized projected notions that the basis of their inferior condition is their skin color. In this context, skin bleaching would manifest as the seemingly most "logical" method through which to approximate the white ideal and thus empower oneself. As the political offshoot of European/white nationalism, global white supremacy continually creates an image of itself in order to perpetuate itself, and thus continues to employ and rely upon the fabrication and projection of imagery to forcibly convince the masses, particularly those oppressed under its systemic exploitation, that the white ideal is in fact the human ideal.

KEY TERMS

White Supremacy
White nationalism
Skin bleaching
Commodity racism

PART II

FORCED MIGRATIONS IN THE ATLANTIC BASIN AND INDIAN OCEAN REALM

CHAPTER 4

THE ACQUISITION AND USE OF LABOR IN AFRICA AND THE START OF THE TRANS-ATLANTIC SLAVE TRADE

Jarvis L. Hargrove

As European explorers began to set sail on journeys of exploration and conquest in the fifteenth century, they equipped themselves with the most modern ships of the day. These new and faster ships allowed explorers the ability to set their sights on areas of the Far East, most notably areas of modern day Western Asia, including India and the Middle East. While their sights were set on the Far East, their landing on the coastline of West Africa and decision to explore further the areas along the seaboard, beginning in the fifteenth century, began a chain reaction of trading mass produced and mined goods, particularly gold from the region. This led to a widespread search for the metal by Europeans, beginning in an area which in the coming centuries became known as the Gold Coast.

This initial trading brought together three continents with networks built on partnerships between those trekking from areas of the Arabian Peninsula into Egypt to North and West Africa and eventually into the Iberian Peninsula and areas of Europe. The landing of Europeans in the fourteenth century caused a significant shift away from these previously mentioned connections, removing middlemen whom brought goods across the Sahara Desert. A crucial component to shift was this early search for gold coming after the Portuguese landing along the West African coastline, which predates the hunt for labor. Albeit, while these earliest connections were based on trade of numerous goods from the empires and states before 1400s, the landing of Europeans, beginning with the Portuguese whom were followed by the Dutch, French, Spanish, and British, on the coastline of West Africa, thereafter was tied first to the search for gold but shifted to labor in the coming decades of the century.

In the first half of the fifteenth century, the bond between Africa and Europe was strengthened by several construction projects stretching the West African coastline. The start of these new projects after this early landing of explorers and traders in the 1400s set off a chain reaction of European nations seeking out there place to claim along the coastline. Moreover, these new construction projects, coupled with their expansion across the Atlantic Ocean by the start of the sixteenth century, brought along with it the need for labor. As the need for labor increased, this caused peoples and states across territories of West Africa to shift away from goods and items they were previously producing in mass quantities, to meet the needs of Europeans whom most desired manpower.

Manpower was used by African states in several different capacities which included: the production of goods, family sustainability, protection of state, maintenance of state needs and duties, and finally, the ability to keep authority over their region. Furthermore, those whom were able to govern this power over labor also held a considerable amount of say and wealth within a state and whom control was only circumvented by the chiefs. As such the institution was able to expand across territories due to several factors, namely the demand for labor was there and the market for slave-produced goods was viable and steadily increasing.[1] With this steady increase in both demand for labor and goods produced by this labor, power was placed in the hands of those whom could acquire this workforce.

When discussing the concept of power held by masters and kings across African states Patrick Manning writes, "The emergence of ... slave classes presented a challenge ... while they held power of life or death over their slaves, never ... equal to that of New World plantation owners ... because of the limits on African kings' power to enforce slavery."[2] Nonetheless, having this power over labor allowed those with this control the ability to accumulate family wealth and status within a state and as Europeans expanded in the nineteenth century individual wealth as well.

While this control over labor brought advantages, power was only in the hands of those whom were able to acquire this commodity through specific forms of acquisition. For African states this included the following: through purchase, pawning, and military conquest of smaller states and for Europeans this came in the form of purchase and trade. The acquisition of labor through the numerous channels resulted in power shifting between states, having and immediate impact on the economy of those who maintained control over the most captives. Albeit, by the fifteenth century as more Europeans reached the West African coastline, the Senegambia region to Angola played a crucial role in the start of the Trans-Atlantic Slave Trade. As a result of their arrival, a shift occurred again in who controlled the ability to obtain and possess the most labor: from African states to Europeans establishing plantations across the Atlantic Ocean. Thereafter, this labor once used by African states was now used by Europeans to expand their economic opportunities both at home and abroad in two unknown territories, Africa and the Americas.

Along the coastline of West Africa, the start Trans-Atlantic Slave Trade set the stage for a global trading phenomenon, making people of African descent and their labor, the chief commodity of trade. European arrival along the coast line of West Africa and the eventual decision to explore and settle areas of the Americas ultimately created a need for labor which they looked to African territories. Moreover, this caused a shift in the ownership and distribution of power between African states and European traders. The central focus of this chapter is institution of slavery in Africa along with the misconceptions associated with its practice and the start of the Trans-Atlantic Slave Trade.

---

[1] Patrick Manning, "Slavery & Slave Trade in West Africa, 1450–1930," in *Themes in West Africa's History*, ed. Emmanuel Kwaku Akyeampong (Athens, OH: Ohio University Press, 2006), 99.
[2] Manning, *Slavery and African Life*, 144.

THE INSTITUTION OF SLAVERY IN AFRICA

The institution of slavery was practiced across all corners of the world, by numerous states and peoples, across religious faiths, and as such the implementation of this man-made tradition does in fact have some variations among each those mentioned. While the states outside Africa in these early centuries began to weaken, the process of holding captives within the continent continued to expand and grow to fit the needs of a new states and a changing economy. In this economy, starting in the seventh century, the Trans-Saharan Trade ushered in a new era of holding captives as their labor became a central component to the growth of three West African empires and several smaller states. Furthermore, this also included an expanding economy from Western Asia into Northeast Africa and a rapidly developing Europe, as they became a heavily traded commodity.

The concept of holding captives or the system of slavery in areas of Africa is not without controversy, as many attempts have been made to make incorrect comparisons with its practice in the continent to its implementation in the Americas. As practiced in the Americas, the institution became a part of first the mercantilist and later the burgeoning capitalist system, leading to conclusion that slavery in this region was born from the economic circumstances of the era. Moreover, this led to the mistreatment of the underprivileged and brought about a new class based on the power held by the master over the slave, or an industrial middle class reliant on slaves or an inexpensive source of labor producing high return products, such as sugar, cotton, rice, and tobacco; commonly referred to as cash crops.[3]

In Africa, holding slaves, pawns, and captives became a key component to social, political, and economic sustainability of nations and families, which become a factor of the revolving power dynamic within these African states. Nonetheless, unlike the forms of slavery practiced in the Americas, the institution in Africa was defined by certain rights, which those held in captivity innately inherited regardless of state or location. Therefore, we must first recognize and understand there are distinct differences between the uses of the term "slave" and "captive" and how they were used could depend on the location. According to Orlando Patterson:

> Because the slave had no … existence outside his master, he became a social nonperson … the definition of the slave, however recruited, as a socially dead person. Alienated from all "rights" or claims of birth … the slave denied all claims … and obligations to, his parents … living blood relations … by extension, all such claims and obligations on his more remote ancestors and descendants. He was truly a genealogical isolate.[4]

Among African empires, this did not exclude his/her impact and influence within the state or rights granted by nation, just a disassociation with the past. In comparison, Akosua Perbi writes, "The war captive as the name implies, was acquired through warfare … The captive, the slave and the pawn invariably performed the same tasks … enjoyed certain rights but the captive and the pawn could be redeemed while the slave could not."[5] Even as a slave in Ghana, individuals still held certain rights and privileges and were still regarded as human beings and not property.[6]

---

[3] Williams, *Capitalism and Slavery*, 5–9.

[4] Patterson, *Slavery and Social Death*, Introduction.

[5] Perbi, *A History of Indigenous Slavery in Ghana*, 8–9.

[6] Ibid., 4.

Captives were integrated into both the state and family acquiring certain privileges, such as becoming a member of their owner's lineage and enjoying rights to an inheritance.[7] Moreover, these individuals are often labeled with the term foreigner, bringing with it misconceptions about the institution in Africa as well.[8]

The institution of slavery or holding individuals as captive labor was not specifically unique or only found in areas of Africa, but its implementation in continent was unlike its practice found elsewhere. Slavery was found not only in portions of Africa but also throughout areas of the Mediterranean in Rome, Greece, Europe, China, and Western Asia and practiced routinely among the earliest of those to practice Judaism, Christianity, and Islam. Many of the most well-known Athenians; Aristotle, Plato, and Euripides all recognized the institution and the flaws associated within its practice. Sophists, those who were teachers in Greece, argued slavery had no basis in the law of nature and it only derived from customs of the state.[9] Moreover, Plato pointed to need to end the possibility of enslaving Greeks and instead enslave only those whom were foreigners.[10] Enslaving foreigners meant these individuals were to never be incorporated into the state, because they were not Greek, unlike those whom were among the many enslaved across African empires.

Furthermore, in its earliest forms, the institution and practice of slavery was not tied specifically to a race, but instead to those of a lower class. According to historian Frank Snowden, "The origin of slavery was based upon the theoretical consideration of inferiority ... barbarian was ... used by the Greco-Roman culture ... sometimes ... by the early Christians."[11] While bondage was tied to the most debased social class of any society, those whom were held in captivity within these earliest societies before the emergence of the aspects of chattel slavery practiced in the Americas, did not keep this status for life and thus the institution could not be tied to specific genetic type.[12] The biblical story about the Curse of Ham, linked slavery to blackness and therefore, slavery was tied directly to a specific race and genetic type.[13] Nevertheless, the modernity of slavery practiced in Africa distinguishes this institution across the continent from any other place in the world.[14]

Moreover, as the institution began to expand within the continent of Africa across the numerous regions, outsiders began to view practice as uniquely one found on this area only. The institution should be viewed as one practiced world-wide and not solely unique to any one place, people, or religion. To understand the idea holding one as a captive or slave, you must understand the power placed in hands of those who held individuals. In areas of Europe, the idea of holding slaves and owning their labor transitioned to serfdom, or tying ones labor to a specific land where they could not be sold. However, in Africa, this transition took on different

---

[7] Ibid., 8–9.

[8] Ibid.

[9] Thomas, *The Slave Trade*, 28–29.

[10] Plato, *Republic*, ed. Francis Conford, (Oxford, 1946), 168; in Hugh Thomas, *The Slave Trade*, 28–29.

[11] Frank Snowden, *Blacks in Antiquity*, (Cambridge, MA: Harvard University Press 1970), 170–71.

[12] Davis, *Inhuman Bondage*, 32–33.

[13] Goldenberg, *The Curse of Ham*, 1. The idea of slavery being tied to blackness crossed the world's three major religions. In the Bible, this is found in Genesis 9: 18–25.

[14] Manning, *Slavery and African Life*, 27–30.

forms as individuals and descendants were members of communal societies and could keep the same status for several generations but more often than not possessed the ability to contribute significantly to the society in which they were held.[15]

Nonetheless, while they did have certain rights within the state, their power was still limited by their status. This gives those individuals certain advantages within the state in comparison to those being held as captives. Orlando Patterson, discussing this concept of power held by individuals and the state over labor wrote:

> Slavery is one of the most extreme forms of the relation of domination, approaching ... limits of total power from the viewpoint of the master, and ... total powerlessness from the viewpoint of the slave ... it differs from other forms of extreme domination ... If we are to understand how slavery is distinctive ... first clarify the concept of power.[16]

To hold control and influence over individuals, one must have complete power and over those being sold but also understand the limitations of their influence. Power held over individuals should be defined as, the ability to control ones political movement, social mobility, and labor across time, generations, and space.

However, in Africa, individuals both held power and understood their control was limited to only certain components of life. Paul Lovejoy in discussing the factors of holding captives and the power possessed by specific groups over labor writes:

> Slavery was one form of exploitation ... slaves were property ... they were outsiders who were alien by origin ... denied their heritage through judicial or other sanction ... their labour power was at the ... disposal of a master ... they did not have the right to their own sexuality ... to their ... reproductive capacities; and ... slave status was inherited unless provision was made to ameliorate that status.[17]

This limitation, if maintained, restricted the control held over a captive to labor and not to the individual body or personal day to day interaction with those within the same state. Therefore, while the individual was held as a captive, they still were able to maintain certain freedoms and rights.

Those held as captives were instrumental to the state in which they were held, as they were crucial in a number of capacities, and according to Claude Meillassoux, "The community is driven to outside recruitment to reconstitute its numbers ... through war, matrimonial or political strategies ... needs of reproduction compel it to define modes of insertion for aliens, alongside matrimonial institutions, and these modes differ ... whether the alien is a man or a woman."[18] Captives were viewed as foreigners or outsiders until they integrated into the state through kinship connections. Until these kinship connections were made, power and influence over these foreigners were in the hands of those whom they were held by.[19] Europeans arriving later did not understand the process of holding captives and used this as one of many justifications to purchase and enslave Africans in the Americas.

---

[15] Rodney, *How Europe Underdeveloped Africa*, 37–38.
[16] Patterson, *Slavery and Social Death*, 1.
[17] Lovejoy, *Transformations in Slavery*, 1.
[18] Meillassoux, *The Anthropology of Slavery*, 28.
[19] Ibid., 33.

CASTLE CONSTRUCTION: FROM GOLD TO SLAVE LABOR[20]

Thirty years after arriving in West Africa, 1471–1472, Portuguese explorers Martim Fernandes and Alvaro Esteves reached three central regions of trade, which became valuable to the exchange of gold, sugar, and in due course the captive Africans. The island of São Tomé and Príncipe, sugar, the Bight of Benin, captives and the area they believed to be the source of the gold crossing the Sahara Desert into Europe, Cabo des Tres Pontas or Cape Three Points, a coastal point on the region they later called the Gold Coast, lying between Cape Three Points, and River Volta.[21]

Reaching the region they believed to be the source of gold and exploring further, they finally settled in Cape Three Points, christening the area *A Mina Do Ouro*, commonly referred to as El Mina. Soon after making landfall at Cabo des Tres Pontas, they immediately began trading for the region's main commodity, gold. People along the West African coastline already connected to one another before the landing of Portuguese, experience their arrival bringing an upswing in the West African economy, and only further expanded these previous connections. The Portuguese landing on the Gold Coast and the establishment of a European trading center, not only connected Europe to Africa, but also linked people and areas hundreds of miles apart from one another to their landing area at Cape Three Points and Mina.

The Gold Coast as one site of the Portuguese extended center of trading, saw states from as far away as Dahomey, Ouidah/Whydah, Cape Verde, São Tomé and Príncipe, the Senegambia region, the Bight of Benin and by 1482 Angola and the Congo, all participating in this growing trade network. Furthermore, this network not only connected each of these regions to one another, but also linked them to Europe and later the Americas. With their numerous trading ships in the fifteenth century, the Portuguese were the only European nation at that time, in Africa and began quickly carving out its niche into the numerous local economies. During its early years in the region, to gain access to gold for export back to Europe, Portuguese traders imported items into the Gold Coast from the previously named locations. Cloths, blankets, and linen from Morocco; brass, iron kettles and bars from Northern Europe; and captives were imported from several areas of Africa.[22] Within only a few short years of hearing news of gold being transported back to Portugal by traders, European nations soon set out to take advantage of this new trading opportunity and by the start of the sixteenth century were daily visible presences along the coastline of the Gold Coast.

Gold acquired was used to finance numerous treks across the Atlantic Ocean between the fifteenth and seventeenth centuries and was so abundantly and readily available to Portuguese traders on their arrival, that the trade in captives was not seen as a vital component to the regions participation in Afro-European commercial network. While such the case along the Gold Coast region, this was not the circumstance of such places as Benin and Angola, where

---

[20] For a more detailed study of the Trans-Atlantic Slave Trade and just before the start of colonialism please see: Hargrove, *The Political Economy of the Interior Gold Coast*.

[21] Cape Three Points is located just to the east of Elmina and stretches to Cape Palamas. See: Thomas, *The Slave Tade*, 345–46.

[22] Anquandah, *Castles and Forts of Ghana*, 52.

they arrived in the same time period.[23] Although well behind Europe as an importer of captives, the Gold Coast still saw a steady influx of captives brought into the region, as Europeans began to bring in captives to trade for gold.

Obtaining captives from Dahomey, Ouidah, Benin, and Kongo, the Portuguese used them to gain gold and finance their expansion into the New World as well as their development as the major European economy. Discussing the Portuguese trade in gold and captives in West Africa and on the Gold Coast, Saidiya Hartman states:

> The Afro-European trade in slaves did not begin in Ghana ... It began with Europeans selling slaves and Africans buying them ... Portuguese ... kidnapped and purchased slaves from Kongo and Benin ... sold them on the Gold Coast ... each slave sold ... the Portuguese received three to six ounces of gold. Slaves fetched better prices on the Gold Coast ... gold transported from El Mina ... rewarded the Portuguese ... the premier place in the Atlantic Slave Trade for ... two centuries.[24]

This exchange of commodities along West Africa, in the coming centuries created a system in which all Europeans nations quickly sought to join.

In 1482, the trade for gold reached new heights, expanding again when the Portuguese began construction of São Jorge da Mina in area they reached ten years earlier, *AMina Do Ouro*. Constructing this trading castle, São Jorge da Mina also referred to as "The Mine," today commonly referred to as Elmina Castle, provided the first permanent residence for Portuguese traders wanting to settle on the African coast to acquire gold.[25] The Portuguese imported both materials and labor for its construction, which according to its original plan was not fully completed until 1486, although it was operational before this date.[26]

With its final completion, John II gave the castle and the Portuguese further authority by granting the newly completed construction all rights and immunities of any city and thereafter established the Guinea Company. Built as a trading center for the buying and selling of gold as well as other highly sought after items found on the Gold Coast, the castle later became a slave trading castle in the sixteenth century. With its construction, the Portuguese officially established a permanent presence in the area resulting in their population expanding shortly thereafter.[27] Akan gold from the Gold Coast remained the most sought after commodity by the Portuguese and the coming European nations between the fifteenth and sixteenth century. Starting with their arrival through the middle of fifteenth century Portuguese traders were able to carry away £100,000 of gold per year. This was later cut with arrival of the French and English in the middle of the sixteenth century, who carried away £50,000 and the Royal African Company £25,000 a year over the two centuries.[28]

---

[23] Walter Rodney, "Gold and Slaves on the Gold Coast," *Transactions of the Historical Society of Ghana*, vol. 10 (1969), 13–14.

[24] Hartman, *Lose Your Mother*, 51.

[25] Holsey, *Routes of Remembrance*, 29.

[26] Anquandah, *Castles and Forts of Ghana*, 52.

[27] Ibid., 53.

[28] Richard Bean, "A Note on the Relative Importance of Slave and Gold in West African Exports," *The Journal of African History* 15, no. 3 (1974): 351–52.

The arrival of Portuguese explorers and traders, coupled with the eventual coming of other European groups in the sixteenth century began a new era in the history of West Africa and the Gold Coast. Each European nation began to specifically refer to the area which they settled as their own Gold Coast region.[29] These early years of European arrival along the Gold Coast, continued to prove central to the development and expansion of each foreign nation's economy in areas West Africa and later their interaction with the emerging economy of the Americas. Through each nations arrival, the Gold Coast areas continued to be a large importer of captive Africans well into the sixteenth century, while surrounding regions to the north, the Senegambia, to the east Dahomey and Ouidah, and as far south as Angola all became exporters of captives.

As the Atlantic Commercial Economy continued to expand, this growing system of exchange found along the Gold Coast continued to impact trading throughout West Africa and the Americas. Furthermore, it was this early exchange of gold between the two centuries that laid the foundation for the expansion of slave trading to and from the Gold Coast. A relatively small number compared to those arriving in Europe and eventually in the Americas, those captives transported into the Gold Coast were put to work. This transportation of captives from one area of Africa to another within a few years of making contact with West Africa decreased due to the need for labor in the Americas.

Ahead of the Trans-Atlantic Slave Trade beginning, most West African nations were already experienced in trading captives across its own land, taking part in the internal African trade in captives. Portuguese traders entering the continent created the occidental trade in captives to the north and eventually the New World.[30] Just as the trade in gold reached its height after the construction of São Jorge da Mina, Christopher Columbus's landing in the New World increased the value of captives, once second to gold to a top priority. The value of Africans increased after European traders realized the possible profits from New World territories.[31] The need for labor in the New World was critical to the trade in Africans across the Atlantic Ocean as the enterprise began boom in the coming years after Columbus' landing. Between 1471 and 1518, not only did the role of Africa, Europe, and the New World change, but the role of the Gold Coast in particular shifted from being an exporter of gold and an importer of captives to mainly an exporter of captives.

The plantation system between the sixteenth and seventeenth centuries created even more competition for West Africa; in particular the Gold Coast as the region was brought into the exportation of captives business. This brought the Portuguese whom were followed by the Danes, French, Swedes, Dutch, and later, the English into the region; resulting in the construction of forty-six forts built along the coast line through the seventeenth century.[32] Ultimately, these forts constructed along the Gold Coast, first used to trade gold later shifted to other

---

[29] Each European nation arriving on the Gold Coast claimed specific points along the coastline as their own. These areas included the Dutch Gold Coast, the British Gold Coast, the Danish Gold Coast, and Portuguese Gold Coast.

[30] Manning, *Slavery and African Life*, 12.

[31] Ibid., 32.

[32] Magnus Huber, *Ghanaian Pidgin English in its West African Context: A Sociohistorical and Structural Analysis* (Philadelphia, PA: John Benjamins Publishing, 1999), 9.

necessities, namely captives, as the plantation economy expanded; the region thereafter was directly seen as an exporter or supplier of captives.

The landing by Christopher Columbus, coupled with the construction of São Jorge da Mina in 1482, expanded the global trade network across the Atlantic Ocean. Furthermore, this also set the stage for a global trading network that in the coming centuries linked four continents and numerous groups throughout each location to one another. Commodities, which European traders coming to the Gold Coast, once only shipped between the coastal territory and Europe in the sixteenth century, were then being transported across the Atlantic Ocean.

The Catholic Church headed by Pope Alexander VI issued a Papal Bull[33], referred to as the Treaty of Tordesillas in 1494, dividing the world between the two nations. For Spain to claim this New World territory, the Pope stated, "To secure the benefits of discovering they must be possessed, that is occupied."[34] Twenty years after the arrival of Columbus in Hispaniola and issuing of the Treaty of Tordesillas by Pope Alexander VI, Father Bartholomew Las Casas, also a member of the Catholic Church called for the introduction of African labor into the region. The first group of Africans arrived in 1518 immediately setting in course a chain reaction. The landing of the first groups of Africans set in motion the transportation and distribution of African captives throughout vast regions of the "New World," eventually comprising of areas from as far North as the New England states of America to the southern tip of South America. Moreover, the landing of Columbus and the years immediately following his arrival served as a starting point for the foundation and emergence of a global system of trade regulated by mercantilism which transitioned into capitalism, and finally European colonial domination of Africa.[35]

Between 1471 and 1518, relying heavily on forts along the West African coast once used for gold trading, the global trade network linked Europe, Africa, and the emerging territories of the Americas. Initially travelling to the West African coast in search of gold, ivory, spices, and other goods, almost thirty years after Columbus' landing, African captives became the chief commodity sought after by Europeans thus signaling the transition to labor being the main and most lucrative commodity leaving Africa. The period of trade and exploration, forever changed the course of history for several continents and people.

Portuguese expansion, into West Africa and later following the Spanish into the New World, to the modern day continent of South America, brought about monumental changes, especially in the need for African labor. The start of Africans being shipped across the Atlantic Ocean helped shift the center of the economic world from the stronghold of West Africa, to Europe and its new territories in the New World. Economically, these changes affecting the entire world, occurred over eighty years beginning first with the Portuguese decision to search West Africa for gold and. Changes continued to occur world-wide after the landing of Columbus and once again after the introduction of Africans into the New World territories, especially those of the Caribbean.[36]

---

[33] Arthur Davis, "Columbus Divides the World," *The Geographical Journal* 133, no. 3 (1967), 3.
[34] Ibid.
[35] John Henrik Clarke, *Christopher Columbus and the Afrikan Holocaust: Slavery and the Rise of European Capitalism*, 3rd ed. (Brooklyn, NY: A & B Publishers Group, 1998), 15.
[36] Eric Williams, *Capitalism and Slavery*, 9.

The Gold Coast became critical to the labor supply being shipped to the New World. Ray A. Kea discussed the importation of captives in the Gold Coast by writing:

> From the beginning … slave trading played crucial roles in the Afro-European commerce … in the Gold Coast … from 1475 to 1540, more than 12,000 people passed through its coastal ports … however, were not slave exports … Rather, people were among the goods … African merchants wanted to buy from their … Portuguese trading partners.[37]

As the Gold Coast transitioned to being an exporter of captives to the New World territories, Ray A. Kea continues by saying, "After … slave imports declined … forts such as Elmina and Axim continued to be major slave markets for slaves brought into the Gold Coast. During the seventeenth century between forty thousand and eight thousand slaves entered the region via the coastal ports."[38] Although the region became an exporter of captives, it still was not the largest exporter of captives.

CAPTIVITY AS PRACTICED IN AFRICA: THE CASE OF THE ASANTE IN THE EIGHTEENTH AND NINETEENTH CENTURIES[39]

Established in West Africa after the start of the Trans-Atlantic Slave Trade, the Asante are just one of the many groups in the region which captives were critical to the maintenance and sustainability of the state; politically, socially, and economically. Formed in Gold Coast region, between the year 1697 and 1701 in the region of Greater Asante[40], the Asante State experienced a series of wars in its expansionary process.[41] As a result of this expansionary process, the Asante began to influence the economy of the interior region and its neighboring states, acquiring captives during this progression. While its boundaries were well established, just as important to the structure of Greater Asante, were the trade routes which linked the region internally as well as externally.[42] Moreover, these routes leading from Kumasi, located in the center of the Asante nation, were crucial to the expansion process of the nation.

Albeit, between early 1800s throughout the latter years of the century explorers kept detailed notes on their interactions in Kumasi and with the Asante themselves. John Beecham one of the earliest travelers who visited the Asante in the mid-1800s described the role captives played in

---

[37] Ray A. Kea, *Settlements, Trade, and Polities*, 197; and Smallwood, *Saltwater Slavery*, 15.

[38] Ray A. Kea, *Settlements, Trade and Polities*, 197–201 in Robert Harms, *The Diligent: A Voyage Through the Worlds of the Slave Trade* (New York: Basic Books, 2002), p. 135.

[39] This is a brief synopsis of the formation of the Asante and the use of captive labor in the state. This will include a short discussion on the role of this labor and its political, economic, and social impact of the state. For a more detailed study of the Asante State, its history, and the use of captive labor in the state before and after the Trans-Atlantic Slave Trade and just before the start of colonialism please see: Jarvis Hargrove, *The Political Economy of the Interior Gold Coast: The Asante and the Era of Legitimate Trading, 1807–1875*.

[40] The term Greater Asante is often used to refer to the Asante Empire, see: Kwame Arhin, "The Structure of Greater Ashanti, 1700–1824," *The Journal of African History* 8, no. 1 (1967), 67.

[41] Ibid.

[42] Garcia Clark, "Class Alliance and the Class Fractions in Ghanaian Trading and State Formation," *Review of African Political Economy*, no. 49 (1990), 75.

the state. Within the state, a captive could rise to power and hold office if he succeeds his master after death acquiring the stool and property of the later.[43] Similarly, other visitors to the region described this notion of inheritance and power, as Robert Rattray states:

> Slaves … did amass considerable wealth and … power. A master encouraged his slave and helped him … because ultimately everything … went to the master. A master could not deprive his slave of his self-acquired property … Lands were also granted to the favorite household slave for life with reversion to the donor … the slave's children … were … allowed … to occupy and use the land after the death of the original grantee."[44]

Moreover, this continues on the previous policy of those within a state captivity maintained certain rights, which were to be protected and respected by both the master and the state. Henry Brackenbury, another of the many visitors to the Gold Coast in the nineteenth century described a similar environment for captives in the state. He describes classes within the state writing, "In the Asante state there were five classes or ranks within the society: 1. Kings; 2. Cabooceers; 3. Sub-chiefs; 4. Sub-chiefs; 5. Slaves."[45] Furthermore, many of these men whom become slaves are victims of war or have become so through extreme circumstances of poverty.[46] This was emphasized earlier by Akosua Perbi in her description of captives and slaves in Ghana.

Nevertheless, slaves within the state of Asante were commonly referred to as odonko a word which is translated to mean "foreigner" or "captive." This same term nnonko or nnonkofo in plural can refer to both a man and woman, describing those expressly purchased to become ones captive.[47] Throughout the state many were taken into captivity through debt, but those whom were foreigners were taken into the state as captives of war. Captives within the state, whether taken on through debt or a captive of war, took on several different roles, but were seen as key contributors to both the state development and individual owner prosperity.

Once the external slave trade was declared officially illegal, the internal trade in captive labor increased quickly to become the mainstay of Asante economic system and was doubtless the main factor behind the success of an ever-expanding farming system in the nineteenth century. As a result of the developing farming units, wealthy elites began to emerge in and around Kumasi, in which two types of elite could be detected; the rural producers of crops and on the other hand, urban traders who conducted the slave trade and owned plantations. Jean Allman and Victoria Tashjian, argue that the use of captives in the nineteenth century by Asante families transformed the wealth of the family aiding them in a successful transition to legitimate commerce.[48]

---

[43] Beecham, *Ashantee and the Gold Coast*, 117.

[44] Rattray, *Ashanti Law and Constitution*, 40–43; in Orlando Patterson, *Slavery and Social Death*, 185.

[45] Brackenbury and Huyshe, *Fanti and Ashanti*, 106.

[46] Ibid.

[47] R.S. Rattray, *Ashanti Law and Constitution*, 35 in Anatole Norman Klein, "Inequality in Asante: A Study of the Forms and Meanings of Slavery and Social Servitude in Pre and Early Colonial Akan-Asante Society and Culture, vol. 1 and 2. (PhD diss., University Michigan, 1981), 95.

[48] Jean Allman and Victoria Tashjian, *I Will Not Eat Stone: A Women's History of Colonial Asante* (Portsmouth, NH: Heinemann, 2000), 11.

The development of an agricultural center to mainly export foodstuffs turned the Asante around Kumasi into major importers of captives and Salaga as exporters of captives, which developed the Asante cash-crop economy of the nineteenth century. Families and individuals in Asante land, and to a great extent in the rest of West Africa, increased their traffic in the internal slave trade over an extensive network of commercial highways.[49] Patrick Manning relates that:

> The … growth of the African slave trade … expanded the scale of African slavery, but caused a new set of institutional transformations … slave mode of production flowered … until it was ended … slavery in the Atlantic world correlated … with the development of industrial capitalism … abolition of slavery in Africa was an aspect of the world-wide movement for abolition … abolition of the slave trade in Africa … The abolition of slavery in Africa—quite a different matter from the abolition of slave trade—was slowed by the establishment of ties between European colonial rulers and African slave owners.[50]

Moreover, the later transition into the so-called legitimate trade was not a crisis of adaptation as argued by A.G. Hopkins [51] but instead one necessitated by three different systems of trade carried out in Africa generally. First, there was the inter-state trade, that is, trade to markets within a particular region. Second, there was intra-state trade or trade conducted between two or more states. Third, there was long-distance trading, or trade covering a number of states over long distances.[52]

The start of the nineteenth century following the closure of the Trans-Atlantic Slave Trade by the British and the Americans, the institution of slavery as comprised in Africa was under attack by those whom did not fully understand its practice across areas of the continent. On the Gold Coast, and within the Asante state, these changes had a far-reaching impact in the years following the closure of the trade. Several of these early changes occurred under nevertheless, the impact of abolition on the Asante and the Gold Coast did not occur right away. In fact, the changes in slavery within the state and the export slave trade were not felt until the time when the Industrial Revolution, increased the need and desire for other commodities.[53] In Chapter 8 of Joseph Inikori's monumental work, *Africans and the Industrial Revolution in England: A Study in International Trade and Economic Development*, he highlights the rise in the imports of raw materials into England during this era, which on the Gold Coast meant an increase in mining.[54]

Moreover, as the Asante state continued to trade heavily in captives with Northern traders entering Salaga, after the turn of the nineteenth century, the trade of bulk goods became critical to the developing trading relationships with traders as they began too desire other commodities.[55] This change in trading patterns between the Asante state and Northerners became very

---

[49] Manning, *Slavery and African Life*, 10.

[50] Ibid., 23.

[51] A.G. Hopkins in his work, *An Economic History of West Africa* argued the transition to legitimate traded items was not a seamless transition but instead one that created chaos in African societies.

[52] Akosua Perbi, *A History of Indigenous Slavery*, 78–79.

[53] Kimble, *A Political History of Ghana*, 2.

[54] Inikori, *Africans and the Industrial Revolution in England*, 404.

[55] Kwame Arhin, *West African Traders in Ghana in the Nineteenth and Twentieth Centuries* (London: Longman, Inc., 1979), 1.

similar to the change in traded commodities to the south of Greater Asante. To the south, the Asante export economy was able to successfully modify itself to meet the changing external needs of markets in Europe and the Americas.[56] Similar to the changeover from gold to captives experienced centuries earlier, the states along the Gold Coast had now transitioned from captives to bulk commodities. For that purpose, they continued to use the established trading routes that crisscrossed the entire region.[57] Nevertheless, as more bulk goods were transported across the many trade routes of the Gold Coast, captives still remained a sought after commodity for several decades to come.

While the large scale changeover that occurred on the Gold Coast from gold to captives was carried out within a matter of years, the transition from trading captives to manufactured items, raw materials, and cash crops lasted a period of nearly eighty years.[58] The one time centers of trade on the coastline, that is numerous castles constructed by European nations, remained valuable assets to trade as more outsiders became willing to venture into the interior of the Gold Coast. An area in the eighteenth century that seemed off limits, by the nineteenth century welcomed many of its first European visitors.

Albeit, as the trade in captives went on unabated throughout the years following abolition, local and long-distance trading in legitimate agricultural goods was greatly determined by seasons. The time of planting crops and harvesting depended on the dry and wet periods. The wet period or rainy season lasted from March to October, while the dry period occurred between November and March.[59] The increased trade in agricultural goods along with hand-made commodities resulted ultimately in the growth of professional and independent traders, who were able to accumulate sums of wealth. Consequently, the Asantehene stepped in to limit the large accumulation among individuals and families by establishing full control over the long-distance trade routes.[60] Moreover, the growth of professional traders led to the development of private ownership of land among the Asante state and the Gold Coast population in general.[61] The Asantehene stepped in once more determining who acquired land and what land was to be assigned to each individual.[62]

The changes that took place among the Asante continuously placed great emphasis on the use of captives to satisfy the rapidly growing need for other products. Captives were utilized in sharecropping and urbanization, making them vital to the commercial success of Asante economy in the nineteenth century.[63] Ownership of slaves in the Gold Coast and throughout Africa was a family business. Akosua Perbi writes:

---

[56] McCaskie, *State and Society in Pre-Colonial Asante*, 26.

[57] K. B. Dickinson, "Trade Patters in Ghana at the Beginning of the Eighteenth Century," *Geographical Review* 56, no. 33 (1966), 417.

[58] Rodney, *How Europe Underdeveloped Africa*, 99.

[59] Arhin, *West African Traders in Ghana*, 2.

[60] Ibid., 1.

[61] Gareth Austin, "No Elders Were Present: Commoners and Private Ownership in Asante, 1807–1896," *The Journal of African History* 37, no. 1 (1996): 3–5.

[62] Austin, *Labour, Land and Capital in Ghana*, 100.

[63] Ibid., 104.

> Labour in ... Ghana, as in most of Africa, was organized on the basis of households and slave ... labour requirements of families ... Indeed the development of legitimate trade in raw materials fuelled an extensive use of domestic slaves in local production to meet the demands of the international market. Farming expanded ... during the second half of the 19th century ... to meet the demands of external markets. As farming expanded so too did the use of slave labour.[64]

Wealthy families in Kumasi maintained large numbers of captives in their farming units while the less fortunate were forced into a system of sharecropping.[65] Albeit, the acquisition of size-able plots of land and the importation of a large number of captive labor turned the Asante economy into a commercial enterprise geared toward the export of goods.[66] The rising demand for Asante agricultural products necessitated the introduction of an extensive farming system for the production of: cassava, cocoyam, yam, plaintain, and maize.[67] In the latter part of the nineteenth century kola, palm oil, and rubber became the major items produced by captives. It is said that the production of palm oil toward the end of the nineteenth century was so great that it defined the era of legitimate commerce.[68] Moreover, trade in gold, which flourished in the eighteenth century, declined substantially by the nineteenth century giving way to agricultural goods.[69]

Asante families who owned captives used them as field workers as well as domestic servants. Although the captives were generally accepted into the families of the owners, still they did not have the same social status.[70] While many of these captives could ultimately be adopted into a family, or marry into a family, elders of the family never forgot the roots of the individual. Within the family, captives were entitled to fair treatment, and were governed by a set of rules: captives were deemed a part of the family, they were entitled to food, clothing, and shelter, children were to be polite to them and captives could not be treated unfairly harsh.[71] Although these were the laws of the Asante, captives of the first generation were often treated more harshly often bearing the marks resulting from scarification practices.[72] The practice of domestic and farming slavery within the Asante state continued until it was outlawed by the British in 1874. Moreover, the British "codified notions of the kinship of slaves by declaring all former slaves family members."[73]

Nonetheless, while abolition laws were passed to officially close the Trans-Atlantic Slave Trade, this did very little to slow the trade in captives from the Gold Coast. For several centuries,

---

[64] Ibid., 70.

[65] Ivor Wilks, *Forests of Gold: Essays on the Akan and the Kingdom of the Asante*, (Athens, OH: Ohio University Press, 1995), 55.

[66] Inez Sutton, "Labour in Commercial Agriculture in Ghana in the Late Nineteenth and Early Twentieth Centuries," *The Journal of African* 24, no. 4 (1983), 464.

[67] Wilks, *Forests of Gold*, 55.

[68] Patrick Manning, "Slaves, Palm Oil and Political Power on the West African Coast," *African Historical Studies* 2, no. 2 (1969), 281.

[69] Gwedolyn Mikell, *Cocoa and Chaos in Ghana*, (New York: Paragon House, 1989), 24.

[70] Perbi, *A History of Indigenous Slavery in Ghana*, 113.

[71] Ibid., 118.

[72] Holsey, *Routes of Remembrance*, 42.

[73] Ibid.

the relationship between Africans and Europeans on the coast was highlighted by the trade in captives. In the years which followed its closure, on Gold Coast the relationship between Africans and Europeans continued to rely on this trade in captives, although illegally traded. Nevertheless, while the trade in captives was officially closed captive labor continued to remain a valuable commodity and labor force within the Gold Coast and interior of the Asante state.

While the British did not invade the interior territory of Greater Asante and the city of Kumasi until 1874 they were only officially able to take the region in 1896. Thereafter, the entire region from the Southern coastline to its Northern border was renamed the Gold Coast Colony after several more armed conflicts. As late last years of the nineteenth century approached slavery within the state and region remained an issue which concluded with the eventual agreement of the Anglo-Ashanti Treaty of 1896. Moreover, the passage of this treaty ended slave trading and human sacrificing, but not the acquisition and private ownership of captives with the newly named Gold Coast Colony, notably those owned by the state.[74]

CONCLUSION

The Trans-Atlantic Slave Trade resulted in the purchase and transport of several million captives across the Atlantic Ocean. Albeit, the start of this trade coincides with the need and demand for labor in areas of west as profits steadily increased for cash crops tobacco, cotton, rice, sugar, and indigo. This period also witnessed the expansion of manufactured goods, weapons, textiles, and similarly produced metalcrafts.[75]

Once captured, African captives were trekked hundreds of miles to the coastline of Africa, where they were held in forts and castles before being packed on board the slave ship. As soon as they arrived, families were torn apart, separating males from females; women were subjected to the loss of a spouse, child and the abuse white men whom over saw the day to day operations of the castle. Arriving in one of the hundreds of forts which lined the coast of West Africa begins not only the separation of the family unit but also the transformation of individuals into members of the African Diaspora.

Boarded and packed into the hulls of the numerous slave ships Africans were transported across the Atlantic Ocean into a life of slavery, one which varied between the numerous locations people were taken. While on board, bonds were formed between people, which became a mechanism for survival. This Trans-Atlantic Slave Trade which could take months between departure and arrival lasted over four hundred years. The results of this trade were sale of millions of men, women, and children into a life of slavery in North America, the Caribbean, Mexico, and South America. On their arrival, men, women, and children were first prepared for sale and then marched to the selling block and sold at auction. Once sold, Africans were subjected to the second humiliating process of seasoning, stripping them of their African identity. While portions of the familiar family units were lost during the travel from Africa to

---

[74] Raymond Dummet and Marion Johnson, "Britain and the Suppression of Slavery in the Gold Coast Colony, Ashanti, and the Northern Territories," in *The End of Slavery in Africa*, ed. Suzanne Miers and Richard Roberts, 96–97.
[75] Getz, *Cosmopolitan Africa*, 72.

the auction block, certain aspects were able to survive. New families emerged and as people began to fuse cultures, customs, and adopt new characteristics they began to unite new and old customs.

This process of being sold at auction was a humiliating experience, as people were measured, probed, and prodded for noticeable defects. Their final sale resulted in the further separation of any bond which remained between family members. Nevertheless the purchase and sale of African captives from the interior of Africa to the shores of the Americas resulted in a worldwide economic boom, giving numerous individuals, companies, and states a vast amount of wealth. Thereafter, Africans were subjected to the second humiliating process of seasoning, stripping them of pieces of their African identity. While portions of the family unit were lost during the travel from Africa to the auction block, aspects of the family unit were able to survive life on the plantation. New families emerged, adopting characteristics of the life people left behind in Africa.

KEY TERMS

Power
Slave
War Captive
Pawn
Asante

CHAPTER 5

THE ATLANTIC SLAVE TRADE: A COMPARATIVE CRITIQUE OF THE LITERATURE SINCE CURTIN

Charles D. Johnson

INTRODUCTION

The publication of *The Atlantic Slave Trade: A Census* in 1969 and its then astonishing conclusion that only 9,556,000 Africans were imported into the Americas during the period 1451–1871, set in motion a whirlwind debate that maintained its momentum for four decades. Previous estimates of African captives taken out of Africa had been much higher and popular opinion higher still. At the heart of the debate, but most often not articulated, is the implication that if one reduces the number of Africans forcibly removed from their homelands, then the impact of their removal on African societies and European societies is likewise proportionally reduced. So, a smaller reduction in population loss would again mean a smaller negative influence on those African societies that the trade impacted, and it would then be a small step to the view that the current economic disparity between western Europe and Africa south of the Sahara cannot be explained by reference to the Atlantic Slave Trade.[1]

It is clear then that the debate inextricably links any discussion of the volume of the trade to the impact of the Atlantic Slave Trade on the overall health and development of societies in Africa. In a similar manner, the significance of the debate also extends to discussions over the trade's profitability, to the configuration of age and sex ratios of captives carried to the Americas as well as to the trades' mortality rates as a result of losses at sea, which again have implications for the salubrity and growth of those societies that the trade impacted. In short, the importance of the discussion over the volume of the trade is central to a wider understanding of the trade's subordinate parts. Consequently, since the publication of *The Atlantic Slave Trade: A Census* historians have endeavored to disaggregate the trade into its subordinate parts and then to deconstruct each component, for example, mortality and profitability. Though important, the

---

[1] For a good discussion of the negative demographic effects of the Atlantic Slave Trade, see Patrick Manning, *Slavery and African Life: Occidental, Oriental, and African Slave Trades* (Cambridge: Cambridge University Press, 1990). Also see John Thornton, *Africa and Africans in the Making of the Atlantic World, 1400–1800*, 2nd ed. (Cambridge: Cambridge University Press, 1998). John Thornton, "Sexual Demography: The Impact of the Slave Trade on Family Structure," in *'We Specialize in the Wholly Impossible': A Reader in Black Women's History*, eds. Darlene Clark Hine, Wilma King, and Linda Reed (New York: Carlson Publishing Company, 1995), 57–65.

ancillary parts of the slave trade economy fall outside the focus of this literature review, but readers are strongly encouraged to investigate them because so much about the trade remains a mystery to the wider public.[2]

PROVENANCE AND THE BUTTERFLY EFFECT

Most Americans do not have a depth of understanding about the Atlantic Slave Trade or slavery in the Americas. Without having a real grasp of what took place allows for illogicality to pass for reasoned conclusions. Our aim is to introduce readers to some of the literatures on the volume of the Atlantic Slave Trade, to the principle scholars in the debate on the volume of the trade, and to descry the contours of their main arguments, and though I am not without my own opinion on the matter, readers can reach their own conclusions. Before turning to the review, it is necessary, however, to address some fundamental issues concerning the trade and the institution of slavery in the Americas. In reading this review of the literature on the volume of the trade, one should never lose sight of the value of a single human life. Each number herein discussed corresponds to one human existence, and each individual had ties of kinship and love to whole families and communities of other people. Hence, there is no way possible to measure the emotional cost of the Atlantic Slave Trade on African peoples, and yet for many people, perhaps most, it is the emotional impact that we tend first to regard. This tendency is a function of our humanity and our identification with human suffering, which makes the debate that much more redolent, and it is natural to have an emotional response to such a large human tragedy where there were so few winners and so many losers. How you feel about the trade and slavery is directly related to where you perceive to stand on the won/loss divide. In reality, there were winners and losers both among Europeans and Africans, but there can be no doubt to the essential understanding that Africans lost far more than they won.

So what was lost? People of European descent in the Americas lost economic opportunities that were taken by enslaved labor. This is not a small matter. According to the 1860 Census, at the highpoint of slavery in the United States, for example, approximately 13% of whites owned slaves. That is roughly the same percentage as own luxury cars in the state of

---

[2] There are a number of articles that address these issues. For Mortality see Robert Stein, "Mortality in the Eighteenth-Century French Slave Trade," *The Journal of African History* 21 (1980): 35–41; Joseph C. Miller, "Mortality in the Atlantic Slave Trade: Statistical Evidence on Causality," *Journal of Interdisciplinary History* 11, no. 3 (Winter 1981): 385–423, Miller argues that slave mortality at sea was adversely affected by pre-embarkation conditions. Specifically, the journey to the coast and the conditions in the baracoons caused mortality rates to be higher at sea then they otherwise would have been; An opposing view to Miller's can be found in R. Cohn and R. Jensen, "Comment and Controversy: Mortality in the Atlantic Slave Trade," *Journal of Interdisciplinary History* 13, no. 2 (Autumn 1982): 317–29; Richard H. Steckel and Richard A Jensen, "New Evidence on the Causes of Slave and Crew Mortality in the Atlantic Slave Trade," *Journal of Economic History* 46, no. 1 (March 1986): 57–77. Discussions of sex ratios of captives taken can be found in David Eltis, "The Volume, Age/Sex Ratios, and African Impact of the Slave Trade: Some Refinements of Paul Lovejoy's Review of the Literature," *The Journal of African History* 31 (1990): 485–92; see also David Eltis and Stanley Engerman, "Was the Slave Trade Dominated by Men," *Journal of Interdisciplinary History* 23, no. 2 (Autumn 1992): 237–57. For an alternative approach to localizing African origins of African Americans, see Walter A. Schroeder, Edwin S. Munger, and Darleen R. Powers, "Sickle Cell Anemia, Genetic Variations, and The Slave Trade to the United States," *The Journal of African History* 31 (1990): 163–80.

Georgia, a former slaveholding state in the Deep South. What this means is that enslaved labor was concentrated in the hands of a relatively small number of people and that it replaced free laborers, many of them were white. This should not be taken to mean that whites who did not own slaves did not benefit from slavery. Economically slavery spurred the growth of the economy and a rising tide floats all boats. From a social stand point, all whites and no blacks benefited from enslavement because slavery, and its stigma, came to be identified with people of African descent.

People of African descent lost economically and socially. Most perceptibly we should say they lost their African identities, their memory of Africa as their homeland, their African Worldview, and, from the vantage point of western society, their value as members of the human family. By a thousand examples we could reify this social degradation and this dilution of the dignity of the African's humanity. It was lost in the village raid that killed family members who fought to their bitter end to be free. It was lost on the perilous journey under a burning hot sun often over many miles to the coast shackled ankle to ankle, hands to waist, and with a coffle around the neck connected like a necklace of beads to the surviving sad souls that once comprised a proud village. It was lost in the scathing heat of the tropics waiting in the dark dungeon of misery where branded and bemoaning Africans anticipated an unknown fate. It was lost chained in the hellish hold of the rolling slave ship, bathed in human excrement and secretions of all kinds, unable to sit upright or to stretch one's legs to their fullest extent while discordant dirges of despair echoed perpetually through the pitch darkness. It has been said that if the wind was right one could smell a slave ship before it could be seen. It was lost on the slave auction block standing naked—man, woman, and child—before a gathering of unfriendly onlookers as slave speculators poked and examined every orifice and made bend every joint to insure the quality of their precious merchandise. It was lost in the loss of husbands, wives, and children who died along the way or who were sold apart never, in all likelihood, to see each other again. It was lost in the four posts, the gallows, the rack, the whipping post, and the many other mechanisms of torture and death. It was lost in the compulsory discarding of African culture—names, languages, religions, values, and beliefs—and the forced acceptance of European names, languages, religions, values, and beliefs. Thus, were Africans in the Americas transformed from their many honored ethnicities (e.g., Mende, Kru, Asante, Ewe, Fon, Yoruba, and Ibo) to negro.

A negro identity was in part a creation of slave societies. Africans had to be made pliable in order to be good workers within the slave system. A negro is a marginal and inferior being who lacked a meaningful history or culture or name, all of which the slave society taught him to look to white society for. What identity and culture white society gave to the negro turned him against himself. Carter G. Woodson, the father of African American history and founder of the Association for the Study of Negro Life and History, made the following observation about the impact of education designed to foster inferiority in blacks almost eighty years ago:

> This is slightly dangerous ground here . . . for the Negro's mind has been all but perfectly enslaved in that he has been trained to think what is desired of him . . . the result, then, is that the Negroes thus mis-educated are of no service to themselves[3]

[3] Carter G. Woodson, *Mis-Education of the Negro* (Trenton: African World Press, Inc., 1998; first published, The Associated Publishers, 1933), 24. Today the Association for the Study of African American Life and History is the leading organization promoting research on and teaching of the black experience in the United States.

Woodson's thesis is that education has often served to mis-educate African Americans and perpetuates a form of mental slavery. W. E. B. DuBois, arguably the preeminent African American intellectual of the twentieth century, noted this problem over a century ago in *The Souls of Black Folks* where he talked about the internal conflict that was created in blacks by living in societies that rejected them for being themselves. He stated

> The Negro is a sort of seventh son, born with a veil, and gifted with second-sight in this American world,—a world which yields him no true self-consciousness, this sense of always looking at one's self through the eyes of others, of measuring one's soul by the tape of a world that looks on in amused contempt and pity. One ever feels his twoness—an American, a negro; two souls, two thoughts, two unreconciled strivings; two warring ideals in one dark body, whose dogged strength alone keeps it from being torn asunder.[4]

African Americans have tried to adapt to being "the other" in societies that privilege people with white skin but as Dubois indicates, not without serious challenges. Joy Degruy has noted that many blacks still suffer from *Post Traumatic Slave Syndrome*, a form of post-traumatic stress that causes African Americans to act in ways that are dysfunctional. African American psychological dysfunction is manifest in their decision-making, self-conception, self-negation, reference group identification, social anxieties, and values. Many of their patterns of substance abuse, suicide, and fratricide, are linked to lingering trauma from the past and neglect and abuse in the present. Degruy's work came almost three decades after that of Cedric Clark's who made a similar argument. Not excluding present white Supremacy, Clark believed that "slavery, more than any other single event, shaped the mentality of the present African Americans."[5] Clark attempted to explain how personality disorders could be transmitted across such a lengthy period of time by pointing up an error in the application of Newtonian concepts that are grounded in the idea of a material universe where "a body at rest remains at rest unless acted upon by some external force."[6] Because of this error, social scientists, Clark contends, have looked for a similar temporally fixed "cause and effect" relationship where others that occur across spans of time are possible.[7]

In 1976, in a tome entitled, *The Selfish Gene*, Oxford biologist Richard Dawkins used the expression meme to describe the basic unit of cultural transmission, or imitation.[8] Some of the examples of memes Dawkins advanced included: "tunes, ideas, catch-phrases, clothes fashions, ways of making pots or of building arches."[9] Other memes are more complex and include

---

[4] W. E. B. DuBois, *The Souls of Black Folk* (Chicago: A.C. McClurg & CO., 1903), 4.

[5] Joseph L. White, "Toward a Black Psychology," in *Black Psychology*, 4th ed., editor, Reginald Jones (Oakland: Cobb & Henry Publishers, 2004), 5; Cedric Clark, "Black Studies or the Study of Black People," in *Black Psychology*, 1st ed., ed. Reginald Jones (New York: Harper & Row, 1972), 7–8.

[6] Newton's First Law: Newton's First Law states that an object will remain at rest or in uniform motion in a straight line unless acted upon by an external force. It may be seen as a statement about inertia, that objects will remain in their state of motion unless a force acts to change the motion. http://hyperphysics.phy-astr.gsu.edu/hbase/Newt.html.

[7] White, 7–8.

[8] Richard Brodie, *Virus of the Mind: The New Science of the Meme* (New York: Hay House, Inc., 1996), 4. Psychologist Henry Plotkin defined a meme as the unit of cultural heredity analogous to the gene. It is the internal representation of knowledge.

[9] Ibid., 6.

attitudes and beliefs. Memetics explains how ideas and attitudes from the past could be spread unconsciously from one generation to the next down to the present. Each person has the capacity to be a cultural germ cell capable of transmitting their culture via ideas and attitudes in whole or in part to other people. In this way, Africans in the Americas learned to think like whites, and where whites had issues with Africans then the Africans internalized those negative ideas. This is a hugely important point because it shows how ideas help shape identities over space and time as black parents and grandparents who learned from their forbearers unconsciously passed on values and beliefs learned during enslavement. Again, under enslavement, Africans were forced to accept alien ideas that often came into conflict with who they were innately, such that they came to dislike and even reject as inferior the texture of their hair, the size of their nose and lips, and their complexion.

Dr. Chester Pierce, a Harvard University Psychiatrist, has reached the conclusion that psychological dysfunction in people of African descent is a result of high levels of stress caused by white supremacy, and that this stress leads to dysfunctional behaviors that often take the form of negative coping strategies, such as substance abuse and even intragroup violence. He named this phenomenon Mundane Extreme Environmental Stress or M.E.E.S. Mundane of course means commonplace. The magnitude of the stress on people of African descent is extreme, and white supremacy is a substantial part of the atmosphere of ideas that make up the social environment. The advent of mass media has made that environment essentially global. Stress of course refers to the socially derived cognitive dissonance.

W. E. B. Dubois writing in 1904 mused:

> What was slavery to the slave trade? Not simply forced labor, else we are all in bondage. Not simply toil without pay, even that is not unknown in America. No, the dark damnation of slavery in America was the destruction of the African family and of all just ideals of family life . . . and these ideals slavery broke and scattered and flirted to the winds and left ignorance and degradation in their train.[10]

For sure the African American family did survive slavery, a point not lost on Dubois, and well proved by Herbert Gutman and John Blassingame, but the African family in slavery no longer contained the African ideals that it once held that served in countless ways to sustain it. They had been "flirted to the winds . . . ." In their place were substituted European ideals that privileged European people and created within people of African descent an odious internal conflict. Africans fought to hold onto their culture and their identities. But each successive generation of Africans born in the Americas, born into slavery, was further and further removed from Africa, which became an imagined almost mythical place. Fixed in the minds of the young who learned of it at their mother's feet, they knew of Africa, but they did not know Africa, and it is not reasonable to expect people to embrace what they do not know. This is perhaps the greatest tragedy of the slave trade and slavery: the intentional separation of Africans from themselves, not just the physical separation of Africans from their homeland, but more importantly the separation of each African from her culture.

What then was The Atlantic Slave Trade or European Dominated Trade in African People? Well, to the African, it was cruel and callous. It was a system to be scorned and destroyed, but

---

[10] W. E. B. Dubois, "The Development of a People," *International Journal of Ethics* 14, no.3 (April 1904): 304.

foremost to the European it was a system of coerced labor, an economic undertaking whose aim was to produce profit for its principal stakeholders. Its origin is tied to the diffusion of the knowledge of sugar production from India via what today we call the Middle East, into the eastern Mediterranean, particularly the Island of Cyprus, during the Crusades (1096–1291). On Cyprus, the idea of manufacturing sugar took hold and the need for a source of labor that could do the back-breaking work necessary to harvest and manufacture granulated sugar from sugarcane became a major concern. Feudal custom prohibited workers on Cyprus from working the long hours necessary for refining sugar so an alternative source of labor had to be found. Along the western shore of the Black Sea, the source of labor was located. These Slavic peoples became the initial workers in the nascent sugar industry, which stretched across southern Europe along the north shore of the Mediterranean Sea. By accident of their birth, they had white skin. They did not toil alone; Muslims, north Africans, and Jews who may have likewise been taken prisoners of war or otherwise captured would have in all likelihood toiled alongside them. Prisoners of war, whether in Africa, Asia, Europe or the Americas, were often enslaved and in the Atlantic Slave Trade. This was one of the principle means by which someone could become enslaved.

Slavery in the Atlantic system took on a new form that was far harsher than the indigenous forms of slavery and servitude prevalent on the continent of Africa before the arrival of the Europeans. No system of slavery was desirable to the enslaved, not in Africa or elsewhere, but slavery in traditional African societies was not a permanent status inherited by the progeny of the enslaved. A person of a different ethnicity, and there are numerous ethnicities in Africa, who was taken as a prisoner during battle, would have in all likelihood been compelled to join a family among the victors and to work in support of the sustenance of that family. She would eventually become a member of the new group, and her children would be born free. Chattel bond slavery, the system that Europeans erected in the Americas, differed because it was an institution derived for the purpose of producing profit and not for mere subsistence. Africans had to be "seasoned"; that is, they had to be denuded of any sense of power or control within the white world and to be made to feel as though they needed that world for their very survival. This explains why even today people of African descent support political parties and platforms that do not speak to their interests. They have inherited generations of mental conditioning that leads to the conclusion that come what may their survival rests with the survival of white society. Physical and psychological violence were employed to create the desired effect. Of the two, the psychological trauma has had the greatest and most effective impact.

In the 1960s, Edward Norton Lorenz popularized the idea of the *Butterfly Effect*, where a small cause in one location can produce a large effect at a remote distance. This is precisely what happened to Africans who were taken and sold into the European Dominated Trade in African People. By a cruel turn of fate, in 1453, the Ottomans, a powerful Islamic state at war with the Eastern Roman Empire or Byzantines, captured Constantinople and renamed it Istanbul. Istanbul sits on the western shore of a strait that connects the Black Sea by water access to the Mediterranean. The Ottomans closed the strait to the Christian empires, and in so doing, it cut off their access to the Slavs who were then working in the sugar plantations in the Mediterranean region. Historically speaking, this significant but yet seemingly localized event, about which it is likely that the Africans most affected by it had no knowledge of, was significant to the growth of the use of unfree African labor in place of Slavic labor for the European sugar plantation economy. Slavic slavery was widespread in Europe, North Africa, and southwestern Asia (Middle East), so much so that the word slave is associated with Slav.

During this same period in the fifteenth century, the Portuguese began establishing contact with African states along the coastline of Northwest Africa. Europeans came to think of Africa as a land of gold after the Hajj of Mansa Musa in 1324. Mansa Musa was the Emperor of Mali, a powerful African empire in the western Sudan that covered most of what is modern Mali, Senegal, and the southern extreme of Mauritania. A devote Muslim, Mansa Musa's religious pilgrimage passed through Cairo, Egypt, on the way to Mecca. Mansa Musa's retinue is said to have included a train of ninety camels laden with gold. He spent gold so lavishly in Cairo that it caused the devaluation of the local currency. Europeans took note. Wars in Europe and the Crusades were financially exhausting to the crowns of Europe. New sources of gold were much sought after because they permitted rulers to pay mercenary soldiers to carry out their wars.

These Portuguese adventurers who sailed down the western coast of Africa then were in search of gold and slaves. They initially raided villages along the African coast and kidnapped Sanhaja Berbers and small numbers of Africans who they then took back to Portugal where they were placed on public display and later sold as enslaved laborers. Berbers are nomadic peoples who historically have lived in the Sahara Desert or along its periphery. There are many Berber groups. They played an important role in carrying the long-distance trade across the Sahara from West Africa to northern entrepôts. These north African port cities feed goods into markets that extended along long-distance trade routes that stretched from south of the Sahara into Europe. During their raids, the Portuguese also took back a small amount of gold, which seemed to confirm the legend born the previous century that Africa was a source of gold.

For their part, Africans living along the coast, having learned by experience the intentions of the Portuguese, began to put up fierce resistance to their slave raiding. After Africans began to kill some of the Portuguese who engaged in marauding, the adventurers shifted to a more diplomatic and less dangerous business model. This of course did not mean the end to raiding as a means of capturing humans. This practice continued throughout the era of the slave trade, but it did underscore the fact that there were African states, such as Songhay and Mali, that were powerful enough that the Portuguese could not operate indiscriminately. Slave raiding was often accompanied by the element of surprise, so it was typically enough for the Portuguese to move to an area where their tactics and intentions were not known. It would be the Portuguese who would first dominate the transporting of Africans to the Americas.

The use of the *Butterfly Effect* is not intended to imply that the Portuguese and later European participants in the trade would not have eventually sought Africans as a source of unfree labor had not the Ottomans captured Constantinople; what it does is to underscore how human fortune often turns on decisions and consequences far removed and often beyond the influence of those persons most impacted. This was certainly the case with the Africans. It seems self-evident though that proximity and the costs associated with shipping cargoes of people over shorter distances rather than longer distances would have made the European's decision to enslave Africans inevitable. Again, the slave trade and slavery were big businesses, and businesses desire to maximize profits while incurring the least expense as possible. The profit motive informed almost every decision made with regard to each institution. Nevertheless, the Butterfly Effect does raise the interesting question how might labor arrangements have differed had the Ottoman not captured Constantinople and cut off the supply of unfree white laborers.

What history reveals is that at the outset of the trade the European participants, the Spanish and especially the Portuguese, but over the course of time certainly not limited to them, were not reticent about using black, red, tan, or even white laborers if it suited their purposes. Following the seven-century-long Moorish occupation of the Iberian Peninsula (711–1492), Catholic leaders in Spain promoted the concept of *Limpieza de Sangre* or purity of blood as a way to privilege Spanish Catholics over Muslims and Jews who had only recently converted to Catholicism. Starting with Columbus' first voyage, Limpieza de Sangre was adapted to their colonies in the Americas to create a social hierarchy based on lineage and race.

The Europeans viewed Native Americans paradoxically as both beautiful and savage. Columbus' description of the Arawak with whom he came into contact on Hispaniola (modern Haiti) was that they were well-built, handsome, completely unselfish, but also savages who would make good slaves. So it was that in search for gold, Columbus started the enslavement of the Indians. European diseases and cruelty ultimately killed millions of Indians. Like the volume of the slave trade, scholars debate the total number of Indians who died. Some estimates are as high as one hundred million in the first century of contact. History textbooks often emphasize the idea of a "Columbian Exchange" to convey the idea that both Europeans and Indians were winners and losers through a process of give-and-take, but the reality is that the Native Americans lost the most and that their loss of land and lives were a desired outcome of the Europeans.

A small number of impecunious and less fortunate whites were "spirited" to the Americas as unfree laborers. Prisoners and vagrants were collected and shipped to the colonies to provide much needed labor. Semi-free labor, likewise, was used right alongside unfree labor in America. Perhaps as many as one-half of the European colonists to immigrate to Virginia and Massachusetts Bay, for example, came as indentured servants who were often worked, branded, and beaten like slaves, and when the slaves ran away, the indentured servants often ran away with them. Certainly many indentures completed their contracts and received what they had agreed upon before embarking for the colonies, but many did not. The willingness of Europeans to enslave whites is an important fact of history that is often not adequately acknowledge with regard to the inception of the trade.

European mortality in the tropics was much higher than that of Africans, a fact Philip Curtin noted in *Death by Migration: Europe's Encounter with the Tropical World in the 19th Century*, and that fact alone would have justified the need for laborers adapted to the tropics. But after Christopher Columbus initiated the Spanish conquest and colonization of the Americas in 1492, coerced labor requirements shifted from being almost exclusively based on sugar production to the need to satisfy the demand of Spanish mining interests who were searching for gold and silver wherever they went in the Americas. Thus, a diversification of jobs in the Americas created a selective preference among the Spanish slave traders for Africans who possessed the specific skills, such as the knowledge of mining techniques, that they needed. European slave traders, such as the British and the French, who became active in the seventeenth and eighteenth centuries applied the same logic and, like the Spanish before them, attempted to acquire Africans who had the skills for the specific labor they needed. The trade grew slowly at first, but by the eighteenth century, it had swollen into a tsunami of captive humans that crashed down upon the Americas flooding them with Africans who came from towns and villages that stretched across a diverse landscape that as time passed and the European demand for captive laborers increased and snaked along the West African coastline and even hundreds of miles into its hinterland. From Senegal in northwest Africa south past the Grain Coast to the eastward bend of the continent through the Ivory Coast, the Gold Coast, the Slave Coast, like a giant Boa Constrictor slithering along the shore on and on through the Bights of Benin and Biafra, and then south again along the twenty-five-hundred-mile long coastline south to the Cape of Good Hope and up the east coast on the Indian Ocean side to Kenya near the equator until the giant white serpent had wrapped itself around the entire southern half of the continent. The tighter the snake squeezed the more Africans were taken into the trade. But how many reached the Americas? This was the seminal question Philip Curtin attempted to answer in *The Atlantic Slave Trade: A Census* that would open a debate that for some scholars of the slave trade has lasted four decades.

BACKGROUND AND METHODOLOGY

Curtin's *The Atlantic Slave Trade: A Census* was first published in 1969.[11] Curtin wrote it to revise what he believed was a series of errors that had led past historians to overstate the number of Africans brought to the Americas during the Atlantic Slave Trade. He specifically, attempts to find a reliable estimate of the volume of the trade to the Americas. He states

> Its central aim is to bring together bits and pieces of incommensurate information already published, and to do this for only one aspect of the trade—the measurable number of people brought across the Atlantic.[12]

Following this method, Curtin chose Noel Deerr's estimates of the slave trade compiled and presented in *History of Sugar* as a starting point or baseline for his work. Curtin's decision to select Deerr's figures is important because it sets a starting figure for the volume of the trade. Why then did Curtin choose Deerr's research over Edward Dunbar's and the other existing literature on the trade?

In 1863, Edward E. Dunbar published *History of the Rise and Decline of Commercial Slavery in America, with Reference to the Future of Mexico*. In that short book, Dunbar estimated that 13,887,500 Africans were imported into the Americas. Curtin felt that Dunbar's estimate might have been exaggerated in support of President Benito Juarez, a liberal politician in Mexico, who had opposed United States' annexation of Mexican territory. Curtin found Deerr's estimate of 11,970,000 imports a more reasonable starting point for his study because Deerr attempted to reach a total volume of the trade by anthologizing estimates of several sections of the trade.

---

[11] Philip Curtin, *The Atlantic Slave Trade: A Census* (Madison: The University of Wisconsin Press, 1969), xviii.
[12] Ibid., xvi.

According to Curtin, Deerr is "the only twentieth-century [historian] to attempt to add up piecemeal estimates . . ." of the trade. This methodology is similar to the one that Curtin uses in *The Atlantic Slave Trade*. Deer then had estimated 1,917,500 fewer Africans being imported into the Americas than had Dunbar. Curtin measured the volume of the Atlantic slave trade using import figures collected from *History of Sugar* and the various government agencies that participated in the trade. He divides the trade into different periods and then reports import figures for each period. His research covers the four-hundred-and-twenty-year period 1451–1871, during which time he estimates that 9,566,000 captives were imported into the Americas. Curtin acknowledges that his estimates would probably be revised and that researchers should take them for what they were—estimates.[13]

REVIEW OF THE LITERATURE

Daryl R. Murray was one of the first historians to answer Curtin's appeal to revise his work. Using archival sources from the "customs house records of Havana, covering the years 1790–1821, and the reports of the British Commissioners stationed in Havana from 1819 . . . ."[14] Murray contends that Curtin understated the volume of the slave trade to Cuba. According to Murray, Curtin had accepted the "Havana customs house figures as representing the total number of slaves imported into Cuba, when at best they represent the minimum importation."[15] Murray also believed that Curtin excluded the trade carried to the Cuban ports of Santiago and Trinidad, and that he had discounted the significance of the illicit trade. Murray claimed that "Illicit trade may have existed, but no evidence is available to show its level."[16] Not being able to determine accurately the levels of the illicit trade makes more difficult to determine accurately the volume of the trade. Murray maintains that illicit trading was rampant because of the 1789 *cedula* that from 1791 to 1820 barred foreign slavers from making port anywhere but Havana. A *cedula* was a government decree. Being cut off from Havana was an inducement for contraband trade to the other Cuban ports such as Santiago and Trinidad. Murray therefore suggested a slight upward revision of Curtin's estimation of 700,600 imports into Cuba. Murray's estimate ranges between 766,600 and 801,800. Like Curtin, Murray cautioned that his research was a minimal estimate not a final figure.

The following year, 1972, Herbert Klein published "The Portuguese Slave Trade from Angola in the Eighteenth Century." Klein, like Murray, points to the Curtin's work as a justification for his work. Klein's work estimated the number of Africans shipped from three ports in West Central Africa, that is, Luanda, Benguela, and Cabinda, during the eighteenth century. He relied on two sets of sources to measure the volume of the slave exports: port records and government reports. Klein had few criticisms of Curtin's study, but he did assert that his methodology was preferred to Curtin's because he used contemporary year shipping recordings,

---

[13] See Appendix B for a listing of estimates for the volume of the trade.

[14] See D. R. Murray, "Statistics of the Slave Trade to Cuba, 1790–1867," *Journal of Latin American Studies* 3, no. 2 (November 1971): 131.

[15] Ibid., 133.

[16] Curtin, *The Atlantic Slave Trade*, 36.

whereas Curtin relied on manuscript summary tables that were frequently made a decade after they were first recorded. In 1992, Joseph Inikori claimed that the use of compiled data, such as manuscript summary tables, was problematic because of the probability of errors having occurred when the customs agents originally compiled the documents.[17] Klein's figures are only comparable to Curtin's between the years 1711 and 1780. Klein had no estimates for the beginning of the eighteenth century or for the end. Klein revised Curtin's export figures for the Portuguese trade upward by 21,360 captives.[18]

In 1975, Roger Anstey released one of the first revisions of Curtin's findings on the British trade. Anstey relied on secondary sources and archival materials to revise Curtin's export figure for the period 1761–1810 upward by 9.6% to 3,658,400. That is an increase of 320,100 over Curtin's export figure of 3,338,300.[19] Ironically, Anstey criticized Curtin for his use of secondary material. In 1976, Joseph Inikori published his criticisms of both Curtin's and Anstey's findings and made the first attempt to completely deconstruct the *Census*.

Inikori found that Curtin's formula for calculating French and British imports into the West Indies, minus Jamaica, had what he felt were "some serious weaknesses."[20] Curtin used a two-part-compound-interest formula that measured the growth rate of the slave population of a given colonial state in the Americas. According to Inikori, that method is not accurate where year-to-year movements in the size of the slave population are not uniform. According to Inikori, "By the very nature of the formula, it is incapable of providing a true estimate of slave imports over a very long period of time during which considerable random fluctuations occurred in the slave population and import figures."[21] Another problem Inikori found was that government officials frequently understated imports into the various colonies. He points to the corruption of the French as an example.

> According to Lucien Peytraud, a manuscript note of Moreau de Saint-Mery, c. 1780, shows that by this date Saint-Domingue already had a slave population of 452,000 and all the French West Indian colonies together had 673,400. The slave population of Saint-Domingue in 1779, as stated in the Census, is only 249,000.[22]

The difference here, if one believes Inikori, is in how the French customs officers recorded imports. He contends slave traders paid off customs officials to avoid the high tariffs associated with large cargoes of captives. Historians of the trade, including Curtin, repeatedly confirm the problem with the reporting of shipping data. However, one of Inikori's main contentions is that the *Census* gives the impression that the sources are more reliable than they are in fact, and those historians, such as Paul Lovejoy and David Eltis, for example, often cite findings from the

---

[17] Joseph Inikori, "The Volume of the British Slave Trade, 1655–1807," *Cahiers d'Etudes Africaines* 32, no. 128 (1992): 646–48.

[18] Curtin's total estimate for the period 1711–1780 was 746,900 captives exported. While Klein's total 768,260. These figures were derived from Table 1 of Klein's Article. See Herbert Klein, "The Portuguese Slave Trade from Angola in the Eighteenth Century," *Journal of Economic History* 32, no. 4 (December 1972): 897.

[19] Roger Anstey, *The Atlantic Slave Trade and British Abolition* (Atlantic Highlands: Humanities Press, 1975), 38–39.

[20] Joseph Inikori, "Measuring the Atlantic Slave Trade: An Assessment of Curtin and Anstey," *The Journal of African History* 17, no. 2 (1976): 198.

[21] Ibid., 198–99.

[22] Ibid., 200.

Census with a higher degree of confidence then the evidence supports. Inikori raised Curtin's British export figure by 40% for the years 1750–1807 in order to counterbalance missing data, the clandestine trade, and under reporting of imports by customs agents. Curtin's export figure is 1,616,100 and Inikori's is 2,365,014. Inikori's revision was the largest correction of Curtin's work at that time. It did not go unnoticed.

Anstey used shipping data gathered from British Customs and concludes that 1,529,180 captives were exported between 1761 and 1801. The difference between his findings and Inikori's can be reconciled by looking at the computation of the number and tonnage of ships that Anstey and Inikori record and at the mean number of captives loaded on ship that each employ in their calculations. According to Inikori, the discovery of a new custom series, Custom Series 17, revealed that Anstey had understated the number of ships that cleared out from England for Africa during the period 1761–1801 by 15.6%.[23] Inikori used a higher mean figure for the number of Africans carried on each voyage than did Anstey. Inikori made allowance for "tight packing," a nefarious shipping method where slave traders attempted to crowd as many people on board ship as possible to make allowance for possible deaths of captives at sea.[24] Inikori set the mean per-vessel cargo size at 430 people, which was 106 more than the 324 that Anstey had allowed for.[25]

Curtin took note of Inikori's critique. Inikori had insinuated in his response that Curtin had intentional set out to lower the number of Africans imported into the Americas. In the same year, 1976, and in the same publication, *The Journal of African History*, Curtin responded to Inikori's criticisms of his findings. His remarks were acerbic and direct. In his defense, he claimed that Inikori had only revised his findings upward. As has been shown, other historians had also revised Curtin's findings upward. Apparently, Curtin believed that Inikori had prior intent to raise his findings when he analyzed the *Census*. Curtin retorted, ". . . every suggestion [of Inikori's] claims that the data I assembled and the estimates I made were too low."[26] Curtin continues, "I have, of course, heard the criticism before—though never in print and never before in a respectable journal. It amounts to the claim that I deliberately falsified the estimates so as to minimize the size of the trade."[27] Curtin of course denied the allegation and went on the offensive, by accusing Inikori of only using evidence that increased his estimates and by claiming that Inikori's "attack" implied that he wrote the *Census* to reduce white guilt. Curtin then reminded readers of what he had stated in the *Census* about the morality of the slave trade: "I made the point that a grand total is too all-embracing to have much meaning in history—that it has no meaning at all for the mortality of the slave trade, which has no defenders in any event."[28] This is true enough today, few people would openly defend slavery

---

[23] Ibid., 217.

[24] As the name implies, "tight-packing" was the practice of overloading slave ships with captives. Slaver traders did this in some instances to increase their profits and in others to indemnify themselves against loss from captive deaths at sea.

[25] Ibid., 212, 218.

[26] Philip Curtin, Joseph Inikori, and Roger Anstey, "Discussion: Measuring the Atlantic Slave Trade," *The Journal of African History* 17, no. 4 (1976): 595. It should be noted that this is not from the same issue as the above article but an issue that is two issues removed from the previous issue.

[27] Ibid.

[28] Ibid., 596.

as a moral institution. But as we stated at the outset, the volume of the trade is correlated to the significance of the trade as a negative influence on Africa's development and as a net positive influence on the development of western Europe and its colonies in the Americas including the United States. This is what was lurking behind the debate between Curtin and Inikori and, in part, why it became so contentious.[29] Nevertheless, Inikori did not convince Curtin to change his findings at that time. Curtin acknowledged that his method of calculating imports into the West Indies was not perfect, but I felt that it was effective as he used it.[30]

Anstey did raise his allowance for the number or tonnage of ships cleared from England to Africa, which put his figure for ships cleared more in line with Inikori's. He did so because of Custom series 17. Little was resolved or changed by the dialogue between Curtin, Inikori, and Anstey in 1976. However, 1976 was significant because it brought the real issues relating to the volume of the slave trade to the fore, and consequently more historians began to focus on the debate, particularly as it relates to the British trade.

Two years later, Herbert Klein, using naval lists kept by the Jamaican port officials, reported that the total volume of Jamaican imports for the period 1782–1808 was 600,000.[31] This was an increase of 80,139 captives landed in Jamaica over Curtin's estimate of 519,861 for the same period. The difference, in part, may be Klein's mean number of Africans per vessel, which is 396 for English vessels. A figure considerably higher than the 324 utilized by Anstey for the West Indies trade, but still lower than Inikori's high estimate of 430 captives per vessel. In response to Klein's article on the volume of the slave trade to Jamaica in 1980, Roderick McDonald stated, "No account has been taken, in either of these studies, of the reportedly large numbers of slaves smuggled into and out of Jamaica as a means of avoiding these duties."[32] Interloping was a serious area of contention for Inikori in 1976 and one of the main reasons that his figures were consistently higher than Curtin's.

In 1978, Robert Stein published, "Measuring the French Slave Trade, 1713–1792/93." Stein relied on Captain's reports to revise Curtin's estimates. He believed that Curtin had underestimated the volume of the French trade during that period because of the paucity "of published information on the first half of the [eighteenth] century."[33] Curtin's exports for the period were 17% lower than Stein's for that reason.[34]

---

[29] The question of whom is to blame for the initiation and perpetuation of the slave trade is a major historical and economic polemic. For dissenting views see Walter Rodney, *A History of the Upper Guinea Coast, 1545–1800* (Oxford: Clarendon Press, 1970) and Thornton, "*Africa and Africans*". A strong discussion of the evolution of slavery and the question of its immortality can be found in William D. Phillips Jr., *Slavery from Roman Times to the Early Transatlantic Trade* (Minneapolis: University of Minnesota Press, 1985). Phillips makes a persuasive argument that the moral question of slavery was not raised until the eighteenth century.

[30] This was a fascinating debate. For Curtin's discussion on his method of calculation, see Ibid., 598. His discussion of government recording methods can be found in the same place.

[31] Herbert Klein, "The English Slave Trade to Jamaica, 1782–1808," *The Economic History Review* 31, no. 1 (February 1978): 25.

[32] Roderick McDonald, "Measuring the British Slave Trade to Jamaica, 1789–1808: A Comment," The *Economic History Review* 33, no. 2 (May 1980): 256–57.

[33] Robert Stein, "Measuring the French Slave Trade, 1713–1792/93," *The Journal of African History* 19, no. 4 (1978): 518.

[34] Ibid., 518–19. Total Exports for Curtin equal 939,100. The total exports for Stein were between 1,100,000 and 1,200,000.

David Eltis, who would become one of the key figures in the debate, reached the conclusion that 1.5 million Africans crossed the Atlantic on British vessels between 1821 and 1843. Because of the dearth of direct evidence, Eltis measured the volume of goods used in exchange for captives to obtain a tentative estimation of the volume of captives exported to the Americas during this period.[35] At that time, Eltis did not make a direct comparison with Curtin's findings, but his method shows how creative historians can be when attempting to solve difficult problems.

James Rawley published *The Transatlantic Slave Trade: A History*. Rawley employs archival materials that Curtin omitted in the Census and contends that for that reason Curtin's import estimates are too low. Rawley calculated, using a new data set, that total imports for Africans brought captive to the Americas was 11,345,000.[36] If for a moment we return to Deerr's estimate of 1,197,000, we can see that Rawley's findings were close to Deerr's, which of course was Curtin's starting point.[37] Rawley's estimate was 625,000 captives from Curtin's baseline. With regard to the British trade to the Caribbean, Curtin, Rawley, and Inikori each make different allowances for mortality at sea and African captives lost to interlopers. Curtin had estimated that the total imports into the British Caribbean over the period 1451–1870 were 1,665,000. Rawley estimated them to be 2,443,000, a 68% increase. Predictably, Inikori's total is still somewhat higher because of his willingness to make allowances to compensate for what cannot be accurately measured, namely the illicit trade. Looking at imports over the period 1698–1807, when the British outlawed the trade, Inikori estimated that there were 2,964,511 imports into the British Caribbean.

In 1982, Paul Lovejoy, a former student of Philip Curtin's at the University of Wisconsin, published "The Volume of the Atlantic Slave Trade: A Synthesis." At the opening of his article, Lovejoy gives a brief historiographical essay on the volume of the Atlantic Slave Trade, in which he calls Inikori's methods "dubious." He then uses Curtin's data, in addition to some of David Eltis', and concludes, not surprisingly, that Curtin's final import estimate is an acceptable total. Lovejoy estimated that 9,778,500, captives were imported, an upward revision of Curtin's findings by 212,500 captives. Lovejoy, who appeared to be coming to the defense of his former professor, sacked the analysis and estimates of James Rawley, Joseph Inikori, and Leslie Rout as "extreme."[38]

Probably one of the more mundane and yet incisive articles considered here is David Henige's "Measuring the Immeasurable: The Atlantic Slave Trade, West African Population and the Pyrrhonian Critic." Henige's purpose was to cast light on what can be known by historians attempting to measure the depopulation of Africa because of external influences and to elucidate the danger of making inferences from conclusions based on weak evidence. To illustrate the problem with the evidence and to underscore his conclusions, Henige created the

---

[35] See David Eltis, "The British Contribution to the Nineteenth-Century Transatlantic Slave Trade," *The Economic History Review* 32, no. 2 (May 199): 211.

[36] James Rawley, *The Transatlantic Slave Trade: A History* (New York: W. W. Norton & Company, 1981), 427.

[37] See Curtin, 13.

[38] Paul Lovejoy, "The Atlantic Slave Trade: A Synthesis," *The Journal of African History* 23 (1982): 475–77. Leslie Rout's work is not considered in this essay. See Leslie B. Rout Jr., *The African Experience in Spanish America: 1502 to the Present Day* (Cambridge: Cambridge University Press, 1976), 1973.

following algebraic equation: a + b + c + d + e + f + g + h = X.[39] The variables can be defined as follows:

a is the number of West Africans who arrived alive in the New World as recorded in sources known to historians.
b is the number of West Africans who arrived alive in the New World as recorded in extant sources not yet known to historians.
c is the number of West Africans who arrived alive in the New World as recorded in sources now lost.
d is the number of West Africans who arrived in the New World in the clandestine trade.
e is the number of West Africans who died between the time of embarkation and arrival at some New World port, in both the "legitimate" and the clandestine trade.[40]

At a glance, one can see that *c*, *d*, and *e* can never be known because there is no extant documentation for those variables. By the logic of this formula, therefore, the total number of Africans brought to the Americas can never be known. Henige added that "in no instance can such estimates [about the slave trade] be proved wrong. Inevitably then, none can be shown to be correct."[41] Henige's algebraic equation and his conclusions probably should have ended the debate over the volume of the trade, assuming of course that his logic was sound, at the very least it should have given historians pause, but it did not. Instead, the debate continued.

In 1987, David Eltis produced an annual time series of imports for the nineteenth-century trade to the Americas. Eltis' purpose was "to fill in the gap [in the former historiography] by generating annual estimates of slave imports in the last six decades of the slave trade [1810–1870]. These incorporate research carried out since Curtin's pioneering study."[42] Eltis examined the trade to Brazil, particularly the trade to Bahia, Rio de Janeiro, and Pernambuco, which is significant because the largest number of Africans went to Brazil. He also re-examined the trade to Cuba and the French West Indies.[43] The bulk of his evidence came from "a data set of 5,378 voyages, and partly on contemporary observers."[44] At the time, his data set represented the latest data on those segments of the slave trade. Eltis's total estimate for captive imports into the Americas was 10,267,425, a 488,925 person increase over Lovejoy's 1982 estimate of 9,778,500. Note also that Lovejoy had used Eltis' earlier data in his 1982 synthesis. David Richardson's findings on

---

[39] David Henige, "Measuring the Immeasurable: The Atlantic Slave Trade, West African Population and the Pyrronian Critic," *The Journal of African History*," 27 (1986): 296–302. The only elements of the equation considered here are those that relate directly to determining the volume of the Atlantic Slave Trade, that is, *a*, *b*, *c*, *d*, and *e*. *X* is the total number of Africans removed from Africa during the period of the Atlantic Slave trade, 1450–1870. Variables f through h relate to the trans-Saharan trade and other causes of depopulation in Africa. See Appendix A for the all the definitions.
[40] Ibid.
[41] Ibid., 302.
[42] David Eltis, "The Nineteenth-Century Transatlantic Slave Trade: An Annual Time Series of Imports into the Americas Broken Down by Region," *Hispanic American Historical Review* 67, no. 1 (1987): 110.
[43] D. R. Murray, argues that the Census data for Cuba is weak. Eltis tends not to agree and uses it in his study. See Murray, 130–33.
[44] Eltis, "The Nineteenth-Century," 112.

British exports for this period were also higher than were Lovejoy's findings. Richardson maintained that Lovejoy's total is basically correct but that his decadal estimates of the trade differ significantly from those of Lovejoy.[45] Richardson also revised Lovejoy's total number of British exports upward by 342,700 for a grand total of 3,120,000 exports.[46]

Seven years after the publication of "The Volume of the Atlantic Slave Trade: A Synthesis," Lovejoy published another historiographical essay.[47] This essay, however, primarily focused on the impact of the slave trade on Africa, reflecting a shift in focus from the total volume of the Atlantic Slave trade to its effects and to its subordinate parts, did revisit the debate over the volume of the trade long enough to state his belief that historians had finally reached a consensus on ". . . the new studies on the volume of the slave trade, in which a consensus [among historians] seems to have emerged."[48] Convinced that a "consensus" had been reached, he then stated that "a proper application of statistical theory could establish the probable range of demographic change."[49] Henige's contribution, from the same journal, seems not to have factored in Lovejoy's findings. He went on to state that the pre-Census scholarship on the trade, that of Dunbar, Kuczynski, and Deerr ". . . were nothing but guesses."[50] He did predict that in the future upward revisions would be more probable than downward.

In the 1990s, Joseph Inikori returned to center stage of the debate. His report to the United Nations Educational, Scientific, and Cultural Organization (UNESCO), *The Chaining of A Continent: Export Demand For Captives and the History of Africa South of the Sahara, 1450–1870* addressed itself to three issues: to clarify what can be known about the volume of the slave trade, to demonstrate that the export demand for slaves had a deleterious effect on the economies of Africa, and to show that the slave trade as well as colonialism were directly responsible for the underdevelopment of economies in Africa.[51] According to Inikori, the export demand for captives kept the total population of Africa at a level that was far too low to stimulate economic development at a level commensurate with the human and material resources available in Africa. Export demand prevented African economies from being able to keep pace with the expanding economies of Europe and America that benefitted from the trade more than they were harmed.[52] Depopulation in the areas in Africa that the trade impacted prevented the piecemeal economic development that buttressed long-term and large-scale economic growth.

The five constituent parts Inikori envisaged included the following:

1. widespread development of the division of labor
2. the growth of internal trade

---

[45] Lovejoy, "The Atlantic Slave Trade," 477. Lovejoy's total is 9,778,500.

[46] David Richardson, "Slave Exports from West and West-Central Africa, 1700–1810: New Estimates of Volume and Distribution," *The Journal of African History* 30 (1989): 2–3.

[47] Paul Lovejoy, "The Impact of the Atlantic Slave Trade on Africa: A Review of the Literature," *The Journal of African History* 30 (1989): 365.

[48] Ibid.

[49] Ibid., 367.

[50] Ibid.

[51] Joseph Inikori, *The Chaining of a Continent: Export Demand for Captives and the History of Africa South of the Sahara, 1450–1870* (Kingston, Jamaica: Institute of Social and Economic Research, 1992).

[52] The Far East refers to Japan, South Korea, and Taiwan.

3. the diversification of the economy
4. the transformation of the technology and organization of production
5. class differentiation[53]

It was Inikori's contention that the slave trade and colonialism prevented these necessary antecedents from taking place and that in turn prevented African countries from developing large-scale stable economies. Having delineated the alleged effects of the export demand for captives and by extension the effects of population decrease on the economies of Africa, Inikori then argued that the true volume of the trade cannot be known. He stated, "Given the nature of the evidence, it is clear that the true figure of people exported from Africa by way of the Atlantic trade cannot be produced by anyone," a point Henige made a decade earlier.[54]

A serious problem with the evidence, according to Inikori, is that "there is no systematically kept record of the trade carried by the shipping employed by European establishments on the African coast in transporting slaves repeatedly to the New World without touching any of the ports in Europe after the initial clearance outward."[55] This problem was exacerbated by another one: many of the clerks responsible for recording the data relating to the trade may have falsified their records. Inikori surmises that the genuine desire on the part of the European slave traders to avoid tariffs may have prompted many of them to understate the size of their cargo of captives and, where possible, to bribe willing government customs agents. Another inducement for traders to operate illicitly was the British trading acts of 1788 and 1799, which placed limitations on the number of captives that could be legally transported to the Americas. In many instances, British slavers even flew Dutch flags in an effort to avoid detection. It is easy to imagine slave traders cutting corners and attempting to gain an edge where it would prove profitable, but it would be next to impossible to determine the extent of the problem. It would be like attempting to determine how many corrupt law enforcement officials there are today. We can estimate, but we can never fully know.

Yet another difficult with the evidence was interloping or the smuggling of captives. Inikori posited that there were two primary reasons that there was a lot of smuggling: first, slavers did not want to pay high tariffs on their cargo for the obvious loss in profit that it represented, and second, trade restrictions did not allow foreign vessels to make port at certain harbors.[56] Murray had stated as early as 1971 with regard to Cuba that "legitimate" trade had gone to Havana and that illicit trade had gone to Santiago and Trinidad. Inikori's arguments—if nothing else—demonstrated why current estimates of the trade are based on incomplete data. At the time, few historians of the slave trade took seriously the findings of Inikori's research. Steven Behrendt, for example, disregarded the two major publications of Inikori in his reassessment of the eighteenth-century British slave trade.[57] Instead he used David Richardson's findings as a baseline for his own in the same way that Lovejoy had used

---

[53] Ibid., 2.
[54] Ibid., 5.
[55] Ibid., 7.
[56] Inikori gives a detailed discussion including several examples from primary sources. See Ibid., 10, 11.
[57] Besides the UNESCO report, Inikori also published an article "The Volume of the British". See Steven Behrendt, "The Annual Volume and Regional Distribution of the British Slave Trade, 1780–1807," *The Journal of African History* 38 (1997): 187.

Curtin's and Curtin used Noel Deer's. Behrendt added new sources to the pool of existing evidence including a slave voyage data set from numerous parliamentary documents. Parliamentary records on the trade are a strong source of information, but the records were assembled from still more direct sources.

In 1992, in an article on the volume of the British trade, Inikori discussed what he believed was the most reliable source of documentation for measuring the volume of the slave trade.[58] According to Inikori, port books are the most direct form of evidence. Customs agents used port books at the point of embarkation to report the number of captives loaded on ship and likewise to record the number that were off loaded at the ship's destination.[59] Clearly then from port books one could descry exports, mortality at sea (difference between exports and imports), and imports. Information from the port books was then condensed into quarterly reports and were sent to the Register General of Shipping and to the Office of the Inspector General of Imports and Exports. Parliamentary papers that relate to the volume of the slave trade were in most instances a synthesis of information compiled from these quarterly reports and were usually synthesized as a result of a direct request by Parliament. For example, the acts of 1788 and 1799 were passed as a direct result of these quarterly reports. Parliament requested that government agents gather information on the volume of the trade. Information from the reports was extracted and consolidated into a useful form before it was sent to Parliament. Therefore, Parliamentary papers are not a direct form of primary evidence. Moreover, compilation of the reports for Parliament created the opportunity for errors to occur in the final reports. Admittedly, unconscious errors could be in either direction—up or down. As mentioned above, duties on their human cargo may have been an inducement for slave traders to bribe custom agents to falsify their port books. Historians have had to consider such factors when attempting to assess the volume of the trade.

Behrendt argued that the Parliamentary papers at his disposal were significant enough to reassess the period 1780–1807 for the British trade. Using the parliamentary data set, he reduced Richardson's estimate by 14.5%.[60] The difference in their results is their method of calculating the loss of captives at sea. Richardson used a reduction factor of 10%. Behrendt broke the period into two parts and used 8.9% and 2.8% to calculate losses at sea. His total of captives boarded is 894,998, compared to Richardson's 1,047,011.[61] In the same year, Ivana Elbl attempted to calculate the volume of the early Atlantic Slave Trade.

Elbl examined the period 1450–1521. He asserted that the documentation contains few numerical sources and gives a breakdown of the sources that are available. More importantly, however, he contends that "Any estimate based on surviving numerical data is necessarily minimalist."[62] Elbl's study is important because it is one of the few that attempted to quantify the

---

[58] Inikori, "The Volume of the British," 648. Port books are the records that most directly reflect the volume of the trade. However, even these could be falsified, and it was also possible for errors to occur in recording the imports into the port books. Creating the reports from the port books also created the opportunity for errors to occur.

[59] Ibid., 648. Inikori gives a step by step break down of the recording process in this article.

[60] Behrendt, "The Annual Volume," 194.

[61] Readers should bear in mind that the time period here is shorter than in the previous discussion of Richardson's findings, which explains the smaller figures here.

[62] See Ivana Elbl, "The Volume of the Early Atlantic Slave Trade, 1450–1521," *The Journal of African History* 38 (1997): 31.

earlier years of the trade. Using a variety of primary sources, Elbl concluded that 156,000 Africans were brought to the Americas during this period. Readers should bear in mind that it would be almost another century before the British would land Africans at Jamestown. Students of history have long been taught that the original twenty Africans landed at Jamestown in 1619 came aboard a Dutch Man of War as reported by John Rolfe, but more recent scholarship reveals that in fact it was a British warship, The White Lion. The White Lion commandeered the captives at sea from a Portuguese vessel on its way to Mexico. Rolfe dissembled British involvement in order to place blame on the Dutch for what was in fact an act of piracy. Piracy has not previously been mentioned, but for reasons that should be self-evident the volume of the trade that arrived as a consequence of this activity cannot be assessed with precession. Nevertheless, it does create the clear impression of high-stakes competition between European rivals over control of the trade.[63]

The final source considered was a paper, "The Known, The Unknown, The Knowable, and the Unknowable: Evidence and the Evaluation of Evidence in the measurement of the Trans-Atlantic Slave Trade," Inikori presented at the *Conference on Transatlantic Slaving and the African Diaspora* held in Williamsburg, Virginia in 1998. In sum, Inikori maintained that because of the paucity of information on the volume of the illicit trade there is not enough solid evidence to determine the actual volume of the trade.[64]

CONCLUSIONS

Curtin's work represents one of the single most important pieces of literature on the Atlantic Slave Trade. From its initial publication in 1969, it captivated multiple generations of researchers interested in the Atlantic Slave Trade. During the period of this review, the researchers of the volume of the slave trade were divided and deeply entrenched into either one of two camps: those who supported Curtin's findings or those who believed he understated the volume of the trade. The different camps dug in like the French and the German armies along the Western Front in World War I, and from within their respective trenches they hurled often acid laced barbs across the no man's land that lay between them. Watching each other's every move and looking for ways to counter the findings of the opposing camp. Inikori attacked Curtin's research and Lovejoy attacked Inikori. Brendt found new evidence on the volume of the trade in the form parliamentary reports and Inikori countered by explaining the weakness in the reports and why they could not be fully trusted. Even today few historical debates invoke the kind of impassioned response as those concerning the Atlantic Slave Trade or slavery in the Americas.

It was for this reason that this subject was chosen because it should produce lively discussion and opportunities to better understand how historians wrestle with complex historical

---

[63] "African Americans at Jamestown," *National Park Service*, accessed, June 11, 2016, https://www.nps.gov/jame/learn/historyculture/african-americans-at-jamestown.htm.
[64] The Known, The Unknown, The Knowable, and the Unknowable: Evidence and the Evaluation of Evidence in the measurement of the Trans-Atlantic Slave Trade, speech given by Joseph Inikori, Conference on Transatlantic Slaving and the African Diaspora, September 1998, Williamsburg, VA. Inikori uses a complex algebraic equation to reach the same conclusion as Henige.

issues and to learn from their research. The aftermath of the conflict has been the production of new knowledge on the trade and innovative tools to help us to teach and to learn about the trade. For instance, the Trans-Atlantic Slave Trade Database is one of many scholarly returns that resulted from the debate over the volume of the slave trade. It contains information of over 36,000 slave trade voyages.

After almost fifty years of research, the estimate for the number of Africans imported into the Americas stands at approximately 10.7 million, a little more than 1 million more than Curtin had estimated in 1969.

KEY TERMS

Post Traumatic Slave Syndrome
Memes
M.E.E.S.
Limpieza de Sangre
Ottomans
Butterfly Effect

APPENDIX A

David Henige[65]

a. The number of West Africans who arrived alive in the New World as recorded in sources known to historians.
b. The number of West Africans who arrived alive in the New World as recorded in extant sources not yet known to historians.
c. The number of West Africans who arrived alive in the New World as recorded in sources now lost.
d. The number of West Africans who arrived in the New World in the clandestine trade.
e. The number of West Africans who died between the time of embarkation and arrival at some New World port, in both the 'legitimate' and the clandestine trade.
f. The number of captives who died in West Africa in transit to, or while at, the coast awaiting embarkation.
g. The number of individuals killed in wars fought only to capture slaves for export from West Africa.
h. The number of West Africans shipped to North Africa during the era of the Atlantic trade.
i. The total number of individuals killed in or removed from West Africa in both the trans-Atlantic and trans-Saharan slave trades from the sixteenth through the nineteenth centuries.

---

[65] See Henige, "Measuring the Immeasurable," 296–302.

APPENDIX B

Estimates for total captive imports into the Americas

Year	Researcher	Estimate
1861	Edward Dunbar	13,887,500
1936	R. R. Kuczynski	14,650,000
1950	Noel Deerr	11,970,000
1969	Philip Curtin	9,556,000
1981	James Rawley	11,345,000
1982	Paul Lovejoy	9,778,500
1987	David Eltis	10,267,425
1989	Paul Lovejoy	9,600,000
1989	Paul Lovejoy	10,800,000
1992	Joseph Inikori	13,392,000
1998	Joseph Inikori	11,420,100

The above chart is not comprehensive.

Paul Lovejoy gave a range for his 1989 estimates. The low estimate is 9.6 million imports, and the high estimate is 10.6 million imports.

CHAPTER 6

THE AFRICAN DIASPORA IN EUROPE: THE BLACK PRESENCE IN ENGLAND FROM THE FIFTEENTH TO THE EIGHTEENTH CENTURY

Tony Frazier

The African presence in Europe represents another dimension of the global African Diaspora. The Atlantic Slave Trade involved both Europe and Africa. Africans were present in many parts of Europe, yet the primary focus of this chapter centers on black people in England. This chapter will provide an overview of the black presence in England between the fourteenth and eighteenth centuries. The understanding of the African Diaspora in Europe broadens the understanding and complexity of black's life in the social and political history of England.

Africans figured prominently in European courts from the thirteenth to the fifteenth centuries and begin to appear in significant numbers in England during the late fifteenth century.[1] Black entertainers and musicians were employed by both the English and Scottish courts. King Henry VII of England had a black trumpeter and King James IV of Scotland used a black dancer. These instances would become commonplace in later centuries of English history as blacks would later serve in British regiments as musicians.[2]

Historians mark 1555 as the beginning of a continuous black presence in England, when five Africans were brought to England from Shama on the West African coast, later modern Ghana. Jon Lok, a London merchant, who hoped that by teaching them English he might facilitate trade with the Gold Coast, brought Africans into Britain. The Africans who followed this group were not interpreters but slaves who would form the basis of a permanent settlement of blacks in Britain.[3] John Hawkins first introduced the trafficking of black slaves to England in 1562–1563 during his voyage to the Guinea coast. Hawkins acquired some 300 black slaves whom he sold to the Spaniards in the Caribbean. His voyages in slave trafficking were the initial steps in a system that would explode almost one hundred years later into the organized Atlantic Slave Trade.[4]

This initial foray into slave trafficking introduced blacks into England during the late-sixteenth century in numbers that alarmed Britons. Subsequently, by 1596, the black population

---

[1] Jagdish S. Gundara and Ian Duffield, eds., *Essays on the History of Blacks in Britain: From Roman Times to the Mid-Twentieth Century* (Aldershot, London: Avebury, 1992), 15.

[2] Gundara, *Essays*, 15.

[3] Peter Fryer, *Staying Power: The History of Black People in Britain* (London: Pluto Press, 1991), 5; F. O. Shyllon, *Black Slaves in Britain* (London: Oxford University Press, 1974), 2.

[4] Fryer, 8.

of England was so significant that Queen Elizabeth I felt compelled to issue an edict objecting to the presence of blacks in her realm. She declared: "Several blackamoors have lately been brought into this realm, of which kind of people there are already too many here ... Her Majesty's pleasure therefore is that those kinds of people should be expelled from the land."[5]

There were subsequent arrangements outlined again in 1601 by Queen Elizabeth I to deport blacks from England.[6] These proposed expulsions were due to the belief that black people would taint the purity of English blood and take jobs away from other servants. Another rationale given for the removal of blacks was their status as infidels and non-Christians.[7] Despite the desire of the queen for a black exodus from Britain, their numbers grew due to England's increased role in the Atlantic Slave Trade.

However, these expulsion plans by the queen were unsuccessful and undermined by the contradictory fact that Queen Elizabeth herself employed an African entertainer and page at her court, which reflected a Tudor family tradition in existence since the reigns of Henry VII and Henry VIII, who employed a black trumpeter known as John Blanke. In 1506 or 1507, the Scottish poet William Dunbar wrote "Of Ane Blak Moir," describing a black woman, called Helenor in the court accounts, possibly Ellen More, who reached Edinburgh by way of the port of Leith and acted a principal role in the "tournament of the black night and the black lady," in which the king of Scotland played the part of the black knight.[8] Africans and their descendants were part of the Scottish court during the Jacobean period in the capacity of performers and musicians.[9]

Francis Blackamoore (Blackymore Maide), a black woman was a member of a radical religious congregation in Bristol during the eve of the Putney Debates during the 1640s. She was a leader in her Anabaptist congregation organized by and for women. She was described as a Baptist given to liberty.[10] Another black in Bristol named Pero, a black male servant to Nevis planter John Pinney. Pero lived a comfortable life and was able to make money as a dentist and performing other services. He was able lend money to other servants on a small scale.[11]

This specter of black humanity was very present in the streets of London during the later years of Elizabeth I's reign. Indeed, as the volume of the slave trade increased, the black population grew in England. The African became part of the everyday language of the English society. Even during the sixteenth century, when William Shakespeare wrote *Othello* he was not

---

[5] Folarin Shyllon, "The Black Presence and Experience in Britain: An Analytical Overview," in *Essays on the History of Black Britain: From Roman Times to the Mid-Twentieth Century*, eds. Jagdish Gundara and Ian Duffield (Avebury: Ashgate Publishing Company, 1992), 202; David Bygott, *Black and British* (Oxford: Oxford University Press, 1992), 18.

[6] Shyllon, "The Black Presence," 202.

[7] James Walvin, *The Black Presence: A Documentary History of the Negro in England, 1555–1860* (New York: Schocken Books, 1972), 64.

[8] Martin Kilson and Robert I. Rotberg, eds., *The African Diaspora: Interpretive Essays* (Cambridge: Harvard University Press, 1976), 173.

[9] Edward Scobie, *Black Britannia: A History of Blacks in Britain* (Chicago: Johnson Publishing Company, 1972), 12; and Fryer, *Staying Power*, 4–5.

[10] Peter Linebaugh and Marcus Rediker, *The Many-Headed Hydra: Sailors, Slaves, Commoners, and the Hidden History of the Revolutionary Atlantic* (Boston: Beacon Press, 2000), 71–77.

[11] Madge Dresser, *Slavery Obscured: The Social History of the Slave Trade in an English Provincial Port* (London: Continuum, 2001), 81.

confused about racial identities. He and the audience that attended his plays certainly witnessed this sea of black humanity in the streets of London. During the Elizabethan era, blacks began to appear as characters in literature, plays, and other entertainment. Blacks were often depicted in art and literature as representations of filth, evil, sin, ugliness, and even the devil. This literary development was accompanied by scientific speculation on race that perpetuated negative ideas about blacks as well as theories of black inferiority.[12] The increasing numbers of Africans in early modern England raised ethnic and racial anxieties about England's national identity.

Although English participation in the slave trade was minimal before the mid-seventeenth century, the end of the English Civil War and the Restoration signaled a growing British involvement in the trafficking of enslaved Africans. This was primarily due to the desire for new sources of labor for the various plantation settlements in the English colonies created before the English Civil War, settlements that included Barbados, the Leeward Islands, and the North American colonies. This increasing demand for slave labor resulted in the creation of the Royal Adventures into Africa, a joint stock company, chartered in 1660. The Royal Adventures' mission was to supply the New World colonies with slaves. However, the company disbanded due to severe financial difficulties, reaching its demise in 1672.[13]

The Royal African Company, chartered in 1672, proved to be more successful than its predecessor. Its charter included a monopoly on trade for a period of 1000 years. Possessing the power to seize ships and property of unauthorized slave traders, it was the first large-scale English organization of the slave trade.[14] During its heyday, from 1672 to 1698, John Locke, who owned shares worth €600 in the Royal African Company, and many other prominent Britons made huge profits.[15] Eventually, its monopoly ended, throwing open the slave trade to private merchants. From this point, large commercial ports came to dominate the slave trade.

The importation of blacks into Britain increased further after the War of the Spanish Succession. The War of Spanish Succession (1701–1714) was a dispute about which nation would inherit the disputed Spanish Empire and its territories. France sought to control the Spanish crown and its territories around the globe, but was defeated by alliance of Great Britain, the Netherlands, Austria, Prussia, and Portugal. The peace settlement to the war was the Treaty of Utrecht in 1713. One of the outcomes of the war resulted in the coveted "Asiento" being awarded to England. This was a contractual agreement between Great Britain and Spain whereby each party agreed that the English would supply the Spanish colonies with slaves. Queen Anne placed the responsibility of conducting the slave trade in the control of the South Sea Company, chartered in 1711 by the government of Queen Anne. This company received a lifetime monopoly on trade to South America.[16] This agreement lasted until the "War of Jenkins Ear" broke out in 1739. The war involved a conflict between the British Navy and the Spanish Navy. One British captain had his ear

---

[12] Gretchen Gerzina, *Black London: Life Before Emancipation* (New Jersey: Rutgers University Press, 1995), 2–5; Fryer, 135–146.

[13] Colin A. Palmer, *Human Cargoes: The British Slave Trade to Spanish America, 1700–1739* (Urbana: University of Illinois Press, 1981), 4; Kenneth Morgan, *Slavery, Atlantic Trade and the British Economy, 1660–1800* (Cambridge: Cambridge University Press, 2000), 6.

[14] Palmer, 4–5; Morgan, *Slavery,* 9.

[15] Fryer, *Staying Power,* 151; John Locke managed to reconcile the belief in the inalienable rights of man with the view that black slavery was a justifiable institution.

[16] Palmer, 10.

severed by a Spanish sword. A member of the English parliament used the severed ear in a speech to create anti-Spanish sentiments spurred a new war between trading partners Great Britain and Spain. The South Sea Bubble, a risky financial speculation that sunk the British national government's stock, contributed to weakening the power of the South Sea Company. As a result, in order to avoid future risks, the company reduced its involvement in the slave trade.[17]

The difficulties of the Royal African Company and the South Sea Company did nothing to dampen the zeal of Englishmen who participated in large numbers in the slave trade from the early half of the eighteenth century. These traders, located in the port cities of London, Liverpool, and Bristol, built or bought ships, purchased supplies and goods, and hired crews. The right of free trade of slaves became recognized a fundamental right of Englishmen.[18]

The increased prosperity of the Atlantic Slave Trade linking three continents fueled the growth of the black population of England during the late seventeenth and eighteenth centuries. Africans were sold in the slave port cities of Bristol, Liverpool, and London. In the early period from 1723 to1743, Bristol was England's number one slaving port. The prominence of Bristol was due to its role in the trade of slaves and sugar, the latter produced by slave labor. Its rival, Liverpool, also built on slave labor, surpassed Bristol as the leading slaving port in the in the eighteenth century. Overall, both cities underwent transformations from mere towns to great world ports due to the trafficking of human cargo.[19]

In the eighteenth century, Africans continued to enter England in great numbers. Although London was Britain's smallest slave port when compared to Liverpool and Bristol, it was the largest city in the world with a population that reached almost 700,000 in 1750 and over a million in 1800.[20] While serving as the capital and a major port city of new industries and trade, London had an extremely diverse population, which consisted of not only Europeans but also black Africans, both enslaved and free. By the middle of the century, it was handling almost three quarters of the sugar imported into England, with the profits from this business playing a crucial role in the city's success. Consequently, London became the center for money lending, serving the dual role of broker and banker. It garnered lucrative commissions and interest for accommodating the peculiar needs of planters and slave merchants.[21]

In addition, London represented the vibrant society, which made up the world of politics and fashion. London attracted the best and the worst, the enterprising and the parasitic people who were seeking their fortunes, searching for work, or running away. London had an abundance of everything including heavy traffic, culture, and filth. London was the heart of British political, cultural, commercial, and intellectual life.[22]

During the seventeenth and eighteenth centuries, colonial slavery developed into a mature social and legal institution. The maturity of slavery throughout the Atlantic world ensured that increasing numbers of blacks eventually found their way to England due to a variety of circumstances. For instance, some entered English society as slaves directly from Africa. Others arrived

---

[17] Ibid., 11.
[18] Eric Eustace Williams, *Capitalism and Slavery* (New York: G. P. Putnam, 1944), 30–32.
[19] Madge Dresser, *Slavery Obscured: The Social History of the Slave Trade in an English Provincial Port* (London: Continuum, 2001), 28; Peter Fryer, *Staying Power*, 32–36.
[20] M. Dorothy George, *London Life in the Eighteenth Century* (New York: Alfred A. Knopf, 1925), 171.
[21] Fryer, 44.
[22] Kirstin Olsen, *Daily Life in 18th-Century England* (Westport: Greenwood Publishing Group, 1999), 57–58.

from the Americas where they had already served as slaves. Many blacks entered London in the mid-eighteenth century as slaves or trained domestics in the service of returning colonial governors and West Indian planters who chose to bring their house slaves with them rather than employ English servants.

Blacks also entered London as children and teenagers brought over as menials or body servants to serve rich English families. Their initial use was to serve as fashionable items.[23] Naval captains also returned with black valets whom they then sought to sell.[24] These white Britons brought with them their black chattels and their slave-holding presumptions and practices. Despite these various avenues of entrance to England, the primary occupation of the majority of black slaves in London was domestic servitude.

Under the category of domestic servant, blacks worked as pages, valets, footmen, coachmen, cooks, and maids. Their status was a state of enslavement, because unlike their white counterparts, they did not receive wages. There must have been reasons for this development other than the search for labor, because there was not a shortage of white domestics.[25] Black servants offered more than labor; they were a symbolic representation with which their owners sought to impress society and to reaffirm their social positions or prestige. The most important commodity offered by black servants was a lifetime of unpaid labor.[26] Unlike those in the plantation colonies, which existed under codified law, black slaves in London lived between a station of chattel slavery and domestic servitude.

Domestic servitude and cultural alienation were harsh realities for blacks in eighteenth century London. Even if chattel slavery did not exist in the law, it existed in the minds of blacks and many white people. Blacks in England were in general not producing products through their labor, but represented the means by which some whites enhanced their own status.

Yet a few privileged blacks managed to escape these horrendous conditions which ensnared so many of their fellow blacks. Their routes to London were part of the jetsam of black humanity being dispersed throughout the Atlantic. The most famous triumvirate of eighteenth century blacks in Britain included Ignatius Sancho, Olaudah Equiano, and Ottobah Cugoano. Each of these writers left written manuscripts for posterity. Ignatius Sancho published the *Letters of the Late Ignatius Sancho, An African* in 1782. Olaudah Equiano published *The Interesting Narrative of the Life of Olaudah Equinao, or Gustavuus Vassa, The African, Written by Himself* in 1794, and Ottobah Cugoano published a book called *Thoughts and Sentiments on the Evil and Wicked Traffic of the Human Species* in 1787.

Ignatius Sancho, became one of the first black writers to publish an antislavery work in history. Sancho was born on a slave ship in 1729, the ship was bound for a plantation in Grenada. Sancho became an orphan after his mother died of an unknown disease and his father, like so many enslaved Africans, committed suicide rather than live as a slave. He was employed by the Duke of Montagu after the Duke recognized his quick mind, and gave him books, and

---

[23] Shyllon, *Black Slaves*, 11.

[24] Fryer, 14–25; J. Jean Hecht, *The Domestic Servant Class in Eighteenth-Century England* (London: Routledge & Paul, 1956), 33–35.

[25] Hecht, 1.

[26] Edward Scobie, *Black Britannia: A History of Blacks in Britain* (Chicago: Johnson Publishing Company, 1972), 22.

encouraged his learning. Sancho spent most of his life as a footman and ultimately as a butler. After leaving the service of the Montagu family he later set up a grocer's shop in Charles Street, Westminster.[27]

The leading spokesman for the African cause, and by far the most widely traveled African living in England in the second half of the eighteenth century, was Olaudah Equiano, sometimes known as Gustavus Vassa, the African. Equiano, unlike Sancho, had memory of his experiences of Africa, and been born of Igbo group in Nigeria. He was ten years old when he was captured and sold into slavery. He did not regain his freedom until 1766, when he was twenty-nine years old. Equiano had served as a seaman under two masters, Captain Pascal and Mr. Robert King. He served in various campaigns during the Seven Years' War with France, and made numerous voyages between America and the West Indies. Equiano had visited England several times and was sent to school there by a Misses Guerin, a cousin of Mr. Pascal. Equiano finally settled in London during the 1770s. By the end of the next decade, he had become deeply involved in the politics of the black people, championing their cause and fighting for the abolition of the slave trade.[28]

Quobna Ottobah Cugoano, born on the West Coast of Africa to the Fantee native group. He was kidnapped and sold into slavery, and was later enslaved on the island of Grenada. That memory of enslavement remained central to Cugoano strident antislavery writing. He joined with his friend Equiano to speak out against slavery and the slave trade. They were both instrumental in forming the group Sons of Africa to lobby on behalf of blacks in London and fighting to end the trafficking of their fellow Africans.[29]

The response to the black resistance of slavery through their flight into self-emancipation and a growing concern toward population numbers of blacks was a matter of debate in the middle of the eighteenth century. In 1764, *The Gentlemen's Magazine* an anonymous commentator remarked:

> The practice of importing Negro servants into these kingdoms is said to be already a grievance that requires a remedy, yet it is every day encouraged, insomuch that the number in this metropolis only, is supposed to be near 20,000.[30]

The concern raised about the number of black servants entering England was a signal that the black presence produced mixed responses.

---

[27] Ignatious Sancho, *Letters of the Late Ignatius Sancho, An African*, (London: J. Nichols, 1782), in *Unchained Voices: An Anthology of Black Authors in the English-Speaking World of the Eighteenth Century*, ed. Vincent Caretta (Lexington: University Press of Kentucky, 1996), 77–109.

[28] Olaudah Equiano, *Equiano's Travels: The Interesting Narrative of the Life of Olaudah Equiano, or Gustavuus Vassa The African, Written by Himself* (London: 1789), ed. Paul Edwards (London: Heinemann, 1969), and Olaudah Equiano, *The Interesting Narrative of the Life of Olaudah Equinao, or Gustavuus Vassa, The African, Written by Himself* (London: 1794), in *Unchained Voices: An Anthology of Black Authors in the English-Speaking World of the Eighteenth Century*, ed. Vincent Caretta (Lexington: University Press of Kentucky, 1996), 185–318.

[29] Quobna Ottobah Cugoano, *Thoughts and Sentiments on the Evil and Wicked Traffic of the Slavery and Commerce of the Human Species, Humbly Submitted to the Inhabitants of Great Britain, by Ottobah Cugoano, a Native of Africa* (London: 1787), in *Unchained Voices: An Anthology of Black Authors in the English-Speaking World of the Eighteenth Century*, ed. Vincent Caretta (Lexington: University Press of Kentucky, 1996), 145–184.

[30] *The Gentleman's Magazine*, 1764, 443.

The 1780s witnessed the black population not only being employed as servants but a large percentage as free workers who often were mired in poverty. They were reduced to unemployed, unprotected, and harmless objects of poverty. The numbers in this group increased with the arrival of the Black Loyalists from the Americas after the Revolutionary War. Governor of Virginia, the Earl of Dunmore, in an effort to aid British war aims, issued a political as well as military proclamation stating "I do hereby declare all indentured servants, Negroes, or others (appertaining to rebels) free, that are able and willing to bear arms, they joining his Majesty's troops, as soon as may be, for the more speedily reducing this colony to a proper dignity."[31] This proclamation by Dunmore was viewed on both sides of the Atlantic as a threat to slavery. Those blacks that sided with the British would later come to be known as the Black Loyalists.

These Black Loyalists were the thousands of former slaves who fought alongside the English during the war. The British had promised them freedom in exchange for their military service in the Revolutionary War. Blacks in America recognized their strange position in a land proclaiming freedom from tyranny yet exercising slavery on the other hand. Britain exploited this issue for their military and political gain. The British rewarded the Black Loyalists by evacuating them Canada, the West Indies, and England for their assistance in the Loyalist cause.[32] A few Black Loyalists who entered England applied for their government pensions and property compensation. The claim and pension examiners made no secret of their discrimination against blacks stating on several occasions "blacks ought to think themselves very fortunate in being in a country where they can never again be reduced to the state of slavery."[33]

Black Loyalists became identified with the "Black Poor." This is not to suggest that there were not any black indigent people living in England before the arrival of the Black Loyalist, but this label became synonymous with the Black Loyalists. The "Black Poor" were cosigned to a status of indigent, unemployed, despised, and an alarming sight in the streets of late eighteenth-century London.[34] They had to contend with poor laws, inadequate housing, racism, poverty, and remained a visual reminder of England's role in Atlantic slavery.[35] Poverty was a noted characteristic of the "Black Poor" with the hardships of cold and hunger as constant companions. For those blacks not dressed in livery, the rags worn by them provided a stark contrast between being a servant and those trying to survive free in London.

The Committee for the Relief of the Black Poor was formed in 1786 to alleviate the conditions of misery and poverty for some blacks in London's streets. The Committee sought monetary relief, started a hospital for blacks, and provided clothing and food support for the black poor. The presence of blacks conditioned a response that it was necessary that they be

---

[31] Sylvia R. Frey, *Water From The Rock: Black Resistance In A Revolutionary Age* (Princeton, NJ: Princeton University Press, 1991), 63; John Hope Franklin and Alfred A. Moss, Jr., *From Slavery to Freedom: A History of African Americans* (New York: McGraw Hill, Inc., 1994), 74–75.

[32] Stephen J. Braidwood, *Black Poor and White Philanthropists: London's Blacks and the Foundation of the Sierra Leone Settlement* 1786–1791 (Liverpool: Liverpool University Press, 1994), 23; John W. Pulis, *Moving On: Black Loyalists In the Afro-Atlantic World* (New York: Garland Publishing Inc., 1999), 87; Mary Beth Norton, "The Fate of Some Black Loyalists of the American Revolution," *Journal of Negro History* 58 (1973): 403–404.

[33] Norton, 404.

[34] Norton, 407.

[35] Pulis, 91.

sent/removed from London and no longer occupy the streets of London with their presence.[36] The committee decided on a solution for removal of the "Black Poor," which was the creation of the Sierra Leone colony to expedite an overseas resettlement. This was an attempt to repatriate blacks, but only about 400 blacks were actually involved in the venture to return to Africa. This venture was disastrous to those who did embark on the voyage.[37] Equiano was appointed Commissary of Provisions and Stores for the Black Poor. He favored the proposal to return Africans to their native quarters, but expressed concern over the continued slave trafficking in the surrounding regions of West Africa. Equiano stated that the expedition failed because of mismanagement. The ships arrival in Sierra Leone coincided with the rainy season, and it was nearly impossible to cultivate the land. The black settlers exhausted all their provisions before they could be replenished.[38] Cugoano was more critical of the experiment. He believed that a show of good faith would have been made if a treaty with the African inhabitants of the land had been arranged. He felt that the black settlers would encounter eventual re-enslavement.[39] After the failure of this initial Sierra Leone project, their developed a second attempt with an expedition of Black Loyalists from Nova Scotia in 1792. There was a total of 1100 blacks who were part of the new journey to Sierra Leone. This second attempt proved to be more successful than the original Sierra Leone settlement.

The idea of this chapter was to create a greater interest of the African European experience in the African Diaspora. The black presence in England elucidates the ways in which the black experience was a part of the fabric of English society. Blacks were more than just interlopers, they answered Londoners doors, ran their errands, carried their purchases, wore their livery, played their music, drank in their taverns, appeared in their portraits, novels, poems, diaries, and plays. Moreover, black Londoners attended church, baptized their children, married other servants who were black, white, and Lascars.

Blacks in England were citizens of the African Diaspora. Some of them came directly from Africa, many were former slaves in the Americas, some had served as seamen, and these blacks possessed knowledge of Africa, America, and Europe owing to their displacement throughout the world.

KEY TERMS

Treaty of Utrecht
Asiento
Royal African Company
Black Loyalists

---

[36] Norton, 407.

[37] Stephen J. Braidwood, "Initiatives and Organisation of the Black Poor 1786–1787," *Slavery and Abolition* (1982): 211–227.

[38] Equiano, 285–286.

[39] Quobna Ottobah Cugoano, *Thoughts and Sentiments on the Evil and Wicked Traffic of the Slavery and Commerce of the Human Species, Humbly Submitted to the Inhabitants of Great Britain, by Ottobah Cugoano, A Native of Africa* (London: 1787), 175, in *Unchained Voices: An Anthology of Black Authors in the English-Speaking World of the Eighteenth Century*, ed. Vincent Caretta (Lexington: University Press of Kentucky, 1996), 145–184.

CHAPTER 7

THE SLAVE TRADE AND THE AFRICAN DIASPORA IN THE INDIAN OCEAN: THE CASE OF EAST AFRICA, ARABIAN PENINSULAR, AND THE INDIAN SUBCONTINENT SLAVERY

Azaria Mbughuni

People of African descent live in communities scattered in different parts of the Indian Ocean from the present day Oman and Yemen in the Arabian Peninsula to India and Pakistan in the Indian subcontinent. At least 75,000 people of African descent live in the Indian subcontinent (India and Pakistan) today. These communities of people of African descent have received little attention when compared to their counterparts in the Atlantic Ocean. The Indian Ocean slave trade was the major conduit for Africans who were sent in large numbers to the Middle East, the Indian subcontinent, and to the Far East. The Red Sea and the Persian Gulf also served as the gateway for enslaved Africans from Egypt, Sudan, Ethiopia and Saudi Arabia, Yemen, Oman, and Iran who were transported to and from the Indian Ocean. How Africans were dispersed in the Indian Ocean, particularly to the Indian subcontinent, and what happened to them afterwards, is a subject that is beginning to receive some attention by scholars.

Study of the Indian Ocean Diaspora poses a number of challenges. The Indian Ocean world was part of a much older system of trade and interactions between Africans and other groups along the Indian Ocean that goes back to at least two millennium. Scholarship on the Indian Ocean Diaspora has generally been lagging when compared to the Atlantic Ocean Diaspora. The book *Race and Slavery in the Middle East: An Historical Enquiry by* Bernard Lewis examines race, Islam, and slavery in the Middle East. The seminal book by Joseph E. Harris, *The African Presence in Asia: Consequences of the East African Slave Trade*, traces the African presence in Asia and draws attention to their accomplishments. Harris More recent scholarship has shed more light on the movements and experiences of Africans along the Indian Ocean. Scholarship on the Indian Ocean Diaspora has been challenging because of the difficulty of obtaining Arabic sources. Many scholars have relied on European sources. P. H. Colomb, a soldier in the British Army, wrote a book about his experiences in the British navy in the nineteenth century. Colomb's book, *Slave Catching in the Indian Ocean: A Record of Naval Experiences*, provides one of the few available primary sources for researchers. Shihan de S. Jayasuriya and Richard Pankhurst's *The African Diaspora in the Indian Ocean*, provides various important essays on the Indian Ocean Diaspora. Gwyn Campbell's edited book *The Structure of Slavery in Indian Ocean Africa and Asia* is a collection of essays that attempts to define slavery in different parts of the Indian Ocean and highlights the uniqueness of the slave trade along the Indian Ocean World. Edward A. Alpers' *East Africa and the Indian Ocean* sheds light on the links between India and East Africa and looks at the coastal communities in Somalia and Mozambique. *Slavery and South Asian History*, edited by Indrani Chatterjee and Richard M. Eaton, contains a number of essays that sheds new light on slave trade and slavery in South Asia.

This chapter traces the movement of African people to the Indian subcontinent, mostly to territories that were under Muslim rulers, and shows the interconnectedness of Africa, the Middle East, and the Indian subcontinent in regard to the slave trade as these three territories shared the Indian Ocean. Many enslaved Africans sent to India travelled through the Middle East, mainly through Oman, but also through the Arabian Peninsula. Enslaved Africans who crossed the Red Sea to the Arabian Peninsula were then sent to the Indian Ocean to the Indian subcontinent. If the Caribbean in the Atlantic Ocean was the place that enslaved Africans were "seasoned" before being redistributed to North America, the Arabian Peninsula and Zanzibar appear to have partly played a similar role for many enslaved Africans who were sent to Muslim-controlled territories in the Indian subcontinent. Seasoning was a period of adjustment in which enslaved Africans learned about their new status in society and adapted to the new circumstances. Enslaved Africans brought to the Arabian Peninsula and Zanzibar were given new names, converted to Islam, and expected to learn their new status in society. Buyers from the Indian subcontinent had a preference for enslaved Africans who had undergone the process of seasoning. The quality of life for enslaved Africans in India greatly depended upon the slave owner they served. Some enjoyed the benefits of slave owner's wealth and power, while others lived in poverty; some belonged to kind slave owners while others lived in a constant state of terror.

The slave trade in the Indian Ocean area consisted of numerous routes, ports of launching and final destinations. There were two major routes: a northern and a southern route. The first route was used to send Africans northwards to the Arabian Peninsula and then north and east to India and beyond; the second route moved southwards, southeast to Islands off the coast of East Africa and south around the Cape of Good Hope to the Atlantic Ocean. Africans were captured from inland and brought to the coast for transport. Inland areas where slaves were captured included present day Ethiopia (Abyssinia), Somalia, Kenya, Tanzania, and Mozambique. Once brought to the coast, enslaved Africans were sent to Zanzibar, the Arabian Peninsula, Persia, the Indian subcontinent, and as far east as China. The slave trade in the Indian Ocean spread far and wide, while most of the slaves sent to the Arabian Peninsula and India came from East Africa, many others were transported across the Red Sea to the Arabian Peninsula, particularly enslaved Ethiopians. Arabia Peninsula became the main destination for most enslaved Africans transported in the Indian Ocean and the Red Sea. Majority of enslaved Africans who were sent to Persia or what is today Iran, the Indian subcontinent, and beyond passed through Arabia particularly in the eighteenth and the nineteenth centuries.

The key to unlocking the secrets of the Diaspora communities in the Indian Ocean is to study the slave trade. To understand the culture and religious traditions of African Indians, it is important to have a clear understanding of where Africans came from and how they were brought to their final destination. The following sections will delineate the movement of Africans to the Middle East and India, the impact of enslaved African soldiers, and the experiences of some of the African Indians. Focus will be placed on the involuntary migration of African people to destinations outside the African continent, but will also provide examples of voluntary movements. Emphasis will be placed on the interconnectedness of the slave trade in East Africa, the Arabian Peninsula, and the Indian subcontinent, and examine elements of slavery in the subcontinent as it pertains to Africans.

ANCIENT ORIGINS

Slavery as an institution has existed since ancient times. While the form of slavery that was practiced in Africa and the Arabian Peninsula was not exactly the same as what emerged in the Atlantic Ocean in the sixteenth and seventeenth centuries, slavery as an institution was very common in North Africa and the Arabian Peninsula. A slave was a property that could be bought and sold and was subjected to a life of servitude. Africans from sub-Saharan Africa were enslaved in both ancient Egypt and Arabia. Nubians were enslaved in Egypt during the Middle and New Kingdoms. There are various sources that point to the enslavement of Africans in the Middle East. For example, the *Book of Jeremiah* in the *Bible* speaks of an Ethiopian eunuch named Melech; the Quran mentions Ethiopian slaves residing in Arabia during the seventh century. After the seventh century, Islam provided guidelines for the status and treatment of slaves. Islam sanctioned slavery, while at the same time encouraging manumission and better treatment for slaves. This chapter does not examine ancient slavery in great depth; it however, provides a brief account of slavery in the ancient periods to show that slavery in the Indian Ocean existed as an institution long before the slave trade reached its height in the seventeenth and eighteenth centuries.

THE RED SEA AND THE SLAVE TRADE

Many enslaved Africans who were transported to the Indian subcontinent from the Arabian Peninsula first crossed the Red Sea before they embarked on a journey across the Indian Ocean. The slave trade carried out in the Red Sea was considerable. Africans transported via the Red Sea were Abyssinians (Ethiopians), Nubians, Somalis, and Africans from southern Sudan. The southern coast of Arabian Peninsula served as a hub for the redistribution of these slaves to final destinations in Turkey, Persia, India, and beyond.

The slave trade in the Red Sea dates back to antiquity. Dynastic Egyptians brought slaves from the land of Punt in what appears to be present day Somalia. Expeditions were sent to Punt to obtain slaves, ivory, and perfumes. *The Periplus of the Eritrean Sea* from the third century AD states that "better sorts of slaves" come from what is present day Somalia. Estimations of the extent of the Red Sea slave trade are educated guesses at best. According to one estimate, about two thousand slaves were exported each year between 800 and 1600 AD, giving us a rough estimate of one million and six hundred thousand Africans sent across the Red Sea to Arabia during the 800-year period ending in 1600. It is clear that Africans were exported to the Arabian Peninsula in large numbers over a long period of time through the Red Sea.

As in Arabia and Africa, slavery has ancient origins in India. Slavery existed in India from antiquity. Hindu laws and customs recognizes and sanctions slavery. According to Hindu law, a person can become a slave under several circumstances; for example, as a prisoner of war, for debt, as the offspring of a female slave, or through voluntary submission to slavery. The slave was considered as a property and had no right to own property unless sanctioned by the slave owner. The Hindu codes are very specific about the rights of slave owner/slave and the different kinds of slaves. Muslims who settled in India after the eighth century AD also practiced slavery. However, the significant presence of enslaved Africans in India took place after Muslims established their foothold in southern India after the twelfth century and increased the number of slaves. Islam recognized slavery and provided stipulations on their status and treatment. Thus, enslaved Africans in India served under both Hindu and Muslim slave owners with majority serving the latter.

Enslaved Africans sent to India came from two main regions: first, there was Ethiopia and its neighboring territories; second, there was east Africa, areas along the Swahili coast and its interior between present day Kenya, Tanzania, and northern Mozambique. What initially fueled the demand for larger numbers of enslaved Africans in India was the need for soldiers. The practice of using enslaved Africans increased with the establishment of the independent Sultanate of Fakhr al-Din Mubarak Shah in 1338 AD. It was, however, not until the fourteenth century that we can document a large number of Africans brought to work for Muslim rulers in India. Sultan Rukh al-din Barbak Shah of Bengal was reported to have an estimated eight thousand "Abyssinians" working for him between 1459 and 1474. Most of them were employed as soldiers. The Shah specifically favored Ethiopian eunuchs and brought them in large numbers to guard his many harems. The origin of the so-called "Abyssinians" working for the Shah was not necessarily Ethiopia. Many did indeed come from Ethiopia and neighboring territories; however, there was a tendency to label most enslaved Africans as "Abyssinian," "Habshi," or "Siddis."

The slave trade in the Red Sea was fed by local conflicts that generated captives. There were constant conflicts between Ethiopian Christians and Muslims, particularly, Christian Ethiopians and Muslim Somalis. This tension turned into a violent war in the 1540s when Ibrahim al-Ghazi, the Imam of Harar, a city which would become the center of Islam in the Horn of Africa, sought to conquer territories in Ethiopia; he destroyed cities and enslaving their inhabitants. It was with the help of the Portuguese in 1543 that the Muslim attacks were halted and al-Ghazi was killed. Ethiopia faced civil wars that ravaged the country in the seventeenth and eighteenth centuries; central authority had collapsed and slaving activities increased significantly. Ethiopian warlords fought each other for control leading to an increasing number of captives. The captives were sold into slavery and sent to the port of Massawa on the coast of what is now Eritrea, where many of them were sent to Arabia and some on to India. Order returned to Ethiopia in the nineteenth century. However, wars continued on the borders with Sudan, Somalia, and among the Muslim Galla in the south. The Galla raiders in southwestern Ethiopia sent their captives to the ports of Zeila (Zaila) and Berbera in Somalia for further transport across the Red Sea.

The Ethiopian presence in the Red Sea was not limited to the slave trade. The Ethiopian Kingdom of Aksum conquered Yemen in the sixth century CE and ruled it for close to a century. This provides an example of Africans moving to the Arabian Peninsula as conquerors. Ethiopian highlands produced coffee and other items that were highly prized and sought out. The coffee trade took Ethiopian traders far and wide along important cities in the

Indian Ocean. At the time, Ethiopia was an independent kingdom with considerable power and influence in the region. Ethiopians conducted trade in the Red Sea and the Indian Ocean and maintained diplomatic relations with Ottoman rulers in Turkey, with Europeans, and powerful rulers in India. In 1503, a European traveler, Ludovico di Varthema, observed that a great quantity of goods was transported to the Red Sea port Jeddah from Ethiopia and that there were many pilgrims in Mecca from Ethiopia. Ethiopians traveled freely in the region to trade and make the pilgrimage to Mecca. Ethiopians also traveled to India not as slaves but as traders and businessmen, some of whom settled there. In Calcutta, India, Varthema came across traders from various parts of the Indian Ocean. He inquired as to where they came from; the traders told him they were from Syria, Turkey, and Ethiopia, among other places. Some Ethiopian traders settled in India and established successful businesses. For example, in the beginning of the sixteenth century, an Abyssinian trader went to Gujarat and established an agate factory at Nandod in Rajpipla. He died in Nandod and was buried close to Bawa Ghor. This example illustrates the complexity of African presence in India. While many came to India as slaves, there were those who went there voluntarily, settled there and became very successful. It is clear from this and other evidence left by Europeans that in the sixteenth and seventeenth century India, one was likely to encounter Africans who were enslaved and those who were free walking in the streets.

During the eighteenth and nineteenth centuries, the Red Sea continued to be an important source of slaves that were re-exported to Persia, India, and other final destinations. There was considerable trade carried out between African coast, Red Sea, Gulf of Aden, and the Arabian Peninsula in the nineteenth century. The port of Zaila in Somalia on the Gulf of Aden was one of the most important centers of slave trade in the Red Sea. The port was a hub for trade beginning in the fifteenth century and continued to serve as a point of departure for slaves well into the nineteenth century. From Zaila, Ethiopian slaves were sent to the Arabian Peninsula, Persia, and India. Muslims ruled the city and most of its inhabitants appear to have also been Muslims. According to the European traveler, Ludovico Di Varthema who visited the Zaila port in 1502, slaves, gold, and elephant teeth were exported to India, Persia, Cairo, and the Arabian Peninsula. Residents of this city often attacked Ethiopian territories and carried away Abyssinian slaves. It is these slaves that were sent across the Red Sea to the Arabian Peninsula and over to Persia and the Indian subcontinent.

By the 1880s, it became very clear to the British that Zaila was an important center for slave trade along the Red Sea. British reports looking at the Red Sea slave trade identified Zaila as one of the principal ports for slaves sent to the Arabian Peninsula and beyond. Africans were transported in caravans from the interior, some were small caravans and others were large with as many as three hundred enslaved Africans. The Africans were distributed into groups and spread out among various communities in the area to await transportation across the Red Sea. Enslaved Africans were then transported using small boats at different points in groups of between ten and thirty.

British investigative reports reveal extensive slaving activities in the region. For example, they report that many slaves were sold in Mecca right before and shortly after the annual Muslim pilgrimage. Pilgrims took some of the enslaved Africans directly to India. Some escaped to seek refuge with the British authorities. Resistance to slavery became more common along the Red

Sea and other areas as British vessels frequented the region and British consuls stationed in the Arabian Peninsula started to manumit those who escaped and made their case to the officials. The British sent some of those manumitted to India. In the beginning of 1881, the British agent in Jeddah, Jas Zohrab, manumitted fifteen Africans, newly imported children who were sold in Mecca during the pilgrimage. He claimed that twelve dhows full of enslaved Africans landed at the time, mainly filled with Abyssinian slaves. The children were freed and taken in by a British vessel. The freed Africans were kept by the British in the Arabian Peninsula until arrangements could be made for them. Among the plans in consideration at the time were to entrust them with locals, sending them to India or back to east Africa.

British authorities reported the capture of three vessels full of enslaved Abyssinian in Marawah in Yemen in 1881. One slaver held thirty-one, another forty one, and the third had twenty seven. The slave market was first held in the port of Hodeida, but was eventually moved to Marawah because of interruptions and pressure from the British. The British gave ninety-nine Africans to the Marawah police chief Hassan Agha, who was asked to give them to trustworthy people under bond and promise that they would not sell them into slavery. Agha distributed them among his friends, many of whom sold the Africans into slavery. The incident led the British to change their policy of leaving emancipated slaves with local officials and they began to explore the possibility of sending them to India and other countries along the Indian Ocean.

The slave trade in the Red Sea was complex and interconnected. Enslaved Africans were taken from inland Ethiopia, Somalia, and the Sudan and transported to various ports in Ethiopia/Eritrea, Somalia, and Yemen. From there, they were transported mainly to Arabian Peninsular ports for redistribution throughout Middle East, Persia, India, and beyond. Although the Red Sea slave trade dates back to antiquity, available records document a thriving trade in the seventeenth century that increased in volume during the nineteenth century. Many of the enslaved Africans who were sent through Red Sea to the Arabian Peninsula were later retransported through the Indian Ocean to the Indian subcontinent.

THE SLAVE TRADE AND THE INDIAN OCEAN

In the Indian Ocean trade, enslaved Africans were taken from inland east Africa and shipped to Arabian Peninsula, India, and Persia. The hub of this trade was the island of Zanzibar, where the slaves were brought from the mainland for sale and then transported to other points along the Indian Ocean. It was the monsoon seasons that made slave trade in the Indian Ocean possible; the different seasons facilitated regular contacts between people in the northern parts of the Indian Ocean with those living as far south as Mozambique. From October to April, the northeast monsoon wind blew across the coast of the Indian subcontinent to the Arabian Peninsular coast then southward onto the coast of east Africa all the way to southern Africa. From April to October, the wind reversed its course; the southeast monsoon blows from southern Africa to the northeast, across the east African coast to the shores of the Arabian Peninsula then on to the Indian subcontinent. These monsoon winds created natural routes that seasonally connected India, the Arabian Peninsula, and East Africa. It was the monsoons that allowed sailors using traditional Arab sailing vessels called "dhows" to travel all the way to southern Africa and back.

Slave traders from the Arabian Peninsula, Persia, and India usually set sail in the middle of November for the east African coast. They sailed along the coast from Somalia travelling south to important ports in Mombasa, Zanzibar, and Mozambique. Zanzibar was said to be full of dhows by the middle of December. The dhows came from the Arabia, Persia, India, and Pakistan to trade for slaves and other items.

Africans were captured in the interior and sent to the coast. Many of them were sent in large caravans organized by Arab slave traders in the coast and in Zanzibar. The slaves were obtained using various methods; some were kidnapped from their homes or its vicinity. Others were captured in wars between different groups. There were also bands of men who raided villages for the purpose of enslaving Africans. During the trek to the coast, the weakest among them never made it that far. Young children and those who were weak as a result of illnesses or wounds inflicted in battle were often left behind to die or be killed. Women with young children were particularly vulnerable because they could not always keep up with the caravans. nineteenth century European observers who travelled in east Africa along the caravan routes often reported seeing dead bodies scattered along the way. Some were killed or left behind to die because they could not keep up.

One popular route in east Africa was along Lake Nyasa on the border of Tanzania and Malawi moving east to the coastal town of Kilwa in Tanzania. Most were sent to Zanzibar from Kilwa; others were sent to the islands off the coast of east Africa such as Mauritius and Madagascar or southwards around Cape of Good Hope. A small number were sent directly northwards to various ports along the route to the Arabian Peninsula and beyond. Another route was from Tabora in northeast Tanzania moving east to the coastal city of Bagamoyo. Enslaved Africans were then put on dhows and sent to Zanzibar. At Zanzibar, enslaved Africans were sold at the slave market, many of them were then sent by dhow to the Arabian Peninsula, Persia, and the Indian subcontinent. Enslaved Africans were also collected at various points in Mozambique, Kenya, and Somalia and moved northwards to the Arabian Peninsular markets. Muscat, the capital city of Oman, was the main port for slave trade obtained in east Africa. Most enslaved Africans from regions along the Swahili coast were first sent to Zanzibar and then to Muscat before being redistributed to other regions.

The British naval captain, R. N. Colomb, reported the extensive slave trade from the interior of east Africa to the coast and from there to Zanzibar and the Middle East. Colomb provides seven examples of enslaved Africans who were captured at various points in the interior, sold to Arab slave dealers, transported to the coast and sent to Zanzibar. From Zanzibar, the enslaved Africans were taken by dhows to Oman. One example is an enslaved African named Marazuku. He was kidnapped by Arabs near Lake Nyassa and taken to Kilwa, Tanzania. Marazuku was sent to Zanzibar where he remained for four months. Eventually, he was sold and sent to Muscat, Oman. Another female slave named Sarhea was kidnapped by Arabs in Tabora. She was sent from Tabora to Bagamoyo, and from there to Zanzibar. Sarhea remained in Zanzibar for five months before being sold and sent to Muscat. The slave trade from the interior of east Africa to the coast was extensive. Most of the Africans were captives from wars between one ethnic group and another. The wars were often initiated and supported by slave traders who wanted to obtain captives for enslavement. The majority appear to have been transported from the east African coast to Zanzibar in dhows carrying small number of enslaved Africans mostly in groups less than ten. For example, in 1879 a British vessel, London, captured a dhow carrying twelve enslaved Africans, six males and six females; the same vessel also captured two other dhows, one carrying one enslaved African and another carrying nine. The enslaved Africans were being transported to Zanzibar. Many of them were sent from Zanzibar to Oman before being sent to other destinations, including India.

The volume of this trade is difficult to determine. The Arabs who carried out this trade from east Africa to the Middle East did not leave us with documentation needed for calculating the figures. Most of the estimates are derived from British vessels that captured dhows carrying slaves in the nineteenth century. Robert O. Collins estimated that 2,918,000 east Africans were sent across the Indian Ocean between 800 and 1900. This figure should be seen as the minimum number that could have been transported from east Africa. There are some records that give us an idea of the trade in the second half of the nineteenth century. Of the four hundred vessels that the British navy boarded in 1869, only eleven were carrying enslaved Africans from Zanzibar on their way north to the Arabian Peninsular markets. Those eleven vessels carried a total of one thousand slaves. This figure gives us an idea of the number of slaves that were carried between Zanzibar and the Arabian Peninsula in one year alone by eleven dhows. The British captured only a small fraction of vessels that were engaged in slave trade in the Indian Ocean. Writing in the late nineteenth century, Edward Hutchinson provides us with figures that give us an idea of the volume of the trade between Kilwa and Zanzibar alone in a period of five years. He estimated, using custom house records from Kilwa, that 76,703 enslaved Africans were sent from Kilwa to Zanzibar between 1862 and 1867. While scholars may never agree about the number of enslaved Africans transported through the Indian Ocean, the number provided by Collins of 2,918,000 provides us a working figure for the volume of the east African slave trade.

THE SLAVE TRADE TO THE INDIAN SUBCONTINENT AND ITS AFTERMATH

The slave trade to the Indian subcontinent was very extensive between the sixteenth and the eighteenth centuries. It was not until 1774 that the British began to pass laws to regulate the slave trade in its territories in the Indian Ocean. One of the first regulations prohibited the buying and selling of slaves unless the individual was already enslaved. The law was largely ignored. In 1786, Lord Cornwallis issued a proclamation stating that anyone convicted of involvement in the slave trade would face severe punishment. A law prohibiting the slave trade was finally issued in 1811 for all territories adjacent to the British Fort William in Calcutta. Recommendations were made for similar measures to be taken in Madras (Chennai) in southeast India and Bombay (Mumbai), the largest port on the western coast of India. The government of Bombay issued the order in 1813. Although the regulation was not adopted in Madras, they did, however, pass a law in 1826 that prevented the export of slaves from Madras. In addition to the British, the Portuguese and the Dutch imported enslaved Africans from east Africa. The Portuguese in Goa brought Africans from their east African colony of Mozambique. The Dutch also imported enslaved Africans to Sri Lanka from southeast Africa. It was, however, the

Arabs and Indians who transported the largest number of enslaved Africans, mostly between the fourteenth and nineteenth centuries.

The establishment of laws governing the slave trade differed from one territory to another. Authorities in Fort St. George and Fort William interpreted the existing laws differently. The British Governor of Bombay reported extensive slave trade in the region in 1836. Slaves were imported into Cutch, Scinde, Kattywar, and the Portuguese controlled territories of Diu, Goa, and Dumaon. He denied that slaves were imported into his territory of Bombay, although he reported Arab slave vessels frequenting the area.

British, Dutch, and Portuguese records clearly suggest a widespread practice of slavery in India and neighboring territories. Slavery was an institution that was clearly defined by the Europeans and Indians, both Muslims and Hindus. Africans were just one among various groups of people enslaved in the region. Their presence in India was, nevertheless, important particularly as soldiers and domestic workers. As slaves, Africans in India were considered property and their treatment and status depended on the slave owner. The British have left us some records of enslaved African transported to the Indian subcontinent from the Arabian Peninsula.

During the eighteenth and nineteenth centuries, the slave trade in the Arabian Peninsula centered on the towns of Muscat in Oman and Medina and Mecca in Saudi Arabia. Muscat was an important stop for slaves from east Africa and parts of the Red Sea. Medina and Mecca received slaves who were transported directly across the Red Sea and overland through Egypt to Saudi Arabia. During the time of the pilgrimage, Mecca became a major site for slave trading; enslaved Africans were purchased in Mecca by pilgrims and transported to distant destinations, including Turkey, Persia, and India. However, Oman received a constant supply of enslaved Africans during the eighteenth and nineteenth centuries.

During the nineteenth century, the capital city of Muscat was full of foreigners from different parts of the world. One could find traders from India, Persia, Armenia, Syria, and Egypt. Most of our knowledge of the slave trade at this time comes from vessels captured by British authorities in the Indian Ocean and the Red Sea. In February 1839, a vessel named Kurachee was captured by a British vessel; it was carrying eighteen slaves owned by various people, including an Indian (Banian) from Muscat and a Banian residing in Kurachee (now called Karachi in Pakistan). On January 16, 1842, another vessel belonging to a merchant from Kisheen, on the Gulf of Aden was captured on its way to Kurachee. The vessel carried thirteen slaves and a resident of Hyderabad. Of the thirteen slaves, nine were Abyssinians and four were categorized as "Negroes." Abyssinian or Ethiopian slaves were distinguished from other Africans from sub-Saharan Africa. On January 20, 1842, another vessel was captured with thirty-five slaves on its way to Kurachee. Some of the slaves were Abyssinians and some were "Negroes." On board the vessel were three Indians who had purchased the slaves in Muscat, Oman, and transported the enslaved Africans to various points along the Gulf of Aden before sending them to Kurachee. Three vessels were captured in the late 1830s in Porebunder, India, with a total of seventy-nine enslaved Africans. There were forty-nine boys aged four to ten and thirty girls aged between five and fifteen. The slave traders tried to hide the Africans to avoid capture; some of them were hidden inside boxes and private holding spaces. They had no clothes on them. These reports document a thriving trade in enslaved Africans carried out by Indian and Pakistani merchants between the Middle East and the Indian subcontinent.

Most of the enslaved Africans were employed in domestic work; many were purchased by wealthy merchants and members of the ruling class.

Up to the end of the nineteenth century, it was a common practice for Muslim leaders in India to purchase slaves or "Siddes" to work for them. From the fifteenth century, the Muslim rulers in India had obtained large numbers of enslaved Africans and employed them as soldiers, bodyguards, and domestic workers. By the nineteenth century, most of the Africans brought to the Indian subcontinent were employed as domestic workers. The ruling class in particular kept importing enslaved Africans up to the end of the nineteenth century despite the British blockade of the trade. The leaders in states such as Hyderabad continued to obtain enslaved Africans from the Arabian Peninsula long after the British began to suppress the slave trade. The slaves were officially given freedom obtained under a "Deed of Freedom" so as to avoid arrest by authorities until they reached the Indian subcontinent. The slaves brought under the service of the rulers often did domestic work. They worked as cooks, washed clothes, and did other domestic work. Officials claimed they were well treated and even paid. In reality, they were owned and not free.

There are several examples that illustrate how rulers were able to bring in slaves in the last quarter of the nineteenth century. In 1882, a case was brought against a slave dealer who was arrested by officials for trading slaves. A slave trader named Abdul Kayum was arrested in Bombay with four African slaves. They were named Jamila, Zafran, Zainab, and Noor. Kayum claimed that the slaves were purchased on behalf of the local leader or Nawab, Jehan Befum, who purportedly made a request to have some "Siddees from Jeddah" purchased and brought to India. He further claimed he was acting as an official of the state under orders from his leader. Later, he claimed the four slaves had been manumitted in Arabia or Bhopal in India. The State of Bhopal denied the claim and any connection to the dealer and the slaves brought to the city. The girls were cleared by the Consul at Jeddah as free. The girls told officials that they had been purchased "like sheep" and taken to Bhopal against their will. Despite denying any connections with the dealer, the ruler wrote a complaint against the arrest of the trader and the manumission of the slaves. He claimed that it was a common practice to purchase slaves, manumit them, and bring them to work as domestic servants. He blamed the British officials for overstepping their boundaries in the case. Furthermore, he claimed that he brought female Africans because "some of the negroes have become widowers and they don't like to marry native women." He continued: "for this reason I wish to get six or seven negroes and negreses from Arabia through Sheikh Hossein, an Arab, a native of Hodeida, who is about to return to his Native Country." The account reveals two important points: first, it was a common practice for rulers and pilgrims in general to purchase enslaved Africans in Arabia; second, it is clear from the ruling Nawab's report that the elite had come up with a scheme to circumvent the British blockade of the slave trade. The elite strategy was to obtain document in the Middle East showing that the Africans were free in order to transport them to India and Pakistan. The enslaved Africans were never freed upon reaching their destination. Lastly, the ruler Befum's claim that enslaved Africans and people of African descent wanted to marry other people of African descent and not natives reveals an attempt on the part of the Africans to preserve their community. African Indian males developed a preference for partners who were either African or of African descent. For rulers such as Befum, this was one more reason to justify the importation of more Africans in the end of the nineteenth century.

Furthermore, there are claims that enslaved Africans were transported directly to India from Zanzibar. There was considerable number of wealthy Indian merchants living in Zanzibar in the nineteenth century. The wealthy Indians provided much of the finance for the slave trade from Zanzibar. These merchants also owned large numbers of slaves in Zanzibar. In the last decades of the nineteenth century alone, the British freed many enslaved Africans owned by Indians in Zanzibar; many of them came to the island from Kutch. Colomb recorded these claims in his book published in 1874. Some residents in Zanzibar transported enslaved Africans to Bombay and took back Hindu females to be sold in Zanzibar in 1841. This trade was done clandestinely by transporting the Africans as crew members in small numbers and then selling them off in India. In 1862, a British official resident in Zanzibar also made claims that merchants in Zanzibar were sending enslaved Africans to India as crew. The practice made it very difficult for officials in east Africa and India to detect and prevent it. There is no clear evidence to support these claims; however, it appears likely that such trade did take place clandestinely.

The number of Africans brought to India increased in the second half of the nineteenth century. This increase was partly due to a decision by the British to send emancipated Africans from various points in the Indian Ocean to India. Africans had made freed themselves by escaping to British authors. The British had the legal power to issue emancipation papers and find ways to protect the newly freed Africans. The emancipation of Africans posed new challenges for the British. Numerous proposals were suggested as to how to dispose of the emancipated Africans. One suggestion was to send the Africans to Muscat. In fact, some of the freed Africans requested they be sent to Muscat. Others asked to be sent back to Zanzibar. The final decision was left to the British. The Sultan of Muscat was approached with a request to allow freed slaves to settle in Muscat. He rejected the idea. Another plan put on the table was to send freed Africans to Bombay and from there to Zanzibar. The British government eventually decided on India. Africans freed from the Red Sea, Indian Ocean, and Persian Gulf would all be sent to Bombay.

In 1872, the British steamer Vulture brought one hundred and sixty-four Africans to Bombay. The Africans had been taken at Aden before being sent to India. This was just one incident of Africans being transferred to India; there were numerous occasions between the 1870s and 1880s, in which Africans were sent to India. There were at least two hundred and four freed Africans sent to Bombay by the end of the 1890s. These freed Africans were apparently left to fend for themselves. One agent in Muscat sent sixteen liberated slaves to Bombay. They found employment in the docks. Although their numbers were relatively small, they started to be noticed by the local population. While some found gainful employment, others were not very lucky. A few started to get into trouble and local Indians started to resent their presence. The police complained that some were getting into trouble. A police official expressed fears that they would be in danger if more were brought.

Another major problem for the British was how to deal with emancipated children. Children could not be employed and thus the government had to maintain them. The children were distributed among missionary societies. As the boys grew older, there were cases where the missionaries wanted them removed. A letter from Bombay in 1872 reported the presence of four African youths in asylum. The boys could speak Swahili and English and thus could work as interpreters. The boys wanted to work as interpreters for the Government. They inquired as to their pay and future prospects. One possibility was that the boys could work as interpreters in British vessels employed in the suppression of the slave trade. The British gave priority to interpreters who could speak Swahili because it was spoken widely in east Africa and among Arabs from the Middle Eastern coast. It was further suggested that the interpreter should be able to speak Arabic and if he did not, he should be taught Arabic. Some of the boys were eventually employed as interpreters for the British. These successful youth represent, however, a very small percentage of the Africans who were sent as freed slaves to India. The majority were apparently abandoned and struggled to make a living in Bombay. Thus, it is not surprising that many of them turned to their culture and spirituality to help them cope and survive in this difficult environment. Culture, religion, and their reputation as warriors came to play a major role in their ability to adapt and survive.

The extensive network of routes and exchanges in the Indian Ocean led to the presence of Africans in the Middle East and the Indian subcontinent. It was mostly through the slave trade that Africans were transported to the distant lands. From East Africa along present day Tanzania and Mozambique to Somalia and Ethiopia, Africans were transported to the Middle East and on to the Indian subcontinent.

KEY TERMS

African Diaspora
Slave Trade
Resistance
Seasoning
Slavery
Islam
Indian Ocean
Red Sea
Africans
Emancipation

PART III

FIGHTING BACK AND GROWING NEW ROOTS: SPIRITUALITY, BLACK POWER, AND CULTURAL ADAPTATIONS

CHAPTER 8

COMBATING SLAVERY: THE THREE HUNDRED YEARS WAR IN THE CIRCUM-CARIBBEAN

Carleen Payne Jackson

When you make men slaves, … you compel them to live with you in a state of war.

—*The Interesting Narrative of the Life of Olaudah Equiano (1789)*

To fully understand the modern African Diaspora in North, South, and Central America, it is imperative to study the experiences of enslaved Africans imported into the region from the sixteenth to the nineteenth centuries. The societies to which they were introduced were sustained by the dual impositions of colonialism (the practice of occupying, controlling, and exploiting another territory) and chattel slavery (a form of labor based on property rights in persons). Despite concerted attempts to break their will and subvert their humanity, the history of people of African descent in the Americas is one of resiliency and agency. They "shaped slavery, contributed to its evolution, helped to speed its demise."[1] To be sure, the dynamics of colonial domination and enslavement, and the resistant responses of the enslaved were not monolithic; they varied over time and across geographical space.

The enslaved population of the South American territory of Brazil, for example, endured the most protracted oppression, with the emergence of the plantation system (large-scale agriculture based on sugar production for European markets) as early as the sixteenth century, and the persistence of slavery until 1888. They are renowned for one revolt after another, including the Muslim Uprising of 1835, which featured over 600 black rebels in confrontation with the white soldiers and armed civilians of Bahia. With their meticulously planned assaults and large paramilitary units (or *quilombos*), Brazilian insurgents "kept their owners permanently on edge," and their constant defiance caused slavery and race relations in Brazil to be particularly volatile.[2]

While there is general concession on the infrequency of slave revolts in North America during two and a half centuries of enslavement, enslaved blacks in the United States were by no means docile in their response to oppression. In his pioneering *American Negro Slave Revolts* (1943), Herbert Aptheker managed to uncover 250 revolts and conspiracies between 1526 and

---

[1] Michael Craton, *Empire, Enslavement and Freedom in the Caribbean* (Kingston: Ian Randle Publishers, 1997), 186.

[2] João José Reis, *Slave Rebellion in Brazil: The Muslim Uprising of 1835 in Bahia* (Baltimore: Johns Hopkins Press, 1995), xiii and 40. The Rebellion of 1835 was almost successful in creating another Haitian-style revolution.

1860.[3] The Louisiana Revolt of 1811, in which some 500 black rebels (many of whom had participated in the Haitian Revolution of 1791) marched on the city of New Orleans, is reminiscent of Brazil's 1835 uprising. That United States' revolts were less persistent than those in Latin America and the Caribbean might be attributed to the overwhelming physical presence and control of white enslavers, and the lack of favorable social preconditions including black majorities, large numbers of African-born blacks, and militarized runaway communities.

The Circum-Caribbean,[4] the region centrally located between North and South America, experienced even greater upheaval, subject as it was to the most diverse and competitive European colonial occupation of the early modern period. Indeed, from Columbus' 1492 invasion of the region, it was dominated first by the Spanish, and by mid-seventeenth century by the English, French, and Dutch engaged in securing colonial boundaries and generating wealth for their respective mother countries. The importation of Africans to these slave-worked plantation societies was massive—constituting forty percent of the twenty million brought to the Americas following the inauguration of the slave trade in 1501. This huge rebel contingent was closer to Brazil in terms of extreme restiveness, and a penchant for violent responses to slavery and colonialism. A striking departure in the Caribbean context, however, is an escalation over time to increasingly effective wars of emancipation by the nineteenth century. Indeed, when one surveys the constant threat of uprisings or their actual occurrence, it becomes apparent that there was an almost continuous state of war.

To be sure, the means by which enslaved blacks in the Caribbean challenged enslavement and colonialism were not limited to military-style revolts. They regularly employed a combination of overt and covert strategies against their oppressors.[5] Overt resistance encompassed open rebellion (full-scale revolts, skirmishes, or abortive plots) within the confines of the plantation, as well as guerilla-style assaults by runaway blacks (known as *Maroons*).[6] Covert resistance, on the other hand, refers to the largely unobtrusive ways in which enslaved individuals challenged their enslavement. Such strategies included sabotage or destruction of plantation property, feigning illness, an insistence on African cultural retentions, and even violence turned against one's person or unborn child—self-mutilation, suicide, infanticide, and abortion.[7]

The daily resort to subversive strategies seems more feasible in light of the brutal code of retribution exacted when rebellions (defined here as armed revolt) broke out. Historians, for their part, have paid a greater degree of attention to this category of antislavery activity than outright war. Michael Craton argued, for example, that while resistance was endemic throughout Plantation America, it was overt only in special circumstances—"whenever they could or *had to*."[8] However, what such conservative interpretations often mask is a marked escalation in incendiary responses in the Circum-Caribbean during the last three centuries of slavery: the 1600s to 1800s.

---

[3] Herbert Aptheker, *American Negro Slave Revolts* (New York: Columbia University Press, 1943).

[4] This wider Caribbean includes all of the islands, and some coastal states in Central and South America.

[5] Craton, *Empire, Enslavement and Freedom*, 185–202.

[6] The word "Maroon" is derived from the Spanish word *cimarrón*. It originally referred to domestic cattle that had taken to the hills in Hispaniola, and has strong connotations of being "wild" and "unbroken."

[7] Orlando Patterson, *The Sociology of Slavery: An Analysis of the Origins, Development and Structure of Negro Slave Society in Jamaica* (London: MacGibbon and Kee, 1967), 260.

[8] Craton, *Empire, Enslavement and Freedom*, 185.

A closer look at the Caribbean rebellious tradition reveals that enslaved Africans and their descendants engaged in endemic antislavery combat that climaxed in the nineteenth century. As Richard Hart demonstrated in his *Slaves Who Abolished Slavery* (1985), blacks in the British-colonized Caribbean did not just "test" the chains of slavery; they ultimately broke them. Eric Williams argued in *Capitalism and Slavery* (1944) that abolitionist legislation in Europe was precipitated by the "battle of slavery" in the Caribbean colonies. C. L. R. James likened the militant "Black Jacobins" in St. Domingue (Haiti) to their namesakes in France who orchestrated the overthrow of the *Ancien Régime* in 1789.[9]

While reflecting on enslavement in Barbados, former enslaved African Olaudah Equiano pointed out the inevitability of violence as a response to enslavement: "When you make men slaves, you . . . compel them to live with you in a state of war."[10] A Haitian planter concurred, "A colony of slaves is a town menaced by assault; one lives on top of a powder magazine."[11] Thus, while one might complain about the high rate of failed revolts in the Americas, one can hardly overlook the destabilizing, and potentially revolutionary, effects of persistent warfare. That Caribbean enslavers deployed all available instruments of repression—slave codes, police laws, standing colonial militias, even black West India regiments—reveals that the prospect of armed uprising was their biggest concern.

The idea of slavery as a perpetual state of war does not necessarily imply the dismissal of the importance of covert resistance. If, as it appears, freedom struggles of the enslaved came in waves, the proliferation of day-to-day resistant responses can be viewed as habitual jabs during the trough of the struggle, and revolts as the upsurge or crest. The image of enslaved blacks engaged in a river of struggle invites reconsideration of the long-range implications for the slave societies of the Caribbean. The cumulative effect of the ongoing resort to multidimensional protest and rebellion appears to be that of a full-scale war waged against slavery and colonial domination.

Hilary Beckles, who made the case for the British-colonized territories, asserted that enslaved Blacks launched a "two hundred years war" (1638–1838) against their oppressors; that "there was hardly a generation of slaves in the English West Indies that did not confront their masters collectively with arms in pursuit of freedom."[12] He further contends that the frequent uprisings were indicative of a "self-liberation ethos" on the part of the enslaved. However, Caribbeanists who have tended to study the region on a colony-by-colony basis or else narrowed their historical foci to the various colonial boundaries have failed to appreciate the full extent and implications of the military assault on slavery and colonialism. My sense is that of a more protracted war in the Circum-Caribbean. Indeed, it seems beyond dispute that a will to rebel, demonstrated during the frontier conditions of

---

[9] Craton, *Testing the Chains*.; Hart, *Slaves Who Abolished Slavery*; Williams, *Capitalism and Slavery*; James, *The Black Jacobins*.

[10] Olaudah Equiano, *The Interesting Narrative of the Life of Olaudah Equiano, or Gustavus Vassa, the African* (London, 1789), 225, accessed December 15, 2015, https://history.hanover.edu/texts/Equiano/ equiano_ch5_a.html.

[11] Médéric Louis Moreau de Saint-Méry, *Description topographique, physique, civile, politique et historique de la partie française de l'isle Saint-Domingue* (Paris: Société de l'histoire des colonies françaises, 1779), 123; quoted in Craton, *Empire, Enslavement and Freedom*, 186.

[12] Beckles, Caribbean Anti-Slavery, 2–3.

the first century, escalated into an increasing propensity for violent warfare from the early 1600s to the late 1800s.[13]

A WILL TO REBEL

Africans rebelled against the oppression of enslavement from the very beginning of their forced migration to the Americas. Phillis Wheatley, the first African American poet, provided an apt description of this instinctive response of humans reduced to chattel status: "In every human Breast, God has implanted a Principle, which we call Love of Freedom; it is impatient of oppression and pants for deliverance."[14] This will to rebel inspired the overwhelming involvement of continental Africans in Caribbean slave revolts before 1800. Among the participants in what Monica Schuler called "rebellions of the spear" were the *Yoruba* of Southwest Nigeria and the *Coromantee* (or *Koromantyn*)—an Akan-speaking people from the then Gold Coast of West Africa.[15] According to Lucille Mathurin Mair, rebel women also carried this "fighting spirit" with them across the Atlantic. Queen Mothers (of the Ashanti) like Jamaica's Nanny of the Maroons and Cubah, the "Queen of Kingston," confounded colonial authorities when they emerged as ring leaders of slave revolts and maroon onslaughts.[16] Indeed, one reason why incoming Africans were subjected to the breaking process of "seasoning" was to curb the spirit of rebelliousness.

As impractical or implausible as it seems, these African shock troops put up an intrepid struggle on most voyages during the middle passage of the transatlantic slave trade that brought them to the Caribbean. For example, there was a bloody uprising on the *Tiger* that sailed from the Gambia to Jamaica in 1702. In May 1703, the 273 enslaved Africans on board the *Martha*, bound from Whydah to Nevis, also rose up. The following year (1704), the *Dorothy* experienced an uprising while on its way to Barbados. In 1707, three intractable Africans on board the *Sherbro* were shot during a revolt on the journey from Sierra Leone to Barbados. Due to another shipboard uprising in 1714, *The Duke of Cambridge* arrived in Barbados with only 100 of its original 350 human cargo. And, rebels on board the *Ferrers* in 1722, attempted mutiny three times—once on the ship and twice before they were sold in the Americas.[17]

---

[13] Joseph Holloway alludes to the same periodization in "Slave Resistances in Latin America," accessed December 15, 2015, http://slaverebellion.org/index.php?page=slave-resistances-in-latin-america, paragraph 51.

[14] Phillis Wheatley, "Letter to Reverend Samson Occum," *Connecticut Gazette* (March 11, 1774), accessed December 15, 2015, http://www.pbs.org/wgbh/aia/part2/2h19t.html, paragraph 1.

[15] Monica Schuler, "Akan Slave Rebellions in the British Caribbean," *Savacou*, 1, no. 1 (1970): 9; John Thornton, "The Coromantees: An African Cultural Group in Colonial North America and the Caribbean," *Journal of Caribbean History* 32 (1998): 161–78.

[16] Lucille Mathurin Mair, "The Rebel Woman in the British West Indies During Slavery" in *Caribbean Slavery in the Atlantic World*, eds. Verene Shepherd and Hilary McD. Beckles (Kingston: Ian Randle Publishers, 2000), 984–1000. Cubah was prominent among the plotters of the 1760 Coromantee uprising in Jamaica.

[17] Colin Palmer, "Slave Trade, African Slavers and Demography to 1750" in *General History of the Caribbean*, vol. 3: *The Slave Societies of the Caribbean*, ed. Franklin Knight (London: UNESCO Publishing, 1997), 33–34.

THROWING DOWN THE GAUNTLET

The African presence in the Circum-Caribbean dates from the early 1500s when they were imported by the thousands first into Hispaniola (the cradle of the Caribbean sugar economy) and other Spanish colonies (Puerto Rico, Cuba, and Jamaica). Although the research is still sporadic, active resistance appears to have been intense during the early colonial period when stringent plantation controls were not yet well established. According to the author of the first comprehensive history of the area, "The Spanish colonies were kept in a state of permanent revolution, however sporadic, unorganized, and ill-timed may have been the revolts of the slaves."[18]

The initial center of disaffection was Hispaniola (now the Dominican Republic and Haiti) which received the first Africans in 1502. The first slave revolt on record broke out in 1522 on the plantation of Christopher Columbus' son, Diego Colón. Some forty rebels, conspiring with Africans on nearby plantations, launched an attack that killed at least nine whites. Slave revolts were a regular occurrence on Spanish plantations after that. In 1533, the first known revolt in Cuba took place at the Jobabo mines where four Africans took on a large military force. It was during the first major slave rebellion in Puerto Rico in 1527, that African rebels began exploiting the tradition of *marronage*—escaping to armed camps in the mountains from which they continued their opposition to the plantation regime.[19]

WAR OF THE NEGROES

Long before the seventeenth century rise of the plantation complex (an economic enterprise based on large-scale, slave-based sugar production)[20] in the Circum-Caribbean, enslaved Africans in the Spanish colonies (Hispaniola, Cuba, Puerto Rico, and Jamaica) had devised a viable alternative to servitude and the confinement of the plantation: flight from the estates and the subsequent construction of African-style communities, led by elected chiefs, socially and politically independent of plantation society. The standing armies of the Maroons maintained near impenetrable strongholds in dense forest terrain and bewildered colonial enemies with their guerilla skills. Says Richard Price, "They struck and withdrew with great rapidity, making extensive use of ambushes to catch their adversaries in crossfire. They fought only when and where they chose, relying on trustworthy intelligence networks among non-maroons (both slaves and white settlers), and often communicating military information by drums and horns."[21]

---

[18] Eric Williams, *From Columbus to Castro: The History of the Caribbean, 1492-1969* (New York: Vintage Books, 1984), 65.

[19] Carlos Larrazábal Blanco, *Los Negros y la Esclavitud en Santo Domingo* (Santo Domingo: J.D. Postigo, 1967), 143–45; Leslie B. Rout Jr., *The African Experience in Spanish America: 1502 to the Present Day* (Cambridge: Cambridge University Press, 1976), 118; Williams, *From Columbus to Castro*, 66.

[20] See Philip Curtin, *The Rise and Fall of the Plantation Complex: Essays in Atlantic History* (Cambridge, England: Cambridge University Press, 1998), XI and 10–13.

[21] Richard Price, "Maroons: Rebel Slaves in the Americas," accessed January 10, 2016, http://www.folklife.si.edu/resources/maroon/educational_guide/23.htm, paragraph 8.

From the 1530s on, hundreds of these maroon communities facilitated constant warfare against Spanish-led troops. In fact, the period from 1545 to 1548 in Hispaniola is known as the "War of the Negroes."[22] This is because it was punctuated by bloody assaults from an estimated 7,000 Maroons who had divorced themselves from the enslaved population of 30,000 by 1546, and had chosen the mountains of Hispaniola as their base of operation.[23] In a phenomenon that has baffled historians (due to its unexpectedness), maroon hide-outs subsequently emerged on smaller islands like St. Kitts and Antigua. It was during the 1639 revolt in the French side of St. Kitts, for instance, that more than sixty blacks took a defensive position at a narrow pass on Mount Misery. It took 500 soldiers to put down this rebellion.[24] Undoubtedly, the stage was set for a concerted violent assault on the oppressive plantation complex.

THE EMBATTLED PLANTATION COMPLEX (1600S)

The seventeenth century also saw the emergence of clusters of embattled plantation societies in the British and French West Indies. The introduction of large sugar estates led to the forced importation of hundreds of thousands of resentful, intractable laborers. Most newly arrived Africans were initially carried to Barbados, which had replaced Hispaniola as the main sugar-producing colony. However, when Jamaica was captured from the Spaniards by the British in 1655, it soon superseded Barbados in sugar production and investment in the transatlantic slave trade. As the number of Africans on most islands exceeded whites ten to one, this created a tenuous situation where a minority group of enslavers were surrounded by a majority population, many of whom refused to accept their enslavement. Indeed, when African rebels were unable to escape to maroon communities, they often sought to exterminate their enslavers.[25]

Antislavery combat during the seventeenth century took the form of periodic skirmishes between the British and the Maroons, as well as intermittent waves of revolts. In Barbados, the militia was kept busy in their effort to eradicate "divers rebellious and runaway Negroes lurking in woods and secret places."[26] A 1649 slave revolt, triggered by insufficient food, spread across two plantations before it was subdued. Ten years later, an abortive revolt unleashed paranoia throughout Barbados; the rebels had planned to massacre all the whites. Another conspiracy, planned over the course of three years, came to light in 1675. As Governor Atkins reported in the aftermath, the plot to burn canefields and kill all of the island's whites had apparently been hatched by the "warlike and robust" *Coromantees* who comprised a majority of the enslaved Africans.[27] Abortive plots also came to light in 1683 and 1692. The participants in the latter

---

[22] Holloway, Slave Resistances in Latin America, paragraph 75.

[23] Williams, *From Columbus to Castro*, 67–68.

[24] Richard Frucht, "Emancipation and Revolt in the West Indies: St. Kitts, 1834," *Science and Society* 39 (1975):199–214.

[25] Curtin, *Rise and Fall of the Plantation Complex*, 104.

[26] Jerome Handler, "Slave Revolts and Conspiracies in Seventeenth-Century Barbados" in *New West Indian Guide* 56 (1982), 9.

[27] Hilary Beckles, *Black Rebellion in Barbados* (Barbados: Antilles Publications, 1984), 34–38, citing Minutes of Council, June 1657, Lucas MSS, Reel 1, f. 365 and PRO: CO 1/35 f.23, Governor Atkins to Williamson, 3 October 1675.

conspiracy had anticolonial goals: to kill the governor and planters, and to set up a government of their own.[28]

Perhaps no plantation society during this period was more embattled than Jamaica. Orlando Patterson's summary of the revolts between 1655 and 1832 proves that plots and rebellions were near permanent features on the island.[29] This was, in part, because Gold Coast Africans were often at the forefront of the revolts, and also because (in the aftermath of uprisings) they often chose *marronage* over surrender. In fact, their first anticolonial revolt emerged out a refusal to be transferred from Spanish to English sovereignty. When the British took the island from Spain in 1655, runaways disappeared into Jamaica's dense Cockpit Country where they formed a Windward maroon camp (Nanny Town) and a Leeward camp (Trelawney Town).

The 1673 revolt in the parish of St. Ann was Jamaica's first serious challenge. It involved 300 (largely Gold Coast) rebels who murdered their master and thirteen other whites before fleeing to the interiors where they formed the nucleus of the Windward Maroons. By 1675, martial law was declared and thirty-five rebels were executed for conspiracy. A minor rebellion was suppressed in St. Mary in 1676 and another crushed at St. Catherine in 1678. The 1680s were also dominated by insurrection: a 1683-conspiracy involving 180 rebels and a 1685 uprising in which 150 rebels seized arms and killed several whites in St. Catherine. Perhaps, the most important of these revolts took place at Sutton's plantation at Clarendon in 1690. A 400-strong army of *Coromantees* killed the overseer, fired the plantation, and fled to the Leeward Maroons base of operation, under the leadership of Captain Cudjoe.[30] By the end of the century, the Jamaican militia was "engaged in open war" with the Maroons.[31]

A CENTURY OF PERSISTENT WARFARE (1700S)

Starting with the revolt of forty Gold Coast blacks in July of 1704, hardly a year passed in the first thirty years of the eighteenth century without violent conflict between whites and antislavery warriors on Jamaica. The ten-year campaign known as the "First Maroon War" (1729–1739) was provoked by the British government's attempt to annihilate the Leeward and Windward Maroons. The defense, led by Captain Cudjoe, cemented their reputation for skillful guerilla combat. During what Thomas Higginson referred to as "Cudjoe's War," thousands of "agile and noiseless" troops supplied with arms and ammunition obtained in ambushes waged an all-out campaign against British and black West India regiments, and Mosquito natives from Latin America. Higginson concluded: "It is not strange, then, that high military authorities, at that period, should have pronounced the subjugation of the Maroons a thing more difficult than to obtain a victory over any army in Europe.[32] Ultimately,

---

[28] Beckles, *Black Rebellion in Barbados*, 30–38.

[29] Patterson, *Sociology of Slavery*, 266.

[30] Hart, *Slaves Who Abolished Slavery* (2), 13–14; Patterson, *Sociology of Slavery*, 267–68.

[31] Williams, *From Columbus to Castro*, 195.

[32] Thomas Wentworth Higginson, "The Maroons of Jamaica" in *Travellers and Outlaws, Episodes In American History*, section *Black Rebellion, Five Slave Revolts* (Boston, 1889), accessed January 10, 2016, https://abengcentral.files.wordpress.com/2009/04/themaroonsofjamaica.pdf, paragraph 6.

the British negotiated the 1838 treaty with the Leeward group in which their freedom was recognized, and they were granted rights to 15,000 acres of land. As Eric Williams pointed out, this symbolized "the erection of a state within the colony of Jamaica."[33]

In 1739, the Jamaican Legislature signed a similar treaty with the Windward or Nanny Town Maroons. This group had been ably led by a rebel woman known as Nanny. Originally from Ghana, this Ashanti chieftainess "was foremost among those who resolved never to come to terms with the English."[34] Following the formal end of hostilities (1738–1740), this first national heroine of Jamaica mobilized her clan of three hundred armed men and ultimately out-manoeuvred the British soldiers.[35] The final confrontations of the intrepid Jamaican Maroons with British force of arms yielded mixed results. During the Second Maroon War in 1795, hundreds of Leeward Maroons under their leader, Captain Quao, employed scorched-earth tactics in the combat against 5000 British troops and local militia. However, whites' paranoid fear of a spread of the Haitian Revolution spurred their ultimate expulsion to Nova Scotia and Sierra Leone in 1800.

The maroon wars might have been diffused in Jamaica, but the military assault continued in other theaters throughout the Caribbean. Between 1728 and 1730, the "Bush Negroes" of Suriname, led by Captain Adoe, repelled expeditions sent against them. Eventually, the Dutch concluded peace treaties with them in 1749 and 1761.[36] The "Black Caribs" (offspring of escaped West Africans and indigenes) on the island of St. Vincent also fought a series of bloody wars against the invasion of their land by British planters during 1769–1773 and 1795–1797. In a settlement reminiscent of Jamaica, they consented to a 1773 treaty, only to be forcibly removed to the coast of Honduras in 1797.[37] There were no peace treaties for the *Negres Marons* (escaped blacks) in mountainous Dominica, who, by 1785, had established multiple free settlements and carried out frequent raids on the plantations. It took a 500-strong military campaign the latter part of 1785 and early 1786 to disperse them.[38]

One Maroon threat that remained unchecked during the eighteenth century was that of the French Caribbean territories of St. Domingue[39] and Guadeloupe. By 1750, more than 3,000 escaped blacks populated the mountainous terrain between French St. Domingue and Spanish Santo Domingo[40]—thus setting the stage for the 1791 Haitian uprising. Even when Maroon communities were routed throughout the region, new communities appeared almost as quickly as old ones disappeared. Thus, they remained the "chronic plague" and "gangrene" of many plantation societies right up to nineteenth century emancipation.[41]

---

[33] Williams, *From Columbus to Castro*, 198.

[34] Mathurin Mair, *Rebel Woman*, 1000.

[35] Brathwaite, *Wars of Respect*, 15.

[36] Richard Hart, *From Occupation to Independence* (Jamaica: Canoe Press, 1998), 29.

[37] Sir William Young, *An Account of the Black Charaibs in the Island of St. Vincent's* (1795), reprinted by Frank Cass, (London, Frank Cass & Co., 1971).

[38] Lennox Honeychurch, *The Dominica Story* (London: Macmillan, 1995), 94–97.

[39] In 1697, Spain ceded the Western third of the island to France and it was known thereafter as St. Domingue.

[40] Jan Ragoziński, *A Brief History of the Caribbean* (New York: Penguin Books, 1994), 155.

[41] Price, *Maroons: Rebel Slaves in the Americas*, paragraph 6.

THE GATHERING STORM

The eighteenth century was characterized by even more persistent revolts throughout the Circum-Caribbean. The record of resistance during the first three decades is indicative of this shift. As early as 1702, enslaved Africans rebelled against new slave codes in Barbados. The enslaved in the copper mines in Jobabo, Cuba rose up in 1713. The first slave rebellion on the Dutch colony of Curacao broke out in in 1716. Conspiracies were frustrated and leaders executed in Nevis in 1725. Several revolts involving the destruction of estate property took place in Cuba in 1726, 1727, and 1731. During the 1733 Amina Rebellion on the Danish island of St. John, African rebels burned near half the plantations, killed 49 whites, and controlled the island for six months, before some three hundred plunged to death over a cliff.[42] Although the Antigua Conspiracy of 1735–1736 never materialized into a full-blown revolt, Gold Coast Africans, led by King Court and Tomboy, galvanized the entire island with their contagious plan to massacre all whites and establish a new government.[43]

Perhaps, the two most serious eighteenth century revolts (outside of the Haitian Revolution) were Tacky's Revolt in Jamaica in 1760 and the Berbice Uprising of 1763. The one in Berbice (Dutch Guiana) was a national liberation struggle; an estimated 2,000 African rebels seized the island colony, killed 200 of the colony's 346 whites, and had their *Coromantee* leader (Cuffy) elected governor. They were defeated in 1764 with the assistance of troops from neighboring French and British colonies, and from England.[44] The 1760 *Coromantee* rebellion in Jamaica was precipitated by Tacky (a former Fante Chief) and Asante Queen Nanny (or Nana), both of whom planned "to make the island a Negro colony."[45] Over the course of a year, a thousand rebels burned, killed ninety of their white masters, and spread terror with their appropriation of gunpowder and firearms. Even when cornered by mounted militia, many committed suicide rather than return to slavery. The *Coromantee* threat did not abate; other rebellions broke out all over Jamaica from 1765 to 1798. This gives credence to Michael Mullin's assertion that Jamaica was the place most likely to replicate the Haitian model of black liberation.[46]

In a region renowned for endemic antislavery warfare, the decades after 1770 threw up even more violent resistance than before. For example, conspiracies were frustrated in Montserrat in 1768 and St. Kitts in 1770. Rebellions were suppressed in Tobago in 1770, 1771, and 1774.[47] The first notable uprising in the British Virgin Islands occurred in 1790, and a major slave rebellion broke out in Dominica in 1791 in which rebels pressed for more free days so that they could work for themselves. The numerous conspiracies and revolts all ended in defeat, with one glaring exception—the 1791 Revolution in St. Domingue.

---

[42] Loiuse Sebro, "The 1733 Slave Revolt on the Island of St. John: Continuity and Change from Africa to the Americas" in *Scandinavian Colonialism and the Rise of Modernity: Small Time Agents in a Global Arena*, eds. Magdalena Naum and Jonas M. Nordin (New York: Springer, 2013), 261–74.

[43] David Barry Gaspar, *Bondmen and Rebels: A Study of Master-Slave Relation in Antigua* (Durham: Duke University Press, 1985).

[44] Alvin O. Thompson, "The Berbice Revolt 1763–64" in *Themes in African-Guyanese History*, eds. Winston F. McGowan, James G. Rose and David A. Granger (London: Hansib, 2009).

[45] Cited in Patterson, *Sociology of Slavery*, 271.

[46] Mullin, *Africa in America*, 201.

[47] K. S. Wise, *Historical Sketches of Tobago*, 1934–38 (London, Baines & Scarsbrook, 1936), 91.

LIBÉTE[48] FOR ALL: THE REVOLUTION IN ST. DOMINGUE

The most violent of all the wars, and the critical turning point in the seemingly endless rebellion against slavery and colonialism, was the revolution that occurred in the French colony of St. Domingue (today's Haiti) between 1791 and 1804. This event was made even more dramatic by the fact that it occurred in the richest colony in the world and the one with by far the largest enslaved population in the Caribbean (half a million). It was also significant in that as many as two-thirds of the black population was African born. This might explain why decades of guerilla warfare by Maroons preceded the revolt of 1791.

The unsuccessful Mackandal Conspiracy of 1757 had involved a plan to poison all whites and drive them out of the island. Another intrepid leader arose in the person of Boukman Dutty, a Vodun High Priest, whose congress at *Bois Caiman* in August of 1791 provided the spiritual fortitude and sense of invulnerability that galvanized the thousands who destroyed over 200 plantations in the North Province and massacred 1,000 white masters.[49] The uprising sent shock waves throughout Europe, and for good reason: what had started as yet another revolt had escalated into a war of national liberation. The timing of the outbreak of war against the French was impeccable; it took advantage of the turmoil in the colony caused by the 1789 revolution in France.

Toussaint L'Ouverture, paramount leader of the St. Domingue Revolution, stated as his unwavering aim, "Complete liberty for all, to be attained and held by their own strength."[50] He put together a well-trained, determined, and highly effective army of some 4,000 black troops. Under his influential leadership, they carried out a formidable ground war against French troops using both guerilla and frontal tactics. By 1793, Cap Français, the major port city, was in ruins and more than 10,000 whites were dead. French representatives were forced to take an unprecedented step—declare the abolition of slavery. By 1794, the oppressive plantation system was in tatters. Toussaint himself led the offense against a British expeditionary force in 1798, as well as an invasion of neighboring Santo Domingo in December of 1800. In 1801, he issued a constitution that asserted black autonomy and a sovereign black state.

When France's Napoleon Bonaparte sent an army of 35,000 soldiers to St. Domingue in 1802 to depose Toussaint, disarm the rebels, and reinstate slavery, the "Black Jacobins" of St. Domingue had no choice but to fight for their freedom a second time. Despite Toussaint's treacherous capture, the war of liberation persisted under the leadership of his lieutenants, Jean Jacques Dessalines and Henri Christophe. The St. Domingue warriors mounted a final offensive, matching atrocity with atrocity, until they had succeeded in defeating the French. By 1804, not only had France failed to retake the colony; it had also lost more than 50,000 soldiers.

The enslaved Africans in Haiti eventually brought about the end of slavery during a bloody thirteen-year war. They took control of the island and established their own independent republic—renamed *Haiti*—in 1804. And while the Haitian achievement was unique, the impact of this revolution was profound. It inflicted European enslavers with the fear that what had happened in St. Domingue could happen in other slave-holding colonies. It also "created the

---

[48] "Libéte" is the creolization of the French word "liberté" meaning freedom.
[49] Curtin, *Rise and Fall of the Plantation Complex*, 165.
[50] James, *Black Jacobins*, 107.

context in which the abolition of slavery elsewhere in the Caribbean seemed more certain."[51] In the aftermath of the Haitian Revolution, rebellions accelerated throughout the Circum-Caribbean including the British Virgin Islands in 1790; Guadeloupe in 1793; Cuba, Puerto Rico, Demerara, and Curacao in 1795; and St. Lucia in 1796. Fédon's Rebellion in Grenada (1795–1796) aimed to create a black republic like Haiti.[52] There were even repercussions beyond the Caribbean. Denmark Vesey, Caribbean migrant to North America, plotted in 1822 to murder plantation owners and seize the city of Charleston before fleeing to Haiti.

THE EMANCIPATION IMPERATIVE (1800S)

The abolition of slavery in the Americas is often thought of as the product of an abolitionist crusade in Europe during the early nineteenth century. However, as Eric Williams maintained in 1944, it is a mistake to treat black emancipation in the Caribbean as merely the outgrowth of a metropolitan struggle. Rather, "the most dynamic and powerful social force in the colonies was the slave himself."[53] The escalating revolts up to the nineteenth century constituted an insistence on emancipation that could no longer be ignored. The long-awaited proclamations of emancipation came for the British colonies in 1838, the French, Danes, and Dutch in 1848, and for the Spanish in the late nineteenth century. Although the final legislation came from above (European governments), it was the people from below (rebel men and women) who made abolition inevitable.

The "apprenticeship" arrangement in the smaller English-speaking colonies (where blacks were required to work for forty hours per week) led to another rebellion in St. Kitts in 1834. During this prelude to a century of trade union activism, blacks walked off the sugar plantations and engaged in island wide work stoppage. Some even joined Maroons, led by Markus, "King of the Woods," who had resorted in the 1830s to plantation raids. Jamaica, at the turn of the century, was also on the brink of revolution. African-dominated conspiracies in 1806, 1815, and 1824 alternated with revolts in 1808, 1816, and 1823.

Although the emancipation movement in the French-colonized territories (outside of Haiti) is traditionally not given much historical attention, revolts intensified there in the nineteenth century due, in large part, to frustration on the part of the enslaved that the desired freedom continued to elude them. While Haiti was declaring its political independence in 1802, the other French colonies were in turmoil over the restoration of slavery in 1802. Williams said, "Whites were being massacred in Martinique, and plantations burnt; Guadeloupe was in a state of siege; three-quarters of the slaves had left the plantations in Guiana."[54]

The nineteenth century emancipation imperative in the Spanish territories was largely fueled by beliefs in the imminent abolition of slavery and anticolonial sentiments. In Puerto Rico of 1812, unrest followed a rumor that the Spanish court (*Cortes*) had declared the enslaved freed. By 1821, a conspiracy, planned by enslaved African Marcos Xiorro, called for participants

---

[51] Barry Higman, *A Concise History of the Caribbean* (New York: Cambridge University Press, 2011), 153.
[52] Edward Cox, "Fedon's Rebellion 1795-96: Causes and Consequences," *The Journal of Negro History* 67 (1982), JSTOR 2717757.
[53] Williams, *Capitalism and Slavery*, 201.
[54] Williams, *From Columbus to Castro*, 326.

to set fire to the town and cut the throats of all the whites before marching on the capital. In 1843, a small group of rebels seized the weapons from the Toa Baja Militia and occupied a church for a few hours. Enslaved blacks even participated in *El Grito de Lares*, Puerto Rico's independence revolt against Spanish rule in September 1868. Their resistance efforts led to the dismantling of slavery in 1873.[55]

Official historiography has been slow to acknowledge an epic freedom struggle in nineteenth century Cuba. As in Haiti and Puerto Rico, a series of rebellions targeted a dual emancipation/independence agenda. The revolts led by former slave, José Antonio Aponte, in March 1812, started with unrest over rumors of slavery being abolished. A large African-led rebellion in June 1825 further precipitated a wave of uprisings that crested in the mid-1840s with the 1844 Conspiracy of *La Escalera* (the so-called Ladder Conspiracy), an underground rebel movement of free and enslaved blacks to end slavery and colonial rule in Cuba.[56] In July 1843, African rebels at the Triumvirato sugar mill in Matanzas Province were called to battle with "talking drums," and were led by a machete-wielding Yoruba woman named Carlota. The year-long uprising led to the liberation of enslaved blacks from at least five sugar plantations and the overthrow of the Spanish owners.[57] The Ten Years' War, which erupted in 1868, started when Commander Carlos Manuel de Cespedes made his thirty enslaved workers a part of his army. Under the terms of the Pact of Zanjón, that ended the War in 1878, the enslaved who had fought were set free.

Finally, knowledge of the end of slavery in Haiti and neighboring territories provided the primary rationale for nineteenth century revolts. The 1831 uprising in the British Virgin Islands was driven by a plot to kill whites and escape to the free republic of Haiti. Enslaved blacks living in Dutch St. Maarten more successfully negotiated their freedom in 1848 by threatening to move to the French part of the island, where abolition had already been declared.[58] Although not traditionally included among the recognized "Emancipation Wars," the 1848 uprising on Danish St. Croix featured thousands of enslaved blacks burning down plantations and besieging the city of Frederiksted. This revolt led to emancipation of all enslaved blacks in the Danish West Indies that same year.[59]

Perhaps, more than any other, the three main revolts in Barbados (1816), Demerara (1823), and Jamaica (1831) were inspired by the Haitian Revolution, and had the strongest impact on the mid-century dismantling of slavery in the Circum-Caribbean. The unifying factor in these culminating Emancipation Wars was a demand for unconditional freedom. The first of the three erupted on Barbados on Easter Sunday in April 1816, under the leadership of an Akan-born head-driver called Bussa, and revolutionary ideologue, Nanny Grigg. Grigg was reportedly informed about the Revolution in St. Domingue and was adamant about bringing

---

[55] Baralt, *Slave Revolts in Puerto Rico*.

[56] Childs, *The 1812 Aponte Rebellion in Cuba*; Barcia, *The Great African Slave Revolt of 1825*.

[57] Eugene Godfried, "Carlota: Lukumí/Yoruba Woman Fighter for Liberation, Massacred in Matanzas, Cuba, in 1844" (2006), accessed January 15, 2016, http://www.africanamerica.org/topic/carlota-lukumi-yoruba-woman-fighter-for-liberation-massacred-in-matanzas-cuba-in-1844.

[58] Higman, *Concise History of the Caribbean*, 157.

[59] Gregory Freeland, "Cultural and Political Resistance among Blacks in St. Croix" (paper presented at the annual meeting of the Caribbean Studies Association, Panama, May 24–29, 1999), accessed December 15, 2015, http://ufdcimages.uflib.ufl.edu/CA/00/40/02/04/00001/PDF.pdf

slavery to an end by military means.[60] The island-wide revolt involved 20,000 of the enslaved from over seventy plantations. Within hours, a third of the island was in flames and around sixty plantations sacked and burned. After four days of bloody combat, nearly 1,000 rebels were killed. Concessions came with the 1826 passage of a Consolidated Slave Act that granted the enslaved the right to own property and give evidence in courts.

The Demerara Rebellion of 1823 took place in Demerara-Essequibo (now Guyana) and involved some 10,000 enslaved blacks on fifty plantations. It was fueled by a desire for freedom and the belief that enslavers were concealing news of emancipation. On the evening of August 18, 1823, leaders Telemachus, Quamina, and their followers seized guns on the plantations and locked up the plantation owners during the night. The idea was to send them to the Governor on the following morning to bring back the "New Law." The rebels, who were armed only with knives and pikes, employed little violence. A one-sided battle at a plantation named Bachelor's Adventure left many enslaved people dead or wounded, and ensured their emancipation would be put on hold for another decade.

The Baptist War of 1831–1832, also known as the "Christmas Uprising," is considered the largest and most significant slave revolt in Jamaica. Over the course of ten days, as many as 60,000 of the country's 300,000 slave population fought for "The Free"—an imaginary emancipation proclamation that they believed had been granted in England but not implemented. Samuel Sharp[e], a Baptist preacher and the moving spirit behind the warriors, had devised a plan for the enslaved to refuse to work after their Christmas holiday, with the aim of forcing the owners to pay to cut the cane. When the planters did not agree to their demands, irate warriors burned down houses, warehouses full of sugar cane and more than 200 plantations. It took British troops the whole of January 1832 to restore order at the cost of over 500 black lives. It was this revolt that give impetus to British parliament's inquiries that ultimately led to the passage of the 1833 law to abolish slavery throughout the British Empire.

As Richard Hart has insisted, "the cumulative effect of the nineteenth century slave rebellions and conspiracies is that they forced both the British abolitionists and the British government to revise their approach to the issue of slavery."[61] The emancipation revolts, which involved thousands, helped to end slavery by giving it an urgency it did not have before. Many were reminded of the Revolution in St. Domingue; there were persistent fears of the occurrence of another "Haiti." Thus, terrified enslavers were now ready to accept abolition, rather than risk more widespread war.

CONCLUSION

A broad-based exploration of the antislavery struggle in the Circum-Caribbean suggests that through three hundred years of endemic combat that crested in the nineteenth century, rebel men and women succeeded in unshackling themselves from enslavement and, in the case of Haiti, from colonial oppression. The weapons in their military arsenal were formidable: myriad

[60] Hilary Beckles, *Natural Rebels: A Social History of Enslaved Black Women in Barbados* (New Jersey: Rutger's University Press, 1999), 171–72.
[61] Hart, *From Occupation to Independence*, 38.

acts of covert resistance, hundreds of outright rebellions and a well-established tradition of *marronage* that asserted their humanity and emancipation imperative. By successfully deploying effective guerrilla and frontal warfare, they forced Europeans to negotiate treaties with them as equals, and to significantly revise the terms under which they were introduced into the region. Undoubtedly, consideration of this extensive record of resistance is important in cementing the story of the contribution of the African Diaspora in the Caribbean to black emancipation worldwide.

KEY TERMS

Circum-Caribbean
Colonialism
Chattel Slavery
Plantation Complex
Resistance (Overt & Covert)
Rebellions
Maronnage
Maroons

CHAPTER 9

PRIESTESSES, CONJURE WOMEN, AND OTHER RITUAL EXPERTS IN ORGANIZED RESISTANCE TO AMERICAN ENSLAVEMENT

Iyelli Ichile

A key theme in black women's resistance, and one which black historical sources bring to the fore, is African spirituality. Queen Nanny, as will be discussed in greater detail later in this chapter, was more than a political leader among the Jamaican maroons. She was an African-born "woman of science," a Queen mother, and a priestess. She taught her soldiers guerrilla military tactics, but she also protected them using her metaphysical expertise.

African cultural traditions were a source of empowerment for women, in particular, due to both the critical roles of women in the cultural institutions of precolonial African societies and the limitations placed on women's agency in patriarchal, Christian Euro-American societies. More specifically, African women were empowered by sacred knowledge. In any case, the narrative of Nanny's expert use of spiritual "science" brings out key issues in terms of women's resistance to slavery: (1) that black women's participation in resistance, and the subsequent interpretations of their actions are tied to gender and gender ideology; (2) our definition of organized violent resistance must be expanded to include spiritual and biological weaponry; and (3) this expansion of the definition of resistance increases the visibility of women as participants, if not complementary co-leaders with African men.

This essay explores the roles played by priestesses, so-called "conjure women" and other ritual experts, in organized resistance to slavery. Historian Walter Rucker argues that although traditions like *obeah*,[1] which have been defined along the same lines as conjure may not be considered "full-fledged religious system[s], the ubiquity, longevity, and sheer complexity" of these practices places them on a level above mere "fragments" surviving the cultural devastation of American slavery.[2] Conjure and obeah, are spiritual systems, as are *santería*, *candomblé*, and *vodou*. What unites these African-based systems is the belief in the omnipresence of spiritual forces and the ability of human experts to communicate with spirit to produce certain outcomes, be

---

[1] *Obeah* refers to a spiritual system based largely on Akan models of healing, metaphysical practices, and beliefs. This tradition is found throughout the British and Dutch Caribbean, mainly among people of African descent.

[2] Walter C. Rucker, *River Flows On: Black Resistance, Culture, and Identity Formation in Early America. (Antislavery, Abolition, and the Atlantic World.)* (Baton Rouge: Louisiana State University Press. 2006), 47–48. Rucker is arguing against Jon Butler's notion that a "spiritual genocide" took place when Africans were enslaved by the British, leaving them with few African religious ideas after 1760. See Jon Butler, *Awash in a Sea of Faith: Christianizing the American People* (Cambridge: Harvard University Press, 1990), 129–30, 155, and 157.

they blessings, healing, cleansing, harm, guidance, or protection. On the farms and plantations owned by slaveholders, enslaved women, to whatever degrees they could, utilized the more potent aspects of these spiritual systems in resistance.

No matter where a woman worked, if she had special abilities and knowledge, she may have been called upon to participate in resistance, though it is often assumed that the women who worked in white households as domestics were isolated from their counterparts out in the fields, and much less likely to challenge slavery. With African cosmologies and their attendant spiritual practices as the framework, however, a kind of open, flowing continuum between the "big house" and the fields comes into view. Especially as it relates to direct, aggressive acts against the white slave owners, there was a great deal of collaboration between those who worked in the house and those who did not. If they themselves were not the expert insurrectionists, the cooks, laundresses, and nursemaids were at least the accomplices who granted access to white bodies and personal property.

This essay examines the role played by female ritual experts in organized, premeditated resistance. This may mean small-scale plots like the poisoning of a slaveholder by just two enslaved people or it may mean large, state or nation-wide rebellions, as in the case of Antigua. Whether they were considered royalty or not, African ritual experts commanded a great deal of respect from both the black and the white communities. As W. E. B. DuBois states:

> The priest or medicine man represented the power of religion. Aided by an unfaltering faith, natural sharpness and some rude knowledge of medicine, and supported by the vague sanctions of a half-seen world peopled by spirits, good and evil, the African priest wielded a power second only to that of the chief, and often superior to it.[3]

Few resistance movements are named for the African spiritual leaders who participated, perhaps owing largely to the Judeo–Christian hegemony at work on all of those same historiographical levels as the patriarchal hegemony, which obscures female participation in resistance. Still, the presence of male conjurers and priests like Gullah Jack and Peter the Doctor are well documented in both the historical record and black folk history. Particularly in the United States, women are not recognized as key players in slave insurrections, and if there were women found among the convicts, there is very little information about what they actually *did* in these revolts.

By waging war against slaveholders from within the African spiritual realm that empowered them, and sometimes, from within white households, female ritual experts posed a more immediate and elusive threat to slaveholding society than mainstream American history has previously conceded. This paper will outline several critical functions of priestesses and conjure women in resistance: makers of charms/protections, poisoners, ritual experts, and spiritual guides. Akan women, shapers and practitioners of the *obeah* tradition, will be the focus of much of this essay, but with significant discussion of women ritual experts from other African traditions.

Poison is one of the more frequently discussed resistance strategies employed by enslaved women. Perhaps correspondingly, the scholarly discourse about the use of poisons and other harmful substances has been in very simple terms, as if almost any enslaved person could have done it, at any time. Scant attention has been paid to the expertise and logistical work required

---

[3] W. E. B. DuBois, *The Negro Church.* (Atlanta: Atlanta University, 1903), 3.

to successfully administer these harmful substances. Moreover, although some light has been cast on the actual plant, mineral, and animal materials used in poisoning by the enslaved, the notion of *belief*, which was often vital to the efficacy of a poison or root, has received only brief mention. Most scholars, like the white slaveholders who wrote about their captives, consider poisoning and botanical knowledge as separate from spiritual knowledge. For example, historian Philip J. Schwartz concludes that because "American Indians might have shared their knowledge of local organic poisons with Afro-American slaves . . . in a handful of Virginia cases [of poisoning], the African background is irrelevant."[4] I assert that the African background is always relevant, especially as it pertains to interpreting or using the natural world, since nature and spirit, in African cosmological understandings, are always connected.

Even those enslaved people who learned of the poisonous plant life in the Americas from the Native American population still had to have the proper training, as well as the trust and faith of other enslaved people who may be a part of this act. Poisoning was based on very specialized herbal knowledge, but in many instances, there also had to be a ritual component to bring about the death of the intended person(s). Some black people thought that because whites did not believe in the metaphysical power of the conjurer or African priest, no form of spiritual warfare could not harm them.[5] In fact, some enslaved people chose to poison other enslaved Africans as a form of revenge against their white slaveholders, not because they were afraid to attack whites directly, but because they believed that whites were invulnerable to African poisons. White authorities may not have admitted the existence of sorcery or magic, but they did believe in it. They certainly punished poisoners, whose skills did cause several white deaths.

Poisoning was not simply a last resort, used by those who were physically weak or otherwise powerless. It was, as Schwartz astutely argues, a uniquely powerful threat, on par with violent insurrections, due to the fact that it was "a secret attack against which there was no warning and little defense. It was by nature premeditated as well as efficacious," not to mention difficult to prove.[6] In other words, enslaved people could mount surprise attacks by either hiding in the bushes or by feeding the bushes to the enemy.

Poisoning and other metaphysical means of harming, therefore, deserve a more central place in the historiography of black resistance. Often considered a "woman's" strategy of aggressive opposition, poison, when situated more towards the center, will also bring women into the center. This section will discuss women's use of poison and other "medicines" intended to harm, within the context of African cosmologies and sacred knowledge. The presence of enslaved women in the homes of slaveholders made the threat of poisoning a constant one; they had easier access to whites' bodies as cooks, childcare workers, and personal assistants.

Proper execution of poisoning required a high level of expertise in plant, animal, and mineral interactions. This expertise was acquired through training. As with any specialized knowledge, these women may have taught their children and younger relatives what they knew. There are several examples of intergenerational and even cross-cultural transfer of knowledge concerning

---

[4] Philip J. Schwartz, *Twice Condemned: Slaves and the Criminal Laws of Virginia, 1705–1865*, 7th ed. (Union: The Lawbook Exchange, 1988), 98.

[5] Albert J. Raboteau, *Slave Religion: The "Invisible Institution" in the Antebellum South* (New York, NY: Oxford University Press, 2004), 283.

[6] Ibid., 92.

botanical warfare. Take, for instance the example of a woman named Boukmann, enslaved in Saint Domingue, who is said to have trained her niece, Marie-Louise, in the art of poisoning. In 1773, Boukmann, who was 42 years old, was placed in solitary confinement, and later put to death and burned, but Marie-Louise, who was 26 years old was spared, on account of her youth and value as a laborer. François Lory de la Bernardière, the owner of the Cottineau plantation where these women worked, later expressed his fears that Marie-Louise would poison the other enslaved people with "herbal concoctions."[7] Interestingly, not twenty years later, a man named Boukmann would take his place in history as the priest whose ritual expertise at Boïs Caiman mobilized the enslaved masses to rise up against the French and dismantle slavery in Saint Domingue.

Before either of the Boukmanns made their mark in Saint Domingue, there was Mackandal, a maroon leader, who systematically instructed others in the art of poisoning, intending to wage war on the French, featuring poison as the primary weapon. His plan was to poison the water supply. He was apprehended and executed by burning in 1758.[8]

Mackandal's legacy lived on during the Revolt at Saint Domingue: women may have been the main poisoners responsible for the deaths of scores of French soldiers camped out at the Galiffet plantation, due to poisoned well water.[9]

In Akan societies, medicine, *aduru*, can be good (*aduru pa*) or bad (*adurubone*). Poison (*aduto*) is in a category all its own.[10] In the Americas, Akan ritual experts, often called *obeah* men or women, also used *aduru* and *aduto* to attack their enemies. Medicines intended for harm would have been administered by a person designated as a healer, *odunsini* ("one who works with parts of a tree"), but not a priest (*okomfo*), since traditionally, priests are not allowed to harm or kill anyone, except witches (*obayifo*).[11]

This fact may also suggest an interesting nuance for the term *obeah*, which is thought to have come from the term *obayifo* (witch), because Akans defined witches as those people who have the supernatural ability to take (*yi*) a woman's (*fo*-person) child (*ba*), or her eggs from her womb,[12] and the fact that physical and emotional stresses of enslavement, caused a devastating infant mortality rate in some areas, whites may have been seen as witches, thus giving rise to the *obosombrafo*[13] function among enslaved priests, whose concern with catching witches would have been extremely high. Moreover, many other illnesses among the enslaved were severe and

---

[7] Gabriel Debien, *Les Esclaves aux Antilles françaises* (Basse-Terre: Société d'Histoire de la Guadeloupe, 1974), 405, 408, and Gabriel Debien, *Plantations et esclaves à Saint Domingue* (Dakar: Publications de la Section d'Histoire, 1962), 63, 67.

[8] Gwendolyn Midlo Hall, *Africans in Colonial Louisiana: The Development of Afro-Creole Culture in the Eighteenth Century*, (Baton Rouge: Louisiana State University Press, 1992), 164. The Mackandal conspiracy caused such alarm among whites that throughout the French American colonies, deadly poisons or charms were sometimes called "Mackandals."

[9] Moitt, 252

[10] Rucker, 43.

[11] Kwesi Konadu, "Concepts of Medicine: as Interpreted by Akan Healers and Indigenous Knowledge Archives Among the Bono-Takyiman of Ghana, West Africa: A Case Study" (PHD Dissertation, Howard University, 2004).

[12] Ibid., 45

[13] These are priests who specialize in witch-catching, empowered to do so by *abosommerafo*, spirits who catch witches. Ibid.

thought to be tied to spiritual etiologies. Akan healers, however did not cure serious or spiritually-caused illnesses, priests did.

If *obeah* were in fact priests, who serve specific spiritual entities, and not simply healers, the priestly participation in spiritual-medicinal harming may also be indicative of the transformation of a cultural institution to meet the needs of a people under duress (enslavement). Whether *obeah* is a term that more closely refers to priests or healers, both of them undergo rigorous training, especially since, as Konadu explains "Akan society . . . and Akan traditions, in all its dimensions, allow for the development of specialists or individuals with more than average competency and knowledge."[14] Edward Long, attempted to explain the deep trust that black people had in (and his disdain for) *obeah* and their skills as poisoners:

> The most sensible among them fear the supernatural powers of African obeah-men, or pretended conjurers; often ascribing those mortal effects to magic, which are only the natural operation of some poisonous juice, or preparation, dexterously administered by these villains . . .[15]

This statement indicates that even cultural outsiders, indeed, enemies, recognized that poison, or "bad medicine" required skill, and with the Akan context in mind, it is clear that the obeah practitioners could deliver *aduto* as expertly as they could deliver *aduru pa*. In the historical records left by Caribbean plantation owners, Akan women are perceived as uniquely predisposed to poisoning, especially the old women thought to be *obeah*. Many of these women healers did practice both "good" and "bad" medicine.

There was also a great deal of strategy involved in poisoning. Enslaved women domestics took advantage of any information they may have had about their slaveholders' business and/or professional life. This information was sometimes funneled to the enslaved people who labored outside of the house, and made for a powerful house–field collaboration against the slaveholders. The house servants were often the door-openers, if not the actual poisoners. Dolly, an enslaved woman, probably employed as a childcare worker in South Carolina, was convicted of poisoning the infant of her owner, James Sands, and for conspiring with Liverpool, the "Negro Doctor who created the poison, to kill Mr. Sands in the same manner. Both were burned alive.[16]

Women, who were not necessarily cooks, or who did not have access to easily ingested poisons, used other methods of subduing whites. Those who were charged with drawing water could have worked with Boukmann to poison the local water supply, while housekeepers, laundresses, and seamstresses may have placed poison across doorsills or in white peoples' clothing so that the poison would be absorbed through the skin. Others made poisons that were to be inhaled, perhaps by being rubbed into a pillow or a handkerchief.

Not all people who were poisoned died instantly; some people were exposed to harmful substances over time, so that their murder would look like a gradual death due to illness. Mark and Phillis were tried and executed in Massachusetts, for their gradual poisoning of their owner, Captain John Codman, in 1755: "Robin twice obtained and delivered to Mark a quantity

---

[14] Ibid., 48.

[15] Edward Long, *The History of Jamaica: Or, General Survey of the Ancient and Modern State of the Island: with Reflections on Its Situation Settlements, Inhabitants, Climate, Products, Commerce, Laws, and Government* (London: T. Lowndes, 1774), 416.

[16] Rucker, 112. He quotes from the *South Carolina Gazette*.

of arsenic, of which the women, Phebe and Phillis, made a solution which they kept secreted in a vial, and from time to time mixed with the water-gruel and sago which they sometimes gave directly to their victim to eat, and at other times prepared to be innocently administered to him by one of his daughters. They also mixed with his food some of the 'black lead,' which Phillis seems to have thought was the efficient poison, though it appeared from the testimony that he was killed by the arsenic."[17] Several other enslaved people assisted Mark and Phillis, although they were the only ones convicted of the crime of treason.

Sometimes a poisoning would be scheduled so it would coincide with another organized resistance strategy, like a revolt or an escape plan. Several female domestic workers in the largest estate homes of Matanzas, Cuba, were recruited to poison the slaveholders they worked for, in conjunction with the uprising of 1843–44, and were sometimes given the title of "queen" among the rebels, owing to their high level of involvement in the rebellion.[18] In Trinidad, a plantation nurse named Thisbe was tortured until she confessed to being a poisoner, and a part of a larger insurrectionary plot.[19] It was reported that in Guadeloupe, as a rejoinder to the thwarted rebellion of 1802, several black women came down "from the hills" and volunteered to work at the military hospital at Pointe-à-Pitre, so that they could poison the French soldiers being treated there. When it was suspected that the black nurses were causing the increasingly high mortality rate among the soldiers, and that they were in collusion with the free colored in the military, they were "rounded up and shot."[20] These collaborations challenge the commonly held notion that, poisoning was an individual act of resistance.

Some slaveholders were surprised to discover that their closest, most trusted house servants were ringleaders in movements to destroy them. In early nineteenth century Martinique, the slaveholders were confused and frightened by what they saw as a transition from the "mysterious African obeah master" poisoner[21] to the supposedly well cared-for overseers, sugar refiners, livestock herders, chambermaids, and children's nurses.[22] These "dutiful" servants became the prime suspects in all poisoning plots, which were numerous at this point in history. White fear had reached such a boiling point that it transformed the slaveholders' way of life: white women accustomed to being served began to prepare their own meals, and childcare workers were watched while they nursed white children. Some formerly trusted house servants were

---

[17] Unknown. "The Trial and Execution of Mark and Phillis, in 1755" (reprinted at the Proceedings of the Massachusetts Historical Society, in 1883, and taken from the Massachusetts Superior Court of Judicature), 4–5. Phillis was sentenced to burning, making this the only instance of an individual receiving the common-law penalty for a crime that was considered *petit treason*. Interestingly, Phebe, the other woman involved in the poisoning plot, was married to a man with an Akan name, Quaco (Kweku), which indicates a possible Akan presence— which usually results in an Akan *influence*—in this conspiracy.

[18] Aisha K. Finch, "Insurgency at the Crossroads: Cuban Slaves and the Conspiracy of La Escalera, 1841–44," (PhD diss., New York University, 2007), 69, 242, and 329.

[19] Barbara Bush, *Slave Women in Caribbean Society, 1650–1838* (Bloomington, IN: Indiana University Press, 1990), 76.

[20] Bernard Moitt, Women and Slavery in the French Antilles (Bloomington, IN: Indiana University Press, 2001), 252.

[21] John Savage, "'Black Magic' and White Terror: Slave Poisoning and Colonial Society in Early 19th Century Martinique," *Journal of Social History* (Spring 2007): 637.

[22] Archives Nationales, Centre d'Archives d'Outre-Mer (hereafter CAOM), FM SG Martinique 52/430, Rapport du Général Donzelot, September 28, 1822. Ibid.

banned from entering the houses.[23] John Savage, in an attempt to explain the motivation of these domestic workers to poison their owners, cites an "often retold" confession, given by an accused house servant: "Eh! It's because of your goodness that I committed so many crimes: things were too good for me . . ."[24] Savage uncritically accepts the rationale of the majority of slaveholders, that this "class of poisoners is made up almost exclusively of slaves who are their masters' favorites . . . their crimes are not brought about by despair or excessive labor; rather it is because of laziness and the special advantages they enjoy."[25]

This rationale, unfortunately reinforced by Savage, disempowers female practitioners, even as he reveals their high level of participation in poisoning. He reinforces the "prose of passivity," in the sense that the violent actions of enslaved women are ascribed to some sort of pathological "over-love" for whites, or simple idleness, rather than frustration, rage, and the desire to be free. Savage completely misses the high probability that the many house servants accused of poisoning were masking themselves—resorting to shallow, euphemistic explanations for their crimes, so as to avoid being punished as severely as they would if they admitted their true motives. Enslaved women, who worked in white households, could have had any number of motives to poison their captors, which likely included a desire to put an end to the sexual exploitation they suffered as easily accessible, unfree persons, and retribution for the stripping of their maternal rights, while being forced to care for the children of others.

Perhaps future research will reveal more about the gendered nature of resistance, which is motivated and shaped by the gendered nature of slavery. It would be interesting, for instance, to learn more about the unnamed sorceress, aboard a French slave ship, who allegedly caused the ship's food and water supply to disappear and killed several other enslaved Africans aboard the ship. The ship's doctor performed an autopsy on a man who was supposedly killed by the sorceress, and found his heart and liver dried up and hollow. Shortly after he beat her severely for her alleged offenses and she swore revenge, the doctor died a mysterious and painful death; his autopsy revealed that his testicles were dried up.[26] Did the sorceress train her powers on damaging the body parts that reflected her treatment by each man? Did she shrivel the black man's heart because of unrequited or tainted love? Did she shrivel the white man's testicles because he attempted to rape her? Ultimately, the story indicates that no matter what interpersonal subplots unraveled on the ship, the sorceress' main goal was to return to freedom in Africa, and she took steps to make this happen; the ship was returned to the African coast, and this woman was set free.

In Martinique, the whites felt so surrounded by the invisible threat of poisoning that they had convinced themselves of the existence of a network of secret poisoning societies among the Africans on the island, no doubt, a reflection of both their underestimation of the wide impact that an individual poisoner could have, and residual paranoia about the highly organized poison-based resistance movement led by Mackandal. Such a large network probably did not

---

[23] Ibid., 638.

[24] Rufz de Lavison, "Recherches sur les empoisonnements," *Annales d'hygiène publique et de médecine légale*, 31 (1844): 400. Ibid.

[25] CAOM FM SG Mart. 52/431, Mémoire Rivière, 1829. Ibid.

[26] Robert Harms, *The Diligent: A Voyage through the Worlds of the Slave Trade* (New York: Basic Books, 2002), 268.

exists, however, studying poisoning from their perspective reveals that Africans did organize themselves with their cultural knowledge as their bond and the substance of their resistance.

Akans call a protective charm *asuman*, or *suman*. An *odunsini* works with *sumans* to collect medicines, and to facilitate the healing process.[27] Among the predominately Akan maroons of Suriname and French Guiana, the word for a charm or talisman is *asúmani*.[28] When going to battle with whites, or just going to work for them, enslaved people felt the need for spiritual and physical protection. Again, ritual experts were called upon to provide these things.

In Akan societies, each military unit had its own shrine and priest, who provided the soldiers with protective powders, charms, or amulets, some of which were thought to make them impervious to bullets.[29] Although there is nothing to suggest that women were more frequently asked to provide spiritual protections than men, there is nothing that conclusively indicates that they did not do so at least as frequently as the men. In Cuba, during the 1844 trials of black people accused of insurrection, charms were mentioned frequently. Aisha Finch writes that "in the course of the hearings, witness after witness testified to the fact that amulets and other spiritual protections were bought, sold, solicited, and otherwise provided. It is thus notable that this spiritual arsenal became [one] of the most carefully hidden, but ironically public weapons of the 1844 resistance."[30] In the context of organized resistance to American slavery, as in Africa, these charms were given to enslaved or maroon people to protect them, this time against the weaponry of the whites.

These charms contained a variety of plant, mineral, and/or animal materials, and were also activated, or charged with *sunsum*, *ashé*, or *nyama* (divine spiritual energy), through rituals performed by the ritual expert. In the 1712 New York Slave Revolt, an *obeah* man called Peter the Doctor gave the insurgents, largely Coromantees, a powder to rub onto their clothing, which would make them invincible. In Saint Domingue, these charms were called *ouanga*. They could include a variety of items, from candles to bones from a cemetery, to banana tree roots. In Louisiana, similar protective charms were called *gris-gris* from the Mande word, *gerregerys*, for a negative charm, or *zinzin*, a Bambara term for a supportive, or protective charm.[31]

Towards the very end of the eighteenth century, as thousands of French planters fled to Louisiana from Saint Domingue with their enslaved servants, the word *wanga*, referring to a harmful charm, grew in popularity, although it did not replace *gris-gris*. Mackandal himself, described the sacred invocations that were to be said over a charm, in order to make it do its intended work. Gwendolyn Midlo Hall points out that the "sorcerer" called on both Allah and the Christian God to activate the charm, and how this reflects the "openness" of the African religions brought to the Americas. While this assessment is well-reasoned, it is important to stress that this openness to other versions of the Deity did not interfere with the Africans' interpretation of the Deity. The making of charms involved prayers of thanksgiving to the spiritual essences of the plant and animal life that was sacrificed to make the charm. The Judeo–Christian tradition does not consider plants and animals as beings energized by spirit, hence

---

[27] Konadu "Concepts of Medicine," 49.
[28] Kwesi Konadu, *The Akan Diaspora in the Americas* (New York: Oxford University Press, 2010), 115, table 4.2.
[29] Rucker, 42–43.
[30] Finch, "Insurgency at the Crossroads," 298.
[31] Hall, *Africans in Colonial Louisiana*, 51, 163.

the distinction made by some scholars between the major proselytizing faiths and so-called "animistic" religions. In other words, had the Africans in Haiti, Louisiana, or any other place where charms were used, truly "added" Muslim and Christian beliefs to their own, the Africans would not have been praying to them over *ouanga*!

While charms often involved physical objects and prayers, protective forces also came in the form of people. Priests, conjurers, and herbalists are products of years of training, but also of their natural spiritual gifts. Some inherit these roles, and others are simply called by Spirit. Harriet Tubman, often called Moses, was also referred to as a "charm." Best known for having delivered dozens of enslaved people to the free North along the Underground Railroad, Tubman, credits her 100 percent success rate to her direct communication to heaven. She never lost a "passenger," due to the premonitions, visions, and dreams given to her by God.

In *Priestess, Mother, Sacred Sister*, professor Susan Star Sered describes the predominance of women spirit mediums, in both male- and female-dominated religions. In the male-dominated religions, especially Christianity, Judaism, and Islam, women are thought to have special sensitivity and receptiveness to spirit because they are less rational, more impressionable, and generally weaker than men. Women are associated with nature and spirituality, due to childbirth and lactation, and men are associated with civilization and culture. In some female-dominated religions, the same association of women with nature exists, but instead of being seen as a source of inferiority to men, this connection places women on a powerful level that is on par with that of men. Sered also mentions that in Afro-Brazilian religions—which she categorizes as female-dominated—"natural sites and materials and culturally constructed sites and materials are equally sacralized in ritual.[32] Hence, Afro-Brazilian female spirit mediums are at least equal to men, if not in some instances more powerful. This notion of balanced gender roles in the religious realm is also reflected in what Sered describes as "fairly even numbers of male and female possessing spirits."[33] To some extent, Sered's observations about the relatively gender balanced nature of Afro-Brazilian religions can be used to describe Vodou, *obeah*, and several other African Diaspora spiritual systems.

With this in mind, it is certain that enslaved African women who could connect directly with the spirit realm would have been well respected by their community. What is more, this spiritual guidance would not have been considered as potent by those operating in a Judeo–Christian framework (including present-day historians).

Take, for example, the fact that Harriet Tubman's most recent biographers, such as Kate Clifford Larson, hypothesize that the dreams and visions are side effects of a brain injury resulting from a blow to the head she received from an overseer,[34] despite the fact that this theory cannot also explain why each of the spiritual messages and feelings that Tubman received were accurate, nor can it explain the myriad other spiritual abilities that she possessed and wielded successfully in the name of freedom.

---

[32] Susan Starr Sered, *Priestess, Mother, Sacred Sister: Religions Dominated by Women* (New York: Oxford University Press, 1994), 197–99
[33] Ibid., 177. Information is found in Table 3: "*The Gender of the Deity.*"
[34] Kate Clifford Larson, *Bound for the Promised Land: Harriet Tubman, Portrait of an American Hero* (New York: Ballantine Books, 2004), 42–43.

Tubman, born in Maryland, sometime in the early 1820s, began her life's mission more than one hundred years after Nanny led her maroon soldiers against the British. Like Nanny, however, Tubman—born with the name Araminta Ross—was said to be of Ashanti origin. Her maternal grandmother, Modesty, was born in Africa and brought over on a slave ship, possibly from the Gold Coast of Africa, from which a significant number of Akan speakers were taken into slavery in the Chesapeake during the eighteenth century. Tubman's Ashanti origins are therefore, a strong possibility. An early twentieth century reporter used the testimony of the elder women in Tubman's community to support this theory of her origins:

> . . . the old mammies to whom she told dreams were wont to nod knowingly and say, 'I reckon youse one o' dem "Shantees," chile.' For they know the tradition of the unconquerable Ashantee blood, which in a slave made him a thorn in the side of the planter or cane grower whose property he became, so that few of that race were in bondage.[35]

While the last point about the small number of Ashanti winding up as slaves is questionable, this quote provides some additional clues about her origins, or at least, in what general cultural context her special abilities might be better understood. One of Tubman's supporters summed up how Tubman is viewed in an African cosmological context: "De whites can't catch Moses, kase you see she's born wid de charm."[36]

First, there are her dreams, which she told to the elder women. While the writer, Frank Drake, focuses on the Ashanti' reputation as rebellious Africans, he does not explain why the telling of her dreams might have prompted the old women to label her an Ashanti. Were the Ashanti thought to have special abilities manifested through dreams, or place some cultural emphasis on dreams? What were these dreams about? Perhaps rebellion was a recurring theme in the dreams. Before she escaped from slavery, Tubman had dreams of flying like a bird, and reaching a barrier (a river or fence) above which she lacked the strength to fly. Just when she felt her strength running out, women dressed in white would help her across. She said that this dream was a premonition of her actual flight to freedom, and that when she got there, she met those people who had come to her aid in her dreams.[37] She received an intuition that her brothers were in danger of being sold further south, and arrived to take them to freedom the night before they were to be sold. During one of her "Railroad" journeys, she suddenly *felt* that the group should change course, and led them through a rushing river. While the group balked at the risky and difficult path, they followed her through the water. They found out later that had they stayed on their original path, slave patrollers would have caught them.[38]

Because U.S. narratives of slave resistance tend to focus more on flight than conflict with whites, Tubman's more aggressive methods are downplayed, or seldom mentioned. For instance, while it is common to learn that she carried a gun, this gun is only seen as something that was turned on other black people—the cowards who wanted to turn back to their owners.

---

[35] Frank C. Drake, "The Moses of Her People. Amazing Life Work of Harriet Tubman," *New York Herald*, September 22, 1907.
[36] William Wells Brown, *The Rising Son; or, The Antecedents and Advancement of the Colored Race* (Boston: A. G. Brown, 1874; reprinted in Florida: Mnemosyne Inc., 1969), 538.
[37] Jermaine O. Archer, "'A Breathing of the Common Wind': Cultural and Political Expressions of Africa in Antebellum Slave Narratives," (PhD diss., University of California, Riverside, 2004), 104.
[38] Ibid., 93–95.

This gun was for security and protection, from anyone, black or white. Had she been a pacifist, or against killing, she would not have been a supporter of the radical, violent approach taken by John Brown at Harpers Ferry, Virginia. According to Tubman, her prayers could be used as a weapon. She prayed to soften the heart of her owner, Edward Brodess, and to make him a "good Christian gentleman," so that he would not sell her onto a chain gang in the Deep South. When it appeared that he still intended to sell her, she prayed to God to kill him. "Next ting [she] heard, ole master was dead, and he died just as he had lived, a wicked, bad man."[39] Tubman fits quite neatly into the resistance tradition of the Akan women before her. She was unafraid to be a warrior, and she fought with both physical and spiritual weapons. Her abilities as a diviner would have made her a priestess, but she also had skills as a healer.

During the Civil War, Tubman nursed diseased soldiers back to health through herbal and root-based remedies. She cured everything from smallpox to dysentery, without getting sick herself.[40] Spiritual workers were often seen as immune to common issues and ailments that afflicted the rest of the population. Their connection to the spirit world afforded them knowledge that could protect them.

Protection and warfare were not the only uses of a spiritual guide's abilities in resistance. As messengers for the spirit world, some spirit mediums drew people to participate in organized resistance, by revealing the will of the spirit that they do so. Barbara Bush points out that in the French Caribbean, "grand voodoo priestesses" had an important role, and through spiritual revelations, gave courage to the rebels.[41] John Stedman, described how some women spiritual mediums in Suriname stirred other enslaved people into battle, or caused them to run away, by carrying the spirit in "pagan" rituals. He stated that among the enslaved, there was

> . . . a kind of Sybils, who deal in oracles; these sage matrons dancing and whirling round in the middle of an assembly with amazing rapidity until they foam at the mouth and drop down convulsed. Whatever the prophetess orders to be done, during this paroxysm is most sacredly performed by the surrounding multitude which renders these meetings extremely dangerous, as she frequently enjoins them to murder their masters, or desert to the woods.[42]

It is clear from this vivid description that Stedman has discovered the more threatening aspects of spiritual mediumship, in the context of resistance. DuBois would have called this type of spirit possession "the frenzy."[43] Spiritual messengers were not only given messages telling rebels what time and where to/not to stage a rebellion; the spirits they carried were sometimes the ones calling for the rebellion!

The ritual described in the above quote from Stedman, involving "dancing and whirling round," may have been the *Komfo* ritual, especially if it were taking place at a river. The *Komfo*, or *Cumfo* signified the desire of the enslaved to return to Africa, if not across the Atlantic Ocean, then at least by crossing the cosmic divide (both of which were symbolized by the ritual

---

[39] Georgia Writer's Project, *Drums and Shadows* (Georgia: University of Georgia Press, 1940), 24.

[40] Sarah H. Bradford, *Scenes in the Life of Harriet Tubman* (Auburn: W.J. Moses, 1869), 95–98.

[41] Bush, *Slave Women*, 74.

[42] John Stedman, *Narrative of a Five Years' Expedition against the Revolted Negroes of Surinam*, eds. Richard and Sally Price (1796; reprinted in Amherst: University of Massachusetts Press,1988), 304.

[43] W. E. B. DuBois, *The Souls of Black Folk* (New York: Washington Square Press, 1970), 155.

crossing of the river).[44] This ritual is likely linked to the officiant whose title, *okomfo* is indicated by its name, thus also linking it to Akan culture. Because in the Africans' cosmological view, *every* action taken must call on the aid of Spirit, this and other rituals formed the foundation of black resistance. Theoretically, because women were often equal participants, if not spiritual leaders, their ritual expertise placed them at the scene of nearly every organized resistance movement among enslaved Africans.

In Cuba, when an enslaved person was beaten, all of those who witnessed it would quickly gather, each adding a handful of dirt to a pot. Then, according to Esteban Montejo, "the master fell ill or some harm came to his family because while the dirt was in the pot, the master was a prisoner there, and not even the devil could get him out."[45] Montejo identifies this particular ritual as a form of revenge used by the Congo people. He does not specify this ritual as a men's or women's ritual, and since both genders were flogged, and both genders were forced to watch this brutality, it can be comfortably assumed that women were involved in the "Congo revenge" ritual.

In the case of Antigua, in 1736, there were at least two women involved. One was, as stated Old Queen (mother). The other was a woman named Obbah. Though each likely played important roles in the revolt, neither was tried, executed or banished. Obbah is probably a transformation of the Akan name, Aba. At some point during the planning of the rebellion, Obbah held a feast for her sister and brought "Dirt from her Sisters Grave . . . in a Callabash," which another person mixed with wine. According to Gaspar, these feasts were commonly gatherings used to recruit new rebels into the insurrectionary army, and to swear them to an oath of loyalty and secrecy. In eighteenth-century Akan societies, this oath, the *ntam*, was routinely administered to the military before a campaign, binding all soldiers in an unbreakable pact. The dirt taken from the graves of deceased relatives or other ancestors was used in ritual concoctions to obligate the oath-takers to the *entire* Akan community, which consisted of humans, ancestral spirits, and deities.[46] They were to each drink the mixture from the calabash. Obbah facilitated a ritual that was to ensure the safety and stability of the soldiers.

Moreover, Obbah's use of her sister's grave dirt is a ritual acknowledgement of the spiritual potency of kinship (*abusua*) and land (*Asaase Ya*). In this layering of feminine spiritual power, she reemphasized the distinct sacredness of both her female blood lineage and the earth over her sister's grave. Indeed, many oaths and rituals were performed at gravesites, which in the absence of a sacred grove or clearing, functioned as African sacred space.

Strikingly similar "damnation oaths," were taken by enslaved rebels in Jamaica in 1760, and in New York in 1712. "Coromantee" Africans in New York took blood oaths by sucking the blood from a cut made in each person's hand. Other Akan oath drinks mixed blood, graveyard dirt, and water.[47] A violation or failure to fulfill one's oath brought the ultimate dishonor to an Akan. Although suicide is considered abominable to Akans, the breaking of the *Ntam* may

---

[44] Konadu, *Akan Diaspora*, 146.

[45] Esteban Montejo, *Biography of a Runaway Slave* (1860, reprinted in Willimantic: Curbstone Press, 1994), 27–28. Translated to English by Rice Hill.

[46] David Barry Gaspar, "From 'A Sense of Their Slavery': Slave Women and Resistance in Antigua, 1632–1763," in *More than Chattel: Black Women and Slavery in the Americas*, eds. David Barry Gaspar and Darlene Clark Hine (Bloomington: Indiana University Press, 1996), 218–38.

[47] Rucker, 43–44.

prompt a soldier to kill himself or herself. After the revolt on St. John was thwarted, thirty-six Akan insurgents committed suicide.[48] What can be surmised from each of these swearing rituals is that no matter what physical materials are available, the ritual reflects a soul-deep belief in the spiritually-binding power of blood ties and sacred earth.

At these recruitment gatherings, as well on the battlefield, rebels also depended on women for food, and other kinds of logistical support. One of the main ritual functions served by women in the context of warfare, both in Asante and in the Americas, was to perform *mmo-mommme twe*, pantomime dances and sing dirges in support of the warriors. Kwame Arhin describes this tradition thus:

> It is unclear whether the dances and songs were expected to have magico-religious effects on the enemy. But they had the practical effect of shaming potential war-dodgers known as *kôsaankôbi* into joining the war. Women were also authorized to compose songs that could drive confirmed war-dodgers to suicide. The situation can be summarized by saying that the essential female military role was to give encouragement to men. Giving encouragement could, however, take a dramatic and more positive turn, if a woman of high status seized arms, or as the Asante called it, *bontoa*, as an example to the males in order to arouse their sense of honour and sharpen their martial ardour.[49]

It is also unclear as to whether this wartime women's ritual support is the same as the *momome* ritual, a cleansing ritual also performed by women, to purify the community in "moments of impending crisis."[50] Considering the number of violent attacks, both organized and spontaneous, that were visited upon slaveholding societies, ritual cleansings probably occurred much more frequently than we know. In Congo Village in the Dismal Swamp maroon community, the residents took spiritual baths.[51] There is no information available describing the purpose of these baths, but it can be inferred that if they were used in times of peace, they were certainly used in times of war.

Because African women drew upon their sacred knowledge and cultural institutions to resist slavery, their actions added insult to the injuries they gave to shocked, disgusted, and fearful white observers. It was bad enough that Africans rebelled at all, but the women participating, indeed sometimes spearheading these movements, had stepped completely out of their "place." Women who were treated like brutes, children, and sex objects, declared themselves queens, sovereign citizens and sacred. Women domestics collaborated with field workers, men, deities, and whoever else was interested in freedom. They did these things on their own terms. In the context of American slavery, African women ritual experts turned the very idea of power on its head, forcing white slaveholders to find creative ways to suppress this power, without actually admitting where it came from.

---

[48] Ibid.

[49] Kwame Brempong Arhin, "The Role of Yaa Asantewaa in the 1900 Asante War of Resistance," vol. 8 of *Le Griot* (Kumasi: Kwame Nkrumah University of Science and Technology, Department of African Studies, 2000).

[50] According to an English translation of the abstract for "Exclusion de femmes de la communauté. Le rituel momome du monde akan," author Stefano Boni says that *momome* is a Sefwi variant, and goes on to describe it as a "response to wars and epidemics in the precolonial setting," which involved "dresses, spatial dispositions and movements, chromatic symbolism, metaphoric acts, use of therapeutic herbs, (and) songs." This article can be found in vol. 192 of *Cahiers D' Études Africaines* (2008). Abstract accessed May 2, 2009. http://www.cairn.info/resume.php?ID_ARTICLE=CEA_192_0765#.

[51] Hugo Prosper Leaming, "Hidden Americans: Maroons of Virginia and the Carolinas," (PhD diss., University of Illinois at Chicago, 1979), 499.

CHAPTER 10

BLACK POWER IN THE AFRICAN DIASPORA

Quito Swan

In the summer of 1966, twenty-five-year-old Kwame Ture (Stokely Carmichael) ignited a political rally by calling for "Black Power." At the prodding of Student Nonviolent Coordinating Committee (SNCC) organizer Willie Ricks, Ture electrified his Greenwood, Mississippi audience. Ture, the Trinidadian-born chairman of SNCC, was not the first person to use the phrase "Black Power." Just months earlier, in May 1966, Adam Clayton Powell Jr. referenced Black Power during a speech at Howard University. Richard Wright's book, *Black Power* (1954), was based on his trip to the Gold Coast, three years before it would become the independent nation of Ghana under Kwame Nkrumah in 1957. Yet, Ture's speech launched these two words across the United States and the wider world like wildfire.

What began as a rallying cry for activist black youth in the United States quickly transformed into a powerful political, cultural, and social movement against white global hegemony. Black Power spanned the Atlantic, Indian, and Pacific oceans. Its adherents were justifiably disenchanted with the socioeconomic conditions facing the black world, such as colonialism, class oppression, sexism, and imperialism. In response, Governments such as the US, British, and French mercilessly attacked Black Power through political persecution, violence, and propaganda, leaving a mass of martyrs, political prisoners, and neocolonies in the wake of these assaults. This included governments led by Black heads of state, who, as in the Caribbean, where threatened by Black Power's calls for self-determination.

BLACKS IN POWER

The notion of "Black people having power" is a historical phenomenon. Indeed, Africa has produced a number of "powerful" societies, nations, and peoples since the ancient world. These would include Kemet, Ghana, Zimbabwe, Nubia, Oyo, Kush, Meroe, Ethiopia, Ndongo, Songhai, and Kongo. Mali's Mansa Musa was one of the most powerful persons in the world during the fourteenth century.

A portion of this essay appeared in "Black Power." The SAGE Encyclopedia of African Cultural Heritage in North America, ed. Mwalimu J. Shujaa and Kenya J. Shujaa (Thousand Oaks: Sage Publications, 2015).

The enslavement of African people in the Americas, Middle East, and Asia created a vacuum of "Black Power." Albeit unevenly, this simultaneously reflected the appearance of "white power" on a world scale, the modern creation of "race" and myths of white supremacy. As such, it could be argued that the modern version of Black Power in the Americas began with the forced arrival of Africans who were brought to the Americas by Spanish conquistadors in the fifteenth century. These Africans often escaped captivity and/or formed independent maroon communities among the indigenous peoples outside of the plantation systems. Known by several names, such as *cimarrones*, *palenques*, *cumbes*, and *quilombos*, maroon societies formed the roots of modern black power. Led by Ganga Zumba and Zumbi, Brazil's *quilombo dos* Palmares lasted from 1605–74. Jamaica's maroons were led by Nanny of the Akan, whose experience speaks to the critical presence of African women in maroonage. African people also formed maroon communities in resistance to Arab enslavement in the Middle East. This included the Zanj rebellion of the seventh century, and maritime maroons such as the Siddis of Janjira in the Indian Ocean.

The countless strikes against slavery across the region (South Carolina's Denmark Vesey, Cuba's Jose Aponte, Mexico's Yanga, Venezuela's Jose Leonardo Chirino, and Barbados' Bussa) formed the bedrock of the Black Radical tradition. Still, the most visible example of Black Power in the era was perhaps the Haitian Revolution, marked by the use of Vodun through Cecil Fatiman and Boukman Dutty. This is perhaps why Black Power advocates of the 1960s called upon the names like Toussaint L'Ouverture, Nat Turner, Sally Bassett, and Harriet Tubman.

In the aftermath of slavery, blacks continue to seek power to control their own destinies. The chains of chattel slavery were recalibrated and replaced with new (and familiar) versions of systematic violence—sharecropping, mass incarceration, wage slavery, forced labor, lynching, deportation, police brutality, disenfranchisement, displacement, sexual abuse, incarceration, and colonialism. Africana ideas of resistance of David Walker's *Appeal*, Esteban Montejo's recollections, Mary Prince's *Narrative*, and Frederick Douglass' cry that "power conceded nothing without a demand," helped to shape the pan-Africanism of the nineteenth century.

In 1862, Edward Blyden charged that blacks needed "some *African power*" and a "great center of the race where" black "physical, pecuniary and intellectual strength could be collected" from Paul Bogle's 1865 call for Afro-Jamaicans to *cleave to the Black* to Ida B. Well's position on armed self-defense, blacks argued that armed struggle was a legitimate form of protest against white physical and systematic violence. Activist women such as Wells and Mary Church Terrell foretold of the leadership roles that black women would play in the Black Power Movement.

The turn of the twentieth century was a critical movement for black insurgency and quests for power. Black political organizations included Brazil's Frente Negra Brasileira (Black Brazilian Front) and Cuba's Partido Independiente de Color (PIC). The first black political party in the Americas, Cuba's PIC was ruthlessly repressed by Cuba's government. In 1878, Chief Atai of the Kanaks launched a war against French colonialism in the South Pacific and killed a French commander in doing so. Meanwhile, Ethiopia's 1896 victory over Italy at Adwa, led by Menelik II and Empress Taitu, galvanized Henry Sylvester Williams, W. E. B. DuBois, Ana Julia Cooper, and others who attended the first Pan-African Conference of 1900.

The broadest organizational attempt by blacks to globally claim power in the twentieth century was the Universal Negro Improvement Association (UNIA). Formed by Jamaica's

Marcus and Amy Ashwood Garvey in Jamaica in 1914, the UNIA flourished while headquartered in Harlem. The UNIA claimed to possess millions of members and established branches across the world as far as Cuba, Australia, and Africa. Its political and economic program was grounded in Ethiopianism, black redemption, and repatriation to Africa. It established a newspaper, the *Negro World*, and a shipping company, the Black Star Line.

The UNIA was only the most visible of a number of Black Nationalist surges efforts circa World War I (WWI). Claude McKay's *If We Must Die* reflected a black interwar militancy, marked by Caribbean migration and the emergence of black theorists such as Harlem's Hubert Harrison from St. Croix. Aime Cesaire's *Discourse on Colonialism* reflected the presence of blacks in the French-speaking world in the roll call of black political agency. Italy's invasion of Ethiopia in 1935 resulted in worldwide support for Emperor Haile Selassie, stimulating the rise of Rastafari.

THE BLACK POWER MOVEMENT

The Black Power Movement of the 1960s traversed along the long-standing webs of historic black internationalism. This included black nationalism, pan-Africanism, *Negritude*, Civil Rights activism, *cimarronaje*, African liberation struggles, and "Third World" revolutionary praxis in the post-WWII era. From the fibers of these battle-tested forms of protest it spun new networks of global radicalism, engaging the anticolonial struggles of Africa, Asia, and the Americas. The movement's immediate predecessors were black women and men who traversed the African Diaspora as activists, revolutionaries, cultural artists, students, teachers, scientists, organizers, and agent provocateurs. It would draw on the political experiences and analyses of a number of activists, such as Grace Campbell, George Padmore, CLR James and Claudia Jones, Paul and Eslanda Robeson, and Kwame Nkrumah.

In the 1950s, the "red scare" of McCarthyism pushed several black organizations from the contours of black radicalism. Even still, African and Caribbean independence movements (such as in the Gold Coast), the National Association for the Advancement of Colored People (NAAACP) Robert F. Williams, the Deacons for Defense, Malcolm X's internationalism, and the assassination of the Congo's Patrice Lumumba reflected the intensity of global black protest. In the United States, several Black Power activists cut their political teeth in the Civil Rights Movement. Indeed, the African American freedom struggle of the 1960s emerged as a part of a broader quest for Black Power and self-determination. Martin Luther King Jr.'s own radicalism and questioning of the tactics of nonviolence is seen through his latter denouncement of the Vietnam War, American imperialism, and capitalism. As advisor of SNCC, Ella Baker of the Southern Christian Leadership Conference (SCLC) helped to birth the youth of this movement, reflected in the emergence of SNCC—of whom many would reject the appeal to the moral conscience of the white world.

According to Kwame Nkrumah, the Black Power Movement was "part of the vanguard of world revolution against capitalism, imperialism and neo-colonialism." It called for: a revolution against capitalism, colonialism, and imperialism; self-determination; a class analysis; support for political prisoners; engagement with Africana and Asian liberation struggles; the legitimization of armed self-defense; an overthrow of white systems of power; Pan-Africanism; and political sovereignty, economic self-sufficiency, and Black cultural transformation.

In 1967, Ture and Charles Hamilton's *Black Power* stated that the movement was a call for blacks to unite, to recognize their heritage, build a sense of community, reject racist institutions and values of the society, define their own goals and lead, and support black organizations. Ture told the 1967 Organization of Latin America States in Havana, Cuba, that blacks in America were victims of white imperialism and formed essentially a US domestic colony. Black Power meant that blacks in America would see themselves as "part of the third world."

Black Power came of age in a world of Civil Rights, Vietnam and napalm, Afros, the "angry children" of Malcolm X, the assassination of Martin Luther King, Puerto Rican nationalism, an aging Elijah Muhammad, a young exiled Winnie Mandela, the Cuban Revolution, Black and indigenous liberation struggles across Atlantic, Indian and Pacific oceans, armed struggle in southern Africa, Bob Marley, Frantz Fanon's *Wretched of the Earth*, the Kanaky fight against French colonialism in New Caledonia, Miriam Makeba and antiapartheid, and Muhammad Ali and George Foreman's "rumble in jungle" in Zaire.

In the United States, Black Power gave birth to a number of political organizations. This included the Revolutionary Action Movement (RAM), Republic of New Afrika, Mulana Karenga's US, League of Revolutionary Workers, Black Liberation Army, DRUM, and SNCC. Amiri Baraka (LeRoi Jones) was one of the most significant forces in the Black Power Movement. Operating primarily out of New Jersey, he helped to launch the Black Arts Movement, which, in many ways, was the cultural wing of Black Power. Indeed, Black Power ushered in a cultural and political consciousness among blacks in the United States, galvanizing even those who did not join formal Black Power groups.

The Black Panther Party was the most visible and is the most remembered Black Power organization. In the aftermath of the Civil Rights Act of 1964, SNCC activists such as Ture and local residents formed the Lowndes County Freedom Organization (LCFO) in "Bloody Lowndes," Alabama. The independent black political party adopted a black panther as its symbol. Black Panther formations quickly spread across the nation. In Oakland, California (1966), Bobby Seale and Huey P. Newton created its current and most remembered manifestation, the Black Panther Party for Self Defense. Their direct influences included Robert Williams' *Negroes with Guns*. The Black Party's ten-point program called for freedom and the power "to determine the destiny of our black and oppressed communities," an end to the capitalist robbery of black communities, full employment, land, bread, justice, housing, education, and free health care for black people, justice, and freedom for all oppressed people held in US prisons and an end to police brutality and wars of aggression. Party members were distinct in their wearing of Afros, leather jackets, and Berets. It "captured" the imagination, hearts, and minds of the black masses via survival programs such as police patrols, free breakfast programs, and community clinics. At all levels of the organization, black women were central to the Party's success. Women such as Angela Davis, Assata Shakur, and Kathleen Cleaver also helped to popularize the Panther Party on the global stage.

The sounds, words, and images of the Black Panthers spread across the world via television screens, contraband literature, the hands of activists, radio stations, popular magazines, and mainstream newspapers. Panther formations appeared across the world, including in

London, Trinidad, and India (Dalit Panthers). In 1971, the Polynesian Panthers were formed in Aotearoa (NZ). The following year, Denis Walker formed Australia's Black Panther Party in New Zealand's Pacific neighbor. Algeria became the home of the International Wing of the Black Panthers and offered refuge to Panthers such as Eldridge and Kathleen Cleaver. The Panthers also influenced and worked with groups such as the Young Lords, a Puerto Rican nationalist group based in the United States, the American Indian Movement, and the Chicano Brown Berets.

Black Power literature and symbolism crossed the world in ways both expected and unexpected. For raising their fists at the 1968 Olympics in Mexico, African–American athletes such as Tommie Smith and John Carlos had their medals taken from them. Ture's *Black Power* was read across the Caribbean, Australia, and Papua New Guinea. Fanon's *Wretched of the Earth* became known as the "Bible of the Black Revolution," reflecting the political legacy of the *Negritude* movement on Black Power. Translated in English and French, *Wretched* could be read in Paris and New Caledonia by Kanaky students of the *Red Scarves* as well as Black Power advocates in Dominica.

Black Power manifested itself within London's urban communities such as Brixton. Spearheaded by young West Indians and the Rasta community, Black Power was a political response to police brutality, white xenophobia, the criminalization of black youth, a racist education system, and Britain's support of apartheid and neocolonialism in Africa. London's Black Panther Party (1968) included its founder, Nigerian playwright Obi Egbuna, Trinidad's Althea Jones-Lecointe and Darcus Howe, and Jamaica's Olive Morris and Linton Kwesi Johnson. Numbers of other Black Power and Afro-Caribbean groups spread across London as well, such as the South East London Parents Organization (SELPO).

Black Power filtered into the Caribbean in the late 1960s. It primarily emerged as a youth response to the unfulfilled socioeconomic promises of political independence. It posed a significant challenge to (neo) colonialism and imperialism across the region. Its impact also spread to the Spanish speaking, Lusophone and Dutch Americas. While grappling with cultural, ethnic, economic, and class contradictions across the region, it engaged cultural movements such as Rasta, Islam, Vodun, and the African Hebrew Israelites.

Born in British Guyana, historian Walter Rodney developed into one of the Caribbean's most Black Power activists. In his *Groundings with My Brothers*, he argued that Black Power in the region represented a "break from imperialism," the "assumptions of power by the Black masses" and "the cultural reconstruction of the islands in the image of the Blacks." While teaching History at Jamaica's University of the West Indies (UWI), he grounded with the wider community about Black Power and African history. Rodney had taught at the University of Dar es Salaam in Tanzania. In 1968, while on route from Montreal's Congress of Black Writers, held at McGill University, Rodney was prevented him from reentering Jamaica. This sparked mass uprisings in Kingston. In 1980, after years of government harassment as a founder of the Working People's Alliance Walter, Rodney was assassinated in Guyana.

Primarily organized by West Indian students, Montreal's Congress critically reflected Black Power's transnational spread across the Americas. Its participants included CLR James, Dominica's Roosie Douglas, Michael X, Kwame Ture, Robert Hill, James Forman, Miriam Makeba, the African Blood Brotherhood's (ABB) Richard B. Moore, Michael Thelwell, and

Jimmy Garrett. In 1969, in a protest against racism at Sir George Williams University and Montreal, students took over the school's computer center. Over ninety-seven people were arrested. These included Douglas, Barbados' Anne Cools, Cheddi Jagan Jr, and Bahamas' Coralee Hutchison.

Students were in the vanguard of Black Power. Partly in response to the Montreal incident, large-scale Black Power demonstrations erupted in Trinidad and Tobago in 1970. Led by Mackandal Dagga—a student leader at the UWI—the National Joint Action Committee (NJAC) mobilized over 10,000 people in protest of the neocolonial state and established a "people's parliament." Black Power's impact was visible in the songs and cultural messages produced by Calypso artists and participants in Carnival.

Trinidad and Tobago's Prime Minister Eric Williams implemented a State of Emergency to curtail the movement. When soldiers in the national army mutinied in support of Black Power, he requested US military aid to put it down. As the National Union of Freedom Fighters (NUFF) engaging the state's army in guerilla warfare, it lost members such as Beverly Jones.

Led by the Black Beret Cadre, Black Power in Bermuda aimed to dismantle British colonialism. Launched in 1969 by John Hilton Bassett Jr., it was affiliated with the US Black Panther Party. Through its *Black Beret* newsletter, liberation schools, survival programs, and low-scale urban guerilla warfare, the Berets clashed with the island's colonial officials. Beret associate Erskine "Buck" Burrows assassinated Bermuda's British Police Commissioner and Governor in 1972–73. In 1977, he was hung for the acts, prompting an island wide revolt.

In 1969, Pauulu Roosevelt Browne Kamarakafego organized the first International Black Power Conference in Bermuda, attracting activists such as Acklyn Lynch, CLR James, Queen Mother Moore, and Flo Kennedy. After plans were thwarted to launch a 1970 Black Power in Barbados, Kamarakafego and activists such as Baraka organized the first meeting of Congress of African Peoples (CAP). Held at Atlanta's Morris Brown College, CAP was a critical movement for Black Power internationally. It was attended by an "Aboriginal" delegation from Australia, which included Pat Kruger, Bruce McGuinness, and Bob Maza of the Aborigine's Advancement League (AAL).

Intending to participate in the Barbados conference, the AAL had invited Kamarakafego to Melbourne to advise them on their own Black Power Movement. While there, Kamarakafego propelled Black Power into the public imagination. While Australia's Black Panther Party was formed in Brisbane, Black Power also had a major impact in "Aboriginal" hubs such as Redfern. Activists such as Gary Foley, Bobbi Sykes, and Paul Coe created a number of survival programs in a fight against police brutality and for the reclamation of ancestral lands. Black Power also culminated in a 1972 Tent Embassy, when indigenous persons established in Canberra to demonstrate that they had never ceded their sovereignty to White Australia.

Black Power in Australia emerged out the radical traditions of Pasifika indigenous communities. Across the region, slavery, "black birding," genocide, political incarceration, sexual abuse, stolen generations, police brutality, whitening, violence, colonialism, and ecological devastation were household names as common as breadfruit, sandalwood, canoes, and cassava. Across Melanesia and Polynesia, Black and Brown communities battled these scourges through Black Power, decolonization, and women's movements.

Concerned with colonialism, segregation, and the exploitation of Papua New Guinea's mineral resources, in 1968 students at the University of Papua New Guinea (UPNG) formed the Nuigini Black Power Group (NBPG). The NBPG was a political manifestation of Melanesian nationalism, and consisted of an emerging core of nationalist poets, politicians, playwrights, and novelists who studied African literature. They studied Negritude's *Presence Africaine*, Soyinke, Achebe, and Senghor. They published Melanesian nationalist works through journals like *Kovave*. NBPG held demonstrations, lectures, and debates on Black Power, investigating how the ideas of Nkrumah, Carmichael, King, and Malcolm X could be applied to the Melanesian context. In 1971, it presented a UN delegation with a statement on decolonization and racism. NBPG forged relationships with other Pasifika activists, such as Cheryl Buchanon, Bobbi Sykes and Fiji's Claire Slatter, and Vanessa Griffen.

Black Power was as much cultural as it was political. The music of African American artists like Curtis Mayfield, Nina Simone, and Marvin Gaye all expressed Black Power themes. The poetry of Gil Scott Heron, the Last Poets, Nikki Giovanni, and Amiri Baraka are only a few visible examples of the powerful role that Black Arts played in the movement. Afro-Brazilians identified with positive black imagery in *Ebony* magazine, Soul Music, and Reggae. In 1974, influenced by Black Power and African liberation struggles the African-centered Carnaval group, Ilê Aiyê, emerged in Liberdade, Bahia. Ilê Aiyê was particularly drawn to African struggles against Portuguese imperialism, as in Amilcar Cabral and the PAIGC of Guinea-Bissau and Cabo Verde and Mozambique.

Pan-African spaces such as Algeria's Pan-African Cultural Festival (1969), Tanzania's Sixth Pan-African Congress and Nigeria's Second World Festival of Black and African Art and Culture (1977) demonstrated the connection between culture, Black Power, and Africa. In Africa, Black Power reflected a mass struggle against neocolonialism. Nigerian Afro-Beat artist Fela Kuti made several references to Black Power through songs like *Water No Get Enemy*. He became politicized after African American activist Sandra Smith introduced him to the world of Black Power through literature such as the *Autobiography of Malcolm X*.

In 1979, Reggae group Steel Pulse released *Tribute to the Martyrs*. The iconic album included recordings like *Uncle George* in memory of Black Panther field Marshall George Jackson. Jackson, author of *Soledad Brother* and *Blood in My Eye*, was murdered in California's San Quentin Prison in 1971. Jackson's tragic death speaks to violent assault launched on Black Power by Western governments across the world. In the United States, J. Edgar Hoover and the Federal Bureau of Investigation's (FBI's) Counter Intelligence Program (COINTELPRO) viciously targeted the Black Panthers. Several Panthers were murdered at the hands of local and state security forces, including Fred Hampton and Mark Clark of the Illinois chapter of the Panther Party. Leaders such as Eddie Marshall Conway, Safiya Bukhari, Geronimo Pratt, and Dhoruba Bin Wahad were wrongly incarcerated as political prisoners. Unlike those such as Mumia Abu Jamal, Jalil Muntaqim and Russell Maroon Shoats, they have since been released. Bukhari, who founded the Jericho Amnesty Movement in support of political prisoners, passed away in 2009. Others secured Wanted former political prisoners include Pete O'Neal, who lives in Tanzania with his wife Charlotte O'Neal. Julius Nyerere's Tanzania hosted a number of Panthers and southern African revolutionaries.

The British, US, and Canadian authorities sought to sabotage Bermuda's Black Power Conference. Black Power activists in London were incarcerated and harassed as well. Australia's government placed activists under tight surveillance and State Police attacked the Tent Embassy. In Vanuatu, French and British colonial officials deported Kamarakafego from the Pacific political condominium for spreading "Black Power doctrines." Activists were denied entry into a number of Caribbean islands. Kwame Ture was prevented entry in a number of countries across the world, including his land of birth, Trinidad. In 1977, South Africa's apartheid government murdered Steve Biko, leader of South Africa's Black Consciousness Movement.

In spite of this, Black Power forced several concessions from the state. The movement dovetailed into the formal creation of Black Studies as an academic field. This also occurred through the black student movement. Decades later, as black communities still face police brutality, mass incarceration and (neo) colonialism, the question of Black Power remains relevant. It has also been remembered through movies such as Sam Greenlee's *Spook who Sat by the Door* and Haile Gerima's *Bush Mama*. It is continued through the emancipatory journalism of media personalities such as Jared Ball (https://imixwhatilike.org). Its legacy lives through the political messages of Hip-Hop, R&B, Reggae, and spoken word artists such as Public Enemy (*Fear of a Black Planet*, 1990), Dead Prez (*Let's Get Free*, 2000), Kendrick Lamar, Queen Ifrica, Rebel Diaz, Janelle Monáe and Wondaland, Yasiin Bey, *Les Nubians*, Sizzla Kalonji, Jasiri X, Sunni Patterson, Youssoupha, Erykah Badu, Chronixx, and Tupac Shakur. Shakur's mother and stepfather, Afeni and Mutulu Shakur were Panthers. Mutulu Shakur remains a political prisoner.

The ideas of Black Power continue to be engaged by contemporary activists and artists. In an era of mass incarceration, social media, police brutality, the ending of Barack Obama's presidency, and mass deportations, the Black Lives Matter Movement is raising critical questions about power, race, class, and gender. The controversy sparked by Black Panther imagery in Beyonce's Formation video during the 2016 Super Bowl demonstrates the tremendous weight that the idea of Black Power still holds in the public memory and social consciousness of the white and black worlds. This is unsurprising, as Assata Shakur, former Black Panther and member of the Black Liberation Army remains in exile in Cuba. RIP Ali.

KEY TERMS

Black Power
Decolonization
Self-Determination
Black Arts
Liberation
Nationalism
Maroonage
Pan-Africanism
Neocolonialism

CHAPTER 11

THE LANGUAGE OF US

Msomi Moor

Many of Us are unware of the Black history of South America's Spanish-speaking countries. Once exposed to this five hundred year-long period, it soon becomes evident that throughout all of the Americas indeed, Afrikans have created their own unique ways to communicate their relationship between their environments and themselves. Out of those aggregated experiences have come innumerable musical genres, linguistic patterns, culinary ensembles, aesthetic representations, religious practices, spiritual traditions, among countless other profound cultural expressions. Together, these expressions constitute our language as Afrikan persons here in the Americas, they are the Language of Us.

The Language of Us construct examines some of those phenomena which comprise our everyday lives here in the western hemisphere and presents them in an understandable way to those whom are able to recognize them as their own. In other words, we use our own perspective—the amalgamated sum of our ancestral memory as Afrikan persons here in the Americas—to navigate the present, understand the past, and chart our course toward a readily sustainable future for our community.

In that light, this chapter will present three phenomena which highlight some of the unique Afrikan cultural dimensions of Black communities, principally found in Colombia and South America. The Afrikan Colombian community ranks as the third largest of all Black communities in the Americas, and it numbers anywhere from twelve million at its most conservative official estimate, to well over 25 million persons approaching its more accurate total.[1] Only the Black populations of Brazil and that of the United States are larger. The three different phenomena to be highlighted are the following: 1) *Palenquero*—the Black Spanish language of the Colombian Maroons, 2) *Castas de Nación*—Black Colombian surnames of continental Afrikan origin, and 3) *Cabildos de Nación*—Black Ethnic-based brotherhoods during the period of legal slavery in Colombia.

---

[1] See the following: El Mundo website article: Afros se preparan para reconocerse en Censo de 2016 http://www.elmundo.com/portal/noticias/poblacion/afros_se_preparan_para_reconocerse_en_censo_de_2016.php#.V4pEFvkrIy4 accessed 7/16/2016 *El Pais* Colombian newspaper online: El 10,62% de la población del país es afrocolombiana, dice el Dane accessed January 17, 2016, http://www.elpais.com.co/elpais/colombia/noticias/1062-poblacion-pais-afrocolombiana-dice-dane.

PALENQUERO

From the earliest years of the introduction of Afrikan captives to the Americas, Blacks have been subjected to the racialized viciousness of white supremacy and the vile European slave empires of the Americas. In that unholy context, thousands of differing ethnic groups from the Afrikan continent found themselves existing in close proximity as enslaved bondsman among the American sugarcane haciendas, coffee and cotton plantations, tobacco fields, lowland rice and indigo swamps, and in some areas, they found themselves on extensive cattle ranches and in precious metal mining districts. One such region of note was the Caribbean coastline of northern Colombia. As early as the mid-sixteenth century, Afrikan captives were already slaving in that Spanish-held territory which comprised part of New Granada. They had entered the region through the leading slave-port entrepôt of all of Spanish America: Cartagena de las Indias.[2]

Very soon after their introduction in the sixteenth century, Afrikan men and women from the Senegambia region, the Congo and Angola, as well as modern day Ghana were stealing themselves away to the remote mountains and isolated swamps of the interior portions of Cartagena Province. They all spoke their own languages and yet somehow forged a way to communicate among each other. Through a cohesion of mental acuity and spoken word, these ancestors fashioned their own unique languages—we recognize them by the following names in different countries: Ebonics, Gullah, and Geechee in the United States; Patwa in Jamaica; Kreyol in Haiti; Dialect in Barbados; Papiamento in Curacao—and Palenquero in Colombia. *Palenquero* takes its name from the term used to reference the villages or fortified settlements of maroons[3], *palenques* as the Spanish called them. This term is particularly used in the countries of Colombia, Panama, Mexico, and Ecuador. Founded by the renowned Afrocolombian maroon leader Benkos Bioho and christened as the town of *San Basilio de Palenque* or "St. Basil's Maroon Town" loosely translated into English, this town maintains perhaps the most successful spoken version of Afrikan languages mixed with Spanish and Portuguese lexicon from the sixteenth century captives brought the Spanish Americas. These self-liberated Afrikans from distinctly different parts of the Afrikan continent constituted the foundational layer of Afrikan ethnography for the Black Colombian community. The language they produced as stated previously, still in use today and as of late being taught in schools in of one of Colombia's oldest Black communities, is called *Palenquero*. This could be loosely translated to "runaway language" or "maroon language."

A number of texts have come out on this language, some from linguists and others from anthropologists. Mostly written in Spanish, they provide intriguing insight into some of the Bantu lexicon and grammar sequences used in this historic form of communication. Black Spanish is indeed one of the more intriguing components of Black South American history which is still to this day an acutely understudied form of expression. Today, one can hear *Palenquero*

---

[2] The former director of the Archivo General de la Nación (Colombia's largest archive) Jorge Palacios Preciado places the number of captive Afrikans having passed through the port of Cartagena at 1,100,000 beings in his work: Jorge Palacios Preciado. La Trata de Negros por Cartagena de Indias. Tunja, Colombia: Universidad Pedagógica y Tecnológica de Colombia, 1973.

[3] Maroon: from the Spanish *cimarrón*—runaway

spoken principally in four places, they are: 1) on Cartagena's tourist beaches, 2) in the village of Palenque de San Basilio itself (about fifty miles southwest of Cartagena, Colombia in the Department of Bolivar), 3) in the city of Barranquilla, travelling northeast along the Caribbean coastline from Cartagena, and 4) reaching as far as the migrations of *Palenqueros* have gone hundreds of miles to the east, strung throughout the Caribbean coastal cities of neighboring Venezuela. This communicative form of expression remains a human patrimony to our Afrikan heritage and valiantly constitutes a living example of the Language of Us.

Intriguingly, one of the linguistic dynamics of this language's Bantu morphology can be immediately identified in spoken *Palenquero*, and it is the word for "cows." Firstly and for the sake of contrast, the word "cow" in Castillian Spanish is *vaca*. That same word in *Palenquero* however is *ngombe*—pronounced (*in gohm bay*). Importantly, it is when both words are pluralized that the Afrikan background comes to light. The plural of *vaca* in Castillian Spanish is *vacas*. Here the pluralization of words comes as a suffix, with the additional letter of 's' being added to the *end* of the word. In Palenquero, however, as seen in the case of *ngombe*, the pluralization of this particular word comes at the *beginning*, and it becomes *mangombe*—"cows." Just like in Ki-Swahili, Lingala, Lunda, or any of the other Central Afrikan Bantu languages spoken today, the pluralization comes at the beginning, as a prefix or letter substitution in those languages as well. *Mtu—person, Watu—people*; *Kitabu—book, Vitabu—books*; *Ngombe—cow, Mangombe—cows*; these are all examples from the Ki-Swahili language demonstrating the use of prefixes or changes at the beginning of words to establish plurality. This is but one smoking gun demonstrating evidence of Afrikanity in the Palenquero language providing a readily accessible ancestral vestige for our generations to cherish. Several authors have written more profoundly into the Afrikanity of the *Palenquero* language and the cultural practices of the *Palenquero* people, including musical genres such as *Mapalé*, funerary rituals such as *Lumbalú*, and male age-grade affiliations such as the *Cuagros*.[4] Within these musical, spiritual, and social practices there is communicated a deeper understanding of our relationship as Afrikan persons to our environment, this knowledge constitutes a higher quality of intelligence communicable among Afrikan peoples. It is part of the Language of Us.

CASTAS DE NACIÓN—NATION CASTES

Already by the late fifteenth century, the Iberians—whom are constituted by the Portuguese and the Spanish—had developed a system of classification of Afrikan persons based on numerous ethnographic, geographic, and topographic associations relating to the Afrikan continent. When they began trafficking *en masse* the Afrikan branch of the human family across the ocean to the Americas, they at first did so by attempting to subdue villages and isolated hamlets via raids and the via use of the latest military advancements in firearms technology. Their tactics were unsuccessful, and were subsequently forced by local chiefdoms to pay rent on the coastlines where they were engaged in docking their ships. As a result, the Iberians began a

---

[4] Nina S. de Friedemann, *Ma ngombe: Guerreros y ganaderos en Palenque* (Bogotá, Colombia: C. Valencia Editores, 1979); Armin Schwegler, *"Chi ma nkongo": lengua y rito ancestrales en El Palenque de San Basilio (Colombia)* (Frankfurt am Main: Vervuert; Madrid: Iberoamericana), 1996.

centuries-long bartering system of firearms, European liquors, metals, local shell currencies (strings of cowry shell beads for example), and other goods in return for the dominant local chiefdom and kingdoms to acquire captives from neighboring villages and population centers for sale to the Americas. These activities eventually changed the cultural traditions of Afrikan kingdoms forever and started the downhill regression toward administrative corruption and complete lack of communal welfare that we see in the aftermath of today's neo-colonialized Afrikan societies.

Consequently, by the sixteenth century if not before, the Iberians were well aware of the different technologies that existed in certain regions of western, central, and eastern Afrika. They applied this knowledge to their advantage, and created a highly efficient, deliberate practice of firstly acquiring Afrikans from regions where traditional cultural technology fashioned them experts in specific skill sets such as: rice cultivation, the mining of precious metals, open-range ranching of large livestock herds, or the cultivation of cotton; then, in subsequent fashion they would sell those captives to the regions in the Americas where their expertise was in great demand and could optimize their chances for the best return on their investments. For example, the rice plantations of low-country South Carolina and Georgia in the United States were flooded with Afrikan captives from the rice growing regions of Sierra Leone, Guinea, and Liberia—places where the ethnic groups residing there for centuries had practiced rice cultivation and were notably skilled in the task. Similarly, the precious metal-stocked rivers of the State of Minas Gerais in Brazil saw its enslaved Afrikan population disproportionately comprised of captive Afrikans taken from west-central Ghana and eastern Ivory Coast. Ethnicities there, namely the Akan peoples, were renowned experts in the mining of alluvial gold, and were practitioners of cultural technologies which summarily encompassed the extraction of that precious metal.

Associating different ethnic groups from Afrika with a corresponding expertise or technological know-how, delivered the Iberians a veritable production and profitability database with which to maximize their profits in the trafficking of Afrikan humans to the American plantations, mines, and haciendas. Studying Iberian trafficking and auction block records, provides modern day researchers of Black history a road map of Afrikan regional and ethnic origins from which to start our inquiries toward the investigation of our family genealogies. As will be shown below, the names used to classify the Afrikan captives by their expertise and origin—end up becoming the surnames of the initial, foundational layer of the Afrikan-Colombian population during the sixteenth and seventeenth century; in remarkable fashion, they continue to be so today.

For purposes of clarity then, it should be reiterated that the regional, geographic, and topographic appellatives, which were given to captured Afrikans by their Iberian enslavers from the fifteenth through the nineteenth century, have stayed on as last names of multiple Black populations of South America, principally Colombia and Ecuador, while in Bolivia to a more limited degree. These appellatives were referred to as *castas de nación*, or nation castes. Today, one has just to look at a listing of high school or middle school student registries in certain Afrocolombian school districts and they will be shocked to see not Spanish or Portuguese surnames, but rather easily identifiable continental Afrikan names. Table 1 provides a listing of some of these startling *casta de nación* references with their region of affiliation.

TABLE 1: Afrocolombian Surnames and their Afrikan Provenances

Senegambia Region	Casamán, Casarán
Guinea Bissau	Bran, Viáfara, Balanta, Biohó
Sierra Leone and the Republic of Guinea	Zape, Cangá
Liberia	Cetré
Ghana and eastern Ivory Coast	Chalá, Mina, Guasá
Togo	Popó
Western Nigeria and Benin	Lucumí, Dájome, Arará
Southeast Nigeria	Carabalí, Briche, Ocoró
Congo, Angola, and Central Afrika	Angola, Anchico, Ambuila, Banguera, Cambindo, Congo, Cundumí, Loanda, Loango, Musorongo

Source: Msomi Moor. Captive African Ethnicities and Labor in Colonial Colombia, 1545 to 1750. Unpublished Doctoral diss., Howard University, Washington, DC 2008; Rogerio Velasquez, "Gentilicios Africanos de Occidente Colombiano," *Revista Colombiana de Folclor (Vol. III, Núm.7)* 1962, 109–48.

These modern day vestiges of Afrikanity are priceless. They permit us both to celebrate our survival with a dignified remnant of our actual regional provenance before having been subjected to the greatest crime against humanity, while at the same time providing us an impressively valuable starting point with which to trace our actual Afrikan ethnic provenance and reconnect to our ancestral lineages. Geographically speaking, these surnames are most prevalent within three southwestern Colombian Departments which are: 1) Valle del Cauca, 2) Cauca, and 3) Nariño. Certain municipalities located among these Departments are home to thousands of Afrocolombians with *casta de nación* surnames. Table 2 provides Department and municipal locations identifying some of the more recognizable concentrations of Afrocolombian *casta de nación* surnames.

In the most northern of the three Departments, Valle del Cauca, there are municipalities such as Cali and Buenaventura, the two largest, where these surnames can be found abundantly. In equal measure, some of the smaller municipalities of this Department such as Jamundi, Palmira, and Robles among others have sizable or more concentrated numbers of communities with *casta de nación* surnames among their Afrocolombian citizens. In the Department of Cauca, the Pacific littoral communities of Guapi and Timbiquí are replete with *casta* surnames, as are the interior valley communities of Puerto Tejada, Villa Rica, Guachené, Quinamayó, Suarez, Robles, Santander de Quilichao, and even the capital city of Popayán have notable populations of Afrocolombians with *casta de nación* last names. On the border with Ecuador comprising the southernmost of the southwestern Departments of Colombia lies the Department of Nariño. Within its borders akin to its two adjacent Departments to the north are a host of Pacific littoral and riverine communities of Afrocolombians, many of whom have identifiable *casta de nación* surnames. Namely, the largest Afrocolombian community of this Department, Tumaco, followed by Barbacoas and the much smaller villages of Iscuande, El Charco, and La Tola together with others, have intriguingly concentrated families with *casta* last names. Among them, as is the unique case of the municipality of Guachene in the Department of Cauca, the different families with the distinctly Afrikan *casta* names are known to each other and engage in certain behaviors toward one another. These types of "trope" associations stem directly from the days of slavery in the gold mines and haciendas of the region, where the European slavers would put certain Afrikan ethnic groups against one another, to assure disunity and the lack of

TABLE 2: Departments and Select Municipalities of Southwestern Colombia with Larger and More Concentrated Populations of Afrocolombians with *Casta de Nación*

Department	Municipality
Valle del Cauca	Cali (Departmental Capital)
	Buenaventura
	Jamundí
	Lopez de Micay
	Robles
	Palmira
Cauca	Puerto Tejada
	Villa Rica
	Santander de Quilichao
	Suárez
	Guachené
	Buenos Aires
	Popayán (Departmental Capital)
	Guapi
	Timbiquí
	Robles
Nariño	Tumaco
	Barbacoas
	Iscuande
	El Charco
	La Tola
	Mosquera
	Pasto (Departmental Capital)

Source: Msomi Moor. Captive African Ethnicities and Labor in Colonial Colombia, 1545 to 1750. Unpublished Doctoral diss., Howard University, Washington, DC 2008.

acquisition of racial consciousness among the enslaved. It is a clearly visible vestige of the evils of slavery here in the Americas and is screaming for attention and study from a right-minded cultural anthropologist or sociologist. As it stands then, for clarity's sake, Black Colombian families in isolated areas with *casta de nación* surnames still to this day may carry on hostilities toward one another stemming from plantation owner/slaver induced divide and conquer tactics used on the hacienda during the days of slavery. That unconscious, latent hostility that Blacks in the Americas feel toward one another, carried over from the days of psychological and physical enslavement on the plantation, is another part of the Language of Us.

CABILDOS DE NACIÓN: ETHNIC AFRIKAN MUTUAL-AID SOCIETIES AND BROTHERHOODS IN THE SPANISH AMERICAS

Dance is a highly communicative form of expression throughout all of the Spanish Americas. When duly performed to its customary purpose hailing from a distinct culture, it is in itself, a language. It transmits esoteric information to the knowledgeable observer which it communicates through somatic code. As such, we should look to recognize a great deal of cultural context and pregnant meaning contained within each particular type of dance. This is indeed the case in the Iberian

Americas, where many of the traditional dances performed among the Black populations speak to a deep knowledge of Afrikanity and ancestral heritage. These dances in their essence, provide clues to our specific regional origins on the Afrikan continent.[5] Iconically, many of the dances serve as vestigial remnants echoing visuals from the days of the historically formed *Cabildo de Nación* houses, the sixteenth and seventeenth century ethnic Afrikan mutual-aid societies and brotherhoods.

These Afrikan ethnic mutual-aid societies were formed during the earliest period of forced bondage in the Spanish controlled Americas, most notably in the larger urban centers or ports. The *Cabildos de Nación* as they were called, loosely translated as "Nation Councils or Nation Houses," were in operation since the initial introduction of Afrikan captives in the early sixteenth century there. They became a standard feature in the Spanish Americas as mutual-aid societies, one, for newly arrived Afrikan captives fresh off the slaving ship whom didn't speak any Spanish—termed *bozales* (wild) by the Europeans, and two, for enslaved Afrikans originating from like regions and ethnicities in Afrika whom happened to be slaving in the proximity of the surrounding area of these cities. These societies were not exclusively but significantly visibly in the following Spanish American locales during slavery: Cartagena, Colombia; Portobelo, Panama; Buenos Aires, Argentina; Montevideo, Uruguay; Lima, Peru, and Havana, Cuba.

In the *Cabildos*, ethnic traditions of untold numbers of Afrikan ethnic groups were conserved, celebrated, and passed on to noncontinental born Afrikan populations for a time. Elaborate dances replete with centuries-old knowledge and customary rituals were performed behind closed doors and away from European slavers and society. In Colombia, among the more potent survivals of this tradition of esoteric Afrikan expression are the readily observable syncopations of the Afrocolombian dance called *Mapalé*, as well as the centuries-old *danzas del Congo* (Congo dances) performed during the Barranquilla Carnaval. Both of these traditions can be witnessed today in the north-central Departments of Bolivar and Atlántico, located in Colombia's Caribbean region.

Comparably, Anglophone Caribbean Blacks of the islands of Carriacou and Tobago may be familiar with *Cabildo* dances by associating them with what are referred to as the "nation dances" performed in their respective countries. These dances also stem from a much older tradition of a direct continental Afrikan continuum, where dancers of these cultural expressions have competitions on whom can perform them most harmoniously and accurately, paying keen attention to distinctly identifiable and defining movements. Cheryl Ryman highlighted a similar vein of deep-seated, codified Afrikan cultural expression in her article from the 1980s specifying the particular ethnic-Afrikan origins of the Jonkonnu dances found in certain parishes on the island of Jamaica. As such, the "Nation Dances" as well as other dances of Afrikan origin in these three and other more culturally intact areas of the Anglophone Caribbean are British America's closest counterpart to the *Cabildo de Nación* ritualistic dances from the Spanish Americas of centuries past.

As a hallmark among the *Cabildos* or *Salas de Nación*, distinct drumming rhythms from different Afrikan regions championed to typify each one. In addition to that, they each spoke the exclusive language of their specific Afrikan origin and practiced many of the spiritual traditions of their homelands in the secure locations of their mutual-aid society houses within the confines of the Spanish cities of America. Surprisingly, there still exists a solemn space where vestiges of some of these cultural dimensions can be seen today. In Cuba, among the practitioners of the

---

[5] Cheryl Ryman, "Jonkonnu: A Neo-African Form Part II," *Jamaica Journal* 17, no.2 (1984): 50–58.

Santería way of life, there exists a drumming rhythm called *Lucumí*. This is the same *Lucumí* described above among the *castas de nación* appellatives being used as last names in Colombia and Ecuador. The Lucumí Cabildo is highly visible in the notary documentation of the colonial period and can be found readily throughout the rest of the Spanish Americas as well. Both this drumming rhythm in Cuba, and last name in Colombia, designate a reference to the Yoruba peoples of southwestern Nigeria as shown above in Table 1.

Fascinatingly, in continuation of this theme, there are accounts of *Cabildo* drumming battles from eyewitnesses living contemporary to the time of their existence. The Afrocolombian author Aquiles Escalante privileges us to one such occurrence in the streets of Cartagena during the seventeenth century. He alludes to the *Cabildo* of the Carabali Briche going against the *Cabildo* of the Carabali Viví (the Carabali Viví are known to be constituted by the Ibibio peoples of southeast Nigeria) in a drum battle of epic proportions; an interesting dynamic here is, that both of these groups would have spoken readily communicable languages to each other as they were from the same region in Nigeria (the proximity of the Niger Delta). In phenomenal fashion, this type of historic encounter constituted the weaponized expression of esoteric traditions of Afrikan culture being played out as a neighborhood rivalry via the medium of percussion instruments on the streets of Cartagena. Indeed a spectacular display of cultural technology that must have been. As a side note in today's times, the appellative Briche has survived on and continues as a last name of Afrocolombian families found deep in the interior Department of Cauca, predominantly in the municipality of Puerto Tejada.

Notoriously as history has it in Cartagena, the "Nation Houses" were broken up earlier than in most other Spanish American societies by the Jesuit Order. Friar Peter Claver it is said, used to snatch the drums of some of the percussionists during ceremonial performances if he didn't like what he was seeing or hearing.[6] It was feared at this time during the mid-seventeenth century, and with plenty of evidence to support said notion, that maroon activity was rising to dangerous levels in northern Colombia and that any organized semblance of Afrikanity among the massively concentrated Black population of Cartagena might turn into a veritable powder keg. Contemporaneously, the entirety of the sixteen-hundreds was ominously referred to as the "century of terror" by authors writing about this period in Colombian history due to the incessant and powerful maroon activity of that country's entire northern expanse.[7] Treaties had already been signed in one maroon town of that area, the now famous Palenque de San Basilio, and there had been other treaties signed along the same stretch of adjoining northern coastline both in Panama (King Bayano) and Venezuela (King Miguel) in the century prior. Certainly, ongoing research will enumerate a more extensive listing of the enigmatic *Cabildos de Nación* from around the entirety of the Spanish Americas, providing an even deeper treasure trove of ethnographic data for use in the researching of Afrikan genealogies in the Americas. To date, Fernando Ortiz and Jesus Guanche have elaborated profoundly on the *Cabildos* operating on the island of Cuba, during the notable *Cabildo* activity there from the seventeenth through the early nineteenth century. Table 3 provides a listing of some of the more well recognized *Cabildos* operating in Cartagena, Havana, or Buenos Aires at some time during the sixteenth to the nineteenth centuries.

---

[6] Ángel Valtierra, *Peter Claver: Saint of the Slaves* (Westminster, England: Newman Press, 1960), 206.

[7] Jaime Jaramillo Uribe, *Ensayos Sobre Historia Social Colombiana* (Bogotá, Colombia: Universidad Nacional de Colombia), 1968, 59–60; Nina S. de Friedemann, *Lengua y Sociedad en el Palenque de San Basilio* (Bogotá, Colombia: Instituto Caro y Cuervo), 1983, 38, 47.

TABLE 3: *Selected Cabildos de Nación* and their Continental Afrikan Regional Affiliations

Cabildo de Nación (Afrikan Nation Houses)	Continental Afrikan Regional Affiliation
Arará	Benin
Carabali Ibo	SE Nigeria
Carabali Briche	SE Nigeria
Carabali Viví	SE Nigeria (Ibibio peoples)
Congo	Congo River basin
Congo Luango	Congo River basin
Congo Mondongo	Congo River basin
Gangá	Republic of Guinea
Lucumí	SW Nigeria (Yoruba peoples)
Mandinga	Upper Guinea Mande speakers
Mina Achanti	Ghana (Ashanti peoples)
Mina Fanti	Ghana (Fanti peoples)
Mina Guaguí	Ghana (Wenchi peoples)

Source: Fernando Ortíz. Los Negros Esclavos. La Habana: Editorial de Ciencias Sociales, 1975; Matt D. Childs, "Pathways to African Ethnicity in the Americas: African National Associations in Cuba During Slavery" in Sources and Methods in African History: Spoken, Written, Unearthed. Rochester, NY: Rochester University Press, 2003; Aquiles Escalante. El Negro en Colombia. Bogotá: Universidad Nacional de Colombia, Facultad de Sociología, 1964; Gonzalo Aguirre Beltrán. Obra Antropológica II: La Población Negra de México: Estudio Etnohistórico. México, D.F.: Fondo de Cultura Económica, 1989.

Finally, in the southern cone countries and southern Andean countries as recently as a century and a half ago in majority Black cities (at the time) like Buenos Aires, Argentina, and cities with potent Afrikan traditional practices such as Lima and Callao in Peru, one could find ceremonies for the crowning of kings and queens among the different "Nation Houses" as a recognizably vibrant mainstay during the year's annual *Carnaval* activities. In continuity today, fast forward fifteen decades to the Black barrios of Montevideo, Uruguay, these practices can still be seen and heard in all their splendor during the *Carnaval* season there, recognizable among the activities carried out by what are referred to as the *Candombes* and *Llamadas*—direct remnants of the *Salas de Nación* activities operating in Montevideo from the late eighteenth century; they were Uruguay's version of the *Cabildos de Nación*.

CONCLUSION

The burden is on Us as Afrikan persons to study ourselves wherever we may be found to highlight the quality of culture which we possess as a collective. We have to be able to recognize ourselves in the different languages of the places to which we were taken over the last fourteen-hundred years. In doing so, we will obtain a more complete understanding of both the contributions which our people have made to the nations in which we are now housed, and in addition, reconstitute our former systems of knowledge and nurturing which produced the timelessly powerful cultures from which we originate. Having acquired a more holistic understanding of whom we were, coupled with an accurate understanding of whom we have been forced to become, will allow us to right our mindset as a people and move forward into future via a reconstructed, empowered expression of self. That is part of the raison d'etre of the Language of Us, to present ourselves to ourselves, so that we may see how we have been damaged, and that through the course of evolving via the upcoming generations, we might heal.

This is a vital undertaking; it is a reclamation of spiritual territory and space. If left for others to qualify and quantify our value and contributions as a people, we are ultimately doomed to be written out of history, and slated for a status of eternal inferiority. Along the way, other consequences shall arise such as having our history misrepresented as something that it was not, or as something for which credit is given to an entirely different group of people. In the case of the former, the case of those Afrocolombians with the *casta de nación* last name of *Popó* is a clear example. The *Popó casta* is associated with peoples in and around the coastline of modern-day southern Togo. Centuries ago, during the Iberian trafficking of Afrikans to the Spanish Americas, this appellative was recorded in trafficking manuscripts to designate persons taken from that area, including their distinctive ethnic marks of a bow and arrow near the area of their temples.[8] That is to say, this last name is a vividly clear reference of ancestral heritage, denoting specific continental Afrikan origin from an identifiably documented area. Fast forward to the twenty-first century, and Black Colombians with that last name are a under constant ridicule and subject to continual humiliation. Non-Black Colombians associate their last name, vulgarly and crassly with their word for fecal material, and are shamelessly quick to point that out in public settings. Our job is to create a platform for the elevation of our collective consciousness via providing competent, pertinent, timely, and empowering information revealing more and more of the totality of our contributions to global civilization, via the same ancestral optic which has been muted for the last fourteen centuries. We are engaged in the task of opening up our present community's mind eye, and are putting on future generations on watch, that it might never be closed again.

Having had the opportunity to be a student in Dr. Joseph E. Harris' class was a timeless experience which provided the security of a psychologically nurturing space for Afrikans to study ourselves, his orientation polished those whom had the opportunity to access his brilliance a clear and coherent charge to serve as edifiers in our community. This author takes that charge as a spiritual responsibility regarding Afrikan communities worldwide, and I can think of no more noble a task to carry out during this lifetime.

KEY TERMS

Afrocolombian	Iberian
Bantu	Maroon
Cabildos de Nación	Palenque
castas de nación	Palenquero
Candombes	Sala de Nación
cimarrón	Santería

---

[8] Valtierra, 106

CHAPTER 12

BLACKNESS IN THE SPANISH CARIBBEAN

Pedro R. Rivera

The Spanish Caribbean comprises Cuba, Puerto Rico, and the Dominican Republic, a nation which shares the island of Hispaniola with the Republic of Haiti. Even without Jamaica, an island of the British Caribbean, these Spanish islands (and including Haiti) represent the bulk of the Caribbean story. In other words, their histories, cultures, and societies are representative of the complexities of a region shaped in resistance and racial mixtures, for it was here where colonial settlement by Europeans first took place in 1492 and where an insurrection by African descendants in the 1790s shattered colonialism.

Cuba is the largest island in the Caribbean basin. But Hispaniola, which is second in size, is the most populous with twenty million people. Hispaniola sits somewhere in the center of a Caribbean crescent where Cuba and Puerto Rico (the smallest of the three) are positioned at its ends. The near linear sequence of these islands may help explain how Spanish ships came across them by maritime intuition or by following the winds. The Spanish settled them and changed their social order with industries that rested on the labor of Africans.

After wars with the natives and the end of hostilities, the three territories were repopulated with Europeans and Africans. Out of unequal economic and social relations, blacks and whites would come to form the racial basis of the general phenotypes one may find at present in these islands. Coffee, mahogany, cinnamon, copper, bronze, tobacco, chocolate, and sugar played roles at various stages in these economies. These products persisted through slavery and freedom, and they often were signifying terms that came to be used to refer to the colors of the people that emerged through racial mixture.

The Spanish Caribbean, and if one is to include Haiti, is a collage that pieces together a mulatto identity and demography. In Cuba today, people of African descent are about 35 percent (in a population of eleven million). In Puerto Rico, the numbers range from 6 to 20 percent (in a population of 3.6 million). In the Dominican Republic, the story is more pronounced; blacks and mulattos compose as much as 85 percent (in a population of 10.2 million), while in Haiti blacks are 95 percent (in a population of 9.8 million).

The numbers aforementioned tell the story. Blackness is both common and unique in each territory. Conversely, African cultural influences are widespread and their degrees vary according to time and context. Anachronistic language, such as "bozal," "ladino," and "creole" can help sketch history and the modern picture of race in the Spanish Caribbean, taking into account that Africans, who came to the region from many ethnic groups, such as Congo, Yoruba, and Carabalí, did not always identify themselves in those terms.

BOZALES, LADINOS, AND CREOLES

"Bozal" is a term used by the Spanish during colonialism to speak of Africans born in Africa and brought directly to the Americas. The so-called "bozales" spoke their original languages, brought their own customs and ancestral traditions, and they also had fresh memories of the homelands from which they were taken forcefully. "Ladinos" was a term used by the Spanish to refer to blacks or Africans who had gone through some level of acculturation in the Iberian Peninsula (Spain and Portugal). "Ladinos" came to the New World (often not as enslaved people) speaking European languages and having gained exposure of Spanish culture. "Creoles" were blacks born in American territories; the term applies also to Europeans or mixed people born in the New World. Both "ladinos" and "creoles" often exhibited generational carryovers from the cultures of their forebears.

"Ladinos" were among the first black people to arrive in the Americas. Among the three groups, they had arguably the smallest impact. There are records and stories of "ladinos," such as that of Micaela, a black woman in Santo Domingo who reportedly became responsible for creating in 1501, a medical dispensary. Besides a contribution in the realms of medicine, historian Celsa Albert Batista interprets her initiative as a challenge to the colonial discourse, helping lay the roots for a culture of human rights.

"Ladinos" were a relative minority among the communities of blacks forming in the Americas. Sometimes they did not consider themselves part of the enslaved people or identified with their plight. Take the complex example of Esteban de Dorantes (also known as "Estebanico" and other names). He was born in Africa, sold into slavery in Spain, and is reported later to accompany or join the ranks of the Spanish conquistadors and slavers who traveled through the Spanish Caribbean, Mexico, Florida, and beyond. His case is not unique, although "ladino" conquistadors are probably under reported.

During the first one hundred years of colonization, "ladinos" were succeeded in numbers by Africans who were captured and transported directly from the continent of Africa ("bozales"). They were brought to work as slaves in short-lived sugar industries in Santo Domingo, Cuba, and Puerto Rico. By the 1550s, their presence in the population of these islands was considerable. In response to slavery, some ran away and established maroon communities, where these fugitives replicated their African customs to the extent that their memory, distance, and diversity of cultural and social components allowed.

These maroon communities have been described by specialists as taking the form of military encampments. African maroons had to exercise vigilance to guard against colonial incursions. As such, they became informed on the ways of colonial centers over time. Accounts by priests who visited some communities reported adoptions of language and religion.[1] Adoptions happened also in the colonial towns as captives participated in *cofradías* or *cabildos* where they socialized and practiced

---

[1] See the reference to Archbishop Portillo to Los Naranjos Palenque (a maroon settlement) in Andujar (2012).

Christianity or their traditions under Spanish supervision.[2] Colonial culture was influenced by African fraternities as they became more syncretic in practice. Today, the *solar de los Arará* in Cuba is seen as a landmark of one such society organized in 1691; it was not the first or only one, however.

From 1600 to 1800 came the rise of the black "creoles." Sugar production went down to subsistence levels and while importation of Africans from the old continent took place, population increase also came along natural reproduction. The Spanish Caribbean islands were caldrons of "creolization," where locally born blacks will have a presence. Documents during these centuries show black people with names associated with African groups and regions, some of which were passed from Africans to "creoles."

In addition to the assimilation of European culture by "creoles," these blacks showed also African retentions as they moved into the national period. Some "creoles" did not make use of the label and rather became radical in upholding the African side of their heritage and as they negotiated their identities as citizens of the nation. As the Gullah Geechee people in the coastal regions of present day Georgia (USA), there are communities of living people in the Spanish Caribbean that have become symbols of endurance. One example is Villa Mella, home in the Dominican Republic to the Brotherhood of the Holy Spirit of the Congos, a *cofradia* of Afro-Dominicans who continue to practice ancient rituals and traditions of culture and spirituality.[3] The Congos of Villa Mella in Santo Domingo was declared by UNESCO a patrimony of humanity.

THE HAITIAN REVOLUTION: RECONFIGURATION OF THE SPANISH CARIBBEAN

By 1790, the population in Cuba was about 250,000, Puerto Rico 150,000, and Santo Domingo around 125,000.[4] Despite the more considerable proportion of whites in Puerto Rico, black "creoles" and/or "colored" people in the Spanish Caribbean islands were the likely majority for the combined populations. With the Haitian Revolution, the black ethno-racial makeup of each territory will change in as far as it created the conditions that altered the course in societies that until then were shaped largely by black "creolization."

The background story is well known. The frontiers of the Spanish Caribbean were breached by French pirates in 1697. The colony of Saint Domingue was established in the western parts of Hispaniola with large numbers of blacks. Within a century, the French were operating a sugar industry with 500,000 captives, many imported directly from Africa. This means that by 1790, Hispaniola was effectively divided into two European colonies (Santo Domingo in the east, Saint Domingue in the west), populated largely with African descendants of different acculturations. The peoples and cultures often mixed.

The uprising of the enslaved people in Saint Domingue brought the collapse of the French sugar industry and the emergence of the Black Republic of Haiti, governed by freed people.

---

[2] For a discussion on *cabildos de nacion* in Cuba, see Lovejoy (2012).
[3] Persinal (2002).
[4] For the Cuban population, see Benitez-Rojo (1992) and Murray (1971), printed in Great Britain p. 136; For Santo Domingo, see Selwyn H. H. Carrington's book manuscript and Saez (1997); for Puerto Rico, see Curtis and Scarano (2011).

The implications were critical for the region. Haiti no longer supplied the sugar market. At this, the Spanish in Cuba and Puerto Rico picked up on sugar making; those in Santo Domingo did not. This was a defining moment. Sugar production brought racial consequences as it required slavery and reintroductions of Africans as captives. As a result of importation, Cuban society began to look like old Saint Domingue. In time, the Dominican Republic took after the new Haiti. Puerto Rico will follow the Cuban model.

From 1790 to 1865, Cuba and Puerto Rico imported a combined figure of about 750,000 captives, a large number of who were "bozales." Again, this rise of slavery did not happen in Santo Domingo although the colony had a change of status quo; given its proximity to the former Saint Domingue, Santo Domingo was hit by the revolutionary war and lost approximately half or two thirds of its population. This was a dramatic change. Its society and population will be reconstituted along natural reproduction and migrations of other "creoles" that were born in or already were familiar with the region.

CUBA AND PUERTO RICO

Meanwhile, this new entry of Africans to Puerto Rico, and in Cuba more particularly, led to the reinforcement of slavery and racial codes. As it was always the case, Africans tried to preserve their dignity in the face of slavery, strengthening a discourse on racial consciousness that was conditioned by the same dehumanizing circumstances that denied them freedom and social equality. This was a peculiar reversal, because slavery is strengthened in Cuba at a time when it was fading out in the region as a labor system.

The numbers of enslaved blacks in Cuba during the first half of the nineteenth century were such that they are comparable to the numbers in Jamaica and former Saint Domingue. The cultural consequences are predictable. Some analysts of this period argue that Afro-Cubans may have developed an African-Spanish language in the nineteenth century as structured as is Haitian Creole or Jamaican English.[5] The language was lost increasingly with the next generations of speakers. But contributions in religion and music remained vibrant as elements of the national culture, the roots of which are reshaped in the 1800s.

African influences in Cuba and Puerto Rico are easy to identify today perhaps because of their more recent period of reintroduction. This late period of entry had an impact on the collective narratives. For example, Cuba and Puerto Rico have more recent memories with slavery and exclusion whereas in the Dominican Republic the memory is in the more distant past. The Dominican Republic emerged in the twentieth century as a highly mixed society with Haitians and other West Indians partaking in its formation.

THE DOMINICAN REPUBLIC AND HAITI

Santo Domingo was the Spanish territory most affected by the Haitian Revolution. In the 1790s, the population was 125,000.[6] By 1809, the population declined to about 70,000. The

---

[5] See the reference and commentary by Lipski (2001).
[6] The numbers vary between 125,000 and 180,000. Pons (1998); See Saez (1997).

colony was marooned as it was caught in the conflicts of Haiti and France; deaths and emigration occurred as Spain ceded the colony to France by treaty. The isolation of Santo Domingo continued as the Spanish crown was refocused in Puerto Rico and Cuba. As the community was left to fend for itself, the dwellers looked to Haiti as new partners.

Before this, there were indications that slavery was dying a natural death. But the 15,000 enslaved people had different opinions. As the uprising in Saint Domingue took its course, blacks in Santo Domingo also made a statement. Revolts were launched in 1796 and in 1812.[7] The conspiracies failed, but they were flashpoints of a rising mood to join with Haiti. Hence in 1822, this happens; the island is unified.

The Dominican Republic gained independence from Haiti in 1844, and its constitution and land tenure system would bear the marks of Haitian influences. Slavery was abolished. Haitian residents stayed in the Spanish side and became Dominicans. The state embarked on modernization absorbing influences from the region.

By the 1880s, a sugar industry was established with investors from Cuba, Puerto Rico and the United States. Rather than slavery or African importation, sugar production started with workers from the Lesser Antilles. In 1916, this labor force was supplanted with new Haitian immigrants; these "creoles" became contributors to the local black culture. Changes in the language, religion, music, visual arts, and the culinary arts are registered along with the participation of Haitians and other Caribbean peoples.

AFRICAN INFLUENCES AND THEIR PERIODS

Taking cue from the preceding context, the Spanish Caribbean story is marked with the imprint of the African journey. Africans changed during colonialism, transforming also the colonizers. Together, they forged the nations of the Spanish Caribbean. Their legacies or formation can be catalogued along historical periods. An overview can be attempted although generalizations can never be perfect. But a few things can be observed.

Prior to the rise of the nation state as a modern entity in the nineteenth century, African religions experienced a high period. From 1500 to 1800, African religions in their more unadulterated forms had a different purpose or appeal for those who practiced them; they were essential vehicles of identity during a time of exclusion. In Cuba, as stated, *cabildos de nacion* were important religious societies organized along African ethnicities. The *cabildos* declined during the nineteenth century due partly to attempts by officials to outlaw some African practices, to rising discourses on integration and nation building, and partly to increasing attacks on slavery as an institution and even fears of uprising. In Haiti, as happened in Cuba, appeals were made by leaders of the revolution, such as Toussaint L'Overture for people to give up Voodoo. This did not work, of course.

Attempts at erasure did not translate into elimination. Africans' religions and their influences continued in other forms. Haiti and the Spanish Antilles are officially Catholic today, but there is little disagreement on African influences persisting in songs, worship, and the dual identities of Catholic saints. *Santeria* in Cuba and Puerto Rico, *Voodoo* in Haiti and *Palos* in the Dominican Republic are alternatives ways of worship for the casual consultant; these also are

---

[7] Franco (2003).

established religions fulfilling the spiritual needs of many people. In most instances, these religions combine African and Spanish traditions; some use African languages as liturgy, as in the case of Santeria, to call on the deities.

No African language is widely spoken in the region. However, African words and idioms are part of what some specialists have called the "Africanization" of the Spanish language in the region. The Royal Academy of the Spanish Language usually reports how Cuba, the Dominican Republic and Puerto Rico contribute with dozens of new words to the Spanish language. In similar ways, Africans expanded the vocabulary of Caribbean Spanish. There are studies listing African words, or "Africanisms" in the general lexicon. Fernando Ortiz' *Glosario de afronegrismos* and Carlos Esteban Deive's "Glosario de Afronegrismos en la Toponimia y Español hablado en Santo Domingo" are examples.

The more fundamental question remains. How did African structures of language or speech contribute to the accent of Caribbean Spanish? Cubans use a different pace and emphasis from Dominicans whose speech differ from Puerto Ricans and all of whom together speak Spanish differently from people in Spain and the rest of Latin America. For answers on this question, the nineteenth century represents a golden period for academic inquiries, judging by the studies.[8] The documentation on black Spanish seems to be lacking prior to 1800 and some of the analysts cannot determine how Africanized Spanish emerges from colonialism. But with the documents produced on the nineteenth century, experts hint at the African influences on structure even when they do not all agree.

Perhaps the debate on verbal communication will never reach the consensus that seems to exist on the African dominance of the language of sound. While the debate on Spanish language goes on, there is little doubt that Africans conquered the form of communication that intertwines body and soul in the Antilles—music, of course. Their intervention in this direction gives the distinct flavor that puts the region in a world stage.

Music is the most mainstream vehicle of African influences, and the twentieth century marks an explosion. From very early, the omnipresence of African sounds disquieted the Spaniards to the extent that they tried to ban religions and the drum. But if religions went into decline, music went on the rise. In 1980, Nicolas Guillen's *Motivos de son* is seen in line with the woks that channel the 1580 story of black sisters Teodora and Micaela Gines who are presumed to have laid some of the seeds that flourished into Cuban music.

The sisters' role in Cuba music is discussed by Alejo Carpentier in the 1940s who also coined the term "transculturation" to mean the amalgamation of elements.[9] However, the Gines musical ingenuity is estimated by mostly left to the imagination as there are no actual record of the sounds they produced. Africans, no doubt, passed music through oral traditions, but these channels of transmission were disrupted (not fully destroyed) in the Caribbean under slavery. The fact is that colonial black music can hardly be reproduced today. The lack of musical transcriptions easily prevents due analysis and appreciation. For the historian, African innovation becomes more visible, tangible, and much more estimable as it is captured in the musical staff and the Cuban *contradanza* of the 1800s.

---

[8] For a discussion about African influences on the Spanish language spoken in the Caribbean see the studies by Lipski (1994); and see Footnote 5.

[9] Carpentier's (2002) seminal study has been reproduced and translated into English.

Musicologists discovered in this period the *cinquillo*, a musical structure and underlying basis of Cuban music. The *cinquillo* reveals African syncopation as an underlying basis.[10] The *contradanza* was popular in the 1800s but the twentieth century represents a sort of renaissance. Prior to the phonograph and the recording industry, some genres such as *son montuno* in Cuba were seen as the music of the lower classes until the recording industry proved their local and international acclaim. This is similarly the story of *merengue*, the music of the Dominican Republic. Before it became a national symbol, *merengue* was rejected in the late 1800s by members of the elite for its African elements, and then accepted in the 1920s as it was considered as an appropriate representation of Dominican culture. When this happened, the official narratives tried to deny the roots.

Puerto Rico has an equally undeniable history of Africans playing a role in the creation of its musical identity, which includes *bomba* and *plena*, and other genres. From singers Ismael Rivera to Tego Calderon, one may find embodiments of African traditions and innovations in shaping the past and future of music in the island. Rivera was an icon of *son* and *salsa* (both African-derived rhythms) whose style and phraseology were unmistakable, and Calderon is a *regetonero* of the new age who channels Rivera and embraces his Lucumí and Carabalí heritage in hit songs like "Salte del Medio." The book of late scholar Juan Flores *From Bomba to Hip-Hop* offers a glimpse of this evolution.

CONCLUSION

In 1983, the Dominican former president, Joaquin Balaguer stated in one his books that the Dominican Republic was "The most Spanish colony in the Americas."[11] In making such unbelievable pronouncement, Balaguer did not seem to deny the black presence in society, only to refute the possibility of any African contributions to the Dominican soul.

Balaguer was not a historian but a statesman who manipulated information for political ends. This is indicative of a larger problem in the region. In Cuba, discrimination persists along strides in equality, while in Puerto Rico black people seem underreported in the census data as a high percentage of people are listed as white or non-African. The fact is that concept of "racial purity" collapsed very early in the Spanish Caribbean. The Spanish even had to manage a *casta* system in order to catalogue mixed people according to degrees of color and heritage in order to arraign a fleeting concept of white superiority.

The relations among people of diverse ethnicities and skin colors engendered also what Carpentier called transculturation (or syncretism). In other words, Colonialism transitioned into independence absorbing a multiplicity of social and cultural elements that became vital in the cast of new identities, and after a revolution in Haiti, Africans and their descendants continued to shape the communities that emerged to present times. It is a history whose effects cannot be denied: blackness is part of the body and ethos that define the persons of the Spanish Caribbean.

---

[10] Ortiz (2001).
[11] Balaguer (1985).

KEY TERMS

Bozal
Creole
Cabildo
Cofradía
Cinquillo
Ladino
Maroon
Saint Domingue
Santo Domingo
Transculturation

PART IV

TRANSNATIONALISM AND THE TIES THAT BIND

AFRICAN AMERICAN EXCEPTIONALISM AND THE POLITICS OF TRANSNATIONAL RESISTANCE: EARLY ENCOUNTERS BETWEEN AFRICAN AMERICANS AND SOUTH AFRICANS

Charles D. Johnson

INTRODUCTION

Beginning in the nineteenth century, encounters between African Americans and black South Africans, hereafter South Africans, led to a cross fertilization of protest sentiment that would later inform their combined resistance to racial oppression occurring in South Africa. Thus, as small numbers of African Americans began to travel to South Africa, the matrix of social encounters between African Americans and black South Africans gave birth to politics of resistance that were inherently transnational. Most of these blacks came to South Africa from the United States, the Caribbean, and Latin America as sailors. During the twentieth century, interactions between Africans in the Diaspora and South Africans fostered the emergence of politicized opposition that evolved unevenly but in general accord with the ever changing political climate in South Africa, in the United States, and globally. Thus, we can trace the antecedents of the modern antiapartheid movement to the political ideas that emerge as a consequence of the social contact between South African and Diaspora blacks during the late nineteenth and early twentieth centuries. Of those blacks that crossed the Atlantic with whom South Africans had contact, African Americans had the greatest influence on them.[1]

CREATING A POLITICS OF TRANSNATIONAL RESISTANCE

In the United States and in South Africa, transnational contact between African Americans and South Africans took place in the long shadow of systemic white supremacy. White supremacy is a global system of thought, belief, and action that assumes the inherent superiority of people who have historically defined themselves as white or persons of European ancestry. Because white supremacy is an ideology, it impacts the thinking of all people regardless of color. Which means, for example, that a person of African descent or Asian descent can harbor white supremacist beliefs and often do. Today, we understand that the idea of white supremacy is a myth because

---

[1] A good examination of how social advancements and transformations impacted the South African liberation struggle can be found here, see Audie Klotz, "Norms Reconstituting Interests: Global Racial Equality and U.S. Sanctions Against South Africa," *International Organization* 49, no. 3 (Summer, 1995): 451–78.

modern science, especially in the field of genetics, has shown that no group of human beings is inherently superior to any other group and that in fact genetically speaking human beings regardless of their physical characteristics are virtually twins. Yet, the impact of white supremacy, which birthed modern racism, is real and has come to have a tremendous influence on shaping the contemporary world including the experiences of South Africans and African Americans.

Interestingly enough, white supremacy was not the sole or even the primary cause of the Atlantic Slave Trade or in the European colonization of the Americas, Asia, and Africa. The Atlantic Slave Trade and colonization were first and foremost European economic systems and white supremacy became a means for Europeans to rationalize economic schemes that brutally exploited people of color for their labor and the resources of their land. Slavery and colonization raised many vexing moral questions in Europe about the right of Europeans to dominate non-European peoples. Yet, once in motion, white supremacy acting as a justification lubricated the economic engine of slavery and colonialism, but it was the profit motive that served as the fuel that drove the system. By creating the idea of "race" as a natural phenomenon and then elevating whites or people of European ancestry to a privileged position among the people or "races" of the world, European intellectuals were able to fashion the idea of the natural entitlement of global white hegemony or white supremacy. Logically, then the African Diaspora politics of transnational resistance that emerged in the nineteenth and twentieth centuries was a response to these hegemonic forces emanating from the United States andEurope, especially those countries that were participants in the Atlantic Slave Trade and later European colonization, such as Great Britain, France, Spain, Portugal, and the Netherlands (Dutch).

African Americans sowed many of the seeds of transnational protest. George Shepperson traced the emergence of African nationalism to what he called a Commerce of Ideas. A Commerce of Ideas refers to the exchange of information that took place between Africans and people of African descent when they came into contact with one another either in Africa or the Americas. African nationalism is the idea that African peoples should control their own nations and the resources of the nation including their labor. It developed in response to European imperialism. Beginning in the late nineteenth and throughout the twentieth century, this Commerce spanned the Atlantic connecting blacks in Africa, the West Indies, and the Americas: North, South, and Central.[2] South Africans and African Americans were a part of this larger transatlantic system and out of these contacts, a politics of resistance emerged as each group shared their experiences living under similar forms of racially based economic exploitation. Thus, African Americans came to identify with the courageous struggle of the South African people for freedom and democracy because it reminded them of their own struggle for civil rights.[3]

---

[2] George Shepperson, "Notes on Negro American Influences on the Emergence of African Nationalism," *Journal of African History* 1, no. 2 (1960): 299.

[3] With the understanding that the largest populations of people of African descent in the Americas live in South America, African Americans herein refers to blacks in the United States. I have chosen to use the less cumbersome South Africans when referring to Africans in South Africa.

Scholars have debated the extent to which historically Africans and African Americans identify and associate with one another.[4] Some, such as Harold Isaacs for example, have argued that in the period from 1865 to 1935 or from emancipation to the Italian invasion of Ethiopia, African Americans were not interested in the affairs of Africans and that Africans were not interested in the affairs of African Americans.[5] There is plenty of evidence to support Isaacs' view, but there is considerable evidence to support the opposing view. Horace Mann Bond, for example, challenged Isaacs and published research showing amicable relations between Africans and African Americans during the nineteenth and the twentieth centuries. More recently, writers such as Penny Von Eschen, Kevin Gaines, and Francis Njubi Nesbitt have given support to the argument Bond made in the 1960s that Africans and African Americans did identify with one another. So, who is correct? In a manner of speaking both Isaacs and Bond are correct because there is evidence supporting both sides of the argument. For our purposes, what is important to understand is that European systems of coerced labor and colonization exacerbated the social distance between African peoples on either side of the Atlantic and contact between African peoples helped to heal misunderstanding and to close social distance. It is the case that in spite of the centrifugal influence of slavery and colonialism on relations between Africans and African descendants, their ties remained intimate and very strong throughout the twentieth century, such was the case with African Americans and South Africans.[6]

Several of the African National Congress's (ANC) original members studied in the United States and some later belonged to the African Methodist Episcopal Church (AMEC) in South Africa. Africans in South Africa established the ANC in 1912. It was the first African protest organization in South Africa and was originally known as the South African Native National Congress. In 1923, the name was changed from South African to African to reflect the wider concern of its early leaders for persons of African descent outside of South Africa, especially those struggling against different forms of colonial and racial oppression. Several of the ANC's founding members had social ties to African Americans. These connections multiplied and grew stronger throughout the twentieth century. As African Americans visited and settled in South Africa, South African leaders combined their ideas about political resistance and education with those of the African Americans with whom they came into contact to help to give shape to the politics of transnational resistance.[7]

---

[4] For a point of view that sees relations between Africans and African Americans as contentious, see Harold Isaacs' "Back to Africa," New Yorker, May 13, 1961. Isaac discusses this in his correspondence with James Davis, in Harold Isaacs, box 1, folder 20, American Society of African Culture Collection, Moorland Spingarn Research Center, Howard University, Washington, DC. For a perspective that sees those relations as congenial Horace Mann Bond, "Howe and Isaacs in the Bush: The Ram in the Thicket," The Negro History Bulletin" in Africans and American Negroes, Box 19, American Society of African Culture Collection, Moorland Spingarn Research Center, Howard University, Washington, DC., see Adelaide Cromwell Hill and Martin Kilson, Apropos Africa: Sentiments of Negro American Leaders on Africa from the 1800s to the 1950s (London: Cass, 1969).

[5] Yekutiel Gershoni, Africans on African-Americans: The Creation and Uses of an African-American Myth (New York: New York University Press, 1997), 1.

[6] Bernard Magubane, The Ties that Bind: African-American Consciousness of Africa (Trenton, NJ: Africa World Press, 1987), 207. Magubane dedicates a chapter to the discussion of African American involvement in the South African liberation struggle.

[7] For a South African perspective on the relationship between African Americans and South Africans, see Magubane, The Ties that Bind. He dedicates a chapter to African American interest in and efforts in belief of the South African freedom struggle. See The Ties that Bind, 211–12.

AFRICAN AMERICAN EXECEPTIONALISM

South Africans viewed African Americans as exceptional, a people worthy of being emulated, and this mutual attraction drew the groups into intimate overlapping circles of social relations based on their shared African ancestry, religion, educational aspirations, and protest against racial oppression. African American Exceptionalism was the idea that blacks born and raised in the United States were modern—more refined, sophisticated, and advanced than Africans or their cousins living in other parts of the African Diaspora. African Americans were assumed to be succeeding in the white man's world better than other people of African descent. This was of course partly a myth, an illusion African Americans themselves fabricated and disseminated. Yet, a myth acted out becomes real, and certainly there were accomplished African Americans, such as the dynamic AME Church Bishop Henry McNeil Turner and the "Wizard of Tuskegee," Booker T. Washington with whom South Africans were familiar. Turner was perhaps the first black Bishop that South Africans meet in person. He visited South Africa in the 1890s. Washington was the founding president of Tuskegee Institute in Alabama and a champion of industrial education, a form of education that emphasized learning a trade such as carpentry, plumbing, or fitting. Through the Commerce of Ideas South Africans became familiar with both.[8] In response to colonial repression and few opportunities for higher education in Africa and perceived African American achievement in the United States, many Africans were drawn to images of America and African Americans in particular. African Americans had built schools, churches, and businesses that supported the idea of African American advancement. Even African American women, like Annie Turnbo Malone, Madam C. J. Walker, and Maggie Lena Walker, had become rich through their own businesses. This was virtually unheard of in South Africa. Inevitably an entire mythology slowly emerged among South Africans that revolved around the idea that African Americans were more advanced.[9]

Contrary to the image of the exceptional African American that was well-known among South Africans in the later half of the nineteenth and the first few decades of the twentieth century, most African Americans were not in fact doing well financially. Rayford Logan called the period of African American history from the end of Reconstruction to the Presidency of Woodrow Wilson "the Nadir" or the lowest point of the African American experience. African American Exceptionalism was therefore at least partly a myth, and as a myth it became a form of African American resistance, a counter narrative whose purpose was to liberate and empower through a process of self-redefinition: the logical means of escaping from the myth of white supremacy was to elaborate and enter into a new self-affirming myth or reality.[10] So, African Americans who visited South Africa extolled their achievements, and those achievements came

---

[8] Manning Marable examines the influence of Booker T. Washington on South Africans in "Booker T. Washington and African Nationalism" *Phylon* 35, no. 4 (4th Qtr. 1974), 398–406. James T. Campbell work on the AME Church in South Africa is comprehensive. He discusses Bishop Turner's influence in *Songs of Zion: The African Methodist Church in the United States and South Africa* (Chapel Hill, NC: University of North Carolina Press, 1998), 136–37.

[9] Gershoni, 1.

[10] Quote by Sterling Lecater Bland, Jr. in the Introduction of Harry Dean, *The Pedro Gorino: The Adventures of a Negro Sea-Captain in Africa and on the Seven Seas in his attempts to Found an Ethiopian Empire* (Yardley, PA: Westholme Publishing, 2011, originally published by Houghton Mifflin Company 1929), xiii.

to overshadow the condition of the majority of African Americans then living in the Deep South who struggled in unfair labor arrangements as tenant farmers or sharecroppers.

Because white America rejected African culture as deficient, African Americans were forced to develop multiple identities: one public and one private. Competing narratives of self or self-definitions posed real challenges for people of African descent. W. E. B. Du Bois eloquently describes the complications of this process in *Souls of Black Folks* when he alludes to the "two unreconciled strivings" and "two warring ideals."

> The history of the American Negro is the history of this strife—this longing to attain self-conscious manhood, to merge his double self into a better and truer self. In this merging he wishes neither of the older selves to be lost.[11]

African American identity had been forged in three hundred years of chattel slavery and an equally long de facto but systemic racial oppression ensconced in the myth of white supremacy that was as brutal as it was inexorable and ubiquitous, which in small steps, generation after succeeding generation, transformed their values, beliefs, and culture from those based in an African reality (or worldview) to those adapted to serve the interests (or worldview) of white people.[12] This new Eurocentric reality pervaded the entirety of the black community in the United States and helps us to understand the true basis of the social distance between continental Africans and those in the African Diaspora where it in fact exists, which is why social contact between Africans and Africans living in the Diaspora proved to be so important.

Certainly, the efforts of slaveholders to transform Africans into negroes was not entirely successful in erasing the former African cultural elements, but slaveholders went to great lengths to mold a new identity and personality for their captive laborers with the hope that it would make them easier to control and more efficient workers. During the process of "Seasoning" Africans, which included both psychological and physical violence, the fabric of their cultural was torn into pieces and callously scattered beyond the horizon of their now fragmented collective conscious: some pieces were lost, some pieces the whites hid to later reclaim as their own cultural innovation, and other pieces were damaged beyond repair. African Americans struggled to hang on to their African culture, to gather, and reassemble what pieces of their cultural fabric they could find, but without all of the original pieces some parts had to be substituted. Replacements were found within the culture and values of white society, for example, argyle and tartan were substituted for the former kente and adire fabric of African memory and culture. As a result, the African American elites that black South Africans viewed as exceptional and modern were in part a creation of two competing myths: the myth of white supremacy and the myth of African American exceptionalism. Yet, in the United States because of the powerful repressive forces militating against the use of African culture, in many ways African Americans were more American than African. Their language, English; their religion, Christianity; and

---

[11] W. E. B. Du Bois, *Souls of Black Folks* (New York: Vintage Books, 1990), 8–9.

[12] African cultural retention in the United States was hotly debated, see for example, Melville Hertsokvits, *Myth of the Negro Past* (New York: Harper & Brothers, 1941 reprinted 1990) and E. Franklin Frazier, *Race and Culture Contacts in the Modern World* (New York: Knopf, 1957); More recent monographs include Sterling Stuckey, *Slave Culture: Nationalist Theory and the Foundations of Black America* (New York: Oxford University Press, 1987) and Michael Gomez, *Exchanging Our Country Marks: the Transformation of African Identities in the Colonial and Antebellum South* (Chapel Hill, NC: University of North Carolina Press, 1998).

their values, a mixture of European cultures that were heavily Victorian, reflected those of their oppressors, which privileged whites in terms of beauty, intelligence, and in almost every area of human endeavor. In as much as South Africans followed African Americans, they too would be emulating the values, norms, and behaviors that were as much European as they were African.

This leads to the obvious question, why was it a problem for African Americans to have taken on European values and beliefs and by extension South Africans? European values and beliefs privileged European culture and denigrated African culture. Taking on those values and beliefs created an internal conflict within Africans. As a consequence of cogitative dissonance then African Americans and South Africans were teeming with social and psychological pathologies—a negative self-image, self-destructive coping strategies, such as alcoholism and substance abuse, and self-hatred.[13] Grace Carroll studies the impact of racism on African Americans and she found that:

> This feeling of being unwanted in America, the stigma of being African in a society dominated by anti-African thought and Eurocentric ideas of beauty, dominance, and entitlement, creates a unique stress for African Americans. This stress is present in all identifiable African Americans and/or all who identify with being of African descent.[14]

Carroll has a name for the social tension that grows out of having identities in conflict: Mundane Extreme Environmental Stress (M.E.E.S.). M.E.E.S. is described as "an environment in which racism and subtle oppression are ubiquitous, constant, continuing, and mundane."[15] It was no small triumph then that through enslavement and racial segregation in the United States, African Americans identified with Africa at all, and many did not, but there were a large number of blacks from the United States and the Caribbean who did and who traveled to South Africa carrying with them a host of ideas that were a product of the environments out of which they came. These ideas combined like molecules with those of the South Africans to form new structures to resist racial segregation and discrimination.

ENCOUNTERS

African Americans went to South Africa for a variety of reasons. In the nineteenth century, many were sailors seeking adventure and opportunities not open to them at home; others were religious zealots set on beating the devil loose of the "natives" and redeeming their souls for Christianity. Still others were members of African American choral groups that toured South

---

[13] The existing literature on the impact of racism and colonialism on blacks is rich. Franz Fanon is arguably the best-known writer in regard to the impact of colonialism but Amie Caesar and Albert Memmi also made important contributions. See for example, Fanon, *Black Skin, White Masks* (New York: Grove Press, 2008, originally published by Editions du Seuil in 1952); Caesar, *Discourses on Colonialism* (New York: Monthly Review Press, 2000, originally published by Presence Africaine in 1955); Memmi, *The Colonizer and the Colonized* (Boston, MA: Beacon Press, 1991, originally published by The Orion Press in 1965). African American social scientists E. Franklin Frazier and Nathan Hare have written acerbic critiques of the behavior of the African American middle class in Frazier, *Black Bourgeoisie* (New York: Macmillan Publishing Company, 1962) and Nathan Huggins, *The Black Anglo-Saxons* (Chicago: Third World Press, 1965, 1991).

[14] Grace Carroll, *Environmental Stress and African Americans: The Other Side of the Moon* (Westport, Connecticut: Praeger, 1998), 3.

[15] Ibid., 4.

Africa and sang Heaven down on their native audiences in the later part of the nineteenth century. As racial segregation became institutionalized in South Africa through the elaboration of restrictive and punitive legislative acts in the twentieth century, African American visitors took note and closed ranks with black South Africans. Seeds of transnational protest were sown that would grow to maturation decades later and eventuate into the modern antiapartheid movement. Hence, the transnational struggle against racialism in South Africa started even before the National Party in South Africa inaugurated apartheid—literally apartness or separateness—in 1948. Apartheid, like its cousin Jim Crow, was a system of laws and norms designed to extract labor from people of color and in all social settings and interactions to privilege whites over people of color. It took a tremendous effort to overcome the tyranny of institutional racism in South Africa, and the roots of that resistance extend to the nineteenth century and is part of the Commerce of Ideas that black sailors from the Caribbean and United States cultivated with South Africans, who did not wait for the arrival of their seaborne brothers and sisters from across the Atlantic to begin fighting back. South Africans were always at the head of their struggle for liberation, but it was a fight they did not fight alone.

For men with ample courage and not much else, the sea held out hope and a promise of something new. As early as 1813, black sailors manned merchant and whaling ships that made port in South Africa and, as a consequence of the War of 1812, a small number of African American sailors had been jailed in South Africa.[16] It was during this period that the "first significant evidence of sustained contact between these foreign black sailors [African Americans and Caribbean Blacks] and the black port residents [of South Africa]" was established. From 40% to 50% of the crewmembers of American whaling vessels cruising the South Atlantic from Walvis Bay around the Cape to Natal and as far north as Delagoa Bay were African Americans.[17] Many of the American whaling vessels made port at Table Bay to obtain provisions and to give their crews liberty. Cape Town was an open port that permitted the landing of black sailors, and therefore had a long established African Diaspora presence. Black sailors from the Caribbean could be found in the ports throughout the Atlantic littoral and were a significant portion of the total population of black sailors in Cape Town.[18] These seamen frequented the local lodging establishments, taverns, and bordellos, where they mingled with the locals: Africans and Coloureds. South African Coloureds were the interracial offspring of Africans and Europeans. Europeans in South Africa, Afrikaners, and British, placed them higher on the social hierarchy of races than Africans. Coloured shared some of the same social spaces as Africans. These informal meeting places permitted the free exchange of ideas and experiences that help to build a matrix of social relations based on a common adversary and similar circumstance. Racial hostility from whites toward the black sailors on the high seas and at port bound the black sailors

---

[16] Keletso Atkins, "Questionable Haven: African American Emigrants in South Africa," a paper delivered at the African Studies Association meeting, St. Louis, November 1991 quoted in James Campbell, *Songs of Zion: The African Methodist Episcopal Church in the United States and South Africa* (Chapel Hill, NC: University of North Carolina Press, 1998), 126. The evidence for earlier African American visitors to South Africa is sparse according to Atkins. See Keletso Atkins, "The 'Black Atlantic Communications Network': African American Sailors and the Cape of Good Hope Connection," *Issue* 24, no. 2 (1996): 23–5.

[17] Ibid., 23.

[18] Alan Gregor Cobley, "'Far From Home': The Origins and Significance of the Afro-Caribbean Community in South Africa to 1930," *Journal of Southern African Studies* 18, no. 2 (June 1992): 352–53.

into a tightknit group, the boundaries of which extended into the local black communities in South Africa.[19]

Of all the black sailors to make port in South Africa during the latter part of the nineteenth century, Captain Harry Foster Dean is one of the most fascinating.[20] In his autobiography, *The Pedro Gorino*, Captain Dean claims to be a direct descendant of Captain Paul Cuffee.[21] Born in Philadelphia, Pennsylvania in 1864, Dean claims that he went to sea at the age of twelve and over the next three years circumnavigated the globe with his uncle Silas.[22] He attended the first pan-African conference in July 1900 in London, where he suggested to W. E. B. Du Bois that he "lead a black army across the Strait of Gibraltar to liberate the continent [of Africa]." Du Bois did not support Dean's plan for a military invasion to liberate Africans from the European colonial powers then in control over much of the continent, so Dean began to formulate a new stratagem to free Africa.[23] With the assistance of a Captain Forbes, Dean acquired a ship, The Pedro Gorino, and set sail for Cape Town as owner and captain with a motley crew of mainly West Indians and South Americans. They arrived in the midst of the second Anglo-Boer war (1899–1902).[24] During his long stay at the Cape, Dean and his crew operated their tramp steamer among the ports that lie between Cape Town and Delagoa Bay (now Maputo Bay) in Mozambique. Remarkably, Dean claims that Portuguese colonial agents offered to sale him Portuguese East Africa including Lorenco Marques (modern Maputo) for 50,000 Pounds Sterling.[25] He attempted to raise the necessary financial support, but the African Americans he solicited were not interested. In an angry statement charged with nationalist undertones aimed pointedly at African American elites at that time who he believed were under the spell of Eurocentric ideas and influence he lamented:

> Why did you not respond, men of my race? You did not respond because you were born in a land where the Caucasian is in power and the Ethiopian can only imitate. You did not respond because of the centuries during which you have labored under the hypnotic influence of false ideals, false logic, false education, and false code of morals. You did not respond because the spirit had been beaten and whipped from your black bodies until you could no longer hold up your heads.[26]

Dean claims also to have been offered land to build a school in Basutoland (modern Lesotho), but before he was able to complete the school or raise the money for the purchase of Portuguese East Africa colonial agents in South Africa foiled his plans by setting ablaze the warehouse in Cape Town where all of his valuable cargo was stockpiled. This ruined Dean

---

[19] Ibid., 351.

[20] George Shepperson makes a passing reference to Captain Dean in 1952, see, Shepperson, "The United States and East Africa," *Phylon* 13, no. 1 (1st Qtr., 1952): 25; John S. Burger, "Captain Harry Dean: Pan-Negro-Nationalist in South Africa," *The International Journal of African Historical Studies* IX, no. 1 (1976). Burger also wrote his Master's thesis on Dean in 1973.

[21] His linage according to Dean can be found in Dean, *The Pedro Gorino*, 8–13.

[22] Ibid., 16.

[23] John S. Burger, 84.

[24] Dean does not state which Anglo-Boer WarDean, *The Pedro Gorino*, 89–0.

[25] Dean, 115–16.

[26] Ibid., 124.

financially, and insolvent he was compelled to hand over the title of The Pedro Gorino to creditors, to leave South Africa, and return to the United States in 1914.[27]

Captain Dean is a charismatic and affable historical figure, a bright shining example of the exceptional African American. Reflecting back on his feats, he recalled walking down one of the main streets in Cape Town with his first mate, a man that all the women thought was "pretty." Dean exclaimed, "We were Dark Brown Vikings on an African Coast" implying clearly that they viewed themselves as men, that they were home, and that they were not inferior to any other men. Dean appears to be among the black sailors who were weaving the transnational web of the Black Atlantic Communications Network spreading ideas of resistance and African nationalism. Yet, his extraordinary adventure is based largely on his own personal testimony, and census evidence suggests that Dean may have engaged in a bit of mythmaking in parts of his autobiography. The concept of Usual Residence requires that citizens of the United States who are working out of the country in nongovernmental positions be omitted from the US Census. Yet, a Harry Foster Dean whose place of birth, birthdate, and date of death correspondences with that of Captain Dean appears prominently in the US Federal Census as a resident of Chicago Ward 3, Cook County, Illinois in 1900 and 1910.[28] In addition, the Marriages Index for Cook County, Illinois indicates that a Harry F. Dean married Henrietta Davis in 1904.[29] Dean did apply for a passport in 1907 and again in 1912, which suggests that he was traveling or planning to travel internationally.[30] The census evidence upsets Dean's chronology of his time in South Africa and seems to contradict his claim that he only returned to the United States from South Africa in 1914. This does not mean necessarily that Dean did not travel to South Africa or even that he was not a captain of a tramp steamer who engaged in memorable adventures in southern Africa. Captain Dean is an example of how African American myth making acts as

---

[27] Ibid., 78.

[28] Across the census data several birthdates are given for Dean, all of them within a few years of his assumed birthdate of 1864. That is typical. His name also appears as Harry F. Dean and Harry Dean. Dean's date of birth, place of birth, and date of death can be found in Ancestry.com, Illinois, Deaths and Stillbirths Index, 1916–1947 (Online publication—Provo, UT, USA: Ancestry.com Operations, Inc., 2011. Original data –"Illinois Deaths and Stillbirths, 1916–1947." Index. Family Search, Salt Lake City, Utah, 2010. Index entries derived from digital copies of original records), accessed June 1, 2012, http://www.ancestry.com. Ancestry.com Operations Inc, 2004. Original data—United States of America, Bureau of the Census. Twelfth Census of the United States, 1900. Washington, DC: National Archives and Records Administration, 1900. T623, 18), Ancestry.com, Year: 1900; Census Place: Chicago Ward 3, Cook, Illinois, accessed June 1, 2012, www.ancestry.com. Also see, Ancestry.com, 1910 United States Federal Census (Online publication—Provo, UT, USA: Ancestry.com Operations Inc, 2006. Original data—Thirteenth Census of the United States, 1910. NARA microfilm publication T624, 1,178 rolls). Records of the Bureau of the Census, Record Group 29. National Archives, Was), Year: 1910; Census Place: Chicago Ward 3, Cook, Illinois, accessed June 1, 2012, www.ancestry.com.

[29] Ancestry.com, Cook County, Illinois, Marriages Index, 1871–1920 (Online publication—Provo, UT, USA: Ancestry.com Operations, Inc., 2011.Original data –"Illinois, Cook County Marriages, 1871–1920." Index. Family Search, Salt Lake City, Utah, 2010. Illinois Department of Public Health records. Marriage Records, 1871–pr), accessed June 1, 2012, www.ancestry.com.

[30] His application in 1907 can be found at US Passport Applications, 1795–1925, National Archives and Records Administration (NARA); Washington, DC; Passport Applications, January 2, 1906–March 31, 1925; Collection Number: ARC Identifier 583830/MLR Number A1 534; NARA Series: M1490; Roll #: 41; his 1912 application can be found at US Passport Applications, 1795–1925, National Archives and Records Administration (NARA); Washington, DC; Passport Applications, January 2, 1906–March 31, 1925; Collection Number: ARC Identifier 583830/MLR Number A1 534; NARA Series: M1490; Roll #: 163, accessed June 1, 2012, www.ancestry.com.

a counter-narrative to the colonial exploitation of blacks at that time. If Dean's story is even partly true as told, he would be an extraordinary example of the exceptional African American that has done so much to capture the imagination of South Africans.

Another impressive African American visitor to South Africa was George Washington Williams. Williams was an African American historian and politician, who visited South Africa in 1890. Born in 1849 in Bedford Springs, Pennsylvania, Williams attended Howard University in Washington, DC, briefly before transferring to and graduating from Newton Theological Seminary. In 1874, after finishing Newton as its first African American graduate, Williams assumed the pastorate of the twelfth Street Baptist Church in Boston, Massachusetts. He is considered by some the first African American professional historian. In 1882, he published his magnum opus, *A History of the Negro Race in the United States.* Williams went to South Africa on a fact-finding mission to collect information about possible investment opportunities for Collis Huntington, the American railroad magnet. He visited Cape Colony, Natal, and the Orange Free State where he met with South African blacks as well as white politicians. Williams was a conscientious chronicler of the debilitating impact of colonialism on Africans. In central Africa, for example, his observations of the cruel brutality of the Belgian Force Publique in compelling Africans to harvest rubber in Congo pushed him to write an open letter to King Leopold II, the self-appointed leader and sole owner of the so-called Congo Free State. In "An Open Letter to His Serene Majesty Leopold II, King of the Belgians and Sovereign of the Independent State of Congo," Williams exposed publicly for the first time the atrocities that were being committed against Africans under the auspices of King Leopold II.[31]

Sylvia M. Jacobs has written extensively on African American missionaries in Africa. She found that by the 1890s they had come to have a significant presence and influence on affairs in South Africa.[32] The Black Baptists were the first of the major African American denominations to arrive in South Africa. In 1894, Reverend R. A. Jackson and his family from Hot Springs, Arkansas established a Baptist Mission Station in Cape Town. Jackson raised the money to go to South Africa, and "At that time, Jackson was apparently the only American black Baptist missionary serving on the African continent."[33] That would change in part because of the tremendous evangelical work of Jackson. By 1900, Jackson had established four Baptist mission stations in South Africa. In 1896, the National Baptist Convention became Jackson's sponsor in South Africa. John Tule, a black South African, became one of Jackson's earliest African converts. Following the path that many South Africans would take, Tule came to the United States for his education. While in the United States he met and married Mary Branton, an African American woman who was born in Chatham, Canada West. Branton too was a dedicated

---

[31] John Hope Franklin, *George Washington Williams: A Biography* (Chicago: University of Chicago Press, 1985), 196–97. See George Washington Williams, *An Open Letter to His Serene Majesty Leopold II King of the Belgians and Sovereign of the Independent State of Cong* (Stanley Falls, Central Africa: s.n, 1890). Franklin included a complete rendition of the letter in the appendix of his biography. See also, Adam Hochschild, *King Leopold's Ghost: A Story of Greed Terror and Heroism in Colonial Africa* (Boston, MA: Houghton Mifflin, 1998).

[32] Sylvia M. Jacobs, ed., *Black Americans and the Missionary Movement in Africa* (St. Barbara, CA: Praeger, 1982) and also *Black Nexus: Black American Perspectives on the European Partitioning of Africa* (St. Barbara, CA: Praeger, 1981).

[33] Kenneth C. Barnes, *Journey of Hope: The Back-to-Africa Movement in Arkansas in the Late 1800's* (Chapel Hill, NC: University of North Carolina Press, 2006), 118.

missionary and member of the Second Street Baptist Church Mission in Detroit, Michigan. She attended Spelman College in Atlanta, Georgia, before traveling to South Africa in 1897, where she continued her mission work by training and educating women and children. African American women missionaries were not permitted to Baptize, which was a privilege reserved for men. An obvious affront to African American women missionaries, it did little to slow down their enthusiasm for their mission work. While protesting within the church for more responsibilities, they found other means to spread God's word. African American women have been remarkable institution builders within the United States and even overseas as transnational change agents that sought to ameliorate the condition of Africans. For instance, while her husband was out "converting 300 Africans," Mary Branton Tule established a school in her name in Cape Town for the education of young people of color. In 1913, the South African government passed the Native Land Act, which broke labor arrangements between African agricultural workers and their Afrikaner employers. At the same time, it limited Africans from renting or purchasing land except within the "native reserves," which were unproductive, overworked, and overcrowded. In effect, this made the majority of Africans landless with almost no legitimate means of protesting. The Tules, husband and wife, joined with South Africans in challenging these unjust laws and did so with such vigor that by 1922 the government banned them from the country.[34]

The presence of the AMEC in South Africa can be traced to its merger with the Ethiopian Church of South Africa in 1896. Mangena Mokone founded the Ethiopian Church in South Africa when he broke away from the white Wesleyan Church in 1892. Charlotte Manye, a South African student at the AMEC-affiliated Wilberforce University in Ohio, helped to make the union possible by putting Mokone in contact with AMEC leaders. In 1898, AMEC Bishop Henry McNeal Turner visited South Africa. An outstanding orator, Turner took considerable pride in people of African descent and made speeches to packed audiences of South Africans. He exhorted African American achievement and education as a vehicle for fostering hope and ambition among the Africans, undoubtedly contributing to the notion that African Americans were exceptional. Membership in the AMEC doubled during his six-week visit.[35]

Bishop Levi J. Coppin, a prominent Bishop of the AMEC who had presided over Mother Bethel Church in Philadelphia, PA, and his wife, Fanny Jackson Coppin, an Oberlin graduate and preeminent educator, arrived in Cape Town in 1902.[36] Bishop Coppin assumed leadership of the Fourteenth Episcopal District of the AMEC in South Africa. In addition to his responsibilities as leader of the AMEC, he established in Cape Town a school, Bethel Institute, and wrote fondly of his South African experiences in *Unwritten History*.[37] Bishop Coppin traveled throughout southern Africa giving sermons and tending to the needs of his large flock. Huge crowds often gathered "to see a colored Bishop" and to hear his orations. He recalled

---

[34] Vaughn J. Walston and Robert J. Stevens, eds., *African-American Experience in World Mission: A Call Beyond Community* (Pasadena, CA: William Carey Library Publishers, 2003), 42. See also, Gerald H. Anderson, *Biographical Dictionary of Christian Missions* (Grand Rapids, MI: Wm. B. Eerdmans Publishing, 1999), 683.

[35] Campbell, *Songs of Zion*, 136–37. Turner even met with President Paul Kruger.

[36] Fanny Jackson Coppin states they arrived in Table Bay on Sunday, November 30, 1902. See Fanny Jackson Coppin, *Reminiscences of School Life, and Hints on Teaching* (Philadelphia, PA: A.M.E. Book Concern, 1919), 123.

[37] Levi Jenkins Coppin, *Unwritten History* (Philadelphia, PA: A.M.E. Book Concern, 1919), 311.

in going to Mafateng, Basutoland (Lesotho) in 1903 for a church dedication that "Rev. Paul M. Shupinyaneng . . . had planned to have a big crowd." He was not disappointed. When the day came they were there from far and near. Some had come as far as a three days' journey on horseback.[38] Such was the success and popularity of the AMEC that even though the church had a standing order not to accept members from another church the white ministers in South Africa still accused the AMEC leaders of "sheep stealing." Coppin recalled:

> After the advent of our Church, the Native people would leave their former Church relations with the white people, and come to us.[39]

While Bishop Coppin spread the gospel, "Miss Fanny," trained the native and colored women for Christian work. Apparently, "Miss Fanny" made quite an impression as some of the women helped to raise $10,000 for the construction of Fanny Jackson Coppin Hall at Wilberforce Institute, a school Charlotte Manye and her husband Marshall Maxeke established outside of Johannesburg.[40]

In the nineteenth and early twentieth century, mission work was one of the main reasons African Americans went to South Africa. Most of those who went, like Manye and Maxeke, were Methodists who had studied at historically black schools.[41] Horace Mann Bond, a prominent African American educator and former President of Lincoln University, did extensive research on African and African American relations during this early period. He found that it was "Methodist Bishop William Taylor, who, in 1885, proposed a mass-missionary movement to evangelize Africa."[42] To prepare the missionaries for their work, in 1887 Taylor help start at Central Tennessee College, in Nashville, Tennessee, what Bond believes is the first "African Studies Program" in the United States. The college catalog claimed this "School for Africa" was to train the students for their mission work in Africa.[43] Fisk University, also in Nashville, had a close relation with the American Missionary Association (AMA). In 1878, the first two of what would be many Fisk graduates went on a mission to Sierra Leone. In 1903, John Jackson, a graduate of Fisk University, became the first of their former students to travel to South Africa. Jackson was just one of an army of African American missionaries who went to South Africa looking to save souls and to stamp out racial discrimination. Their presence in South Africa had a profound effect on South Africans. Many blacks converted to Christianity, joined African

---

[38] Coppin, *Unwritten History*, 321.

[39] Ibid., 311.

[40] "Miss Fanny" was a cognomen of Fanny Jackson Coppin first given to her by the girls at the Institute for Colored Youth. See Coppin, *Unwritten History*, 361–63. Also see Coppin, *Reminiscences of School Life, and Hints on Teaching*, 126.

[41] In the United States, there are a category of schools known as Historically Black Colleges and Universities or HBCUs. Founded in the nineteenth century, white philanthropist give much of the initial funding to establish these schools to support the education of freedmen. See Charles L. Betsey, ed., *Historically Black Colleges and Universities* (Piscataway, NJ: Transaction Publishers, 2008).

[42] Horace Mann Bond, "African-American Relations Seen Through African Students Enrolled in American Negro Colleges: A Progress Report of a Historical Study," [1961], in box 36, folder 4, Third AMSAC Conference Papers, American Society of African Culture, Moorland Spingarn Research Center, Howard University.

[43] Ibid. Central Tennessee College later became Walden University but is now defunct. This school supported by Methodist offered courses in African agriculture, African health problems, African languages, African religions, and African art.

American lead churches in South Africa, and scores came to the United States to earn a college education, often from schools affiliated with their African American church in South Africa.[44]

Music is a universal form of communication that has the capacity to transcend lingual differences. It is deeply important to people of African descent, and the cornerstone of every black Christian denomination. For most black Christians, to not have music as part of the worship service is to not have church. During the final two decades of the nineteenth century, Orpheus McAdoo and his Jubilee Singers from Hampton, Virginia toured and performed in Cape Town and other parts of South Africa. Their influence in South Africa contributed indirectly to the merger of the Separatist Church in South Africa and the AMEC in the United States.[45] The presence of the AMEC in South Africa paved the way for a large number of South African students to study at historically black schools in the United States. The McAdoo Singers toured South Africa for a year and a half, visiting and performing in many of the towns in the Eastern Cape, including Grahamstown, Alice, and King Williamstown. Press accounts of that period reveal that black South Africans were not only impressed by these performances but some thought they were better than the best British choral groups. Africans who attended these concerts viewed the African American performers with a sense of racial pride. So significant was the influence of the Jubilee Singers that they changed the landscape of choral music performance among blacks in South Africa from the staid and sterile British form to an expression of music that embraced the impassioned and emotional style common to African American church music.[46] Mangena Mokone, a leader of the Ethiopianist movement, attended a performance by the McAdoo Singers in Pretoria, and H. R. Ngcayiya, like Mokone, a founder of the Ethiopian Church but also a founder of the ANC, actually joined a local jubilee group in Burghersdorp.[47]

As noted above, black spirituals played an important role in fostering relations between black South Africans and African Americans in the last decade of the nineteenth century. In the 1920s jazz would play a similar role. Music is important throughout Africa and the African Diaspora, and was important in linking diaspora blacks to blacks in South Africa. For many South Africans, African American music was often their first introduction to African American culture. Jazz took root in Queenstown, in the Eastern Cape Province among mission educated Xhosa. By the 1920s, Queenstown became known as "Little Jazz Town" and is currently referred to as the "New Orleans of South Africa." Two of the bands included Meekly Matshikiza's "Blue Rhythm

---

[44] Ibid.

[45] See Johann Buis, "Black American Music and the Civilized-Unciviled Matirx in South Africa," *Issue* 24, no. 2 (1996): 28–30; David Coplan, *In Township Tonight: South Africa's Black City Music and Theatre* (New York: Longman, 1985), 38. See also, Veit Erlmann, "'A Feeling of Prejudice': Orpheus M. McAdoo and the Virginia Jubilee Singers in South Africa 1890–1898," *Journal of Southern African Studies* 14, no. 3 (1988): 331–40. McAdoo had traveled abroad with the Fisk University Jubilee Singers in the 1880s, and consequently, patterned the Virginia Jubilee Singers after the Fisk University group. Hotep Idris Goleta, "The Development of Jazz in South Africa," manuscript is in the possession of the author. Goleta is a South African Jazz pianist who fled to the United States in 1963. He lived, performed, and taught Jazz in the United States for thirty years before returning to Cape Town. He is the author of several Jazz CDs as well as articles on Jazz history in South Africa.

[46] Buis, "Black American Music and the Civilized-Uncivilized Matrix in South Africa," 28.

[47] Campbell, *Songs of Zion*, 129. Sacred music was an important feature of the Ethiopian Church movement and familiarized black South Africans with African American religiosity.

Syncopators" and William Mbali's "Big Four."[48] African American merchant seamen brought jazz to Cape Town. South African youngsters would frequently go to the docks to meet the black sailors coming from the Caribbean and United States to get first dabs on the most recent music or news. The black sailors brought music recordings of African American jazz musicians such as Louis Armstrong, Bessie Smith, Duke Ellington, Count Basie, Ella Fitzgerald, and Cab Calloway. Jazz was a revolt against the predominant British and Afrikaner music in South Africa. For African Americans who listened to it in the swank parlors uptown in Harlem having migrated from the dusty roads of the Deep South, Jazz was an affirmation of their modernity. It had the same effect on South Africans who embraced it. How could it not? Jazz is dynamic and requires the musician to have creative freedom. Their audiences experience this freedom vicariously through the music and by extension the musician. So, like other forms of black music, Jazz was often pregnant with rhythms and verses of black resistance. South African Jazz musicians of the late twentieth century such as trumpeter Hugh Masekela, songstress Zenzile Miriam "Mamma Afrika" Makeba, and pianist Hotep Idris Galeta represent a continuity of artistic expression that weds South Africans and African Americans across time and space.[49]

Black sailors from the Americas and Caribbean were the carriers of African Diaspora culture. Whether it was, for instance, Jamaican sailors bringing knowledge of how to prepare Jerk chicken or, much later in the twentieth century, Reggae music and Rastafarianism or whether it was African American sailors bringing Jazz, black South Africans were interested and most often receptive. Port cities were where the greatest concentration of African Diaspora culture can be found throughout the Atlantic realm including of course South Africa. This is true for European culture as well. Port cities the great meeting place for culture: Xhosa, Khoisan, British, French, Jamaican, Trinidadian, Dutch, African American, and many other cultures came together in the cities by the sea. Local residents collected bits and pieces of it—a word here, and expression there, a song, a dance, a value—and they passed it along until that cultural element had diffused to even the remote corners of country. One is reminded of this today, when a Coca-Cola can is found in a remote location only accessible via foot. Culture travels.

As much as anything, the sailors brought news from the African Diaspora. Newspapers such as the *New York Amsterdam News*, the *Chicago Defender*, the *Pittsburgh Courier*, the *Afro America*, and Marcus Garvey's *Negro World* were passed from person to person throughout the South African Townships. Periodicals such as these help to mitigate the isolating effects of racial segregation in South African by providing a window to the wider African world. Beginning in the 1940s, *Ebony* magazine and later *Jet* magazine played a critical role in conveying the experiences

---

[48] David Coplan, "The Urbanization of African Music: Some Theoretical Considerations," *Popular Music* 2, Theory and Method (1982), 115. From Hotep Idris Galeta, interview by author, May 19, 2001, Cape Town, South Africa, tape recording in the possession of the author. See also, Hotep Idris Galeta, "The Development of Jazz in South Africa," on All About Jazz.com, November 25, 2003. Accessed June 5, 2012, http://www.allabout-jazz.com/php/article.php?id=889&page=1,.

[49] Buis, "Black American Music and the Civilized-Unciviled Matirx in South Africa," 29. South Africa produced its own jazz greats who though influenced by African American artists created their own sound and have left their own remarkable legacy, some of them include the Manhattan Brothers, Dorothy Masuka, the Dark City Sisters, Dollar Brand/Abdullah Ibrahim, Jonas Gwangwa, Letta Mbuli, Caiphus Semenya, Miriam Makeba, and Hugh Masekela. Makeba's experience is considered more closely in the section on South Africans in the United States.

of black Americans. Their articles and images celebrating black achievement, often cast against a backdrop of Jim Crow segregation, built on the already prevalent idea in South Africa of Africa American exceptionalism. South Africans cheered for Jesse Owens, Joe Louis, and, later, Muhammad Ali from having first learned about them and their achievements through news shared across the Black Atlantic Communications Network.

In the 1920s, black sailors brought the teachings of Marcus Garvey to South Africa. Garvey, who was born in Saint Ann's Bay Jamaica in 1887, established the Universal Negro Improvement Association and African Communities League (UNIA) in Harlem, New York in 1914 with the specific aim of liberating Africa and peoples of African descent from European colonialism through economic empowerment.[50] In the 1920s, the UNIA was the largest organization of people of African descent in the world. Garvey got inspiration for the name of his organization after learning about the horrible treatment of natives in southern Africa. Garvey stated:

> It was while speaking to a West Indian Negro who was a passenger on the ship with me from Southhampton [in 1914] who was returning to the West Indies from Basutoland [modern Lesotho] with his Basuto wife, that I further learned of the horrors of native life in Africa. Retiring to my cabin…the vision and thought came to me that I should name the organization the Universal Negro Improvement Association and African Communities (Imperial) League.[51]

Max Yergan, a Christian missionary from Raleigh, North Carolina, who graduated from Shaw University, traveled to South Africa as Foreign Secretary of the Colored Work Department of the Young Men's Christian Association (YMCA). He arrived in South Africa with his wife, Susie Wiseman Yergan, and two small children in January 1922 and lived there for the next fourteen years, working from the campus of the African Native College at Fort Hare in the Eastern Cape Province.[52] Situated in the tiny rural town of Alice in the same community as the long established Lovedale Institute, Fort Hare was erected in 1916 to promote education for Africans and other non-Europeans in the spirit of Booker T. Washington. Yergan's work as a YMCA officer revolved around training black students, promoting Christianity, and harmonizing interracial relations. He therefore traveled throughout South Africa, giving sermons, lecturing, meeting with local as well as high-ranking officials, and organizing conferences to promote the missionary agenda of the YMCA.[53]

Being a Christian missionary, Yergan miscalculated the effectiveness of moral suasion to alter deeply held racial beliefs among the white South Africans. As his failures and frustrations

---

[50] Robert Trent Vinson, "'Sea Kaffirs': 'American Negroes' and the Gospel of Garveyism in Early Twentieth-Century Cape Town," *Journal of African History* 47 (2008), 281. For an in depth look at the influence of Garveyism in South Africa, see Robert Trent Vinson, *The Americans Are Coming!: Dreams of African American Liberation in Segregationist South Africa* (Athens, OH: Ohio University Press, 2012), Chapter 3.

[51] Tony Martin, *The Pan-African Connection. From Slavery to Garvey and Beyond* (Dover, MA, 1984), 134; quoted in Cobley, "'Far From Home': the Origins and Significance of the Afro-Caribbean Community in South Africa to 1930," 366.

[52] David Henry Anthony, *Max Yergan: Race Man, Internationalist, Cold Warrior* (New York: New York University Press, 2006), 45–6. See also, David Henry Anthony, III, "Max Yergan in South Africa: From Evangelical Pan-Africanist to Revolutionary Socialist," *African Studies Review* 34, no. 2 (1991), 32.

[53] Anthony, III, "Max Yergan in South Africa," 32.

mounted, he began to look for solutions by other means.[54] On furlough in London in 1931, Yergan met the black titan of the stage and cinema, Paul Robeson, who with his wife Eslanda, befriended Yergan. Convinced that the Soviet Union had eradicated their race problem, the Robesons arranged for him to meet several people who had visited behind the "Iron Curtain."[55] By the middle of the 1930s, some of Yergan's students detected a change in him. One such student was Govan Mbeki. Mbeki was born in South Africa in 1910. He was a student of Yergan, and a future leader of the South African Communist Party (SACP) and the ANC. In 1999, his son Thabo would be elected the second president of the Republic of South Africa. In 1963, alongside Nelson Mandela and others, Govan Mbeki was tried for treason and sent to prison. Mbeki recalled that Yergan had an entire secret library of socialist literature at his house on Fort Hare's campus. Mbeki credits Yergan's lessons with helping to mold many of his early political ideas and in his decision to become a communist.[56]

Paul Robeson was a true Renaissance man. His family was from North Carolina, but by the time of his birth in 1898, the Robeson family had relocated to New Jersey. Robeson graduated from Rutgers where he won twelve varsity letters in sports, was a three-time Walter Camp All American in football, and the valedictorian of his graduating class. He graduated at the top of his law school class at Columbia, but chose a career of professional singing over the practice of law. Robeson used his talent and influence as a mighty humanitarian sword against tyranny, fascism, and racism. He fought for all races of people from all around the world, but he took specific aim at South Africa because it was believed to be one of the most racially repressive countries in the world. Committed unflinchingly to the human right struggle, he sacrificed a lucrative career in entertainment and international stardom for the anticolonial campaign. Robeson never actually visited South Africa, but his wife Eslanda Goode Robeson and young son Paul, Jr. made the trip arriving in Cape Town in 1936.

After disembarking from the cruise ship that brought them to Cape Town, a member of the South African press asked Eslanda Robeson why she had come to South Africa. Her answer represented the sentiments of many of the Diaspora blacks who visited South Africa. She replied that since she and Paul were negroes "they were naturally interested in the Negro everywhere" and "in conditions which affect our people." In Cape Town, the Robesons paid a visit to Louise Gow formerly

---

[54] Yergan's work is outlined in Max Yergan to Jesse Moorland, May 15, 1922, transcript in YMCA—Max Yergan—Corr.—January–June 1922, Box 126–64, Jesse Moorland Papers, Moorland Spingarn Research Center, Howard University, Washington, DC. By the end of 1924, Yergan had established 23 associations. See Yergan to Moorland, June 1, 1925, YMCA—Max Yergan—Correspondence 1925, Box 126-65, Jesse Moorland Papers, Moorland Spingarn Research Center, Howard University, Washington, DC. Yergan's frustration is apparent in correspondence with Alfred Xuma. See for example, Alfred Xuma to Max Yergan, June 12, 1935, transcript in Xuma, A.B., Box 206-4, Max Yergan Papers, Moorland Spingarn Research Center, Howard University, Washington, DC. Also, Anthony, "Max Yergan in South Africa," 40.

[55] Yergan discusses his trip to London in correspondence with Jesse Moorland. See, Yergan to Moorland, October 27, 1931, transcript in YMCA—Max Yergan—Correspondence 1928–1929, Box 126–65, Jesse Moorland Papers, Moorland Spingarn Research Center, Howard University, Washington, DC.

[56] Govan Mbeki, interview by the author, July 1, 2000, at the home of the subject, Port Elizabeth, South Africa, tape recording in the possession of the author. Discussion of Eslanda's visit to South Africa can be found in Eslanda Goode Robeson, *African Journey* (Westport, CT: Greenwood Press, 1945), 42; her quote was taken from Martin Duberman, *Paul Robeson: A Biography* (New York: The New Press, 1989), 206. Anthony III, "Max Yergan in South Africa: From Evangelical Pan-Africanist to Revolutionary Socialist," 42.

of Richmond, Virginia. Mrs. Gow was the wife of Reverend Francis H. Gow, who was afflicted with the AMEC and a proud alumnus of Tuskegee Institute. The Gows lived in the Coloured section of the city.[57] From Cape Town, Eslanda and Paul, Jr. traveled to Port Elizabeth to meet Yergan and Roseberry Bokwe. Bokwe was a prominent African physician.[58] Together they traveled on to Alice where they spent several days passing time in the homes of African friends discussing politics.[59]

Before departing from Alice, she participated with Max Yergan in the All Africa Convention (AAC) in Bloemfontein. At that convention, the AAC leadership charged Yergan with the important responsibility of returning to the United States to fight for South African liberation. Yergan would do just that, working with the Robesons, he formed the International Committee on African Affairs (ICAA), which later became the Council on African Affairs (CAA). The CAA was the most important anticolonial organization in the United States from 1940 to 1955 when it collapsed under tremendous repressive pressure from the US government, which had identified the Council as a Communist front organization. After the convention, the Robesons left Bloemfontein for Johannesburg in the company of Alfred Xuma.[60] In Johannesburg, Robeson attended a party at the Bantu Men's Social Club, which was a frequent gathering place for African elites. A young Nelson Mandela took boxing lessons at the social club while living in Soweto, short for Southwestern Township, which is located just outside of Johannesburg. The visit of Eslanda Robeson, the wife of an international African American celebrity undoubtedly contributed to the idea of exceptional African Americans in South Africa.

Madie Beatrice Hall was the wife of Alfred Bitini Xuma, the president of the African Nation Congress from 1940 to 1949. Hall was born in Winston Salem, North Carolina and lived in South Africa from 1940, when she married Xuma, until shortly after his death in 1962. Thereafter, she returned to the United States. Hall became a major community figure in South Africa and a revered symbol of black achievement and pride. Her community work helped to revitalize the Women's League of the ANC. The Women's League during Hall's period of involvement focused on protesting against pass laws, beer halls, and Bantu Education. Pass laws required Africans in South Africa to carry identification or passes that indicated where they lived and where they were employed. If an African was caught without a pass they could be arrested. Bantu Education required Africans to be taught in Afrikaans, a former of Dutch and the language of Afrikaners, and it limited the upward educational mobility of Africans to jobs that would be useful in the service of whites. Hall also helped to launch the Zenzele (meaning literally "work for yourself") clubs. These influential women's groups provided African women with new opportunities for leadership and service.[61] Her years in South Africa exemplify a commitment to the cult of domesticity, which centered on managing household affairs, and social welfare in the larger community. Like many

---

[57] Lewellyn Longfellow Berry, *A Century of Mission of the AME Church 1840-1940* (New York: Gutenburg Printing, 1942), 183.

[58] His sister Frieda married Professor Z.K. Matthews, the first graduate of Fort Hare and a leader of the African National Congress. See Robeson, *African Journey*. For an autobiographical account of Frieda Bokwe see Freda Matthews, *Remembrances* (Mayibuye Books, 1995), 27–28.

[59] Robeson, *African Journey*, 43; Eslanda Robeson, *African Journey* (Westport, CT: Greenwood Press, 1945), 35.

[60] Ibid., 50.

[61] For a more in-depth treatment of Hall see, Iris Berger, "An African American 'Mother of the Nation': Madie Hall Xuma in South Africa, 1940–1963," *Journal of Southern African Studies* 27, no. 3 (September, 2001). Quote is from pages 548–49.

African American women of her era, she believed in the power of women to heal and transform individuals and communities from decadence born of a lack of educational opportunities and endemic poverty. Hall made speeches to women's groups and gave presentations to promote her community work. Dearly beloved by South African women, she left South Africa with the honorary appellation, "Mother of the [African] nation."[62]

CONCLUSION

For the better part of the twentieth century, especially among urban black South Africans, African Americans were exemplars of "urbanity and sophistication." Many black South Africans became convinced that education had given African American elites their perceived advantages. Captain Harry Dean, Reverend R. A. Jackson, Orpheus McAdoo, and a host of other members of the Black Atlantic Communications Network participated in the Commerce of Ideas that drew African Americans and South Africans closer together, into what Bernard Magubane called "The Ties that Bind." These "Ties" are evident in the numerous marriages and close friendships between South Africans and African Americans that have existed for two centuries. Because of the perceived benefits of education and the sense that African Americans were "Hip," many black South Africans adopted aspects of African American culture in the form of music, language, fashion, and even the oftentimes strident attitude African Americans had toward freedom.

Today, this process of cultural sharing continues to play out in South Africa where young South Africans have embraced Hip Hop and have produced numerous outstanding young Hip Hop artists. South African Hip Hop artist Jabulani Tsambo or Hip Hop Pantsula (HHP), for example, raps about the experiences of Blacks in South Africa in a manner similar to Hip Hop artists in the United States. His dulcet lyrics weave together English and Setswana, his first language, while the pulsating and rhythmic bass lines of his music flow in a manner that are universal to Hip Hop music regardless of geographic location. They would be immediately familiar to Hip Hop enthusiasts in the United States or around the world. According to HHP, he learned pattern construction for his rhymes listening to hymns in the Methodist Church in South Africa. African American rappers like Christopher Wallace who went by the stage names Notorious B.I.G. or Biggie and Trevor George Smith who is better known as Busta Rhymes were a couple of the artists who had a significant influence on his music, which he self-described as Hip-Pop. South African influences on his music include Prof. of Baphixie, Our Local Crowded Crew, and Thebe. Rap music at its best is a form of informal education. Education, like music, was a strong attraction for South Africans to come to the United States.

Scores of South Africans came to the United States for educational opportunities beginning in the late nineteenth century and this process continued throughout the twentieth century. The numbers of South African students coming to the United States fluctuated overtime depending on internal and international factors that made it difficult for them to travel or to gain entry into the United States. They attended both Historically Black Colleges and Universities (HBCU) and Historically White Colleges and Universities (HWCU). Of those that attended HBCUs during the period between 1870 and 1930, the majority went to Wilberforce University in Ohio, Lincoln

---

[62] Ibid., 564.

University in Pennsylvania, Tuskegee Institute in Alabama, and Howard University in Washington, D.C.[63] Within the educational setting, even more opportunities presented themselves for South Africans and African Americans to learn from each other and about each other. These early encounters sowed the seeds of transnational protest politics that in the latter half of the twentieth century would topple apartheid and transform South Africa for the first time into a true political democracy.

KEY TERMS

African American Exceptionalism
African National Congress
African Nationalism
Black Atlantic Communications Network
Commerce of Ideas
Paul and Eslanda Robeson
George Washington Williams
Harry Dean
Madie Hall
John Tule and Mary Branton
Max Yergan
Orpheus McAdoo and the Virginia Jubilee Singers
R. A. Jackson
Apartheid
Mundane Extreme Environmental Stress
White Supremacy

---

[63] Edgar, *An African American in South Africa*, 131. Tuskegee Institute is now known as Tuskegee University.

CHAPTER 14

KNOWLEDGE BECOMES POWER: WESTERN EDUCATION AND THE EMERGENCE OF WESTERN-EDUCATED ELITE RESISTANCE IN KENYA, 1840–1950

Jim C. Harper, II

This research will primarily outline the role of European missionaries in the development of western education, which has been referred to as "formal education," in Kenya. Upon their arrival in the region, the Europeans missionaries extended learning the English language to Africans to enable them to read the Bible. They considered their effort in that regard as the essential instrument of the European "civilizing mission." This method ultimately won the missionary converts and produced indigenous catechists that converted their fellow citizens to Christianity. The subsequent expansion of western education in Kenya was the result of the close cooperation between the missionaries and the colonial government. That education aimed at the creation of a skilled low-level work force, rather than being a generous policy to provide educational opportunities for all Kenyans.

Western education expanded once the British succeeded in placing the region under their control. As a result, the white settlers took the most fertile lands from Kenyans and a railway system was constructed to move people, produce, and other items to the coast and other parts of Kenya. These developments required a large army of semiskilled local workers. Hence, vocational education became the focus of missionary and colonial government schools. Vocational education produced farm hands, craftsmen, and junior clerical staff to work in subordinate positions for Europeans. Incidentally, missionary and public education gave birth to the western-educated elites in Kenya or *Asomi*. Some of the western-educated elites reacted to the domination and racial discrimination of the colonial government and the paternalism of the missionaries by establishing political organizations and independent African churches and schools. Their reaction to colonial rule marks the beginning of the western-educated elites' resistance in Kenya.

Formal education in this context is also referred to as modern or western education. It has been used to describe the systems of education that came to Africa first with the Christian missionaries and later colonial governments.[1] There is no question that like Islam, Christianity has had long and continuous presence on the African continent. Christianity came to Africa during the first century. It was arguably introduced by St. Mark. He wrote the second Gospel and founded the

---

[1] European writers define western education as formal or modern education because it takes place in formalized classroom settings or institutions. African education is referred to as informal or traditional since it occurs in a variety of environments including the home, during apprenticeship, initiation ceremonies, through myths, folklore, or legend.

first Church in Africa located in Alexandria, Egypt. Christianity spread up and down the Nile Valley, to Ethiopia, and westward to the Maghrib. St. Mark was not the only great Christian leader produced in Africa. Other leaders included Simon of Cyrene, who is known to have carried the cross of Jesus; Tertulian of Carthage, who was the first to use the word Trinity; Antony of Nubia, who is claimed to have founded hermit life; and St. Augustine, Bishop of Hippo.[2]

Over time, this ancient Christianity on the continent of Africa lost ground to Islam, which began its advance into the continent during the middle of the seventh century. By the fifteenth century, the entire Nile Valley was Islamized with the exception of a small minority Christian group in Egypt known as the Copts. The Copts also survived in Ethiopia as a larger part of the population. Interestingly, in Ethiopia, Christianity remained as the state religion until the fall of Emperor Haile Selassie in 1974.

Christianity began to lay another foundation on the continent of African with the arrival of the Portuguese Jesuits in the early phases of the transatlantic slave trade. By 1494, Portugal led the conversion and commerce in the "newly discovered lands east of a meridian 100 leagues west of the Cape Verde Islands," and was granted the region by the Papal Bulls issued by Pope Alexander, IV.[3] During this period, Prince Henry, also known as Prince Henry the Navigator, was the governor of Ceuta, which was located on the northwestern region of Morocco. This area was captured by the Portuguese in 1415 and used as a base for further exploration of the west coast of Africa. Nevertheless, the work of the Jesuits was mainly focused on the three West African Islands of Cape Verde, Sao Tome, and Principe as well as parts of Luanda, Angola. The islands, the Highlands of Ethiopia, and South Africa remained strong holds of Christianity for the entire period of the Atlantic slave trade. It was not until the nineteenth century that humanitarian and evangelical forces began to intensively pressurize aiming at the abolition of the transatlantic slave trade taking place mainly in West Africa. In the 1840s their attentions concentrated on East Africa. This expansion across the continent was due in large part to the reports from the travels of David Livingston of the London Missionary Society.[4] Livingstone's writings and speeches inspired the European evangelical and humanitarian forces. His writings focused on the inhumane practices of the Arab slave trade in East Africa that led to abject poverty and humiliation for the people of the region. He declared that "for every slave exported, ten other Africans lost their lives" horrified his readers and those listening to his detailed speeches. Livingston advocated for the redemption of the Africa people and demanded the opening of a "path for commerce and Christianity" that would eventually led the people of Africa closer to Europe and to Christianity.[5]

Livingston's message resonated well with the expansionist vision of the British government. The British government had already been laying the groundwork to expand commerce with India and throughout the Indian Ocean. However, their earlier attempts to form agreements with the Sultans of the Omani Empire were unsuccessful. The Sultans had established a stronghold over the region by strategically establishing a base in Zanzibar, off the coast of East Africa.

---

[2] Geoffery Parrinder, *Religion in Africa* (New York: Praeger Publishers, 1969), 103–109.

[3] A league is 3 miles or 4.8 kilometers. Refer to, J.D. Fage, *A History of West Africa* (Cambridge: the University Press, 1969), 55.

[4] I.N. Kimambo, "The East African Coast and the Hinterland, 1845–80," in *General History of Africa*, ed. J.F. Ade Ajayi, vol. 6 (UNESCO, Paris 1989), 264–5.

[5] J.D. Fage, *A History of West Africa* (London: Routledge, 1995), 260.

In an effort to open lines of communication the British appointed Colonel Atkins Hamerton as Consul to Zanzibar. Hamerton was able to persuade Sultan Sayyed Said to sign the Hamerton Treaty in 1945. This treaty sought to limit slavery within the Sultanate but neither the Sultan nor his successors were willing to enforce the treaty.[6] Abolition of slavery would have devastated the economy of Zanzibar. Zanzibar's plantation economy was based on slave labor. In order to force the Sultans to comply, the British applied diplomatic pressure and threats on the third Sultan, Sayyed Bargash, forcing him in 1873 to ban maritime slave trading.

At the same time, white missionaries stepped up their presence on the coast of East Africa, while the explorers traversed the interior. In 1844, the first missionaries arrived in Mombasa, Kenya. These three German missionaries were dispatched by the Church Missionary Society (CMS). J.J. Erhardt and Johann Rebmann served in Kenya while Johann Ludwig Krapf served in Ethiopia. After two years Rebmann joined Krapf in Ethiopia and died soon after his arrival. In 1847, they founded the first white mission station in East Africa among the Mijikenda (nine groups) at Rabai village (Freretown), about 25 km North West of Mombasa.[7] Rabai served several purposes: proselytism, a haven for freed slaves, and a platform from which missionaries launched their evangelical mission into the interior. In 1891, approximately forty-five years later, the Holy Ghost Fathers established their first missionary station in Mombasa.

The mijikenda remained untouched by Islam and were recruited by the missionaries. Asara Opoku asserts,

> Most of the recruits would appear to be those who were regarded by the Africans as social outcasts, and the downtrodden such as lepers and others who suffered various forms of social disabilities in traditional African societies. Included in this category were those who had broken certain traditional taboos and were fleeing from persecution.[8]

The result of the outcast coming to the missionaries seeking assistance supported the racist ideas of Europeans toward Africans. It added to the belief that Africans were culturally backward, miserable human beings and that the white man was justified in his efforts to uplift and transform the continent and its people through conversion and education into a modern Christianized/western society. In fact, the first Kenyan convert to be baptized by the CMS evangelists was Mringe, a dying cripple of Giriama ethnic background.

In addition, Rabai and its sister station in Bagamoyo, Tanganyika became the most important colonies for freed slaves.[9] Some of the newly freed people came from Bombay, India, while others were rescued by the British from slave ships that had originated in Southern or Central Africa. The first group of 150 of so-called "Bombay Africans," arrived at Rabai in 1875. It was not long before Rabai became the largest freed slave compound in East Africa. The resettlement of "Bombay Africans" was an attempt by the British government and missionaries to

---

[6] Kimambo, 263.

[7] The mijikenda, or nine villages included the Chonyi, Digo, Duruma, Giriama, Jibana, Kambi, Kauma, Ribe, and Rabai. Rabai was also given the name Frere after Sir Battle Frere was sent by the CMS to establish a mission station at the village. His mission was to also negotiate a treaty prohibiting the slave trade with the Sultan of Zanzibar.

[8] K. Asare Opoku, "Religion in Africa During the Colonial Era," in *General History of Africa*, ed. A. Adu Boahen,. vol. 7 (UNESCO: Paris, 1985), 527.

[9] Neely Tucker, "Descendants Hold To Ex-Slaves Dream" (Detroit Free Press: Detroit November 1997), 15.

establish communities for freed Africans in East Africa comparable with the settlement of the "Atlantic freed slaves" in Liberia and Sierra Leone. The European missionaries consciously discriminated between the "Bombay Africans" and the free Bantu people of the coast. Unlike the Bantu, most of the "Bombay Africans" mastered different languages, including English, and possessed various skills in trade, carpentry, and farming. Accordingly, they received better treatment from the Europeans than the indigenous coastal Africans. This discriminatory treatment fostered resentment and strained the relationship between the two groups.

The new converts received instruction in reading and writing in English, Bible studies, and learned various skills and crafts such as carpentry and gardening. Nevertheless, the teaching of Christianity and conversion remained the primary goal of the missionaries. The graduates of the missionary schools were expected to become religious and convert other Africans. They were also to undermine traditional African customs and practices such as rites of passage, drumming and dancing, birth and death rituals, pouring of libations and all customs and traditions that European missionaries deemed pagan. In essence, African missionaries were to bring Africans to Christ, imbibe them with European values, and train them in vocational crafts. The missionaries were working hand in hand with the British government to develop a group of Africans that could eventually enter the colonial workforce and use their vocation training to produce goods and services for the British. Eventually, the elements individualism, competition, and elitism that were often not a critical factor in traditional African societies were strongly expressed from the establishment of the early missionary schools. The "Bombay Slaves" and the coastal Africans at Rabai constituted the first group of western-educated elites in Kenya. These western-educated elites were called the *Asomi* which is the Kiswahili term for western-educated elite.

Although there relationship between the "Bombay Africans" and the indigenous coastal Africans was strained the education gained from the missionary schools allowed them the opportunity to become ministers, journalists, trade unionists, craftsmen, and junior civil servants particularly during the colonial period. It has been noted that European accounts on the social conditions and geography of East Africa were based primarily on reports and journals of "Bombay Africans" such as William Jones. Jones and other men, including David George, Jacob Wainwright, and Matthew Wellington, helped in the establishment of missions in East Africa. In other words, missionary education in East Africa, and the whole of Africa for that matter, produced western-educated African elites that eventually became the intellectual and spiritual equals to the Europeans.[10]

It must be noted that there are relative similarities between the fortunes of the "Bombay Africans" and their counterparts in West Africa, that is, the freed Atlantic slave communities that the British and Americans established in Sierra Leone and Liberia. Both the Americo-Liberians and Sierra Leone creoles received preferential treatment from the missionaries and the British administration over the indigenous Africans in the region because of their susceptibility and readiness to accept the patronage of the missionaries and the colonial administration. They were educated by the church and enjoyed the protection of their "liberators," the British.[11]

---

[10] Joseph E. Harris, *The African Presence in Asia: Consequences of the East African Slave Trade* (Evanston: Northwestern University Press, 1971), 73–76; Neely Tucker, 15.

[11] Walter Williams, *Black Americans and the Evangelization of Africa, 1877–1900* (Madison: University of Wisconsin Press, 1982), 141.

Evangelists of the CMS were joined in due time by other colleagues deployed by the University Mission to Central Africa, the Holy Ghost Fathers, the London Missionary Society, the Anglican Church, the Scottish Free Church, the Gospel Missionary Society, and the African Inland Mission. In fact, the last decades of the nineteenth century witnessed the tremendous flow of missionaries from the coast into the interior of the continent. The thrust was made possible by the opening up of the hinterland by explorers and geographers, the discovery of new medicine to combat tropical diseases that killed Europeans and the establishment of European rule. For sure, once the Europeans dug in, their colonial governments considered the missions true partners sharing the same values, culture, and aspirations in transforming African through establishing European hegemony and extending Christian education to the native.[12] Hence, the colonial authorities provided the missionaries with protection and offered them huge subsidies. Consequently, numerous churches and missionary schools sprang up in Kenya and the whole of Africa. In fact, the church also served as a school. Thus, with the relative increase of schools, missionary education became available to a very section of Kenyans.

Europeans believed that missionary education was a great success from its inception. Reports in the Anglican Church newspapers in 1876 proudly described the "African Christian Soldiers as the best examples of what black men may become." But a few years later, in 1881, the same men were dismissed as being "idle and slovenly in their habits and their women spend most of their time gossiping and sleeping." This change in attitude is reflective of the growing menace caused by the newly minted African missionary men who now enjoyed a "privileged" position in their society and viewed themselves and above the general population of Africans. African evangelists aspired to positons with higher status than that of priesthood—positions that were exclusive to European missionaries. No European missionary was prepared to concede this to Africans for it implied subordination to a "lesser" human being. In addition, African missionaries demanded the Africanization of the Church in worship, theology, and understanding. The African missionaries noted that Christianity ought not to be presented to Africans as it was understood and interpreted by Europeans. Such were the revolutionary demands that shocked European evangelism to the core for they entailed the blending of Christianity with what the European missionaries described as "pagan" practices of Africans and subordination of whites to blacks. Further still, African priests resented the fact that European missionaries were paid three times as much as African ministers and demanded equal pay. They decried the audacity of the British missionaries who appointed themselves as legal magistrates in order to administer civil and criminal law on Africans. To place this situation into context, the African missionaries sought out to reconstitute the environment that made the superiority and authority of the Europeans missionaries absolute.[13] In other words, the African ministers actively demanded and fought for a fair distribution of the power with the colonial religious, economic, and political spheres.

The reaction of the European missionaries to the demand of the African missionaries was dramatic. They stopped teaching English, decreased the school day to a half-day, and forced students to spend the majority of their time on farms. The African responded by organizing independent African churches known as Akurinu in Kikuyu language. This was how the western-educated elites lit the torch of African nationalism.

---

[12] Opoku, 525.

[13] Colin Reed, *Pastors, Partners, and Paternalists: African Church Leaders and Western Missionaries in the Anglican Church in Kenya, 1850–1900* (Leiden, NY: E.J. Brill, 1997), 121.

A number of independent African churches began to rise throughout Kenya that cut across ethnic boundaries. Churches included the *Dini ya Nsambwa* (Church of the Ancestors), Nomiya Luo Mission, which was founded in 1910 by John Owallo among the Luo. The *Nomiya* Luo Mission adopted biblical circumcision for men as a necessary tool of salvation, a previously unknown tradition among the Luo.[14] One may also note the following independent churches: the *Dini ya Roho* (Holy Ghost Church), founded in 1927 among the Abaluyia by Jakobo Buluko and Daniel Sande; the *Joroho* (Holy Ghost), founded by Alfa Odongo among the Luo, and the Independent African Church, founded in 1929 among the Maasai in Narok by Ole Sempele.[15]

The rise of the Independent Maasai African Church (IMAC) under the leadership of its founder, Molonkett Olokorinya Ole Sempele of the Maasai, provides an early glimpse toward the plight of African Americans in the United States. Further, it gives insight into the disenchantment of African missionary educated elites with racist, white dominated Christian societies in Kenya and the United States. It is also a reflection of the fear of its leadership that the same horrifying fate experienced by African Americans in the United States would eventually extend its reach to Kenya, which is steadily being dominated by racists white settlers, colonists, and missionaries. The Maasai were the very first ethnic group in Kenya to whose land was taken by European settlers. As you will better understand later in this chapter, the founding of the IMAC will clearly show the influence of black institutions of higher learning and black communities in the United States on church leaders on the African continent. This is a window to the emerging Pan-African movement and ideology.

Ole Sempele was one of the earliest Maasai converts of the African Inland Mission (AIM), now known as the African Inland Church. He was educated at Thogoto School. In 1908, he accompanied his AIM friends, the Stauffachers, to the United States where he attended a trade school for blacks in North Carolina. He later joined the Boydton Academic and Bible Institute, which was founded in 1878 in Boydton, Virginia.[16] Throughout his studies in Kenya, North Carolina, and Virginia, Ole Sempele held favorable opinions about the positive role that Christianity played in America. However, his attitude changed toward "Christianity" when he heard about the lynching of 230 African American Christians by white supremacists. He instantly resented, not the faith itself, but the hypocritical, racist attitude of its white bearers. On his return to Kenya, he immediately broke away from the AIM and found his IMAC.[17]

African priests did not rise to the highest levels of the established white church until after Kenya gained its independence. A few of the African priests that rose to the highest levels of the church include Archbishop Festo Olang from Abaluyia. Reverend Festo Oland was educated in the CMS School in Maseno and Alliance High. He later attended St. Paul's Theological College in Limuru and was ordained as a Deacon in Nairobi. In 1948, he received a British Council scholarship that helped him attend Wycliffe Hall, Oxford, and Holy Trinity Parish in Bristol. In 1951, he became Dean for Central Nyanza and in 1955 was consecrated as Assistant

---

[14] Owallo is said to have had a vision in 1907 in which he was taken to Heaven by the Arch-Angel, Gabriel. While in heaven, he noticed that the Popes, Europeans as well as Asians were not allowed entry. He therefore came to the conclusion that the white and Asian churches were not for Africans. Hence, he founded *Nomiya*, a church that mixed Christianity with Luo traditional practices.

[15] Opoku, 531.

[16] G.E. Richings, *Evidence of Progress Among Colored People*, 8th ed. (Philadelphia: Geo. S. Ferguson Co, 1902).

[17] Kenneth King, *Pan-Africanism and Education: A Study of Race Philanthropy and Education in the Southern States of America and East Africa* (New York: Oxford University Press, 1971), 245.

Bishop of Kampala, Uganda. Therefore, he became Bishop of Maseno Diocese, and in 1970 was elected as the first African Archbishop of the Anglican Church in Kenya.[18]

Another African priest, his Eminence Maurice Michael Otunga, rose to the high post of Cardinal ten years after Kenya gained her independence. Otunga's father was a traditional paramount chief of the Bakhone who never converted to Christianity. His mother Rosa Namisi, was a renowned diviner. Otunga was baptized at the age of twelve. He studied at Mangu High, one of the oldest Catholic institutions in Kenya, before he attended St. Mary's Seminary in Kakamega and St. Mary's Seminary in Gbaga, Uganda. Thereafter, he joined the Pontifical College in Rome. Cardinal Otunga completed his major seminary training in Italy and was ordained priest in 1950. He finished his studies at the College of Propaganda Fide before he returned to Kenya to join the Kakamega Seminary where he taught Theology for five years.[19] During this period he became diocesan chancellor and staff member of apostolic delegation in Anglophone Africa. By 1969, he was elevated to Bishop of Kisii and then appointed Titular Archbishop of Bormarzo and Coadjutor of Nairobi, with the right of succession.[20] On October 24, 1970 Otunga was named the Archbishop of Nairobi. Otunga was Kenya's first black Bishop, Archbishop, and Cardinal.

Several highly ranked Kenyan evangelists received advanced theological education in black seminaries in the United States. Amongst these were Henry John Okullu and Reverend Thomas Johnson Kahume. Both men climbed to the supreme level of Bishop after independence. Okullu, a Luo from Kisumu was baptized at the age of eighteen and was given the name John Henry. He attended Kima Primary but soon abandoned his studies because of the harsh treatment and discriminatory attitude of his white instructors. Okullu then left for Uganda and worked with the East African Railways and Harbors while continuing missionary training at Bishop Tucker Theological College. He was ordained Deacon in 1957 and priest in 1958. Okullu then traveled to the United States and gained a degree of Bachelor of Divinity at the then "all Negro" institute. Virginia Theological Seminary, in Lynchburg, Virginia, in 1965. He returned to Uganda to become the editor of *New Day*, a Christian newspaper owned by the Church of Uganda. His editorials critiqued one-party political systems as being "tyrannical and unworkable ... made life uncomfortable for President Milton Obote of Uganda who favored one-party politics.[21] Okullu eventually returned to Kenya in 1969 to serve as the editor of *Target* (in English) and *Lengo* (in Kiswahili) that was published by the National Council of Churches of Kenya. His editorials continued to press for multiparty political systems and his objection to monolithic politics. In 1971, Okullu was consecrated the first Kenyan Provost of All Saints Cathedral in Nairobi and from 1974 occupied the post of Bishop of Maseno South Diocese. Throughout his live, Bishop Okullu used the pulpit effectively "to poke barbs a public institutions, including the Chruch, which did not live up to the people's expectations." He was accused by the Kenyan political establishment of being a "leftist," a charge that he simply dismissed by saying, "I do not know what I means to be a leftist, I just preach the truth."[22] He received an honorary Doctor of Divinity degree from Virginia Theological Seminary.

---

[18] The Nation, February 4, 2004.

[19] Sunday Standard, "Catholic Information Service For Africa," Issue No. 255, September 7, 2003, 1–7.

[20] Catholic Information Service For Africa, Issue No. 255, September 7, 2003.

[21] East African Standard, December 15, 2003.

[22] Ibid.

Reverend Thomas Johnson Kalume from the Kamba nation received his advanced missionary education in the United States. He attended Jilore Primary, Bate Sector School, and Katoleni Boarding School in Kenya. In 1950, he joined Kagumo Teachers College and the United Theological College in Lauru. Thereafter, he went to the United States where he received a Master's degree in Religious Education from Union Theological College in 1967. In that same year he was ordained the first Kamba Bishop.

The collective drive of the independent African churches, sometimes referred to as "Breakaway Churches," of Kenya and other sister churches in Africa, brought Christianity home where African ministers interpreted the Bible in accordance with their own independent reading of it. Ironically, by rendering the Bible into African languages, the European missionaries, without realizing it, helped break down their monopoly over Christian spirituality in Africa by their own hands.

With this in mind, it was from the womb of missionary education, in conjunction with colonial education, that western educated African elites emerged. Missionary schools provided the vehicle through which Kenyans not only converted to Christianity but also learned the languages, customs, and methods of the Europeans. In addition, government schools provided a somewhat broader learning in arithmetic, geography, and history.[23] Thus, besides religious leaders, both systems, which Kenyans call "enabling education," produced African elites who filled all kinds of subordinate positions in the colonial administration not only in Kenya but also in regions under colonial rule throughout the continent of Africa. It was from the midst of this group of westernized African elites that colossal figures sprang up to challenge European presence, domination, and rule in Africa. A crop of missionary school graduates not only spearheaded the radical nationalist movements in Africa but also inherited power from the Europeans upon independence. These western-educated elites include Harry Thuku, father of Kenyan nationalism, Tom Mboya, Mzee Jomo Kenyatta, the first Prime Minister of Kenya, Honorable Mbiyu Koninage, Dr. Julius Kiano, Honorable K.K. Nijiiri, Jaramogi, Oginga Odinga, Daniel Toroitich Arap Moi, the second President of Kenya, Jones Beauttah, Jonathan Okiwiri, Jeremiah, Awori Reuben Omulo, Simon Nyendi, Jesse Kariuki, John Machuchu, and Joseph Kang'ethe, to name a few.

There is no doubt that the missionaries and the colonial government were bedfellows. In fact, the march of the European powers into Africa owes greatly to the incessant appeals by the missionaries. Civilizing the natives and promoting commerce and agriculture were beliefs shared by both the missionaries and European policy makers. The missionaries were of the opinion that the task, "the White Man's Burden," could be successfully accomplished under the protection of European governments, preferably their home governments, in territories in which they operated. Hence, British missionaries in East Africa called upon their Imperial Government to intervene in the region. It is thus correctly stated, "on the whole it may be said that Christian missions in Africa were the ally and adjunct of European imperialism and the activity of missionaries were part and parcel of the advance and penetration of the West into the non-western world."[24] Indeed, the immediate educational policy of the British administration

---

[23] R. Mugo Gatheru, personal communication with author, Sacramento, California, October 31, 2003.
[24] Opoku, 525.

in Kenya did not differ from that of the missionaries for both systems sought to produce religious coverts, teachers, laborers for white farms, and junior civil service positions.

Once British rule was established in East Africa with the blessings and support, and quite often at the behest of the missionaries, the best lands were firmly in the hands of white settlers, a new money economy based on plantations emerged in Kenya and the foundation was laid down for decades in missionary schools to develop a human labor force consisting of western-educated elites. It was Saint Austin's missionary school, established in 1898, that pioneered the growing of Arabica coffee on the volcanic slopes of Nairobi. Subsequently, the cultivation of coffee expanded at an astonishingly rapid pace as coffee farms owned and run by white settlers as well as the missions that sprang up throughout the Highlands of Kenya. By 1920, coffee, was considered the black gold became the leading cash crop in Kenya. The other cash crops were tea, pyrethrum, and sisal. Hence, the emerging money economy, the colonial administration and efficient communication systems—railway, ports, and mail and telegraph services that were subsequently developed, and the emergence of urban centers, such as Nairobi and Machakos, required a huge cadre of trained Africans to run them. A skilled and semiskilled African labor force became necessary and urgent particularly as British colonial policy demanded that each colony maintained itself.[25]

For that purpose, the colonial administration subsidized missionary schools to provide the needed workforce. However, it soon became clear that missionary education, because of its heavy concentration on religious subjects and relatively modest number of mission schools, was unable to produce the huge army of African workers the colony required. In fact, by 1910 there were only thirty-five missionary schools in the whole colony. To solve the problem, the British established a commission headed by J. Nelson Frazer who was brought from India in 1909 to serve as advisor to the colonial authorities. The Frazer Commission recommended a dual-educational system: academic for Europeans and vocational for Africans, notwithstanding that the colonial government had been all along solely concerned with the educational provisions for the children of European settlers. In fact the first schools for European students, the Prince of Wales and the Duke of York for boys and the Duchess of York for girls, were opened in 1902 to prepare white students for administrative and professional positions. The Asian community opened its first school, the Duke of Gloucester, in 1910 where students received both academic and commerce oriented instruction that prepared them for positions as accountants, businessmen, and technicians.

The Frazer Commission, in other words, recommended that education be racially segregated. Accordingly, the colonial authorities established the first government school exclusively for Africans in Machakos town in 1913. The school provided technical and industrial education based on the model of African American schools in the United States. At any rate, the Frazer Commission set the standard for education policy Kenya for the colonial era and provided the guidelines that the 1924 Phelps-Stokes Commission and the 1949 Beecher Commission followed faithfully.[26] The Phelps-Stokes Commission emphasized the need to train African youths in agriculture and craftsmanship for the benefit of Africans in the rural areas. The Beecher Commission stressed a curriculum for Africans that prepared them to work efficiently on settler farms and to fill clerical positions in the colonial administration.

---

[25] Sir Andrew Cohen, *British Policy in Changing Africa* (Evanston: Northwestern University Press, 1959), 16.

[26] William R. Ochieng, *Themes in Kenyan History* (Ohio University Press, 1990), 149.

In 1911, the first Department of Education in Kenya was formed and James Orr was chosen as the Director. The department was charged with establishing and overseeing government schools, and by extension, keep missionary education in check. During his tenure in office, Orr advocated and worked diligently to promote "village" industries and craftsmanship to meet the needs of Africans rather than to feed settler plantations. It was under his administration that the first government schools were established in Machakos. African students soon realized that working on settler plantations brought them more immediate financial reward than serving in the small, subsistence "village" economy. Therefore, the majority of young Africans gravitated around white farms after leaving school.

In 1918, the Education Commission formed by Orr recommended that the government should play the major role in education in the territory, while at the same time, allow the missions to maintain some influence in educational activities. The missions were to focus on "character building" or vocational education in order to receive subsidies. This would ensure close government control over missionary schools. Since most of the missionary schools were underfinanced, the governmental subsidies would allow them to continue with their primary objectives of converting Africans to Christianity and at the same time focusing on vocational education. Some missionaries sincerely believed that vocational education was absolutely the correct type of education for Africans. In their opinion, the primitiveness and innate depravity of Africans precluded them from benefiting from liberal education. In essence, technical education would make Africans more industrious and instill in them Christian virtues to offset the lack of morality in African societies.[27] Many missionaries considered plantations as one of the tools that, in their opinion, promoted legitimate trade and commerce that saved the natives from the misery vented on them by the Atlantic and Indian Ocean slave trade and by destitution.

Professor Mugo Gatheru recalls that education in the primary and secondary school was very demanding and that "discipline was imposed severely ... the schools were run like military academies. Social life was discouraged. Corporal punishment and obedience were encouraged (and) the students were overworked." Still, neither the missionaries nor the colonial authorities intended to extend mass education to the masses of Africans, only to the few Africans who were then absorbed into the colonial administration and were paid very low wages. Gatheru further states that the system of education was, "a very solid foundation for those who had opportunities to study abroad for further education ... it also "enabled" many Kenyan leaders to become icons in the Independent African Church movement, the African nationalist movement, and in independent Kenya.[28]

Missionary and vocational education opened the gates for Kenyan elites to enter the arena of employment not only as priests or the cash crop economy but also in the colonial civil and military services. Africans were thus able to unveil the secrets of the power structure. Kenyans worked as clerks, policemen, and hospital staff, and at ports and on railways; they manned the telephone, telegraph, and mail services; they drove motortrucks and were employed as school teachers. It was this early group of western-educated elites that began the fight for later elites to govern independent Kenya.

---

[27] Daniel N. Sifuna, *Development of Education in Africa: The Kenyan Experience* (Nairobi: Initiatives Publishers, 1991), 52.
[28] Mugo Gatheru to Jim Harper, October 31, 2003.

Missionary and government schools in Kenya along with the entire East Africa Protectorate had laid down the foundation for the development of the *Asomi*, western educated Africans that came to react radically in different ways to the realities of colonialism and racism, to European Christianity and its white bearers, and to white settlement. The first reaction of the *Asomi* was directed toward their mentors, the white missions, pioneers of western education in the region. The reaction involved the formation of independent indigenous churches to provide "a place to feel at home for the many Africans who had accepted Christianity but found it intolerable to live under missionary patronage.[29] The independent Churches provided the spiritual inspiration to fight white missionary domination and blend Christianity with African spiritually and beliefs. In other words, the independent Churches were part and parcel of the larger resistance movement against British colonialism. Further still, the *Asomi* were credited with the founding of independent schools and the establishment of political organizations, known as Young Associations, which articulated the grievance of the masses.

In 1929, the western educated Kikuyu ethnic group formed two organizations, the Kikuyu Independent School Organization (KISA) and the Kikuyu Karanja Education Association (KKEA), to look into the possibility of establishing their own schools free of missionary and government control. The Kikuyu elites were reacting to missions, particularly the Church of Scotland prohibition of the ancient custom of female circumcision, to the absence of Kikuyu voice in the administration of missionary and government schools, and to the curricula that these schools offered. KISA and KKEA endeavored to incorporate western culture into their traditional society and contribute mightily to the advancement of the people without their basic values. Thus, the independent schools should be considered yet another expression of resistance to European supremacy. Consequently, the first independent school was founded at Kiambu, in the heart of Kikuyu homeland. The colonial authorities initially viewed the independent schools as a step toward promoting denominational schools rather than yet another tool in the nascent, radical African nationalist movement. However, the authorities soon realized the menace that these schools nurtured toward the colonial situation in their country. By 1931, the colonial government set in motion a plan to take over the independent African schools and extend government control over all schools.

The British government's plan was to increase representation of Africans on Local Native Councils, whose duties included, among other things, overseeing education in their respective districts and providing grants-in-aid to the schools.[30] However, the Great Depression of the 1930s brought with it financial constraints that made it rather impossible for the colonial government to finance and consequently control the independent schools movement that gave the Africans almost complete freedom to open new schools and run them the way they wanted. The independent schools offered their students curricula that fostered the nationalist spirit and provided reasonable or free tuition to students who could not afford it. The development of independent schools represented the rise of cultural nationalism in Kenya. Like missionary and government schools, the independent schools were thus a vehicle of change, different as it may be, and the platform that produced a cadre of elite that challenged the Europeans.

---

[29] E.S. Atieno-Odhiambo, "Politics and Nationalism in East Africa, 1919–35," in *UNESCO General History of Africa*, ed. A. Adu Boahen, vol. 7, 671.

[30] E.B. Wellburn, *East African Rebels: A Study of Some Independent Churches* (London: SCM Press, 1961), 159.

KISA and KKEA were instrumental in founding of the independent Kikuyu African Orthodox Church (AOC) with an African American/Caribbean/South African influence. In 1930, the organizations invited Bishop Daniel William Alexander to visit Kenya. Bishop Alexander was born in Kimberly, South Africa, to an emigrant from Antiqua and an African woman.[31] He traveled to America in 1927 to join the AOC, which had been established in 1921 by Antiguan George Alexander McGuire in close association with the Universal Negro Improvement Association (UNIA) which was founded by Marcus Garvey. During his trip, Alexander was consecrated by McGuire and on his return to South Africa he established his church, St. Augustine of Hippo, in Kimberly. While in Kenya, Bishop Alexander trained and ordained four priests that KISA and KKEA assigned to him. Therefore, Alexander laid down the foundation for the AOC in Kenya. Now, more independent African churches were spouting up at the same time that Independent African Schools and political organizations were being established.

The independent schools received a big boost with the arrival of Peter Mbiyu Koinange, son of the great Chief Koinange, of the Kikuyu nation. Peter Mbiyu Koinange came back to Kenya after attending college in the United States in 1938. Mbiyu, who attended Baxton School and Alliance High School in Kenya, had a long academic sojourn in America, where he studied at Hampton Institute (1927–1931) and Ohio Wesleyan University (1931–1933), and received his Masters of Arts degree in political science from Columbia in 1936. Mbiyu was the first Kenyan student to complete a postgraduate degree in liberal arts in the United States. Moreover, he joined St. Johns College in Britain from 1936 to 1937, where he met with Jomo Kenyatta over the colonial condition in their homeland, Kenya. Kenyatta would eventually become the first African President of Kenya in 1963 once Kenya gained its independence from Britain. While in the United States Mbiyu became a close associate of Ralph J. Bunche and his wife. He also bears witness to the atrocities committed by whites against blacks. Witnessing these events ignited in him the flames for fighting European injustices in his homeland. Hence, upon his return to Kenya in 1938, he embraced the independent church and school movements. Instantly he joined the movement by single handedly founding the Kenya Teachers College at Githunguri as an independent institution under the umbrella of KISA.[32] Mbiyu became one of the strongest advocates that Kenyan students should attend colleges and universities in the United States. He therefore, encouraged and assisted students, such as Julius Gikonyo Kiano to seek higher education in American institutes of higher learning. Julius Kiano was one of the students that followed in his footsteps and became the first Kenyan to receive a Ph.D. Mbiyu participated in the founding of the Kenya African Union and thus became one of the dominant figures in the nationalist movement, as well as in the Cabinet of President Jomo Kenyatta.

With the small expansion in secondary schools (middle schools) in the middle of the 1930s, the British colonial government recognized the need for higher education in their African dominions. Accordingly, a commission, the de la Warr Commission, was appointed in 1937 to determine the necessity for higher education in Kenya. The report of the Commission was criticized for being too focused on technical and vocational education. Nonetheless, the Commission recommended that Makerere institution in Kampala, Uganda, established in 1922

---

[31] Morris Johnson, *Archbishop Daniel William Alexander and the African Orthodox Church* (UK: Rowman and Littlefield, 1999), 15.
[32] Interview with Dr. Julius Gikonyo Kiano, Nairobi, Kenya, June 29, 1999.

to promote skilled trades, be transformed into a college open to secondary school graduates in the Protectorate. Furthermore, the 1945 Asquith Commission recommended the formation of the Inter-University Council for Education in the colonies to establish colleges as satellites of the University College linked to the University of London. Makerere was accordingly raised to the status of a University College linked to the University of London. Finally, general academic "college" education was extended to a few East Africans. Consequently, a small crop of western educated professionals—nurses, technocrats, journalists, and academicians—sprouted. They too stepped forward to raise the level of resistance and the nationalist movement in the region.

Western education fostered the emergence of political organizations, Young Assocations, that addressed by chiefs appointed by the colonial authorities. Their founders in Kenya were a group of youths who graduated from missionary schools.[33] The first Young Association in East Africa was the Young Baganda Association founded in Uganda in 1919 by Z.K. Sentogo. Its secretary, Joseph Kamulegeya had a close relationship with W.E.B. DuBois, Marcus Garvey, and Tuskegee Institute introduced a young Kikuyu from Kenya, Harry Thuku, to his American friends. The Young Banganda Association was founded to protest against the authority that the colonial government vested in appointed chiefs. Some African chiefs were received colonial support and funding to carry out the plans of the colonial authorities. It was this organization that inspired the rise of sister organizations in Kenya such as the Young Kikuyu Association (YKA), The Kikuyu Central Association (KCU), and the Young Kavirondo Association.

On June 11, 1921, Harry Thuku, a young Kikuyu graduate of the Gospel Missionary Society School who lived in Nairobi where he was employed as a telephone operator, launched the YKA, with the assistance of Josse Kariuki, Job Muchuchu, and Abdula Tarrar. Within a couple of months, the founding members realized that the name, the YKA, did not represent the all-encompassing philosophy they hoped to implement. That philosophy was delineated by Harry Thuku who announced that "unless the people of this country form and Association, the Native in Kenya will always remain voiceless."[34] The change in the name became urgent as Thuku canvassed for membership in Nairobi not only amongst the Kikuyu but also the Kamba, the Luo, the Ganda, the Maasai, the Swahili, and the Asian community. Furthermore, Thuku's exposure to the thoughts of DuBois and Garvey helped shape his political awareness and inspired him toward embracing all Kenyans irrespective of their ethnic background. I have been reported that Thuku received copies of the *Negro World*, the publication of the Universal Negro Improvement Association founded by Marcus Garvey. As a result, the name of the YKA was changed to the East African Association in order to encompass all groups. The name change allowed Thuku to receive more support from other Young Associations as well as the Asian community. The political manifesto of the East African Association addressed general issues that were the concern of the entire nation such land alienation, the excessive hut and poll tax, the reduction of wages by the government and settlers, the registration system, and forced labor (*kipande*).[35]

---

[33] E.S. Atieno-Odhiambo, "Politics and Nationalism in East Africa, 1919–35," in *UNESCO General History of Africa*, ed. A. Adu Boahen, vol. 7, 665–72.

[34] Ibid., 669.

[35] *Kipande* or forced labor was imposed by the Colonial Authorities on all adult males to serve in settler plantations and public facilities.

Thuku cabled these issues directly to London. He persisted in bypassing the local colonial authorities, and raised complaints to the Colonial Office. In 1922, he was arrested and incarcerated by the police in Nairobi allegedly as a danger to peace and order. The arrest caused an uproar in the city. A few days after his arrest the masses in Nairobi went on a general strike and surrounded the police station. The police intervened, opened fire, and left twenty-one Africans dead. Thuku was deported to distant Kisimayu where he was detained for nine years. That signaled the death of the first multiethnic, multiracial organization in Kenya. However, a new fractional organization rose, the KCU. The Kikuyu elected Thuku as its leader in absentia. A younger Kikuyu activist, Johnston (Jomo) Kenyatta, who was educated at the Thogoto Missionary School, assumed the leadership position of the KCU. The political agenda of the newly founded Association was to reclaim the land taken by the government, settlers, and missions then restore the land to the Kenyans.

Essentially, the establishment of the mission school of the CMS in 1846 at Rabai, near Mombasa, led to the development of formal education in Kenya. More missionary schools were eventually opened by other denominations. The initial purpose of these mission schools was evangelism and conversion of the local people to Christianity. However, with the colonization of Kenya and the influx of settlers underway, the railway into the interior constructed, a cash crop economy developed, and the country received thousands of immigrants from Asia, the whole fabric of the Kenyan society was transformed. This necessitated a change in the track of the education system for Africans. Hence, mission schools shifted toward the production of laborers for the farms of the European settler population, and clerical staff for the colonial administration. This "formal education" gave birth to educated elites that aspired for a high level in the new system and eventually for replacing it. Consequently, the western educated elites, the *Asomi*, broke away from the established colonial and missionary organizations to develop independent churches that "Africanized" the Christianity of the Europeans, formed Associations that became the voice of the masses in place of the colonial chiefs and white pastors, and built national schools to instill in the young generation a sense of patriotism and pride. Yet, one cannot but notice the small, albeit significant presence of African American influences in Kenya in the first thirty years or so of British control of the country. Although the colonial administration barred black "agitators" in the Diaspora from entry, the Phelps-Stokes Commission was able to establish the Jeanes School, which contributed to the development of educated elites in Kenya. Besides, the views of DuBois and Garvey and the inspiration of Tuskegee and Hampton had a great impact in shaping the political philosophy of some of the indomitable elites such as Ole Sempele, Harry Thuku, and Jomo Kenyatta.

KEY TERMS

Asomi
Formal Education
Informal Education
Kipande
Independent African Church
Independent African Schools
Phelps-Stokes Commission

CHAPTER 15

EDUCATION FOR FREEDOM: BLACK SOUTH AFRICANS IN THE UNITED STATES, 1870–1970

Charles D. Johnson

INTRODUCTION

Black South Africans were both pushed and pulled to leave their homeland. De facto racia discrimination, pervasive racial violence, and consequent pauperization combined with the utter lack of opportunities for social mobility conspired to push many black South Africans to search for better and safer prospects. Many of them would end up traveling to the United States, pulled by the hope that their going would create possibilities for them that were not available to them in South Africa. African American visitors to South Africa made a profound and positive impression on South Africans that informed their decision to travel to the United States. For example, Orpheus McAdoo's entertainers left South African audiences spellbound and desirous of emulating African Americans. According to James Campbell:

> The conclusion that African audiences seem almost universally to have drawn—was that African Americans were more "advanced" than they. This idea was to have an abiding impact on South African black culture… For much of the twentieth century, black America would remain a symbol of urbanity and sophistication among black South Africans, especially in the cities.[1]

Relative to their black South African brothers and sisters, African Americans had *Contemporary Hindsight*, that is, they had in many instances previously experienced the travails that were contemporary for South Africans. Contemporary hindsight was a form of déjà vu. For many African American visitors, going to South Africa was like stepping back in time and walking into their own past. African Americans were a few steps ahead of black South Africans who were following them along a similar trajectory of struggle. Each was fighting to emerge from pervasive systems of racial oppression that were akin. This déjà vu gave African Americans the ability to reflect back through their particular experiences and help South Africans to anticipate, to better understand, and to overcome their racial tyranny.

African Americans had had opportunities for ideological and cultural-creative development that were not readily available to South Africans. As a policy, South Africans were maliciously

---

[1] James Campbell, *Songs of Zion: The African Methodist Church in the United States and South Africa* (Chapel Hill, NC: University of North Carolina Press, 1998), 131.

repressed to keep each successive generation as unenlightened and no further advanced then preceding generations. For white South African society, denying black South Africans to learn and to reach their full potential as members of the human family was a fundamental weapon in their arsenal of racial domination. Slaveholders had similarly kept African Americans in ignorance and some states even made it a crime to teach an enslaved African American to read. In the socially monolithic rural areas of the South, this proved to be much easier to accomplish than in urban areas in the north, where the edifying result of a diversity of opinions existed. This would prove to be true in both the United States and in South Africa.

In South Africa, black South Africans were largely forced to live in the rural areas and kept out of the living spaces in the cities. The Native Land Act (1913) forced Africans to live in reserves, areas similar to Indian reservations in the United States. Of course, there were exceptions such as Sophiatown and Soweto, which were townships that provided living quarters for blacks who worked primarily in service jobs for whites in Johannesburg. For it was the cities that often served as cultural incubators, where an amalgam of ideas and beliefs coalesced in public gathering spaces to form new points of view, new opinions, and new cultures. Port cities in South Africa played an especially important role in the development of black culture and in creating the politics of resistance in South Africa. Cape Town during the nineteenth century, for instance, became a cosmopolitan city as black sailors from throughout the Atlantic realm made port there. Cities also often had institutions frequented by blacks including churches.

The black church in South Africa and the United States have parallel histories, but the formative church experiences of African Americans precede those of South Africans by several decades. Breaking away from white congregations, African American and South African church leaders sought a place in the sun where they could develop their own brand of Christian religious expression and to serve the needs of their parishioners as they best saw fit. Independent religious institutions proved to be an excellent training ground for community and political leadership. Religious instruction, no doubt, prepared church leaders for service to the community.

But what really placed African Americans ahead of their brothers and sisters in South Africa more than the cities or churches were the numerous Historically Black Colleges and Universities (HBCUs). HBCUs were critical to the development of the African America community. They provided educational opportunities that otherwise would not have existed for blacks. They produced its ministers, doctors, lawyers, business professionals, teachers, and many of leaders of the civil rights movement. Booker T. Washington attended Hampton Institute (Hampton University) in Virginia and was the founder of Tuskegee Institute (Tuskegee University) in Alabama. Reverend Dr. Martin Luther King Jr. graduated from Morehouse College in Atlanta, GA. Civil Rights attorney and the first African American Supreme Court Justice, Thurgood Marshall, who tried and won the important Brown v. Board of Education (1954) case that desegregated schools was a graduate of Lincoln University in Pennsylvania. Kwame Ture (Stokely Carmichael) who was one of the principal leaders of the Black Power movement in the United States was a graduate of Howard University. Undoubtedly, then education was critical to freedom because the oppressive demon that had first to be slain was ignorance. South Africans understood this and through their contact with African Americans learned of educational opportunities in the United States.

Logically then, the majority of South Africans to come to the United States came for education. With one exception, only a few of the better-known South Africans who visited the United States are considered here. Starting in the nineteenth century, they made the trip seeking educational opportunities that did not exist for them in South Africa. For those South Africans fortunate enough to receive an education in the United States, their scholastic attainments distinguished them within their race when they returned home and many of them became prominent leaders in South Africa. While sojourning in the United States, Jim Crow racism and segregation meant that black South Africans had to deal with the same hardships as their African American brothers and sisters, experiences that because of the racial situation in South Africa would have been very familiar to them. Being able to empathize with African Americans brought the two groups into a tight web of friendship and alliances upon which they built their struggle for equality and freedom.[2]

ENCOUNTERS

Horace Mann Bond's research suggests that the first South African to attend school in the United States enrolled at Howard University in 1871.[3] Between 1870 and 1950, roughly the time frame of this study, Bond estimates that 106 South Africans enrolled at historically black institutions in the United States. In the period from 1870 to 1910, the largest number of South African students, twenty-three, enrolled at Wilberforce University. Wilberforce's popularity is directly related to its affiliation with the African Methodist Episcopal Church (AMEC) and the work of that denomination in South Africa. During the same forty-year period, Lincoln had thirteen South Africans enroll, Tuskegee had ten, and Howard had seven.[4] Bond's estimate does not represent a grand total because several South Africans were educated outside of HBCUs.

James Campbell has chronicled the AMEC history in South Africa. His work reveals the overlapping relationships that emerge between African Americans and black South Africans as they crisscrossed the Atlantic seeking different types of opportunities. Charlotte Manye made the crossing and became the first African women from South Africa to obtain a bachelor of science degree, which she earned at a Historically Black College in the United States. Manye's circuitous journey began after she observed the Orpheus McAdoo Jubilee Singers in her hometown of Kimberley, South Africa during their 1890 visit. The Jubilee Singers from

---

[2] In the north and the south, whites and blacks clashed, often ending in a tragic loss of life. In the south, it was particularly bad for blacks as whites used extra legal means to maintain their economic dominance and position of social privilege. E. M. Beck and Stewart Tolnay, "The Killing Fields of the Deep South," *American Sociological Review* 55, 4 (August, 1990): 531. See also, Ralph Ginzburg, *100 Years of Lynching* (New York: Lancer Books, 1962, reprinted Black Classic Press, 1988). For a visual presentation see, James Allen, *Without Sanctuary: Lynching Photography in America* (Santa Fe, New Mexico: Twin Palms, 2000).

[3] Horace Mann Bond, Table 1, "African-American Relations Seen Through African Students Enrolled in American Negro Colleges: A Progress Report of a Historical Study" (1961), in box 36, folder 4, Third AMSAC conference papers, American Society of African Culture, Moorland Spingarn Research Center, Howard University. Bond claims to have obtained his findings from the catalogs and archives of the universities he researched including Howard University.

[4] Totals were gleaned from Table 2 in Bond's report. Ibid.

Hampton, Virginia, were an African American entertainment group led by Orpheus McAdoo who spent over a year in South Africa performing minstrel shows and singing black spirituals. South Africans particularly liked their rendering of slave songs. McAdoo had traveled internationally in the 1880s with the famous Fisk University Singers and based his group off of the Fisk Singers. McAdoo regaled their audiences with the achievements of African Americans, and their singing made a significant positive impact on South African choral music. Moved by their singing, Manye joined a white-owned African choral group that toured Great Britain. While on tour in Great Britain, the South African group met African Americans who informed Manye of educational opportunities in the United States.[5] At that time, there were no institutions of higher education in South Africa that would accept black South African students for advanced degrees. It would be almost another two decades before the Native College at Fort Hare opened its doors enabling Africans to receive a college education in South Africa. Having learned of the opportunities for higher education, Manye set her sights on going to the United States to go to college. Regrettably, the tour Manye was a part of ended in financial failure. When the white organizers billed a second tour that included the United States among its stops, Manye was the only returning member to sign up.[6] The financial issues that plagued the first tour also undermined the second, and the singers were left impecunious in Cleveland, Ohio. Reverdy Ransom, an AMEC minister, came to the rescue of the African singers. Believing they would make good missionaries, with the assistance of Bishop W. B. Derrick and Bishop Benjamin Arnett, he got Manye and several of the other singers admitted into Wilberforce University. Manye was also able to make arrangements for several of her South African countrymen to attend historic Wilberforce. Founded in 1856, the Institution was appropriately named in honor of William Wilberforce, the great English abolitionist. James Tantsi, Charles Dube, Henry Msikinya, Edward Tolityi Magaya, and Marshall Maxeke, whom Manye would later marry, joined her at Wilberforce. Tantsi and Maxeke played key roles in establishing the South African Native National Congress (SANNC), which later became the African National Congress (ANC). Charles Dube's brother, John, became the SANNC's first president. At Wilberforce, Manye and the other South African students studied under W. E. B. DuBois, who was then completing his studies for his Harvard PhD and undoubtedly working through his ideas on Pan Africanism. It is reasonable to assume that the South African students shared with DuBois the difficult conditions that Africans and people of color were forced to live under in South Africa.[7] Thus, in 1903, when he made his famous declaration in *The Souls of Black Folks* that "Gentle Reader . . . the problem of the Twentieth Century is the problem of the color-line," he understood that the problem of white supremacy was essentially global.[8]

Manye also played a critical role in establishing the AMEC in South Africa. She sent letters, while at Wilberforce, to her sister Kate who had earlier traveled with her to Great Britain as a member of the African choral tour, but when they returned home Kate elected to remain in

---

[5] Campbell, *Songs of Zion*, 133–34.
[6] Campbell, *Songs of Zion*, 133.
[7] J. A. Millard, "Maxeke, Charlotte Manye, 1872 to 1939, African Methodist Episcopal Church South Africa," in *Dictionary of African Christian Biography* (1999), accessed June 29, 2011. http://www.dacb.org/stories/southafrica/maxeke_charlotte.html. Also see Campbell, *Songs of Zion*, 134.
[8] W. E. B. DuBois, *The Souls of Black Folk* (New York: Vintage Books/The American Library, 1990), 3.

South Africa rather than follow her sister to Wilberforce. Kate read Charlotte's letters about Wilberforce and the AMEC to Mangena Mokone, a relative and Wesleyan Church leader, who took considerable interest. In 1892, owing to racism within the ranks of the white Wesleyan Church in South Africa, Mokone had decided to break away and form an African led church. Church leaders decided to name their new religious institution the Ethiopian Church in recognition of the privileged position Ethiopia, an African nation, has in the Bible. Several other black South African clergymen followed Mokone's example, broke from white churches, and joined the Ethiopian Church bringing large congregations with them. The Ethiopian Church was the first African-led Christian Church of its size in South Africa. After hearing about the work and administration of the black church in the United States, Mokone sought to unite the Ethiopian Church with the AMEC, which had multiple institutions of higher education: Allen University, Columbia, South Carolina (1870); Morris Brown College, Atlanta, Georgia (1881); Paul Quinn College, Dallas, Texas (1872); Shorter College, Little Rock, Arkansas (1886); and Wilberforce University (1856). Beginning in 1895, Charlotte worked to facilitate the union by connecting the AMEC leaders with Mokone, and in 1896 the AMEC and the Ethiopian Church were formally joined when minister James Dwane representing the Ethiopian Church traveled to the United States and was reobligated to the AMEC ministry with the authority to obligate other ministers in the Ethiopian Church.[9]

Charlotte Manye and her husband Marshall Maxeke returned to South Africa in 1903 and worked together as missionaries for the AME Church in the Transvaal and later in the Eastern Cape. With the support of Enoch Mamba, the couple established an industrial school in the Eastern Cape, and in 1908, under the auspices of the AME Church they also established Wilberforce Institute, now Wilberforce Community College, which is still operating in Evaton, a community just outside of Johannesburg. Initially, Wilberforce Institute was based on an HBCU model and included a primary school, high school, teacher training school, and seminary. Manye was also a founding member and president of the Bantu Women's League, which was a precursor of the African National Congress Women's League (ANCWL). South African women used the ANCWL as an instrument for resisting racial oppression in South Africa. South Africa was not immune to gender bias, and men within the South African freedom struggle prevented women from becoming regular members of the ANC, a policy that remained in force until 1943.[10] African women, for their part, fought against their men to end discrimination within their movement while at the same time assisting their men to wage war against racial discrimination at both a national and international level. Nevertheless, the establishment of the AMEC in South Africa precipitated the arrival of scores of South Africans seeking educational opportunities in the United States over the next century.

John Langalibalele Dube was the first President–General of the ANC, and a towering figure on the South African political landscape. Many black South African political leaders, especially those in the ANC, still revere him as a pioneer and a founding father of the ANC.[11] Dube was born in Natal in 1871. He attended mission schools in South Africa before matriculating

---

[9] Campbell, *Songs of Zion*, 117, 128–29, 131, and 135.

[10] Campbell discusses Enoch Mamba in *Songs of Zion*, 203.

[11] Wanda Hennig, "Woza eNanda: Durban Heritage Site Hails South African Heroes Mandela and Dube," *South African Examiner*, May 21, 2010, accessed September 14, 2011. http://www.examiner.com/

in the preparatory department of Oberlin University in Ohio, from 1888 to 1890. His mother arranged his education through the good efforts of William and Ida Wilcox, white missionaries stationed near Durban who were members of the American Board of Commissioners for Foreign Missions (ABCFM). Hopeful education would prepare Dube for mission work, they arranged for his passage to America and for Dube to attend the preparatory department of Oberlin University in Ohio. To pay for his tuition and living expenses, he worked a variety of hardscrabble jobs including on a road gang and for a printing firm. Dube lasted but one day on the road gang, calling it the hardest days' work of his entire life. He never graduated from Oberlin, but his time in the United States was important nonetheless. Upon returning to South Africa he used his knowledge of the printing trade to establish *Ilanga Lase Natal* (*The Natal Sun*), the first indigenous Zulu newspaper.[12] His work experiences in America undoubtedly gave him a sense of how difficult life was for African Americans, who were then struggling through a dreadful period that Douglas Blackmon has described as *Slavery By Another Name*.[13]

After leaving Oberlin, Dube wrote a short book entitled, *A Familiar Talk Upon My Native Land and Some Things Found There*.[14] In it, Dube highlights the tension between his newly acquired Christian beliefs and his former Zulu traditions.

"A double part" is in allusion to what DuBois called double consciousness or conflicting identities. Commonplace in the European colonial setting and within racist societies, this internal conflict was the source of many problems affecting African Americans and South Africans. Whatever reservations Dube may have had at the time about his apostasy, they were fleeting for he became a devote Christian after his conversion and later ordained as a Christian minister in the Congregational Church. Yet, his conversion to Christianity came at the expense of his former beliefs. Many Africans cast off their traditional beliefs once they converted to Christianity and some even looked down upon those former beliefs as "primitive" or even heathen. Rejecting traditional African beliefs was in a manner a negation of one's self because religion explains through spirituality, our origin, and place in the world and because adopting Christianity also meant having to rationalize the numerous irrational interpretations of the faith that Europeans often used as a justification for the exploitation of people of African descent. People of African descent who have adopted Christianity have made it of their own fashion by imbuing its performance with African spiritual practices, such as impassioned singing, and by interpreting its message in ways that sustained and gave dignity to the black experience. Indeed, for many African Americans, the black church was an instrument of both their spiritual and political delivery.

In 1892, Dube returned to South Africa, where he went to work as a teacher at his former high school in Amanzimtoti (Sweet Water). He married Nokutela Mdima and, like his

---

south-africa-travel-in-national/woza-enanda-durban-heritage-site-hails-south-african-heroes-mandela-and-dube-video-slideshow.

[12] Sheila Marks, "Ambiguities of Dependence: John L. Dube of Natal," *Journal of Southern African Studies* 1, no. 2 (April, 1975): 162–63.

[13] Douglas A. Blackmon, *Slavery by Another Name: The Re-enslavement of Black Americans from the Civil War to World War II* (New York: Anchor Books, 2009).

[14] John L. Dube, *A Familiar Talk Upon My Native Land and Some Things Found There* (Michigan: University of Michigan Library, 2005), Digital General Collection, accessed September 14, 2011. http://quod.lib.umich.edu/cgi/t/text/text-idx?c=genpub;idno=ATC4207.0001.001.

father James before him, began work as a Christian missionary. Frustrated with the racism of white missionaries, he and his wife established a separate Christian mission at Incawadi in the Umkomas Valley. His break from the white-led church coincided with Mokone's split from the Wesleyan Church. In 1897, Dube returned to the United States for a second time. This time to attend Theological Seminary in Brooklyn. Providence would have it that while Dube was in New York, Booker T. Washington visited and gave public lectures. Dube attended one of Washington's lectures and was very impressed by Washington's message of self-help. Washington, who was a powerful orator and arguably the greatest exemplar of African American exceptionalism of his era, spoke on the need for skilled labor and the value of industrial education. Deeply impressed with Washington's educational philosophy, Dube visited Tuskegee Institute in Alabama in 1897 to learn more about industrial education and to see the practical application of Washington's teachings. His visit coincided with the institution's commencement exercises, and Washington asked Dube to give remarks. Dube praised Washington's industrial education work, and detailed the need for self-help programs in South Africa.[15] After Dube returned to South Africa, in 1900, he established the Zulu Christian Industrial School based on the Tuskegee model of vocational and industrial education. The name was later changed to the Ohlange Institute to imply that it was a place for new growth and development. Like Tuskegee, the new school emphasized self-reliance. Today, it is the Ohlange High School and the location where Nelson Mandela voted in South Africa's first free elections in 1994.[16]

Washington, who was referred to respectfully as the "Wizard of Tuskegee," had a profound impact on black South Africans. His self-help philosophy was a pillar of the ideology of African redemption: Christianity would transform Africans into moral beings, and industrial education would make them more efficient laborers. Industrial education was not Washington's invention. It was part of the core curriculum of the Institute for Negro Youth in Philadelphia, Pennsylvania. Fanny Jackson Coppin, an Oberlin College graduate and wife of Bishop Levi Coppin, was principal of the institute. The Coppins left their work in Pennsylvania to carry on mission work in South Africa and took with them the idea of industrial education.[17]

The extent to which industrial education would benefit Blacks has been debated down to the present day. Washington of course argued it would make blacks more self-sufficient. In truth, the vast majority of blacks, both in the United States and South Africa, were poor and without the necessary capital to establish their own businesses, which meant that most had to find jobs working for whites. Even where they were able to get a business off the ground, it was subject to the vagaries of often hostile white competitors who might become violent in their opposition. In such an environment, it is easy to understand why Washington attempted to disarm the South by advocating for blacks to keep their social distance from whites while working with them in business. This was of course the core message of his Atlanta Compromise Address of 1895. DuBois and other black progressives took issue with Washington on his warning for

---

[15] Dube's visit to Tuskegee can be found in William Manning Marable, "Booker T. Washington and African Nationalism," *Phylon* 35 no. 4 (4th Quarter, 1974): 401.

[16] Before voting, Mandela went to the grave of Dube to lay a wreath and pay his respect. Chris Mcgreal, "Mandela Realises His Dream," *Mail and Guardian: Nelson Mandela a Tribute to a Nation's Leader*, April 29, 1994, accessed September 14, 2011, http://madiba.mg.co.za/article/1994-04-29-mandela-realises-his-dream.

[17] L. J. Coppin, *Unwritten History* (Philadelphia: AME Book Concern, 1919), 360.

African Americans to stay out of politics and the idea that the preferred form of education for African Americans should be industrial. From DuBois' perspective, politics and business were two sides of the same coin. African Americans needed influence in both. DuBois did not think industrial education was inherently flawed. He appreciated that African Americans needed carpenters, fitters, and electricians, but he also knew that African Americans needed doctors, lawyers, and teachers, and he knew that industrial education would not produce them. Since then writers have had much to say about the difference of opinion between Washington and DuBois, but at Washington's death in 1915, DuBois' remarked that the "Wizard" was the most significant African American of his era. Many South Africans agreed and paid homage by visiting or enrolling at Tuskegee.

In 1898, Pixley Ka Izaka Seme arrived in the United States to attend high school at the Mount Harmon School, in northwestern Massachusetts. In 1904, he visited Tuskegee Institute in Alabama and afterward wrote to Washington, "We need your spirit in South Africa."[18] After completing his course of study at Mount Harmon, Seme earned his undergraduate degree from Columbia University in New York City in 1906.[19] Weary of the insidious influence of racism and colonialism, Seme gave a major address to the Royal Africa Society in London, in 1906, entitled, "Regeneration of Africa". His talk celebrated the major contributions of Africans to world society and provided a counter narrative to the then prevalent myth of African inferiority. Portending Leopold Senghor's Negritude by a half century, he reflected on the unique relationship that African people shared with one another. "The African people," he said, "although not a strictly homogeneous race, possess a common fundamental sentiment which is everywhere manifest, crystallizing itself into one common controlling idea." Seme later earned a law degree from Oxford in London.[20] Dube and Seme returned to South Africa with the norms and values they had adopted while learning from and living among African Americans. They were educated elites who assumed important leadership roles in the African community once back in South Africa.[21]

---

[18] Marable, "Booker T. Washington." Discussion of Washington's influence on Seme and Dube can be found in Marable, "Booker T. Washington," 398–401; Marable, "African Nationalist: The Life of John Langalibele Dube" (PhD diss., University of Maryland, 1976); also see, Mattye Laverne Brandon, "The Interaction of Afro-Americans and South Africans, 1898–1940" (MA Thesis, Howard University, 1971). Brandon's work is a more general discussion on African American relations with South Africans.

[19] See R. Hunt Davis, "John Dube: A South African Exponent of Booker T. Washington," *Journal of African Studies* 2, 4 (Winter, 1975–1976): 505. William Manning Marable, *African Nationalist: The Life of John Langalibalele Dube.* (Michigan: UMI Dissertation Services, 1976), 66–68. There are few works on Pixley ka Izaka Seme because documents of his early life are dearth. For biographical information on Seme see, Tim Couzens and Richard Rive, *Seme: The Founder of the ANC* (Trenton: Africa World Press, 1993), 15–19.

[20] See, speech by Seme, "Regeneration of Africa," given at Columbia University, April 5, 1906. The speech appears in *Journal of Royal African Society* 5 (1905–1906). Also see, William Henry Ferris, *The African Abroad: Or, His Evolution in Western Civilization, Tracing His Development under Caucasian Milieu* (New Haven: Tuttle, Morehouse & Taylor Press, 1913, reprinted New York: Johnson Reprint Corporation, 1968).

[21] For the origins of the African National Congress see, Thomas Karis and Gwendolen Carter, *Protest and Hope, 1882–1934*, vol. 1 of *From Protest to Challenge: A Documentary History of African Politics in South Africa, 1882–1990* (Stanford: Hoover Institution Press, 1972); Andre Odendaal, *Vukani Bantu!: Black Protest Politics in South Africa to 1912* (Totowa: Barnes & Noble, 1984); and R. V. Selope Thema, "How Congress Began," *Drum*, July 1953.

Seme called the inaugural conference to discuss establishing an African protest organization. Convened on January 8, 1912 at Maphikela House in Mangaung Township, Bloemfontein in the Orange Free State province, the conference included 100 delegates. Seme gave the keynote address, and Reverend John Langalibalele Dube was elected the new organization's first President-General in absentia. The delegates chose South African Native National Congress (SANNC) as the initial name of the organization, and that name remained in use until it was changed in 1923, to the African National Congress (ANC) in appreciation for the young organization's connection to the larger struggle to liberate Africa from colonialism. Thus, the principal organizer and the first president of the ANC were educated in the United States and intimately familiar with African Americans, having lived among them for several years. The ANC embodied the idea of self-sufficiency and self-help. Its principle aim was to free South Africa of racial injustice and establish democracy.

Seme and Dube were not the only prominent South Africans to come under the influence of Booker T. Washington's ideas. Professor Davidson Don Tengo Jabavu visited Tuskegee in 1913 at the behest of the South African Minister of Native Affairs. Jabavu would later become the first African on faculty at the South African Native College at Fort Hare. Jabavu was tasked with learning everything he could about industrial education so that it could be adapted to the education of natives in South Africa.[22] During Jabavu's visit to Tuskegee he met a bright young South African student who had just enrolled at the school—Alfred Bitini Xuma. Jabavu observed Washington's industrial education curriculum in action, and when he returned home, he praised Tuskegee for its discipline and teaching methods.[23] What Jabavu learned about industrial education at Tuskegee was later incorporated into the curriculum at the Native College at Fort Hare when it opened in 1916, in Alice, South Africa. Fort Hare would become the preeminent educational institute for Africans in southern Africa. Its former students included Nelson Mandela, Robert Sobukwe, Oliver Tambo, Robert Mugabe, Seretse Khama, Govan Mbeki, and Z. K. Matthews amongst many others.

Xuma entered Tuskegee in the fall of 1913, and began an educational program that combined learning about arts and letters with working with farm implements and livestock. At Tuskegee, instruction emphasized the manual arts, including animal husbandry, farming techniques, and mechanics. During his matriculation at Tuskegee, one of Xuma's professors was the renowned scientist George Washington Carver, who had earned national recognition for his discoveries of the many usages of peanuts.[24]

After graduating from Tuskegee, Xuma studied agriculture at the University of Minnesota in the city of Minneapolis. He lived in an African-American community in neighboring St. Paul and attended St. James AME Church where he taught Sunday school. At St. James he met a young Roy Wilkins, who later became a prominent civil rights leader and the Executive Director of the National Association for the Advancement of Colored People (NAACP) from

---

[22] Marable, "Booker T. Washington," 402.

[23] Matthews discusses Jabavu in his autobiography. See Z. K. Matthews and Monica Wilson, eds., *Freedom for My People: The Autobiography of Z. K. Matthews, Southern Africa 1901 to 1968* (Cape Town: D. Philip, 1981), 51. Jabavu taught Latin and Bantu Languages. Jabavu also visited Hampton Institute. Steven Gish, *Alfred B. Xuma: African, American, South African* (New York: New York University Press, 2000), 28.

[24] Ibid., 97.

1964 to 1977. Xuma joined the YMCA in St. Paul, and in 1919, at a YMCA conference in Des Moine, Iowa, he met Max Yergan. Two short years later, Yergan moved to South Africa where he lived for 15 years and worked as a YMCA missionary.[25] Xuma was active in the small African American student community at the university, joining Alpha Phi Alpha Fraternity, Incorporated at the University of Minnesota. He later became a Charter member of Alpha at Marquette University.[26] His membership in Alpha highlights how connected he was to the African-American community. Founded in 1906, Alpha was the first college Greek-Letter organization among African Americans.[27]

After his graduation in 1920, Xuma enrolled at Marquette School of Medicine in Milwaukee, Wisconsin. Connected with the African-American community through links with the YMCAs in both Milwaukee and Chicago, Xuma learned African-American middle-class values that emphasized "industriousness, sobriety, dedication to family, and active church membership." While in Chicago, a city with a significant and established African-American community, Xuma met and befriended a host of people, including his countryman Sol Plaatje, the founding Secretary of the ANC. In 1922, Plaatje was visiting Chicago as part of his tour through the United States to promote his work *Native Life in South Africa*, to call attention to the plight of his people, and to seek assistance.[28] Xuma transferred to and graduated from Northwestern University. After he received his certificate for having completed the theoretical portion of his medical curriculum in 1925, Xuma interned in general surgery at St. Louis City Hospital No. 2 for one year. Forming similar linkages with the African-American institutions in St. Louis that he had previously formed in Tuskegee, St. Paul, Milwaukee, and Chicago. Xuma graduated medical school in 1926, and the following year he began his roundabout journey back home, stopping in London first to obtain a license to practice medicine in South Africa.[29]

A practicing surgeon in Sophiatown, Xuma was also politically active. His standing as a surgeon won him respect in South Africa among both blacks and whites. He was elected President of the ANC in 1940, a position that he held until 1949. As President, he played a vital role in the organizational development of the ANC during the 1940s and was a mentor to the ANC Youth League members: Anton Lembede, Nelson Mandela, Oliver Tambo, and others. While in the United States, Xuma married Madie Hall Xuma from Winston-Salem, North Carolina,

---

[25] Xuma to Yergan, "Transcript in Xuma," June 7, 1928, A. B., Box 206-4, Yergan Papers, Moorland Spingarn Research Center, Howard University, Washington, DC. When Xuma returned to South Africa Yergan contacted him in writing. Evidently, Yergan did not remember Xuma. His letter to Xuma dated June 4, 1928, states that he learned about Xuma from Grover Little of Chicago. However, in his reply on June 7, Xuma reminds Yergan that he last saw him at the YMCA conference in des Moine, Iowa, and that George Arthur who was connected with the YMCA in Chicago had informed him that Yergan was coming to South Africa. For June 4, letter see "Transcript in Xuma".

[26] Xuma at University of Minnesota. See Gish, *Alfred B. Xuma*, 36. Discussion of Xuma and Alpha Phi Alpha can be found in Ibid., 36 and 39. Other members of Alpha Phi Alpha include W. E. B. DuBois, Paul Robeson, Max Yergan, Martin Luther King, and Thurgood Marshall, a civil rights attorney and the first African American supreme court justice.

[27] See Xuma to Yergan, "Transcript in Xuma."

[28] Discussion of values taught at the YMCA can be found in Gish, *Alfred B. Xuma*, 43. Xuma was a musical performer at the function held for Plaatje. Brian Willan, *Sol Plaatje: South African Nationalist, 1876–1932* (Berkeley: University of California Press, 1984), 280.

[29] Gish, *Alfred B. Xuma*, 45–48.

and Max Yergan served as his best man. Madie Hall moved to South Africa in 1940 and lived there for more than two decades. She left as a revered figure among South African women.[30]

James Saul Mokete Thaele earned a bachelor of arts degree from Lincoln University in 1917 and a theology degree from the same institution in 1921.[31] Thaele was born in 1888 in Basutoland (Lesotho). After finishing Lincoln, Thaele worked as a high school teacher in Philadelphia, where he came under the influence of Marcus Garvey's Universal Negro Improvement Association.[32] "For Thaele, the UNIA epitomized the relative commercial, political, and social organization that South Africans had long admired in black America, and he returned to South Africa a committed Garveyite." In 1922, Thaele returned to South Africa with a militancy that was common to members of the Garvey movement but uncommon among black South Africans of that era. He became a powerful leader of the ANC in the Western Cape and even founded a newspaper, *The Africa World*, which was based on the model of Garvey's *Negro World*. It extolled black achievements and condemned the debilitating impact of European colonialism on African people.[33]

In February 1921, Sol Plaatje, a founder of the SANNC and an avid writer, entered the United States through Canada in hopes of raising funds for his work as a freelance writer, journalist, and newspaper publisher in South Africa. He published *Tsala ea Batho* (*The Friend of the People*), which was chronically in arrears. He also hoped to raise funds for community work in Kimberley.[34] Plaatje visited several major cities meeting with African-American leaders and giving speeches. In New York, for instance, he met Marcus Garvey and spoke to huge gatherings of enthusiastic Universal Negro Improvement and Association (UNIA) supporters. He also addressed church audiences, orating on such topics as, "The Black Women's Burden" and "The Black Man's Burden." He sold pamphlets highlighting racial issues in South Africa and even arranged through DuBois to publish an American edition of *Native Life in South Africa*. Widely read both in his birthplace and in the United States, *Native Life* describes the devastating and tragic effects of the Native Land Act of 1913 on black South Africans.[35] DuBois invited Plaatje to attend the second Pan African Congress session in Paris in the fall of 1921. When Plaatje's financial circumstance prevented him from attending, DuBois read a speech that Plaatje prepared especially for the occasion, keeping its author's identity a secret. Plaatje's speech was a scathing condemnation of South Africa's racial policies. He especially condemned the Native Land Act of 1913, which set aside a mere 7 percent of the total land for Africans and prohibited sharecropping. Plaatje referred to it as, "the most outrageous of the monstrous crimes" that the South African parliament had committed against the "natives." The Act made

---

[30] Heidi Holland, *The Struggle: A History of the African National Congress* (New York: George Braziller, Inc., 1990), 50–51.

[31] Amanda D. Kemp and Robert Trent Vinson, "'Poking Holes in the Sky': Professor James Thaele, American Negroes, and the Modernity in 1920s Segregationist South Africa," *African Studies Review* 43, no. 1 (April, 2000), 143. Special issue on the Diaspora.

[32] Ibid., 147.

[33] Ibid.

[34] For reference to *Tsala ea Batho* see, Willan, *Sol Plaatje*, 158; What Plaatje hoped to accomplish can be found at Ibid., 173; and Plaatje had hoped to raise funds but was disappointment in the small sums of money he obtained. Ibid., 270.

[35] Brian Willan, *Sol Plaatje*, 264, 266–69; Plaatje's role in early ANC politics can be found in Ibid., 150–53.

many blacks landless and homeless.[36] Following in the footsteps of Dube and other South Africans, Plaatje visited Tuskegee and, like his countrymen before him, he was awestruck by the great work that was being done there. Plaatje had not come to the United States to attend school, but he nevertheless came away better informed about the race problem facing people of color. Issues of race drew other South Africans to the United States as well.[37]

Zachariah Keodirelang Matthews first visited the United States after winning a Phelps Stokes Fund scholarship to study race and culture contact at Yale University in the United States for the academic year 1933–34. "Z. K." was born in Kimberley, South Africa in 1901. He was the first graduate of the Native College at Fort Hare, completing his Bachelor degree in 1924. While at Fort Hare, Matthews was a student of D. D. T. Jabavu. He was also the first African to earn a law degree in South Africa. Many years later he returned to Fort Hare and became its first African principal. Active in politics, he was Treasurer and then President of the Cape Branch of the ANC. In the 1930s, scholars were attempting to address what was then called the "Negro problem" or "Negro question." In *The Souls of Black Folks*, DuBois alluded to the idea that whites often perceived the mere presence of blacks in what were to them "white societies" as a problem. The Phelps Stokes Fund was interested in addressing the "quandary" and believed that bringing South Africans to the United States would be a good way for South Africans to learn how Americans were addressing the issue.[38]

Charles Loram, a white South African educated in the United States, directed the interracial educational program on race and culture at Yale. Education was the presumed panacea to the race problem, so Loram took participants on a tour to several of the historically black institutions in the South. The group made stops at Howard University in Washington, DC; Hampton Institute in Virginia; Livingstone College in North Carolina; Fisk University in Tennessee; as well as Talladega College and Tuskegee Institute, both in Alabama. At each institution, the group took a campus tour and met with faculty and administrators.[39] At Tuskegee, Robert Russa Moton, a graduate of Hampton Institute who replaced Booker T. Washington as principal of the institute after his death in 1915, greeted the students alongside the preeminent scientist George Washington Carver. Matthews amusingly observed that it was Carver who had "rescued the humble peanut from obscurity." In Nashville, the group toured Fisk University, which from its early history had missionary ties to Africa and had by 1934 produced graduates such as W.E.B. DuBois (1888); Margaret Murray Washington (1890), wife of Booker T. Washington; Lorenzo Dow Turner (1910), who pioneered research on Gullah culture and African cultural retentions in the Americas; and Charles Harris Wesley (1911), who was the third African American to earn a PhD from Harvard and would later serve as president of Wilberforce University and Central State College, both in Ohio. The group actually met Wesley at Howard University in Washington, DC. where he was then on faculty in the Department of History. At "The Mecca", the cognomen for Howard, an impressive cadre of

---

[36] Ibid., 271–73. See also, Frank Welsh, *South Africa: A Narrative History* (New York: Kodansha International, 1999), 375–76.

[37] Ibid., 278–79.

[38] Racism necessitated that Matthews be effectively co-headmaster alongside Alexander Kerr, a white educator and former principal of the institution. Wilson, *Freedom for My People*, 81 and 96.

[39] Ibid.

distinguished administrators and faculty queued to welcome the touring South African students: Mordecai Wyatt Johnson, a Morehouse College graduate, the first African American president of the institution; Alain Locke, Chair of the Department of Philosophy and "The Father of the Harlem Renaissance"; sociologist E. Franklin Frazier, a pioneer of African American culture and the author of *Black Bourgeoisie*; Ralph Bunche, Chair of the Department of Political Science and later recipient of the Nobel Peace Prize; William Leo Hansberry, father of the historical study of ancient Africa, and the aforementioned Wesley. Both Hansberry and Wesley were in the Department of History.

President Johnson was a Baptist preacher and great orator. Almost indistinguishable from a white man in physical appearance himself, Johnson was known to give lengthy sermons against white supremacy with the passion and courage of the Apostle Paul. In 1930, South African President Jan Smuts spent an afternoon at Howard meeting with Johnson and other black leaders. Robert Edgar and Myra Houser found that The Phelps Stokes Fund arranged the meeting with the hope that it would "enlighten" Smuts on the race question. Smuts left the gathering claiming it was the most insightful discussion he had ever had on the matter of race, but the impression on Smuts was fleeting.[40] The white students on the educational tour were stunned by the talent of the black intellectuals they met at the black schools, and their positive reactions were a source of pride for Matthews, who was likewise impressed.[41]

While touring the South, Matthews and his interracial group of students conformed to the reigning Jim Crow segregationist norms, which for Matthews meant staying in African-American hotels and eating at African-American restaurants, and when these were not accessible staying with an African-American family. He recalled that on at least one occasion, Charles Loram was able to get him admitted to a Whites-only establishment by convincing the proprietors that he was an Abyssinian prince![42]

At the end of the Yale program, Matthews presented his thesis, "Bantu Law and Western Civilization in South Africa: A Study in the Clash of Cultures," which examined the ways that European law undermined native authority. On his way back to South Africa, he stopped in London to visit with Paul and Eslanda Robeson. The Robesons were part of a transnational community of black anticolonial activists in London that included Jomo Kenyatta, George Padmore, C. L. R. James, Eric Williams, Ras Makonnen, and I. T. A. Wallace-Johnson.[43] Matthews strengthened ties with the Robesons during his brief visit. Eslanda and Paul Jr. visited with Z. K. and his wife Frieda when they visited Fort Hare for Roseberry Bokwe's wedding in 1935.

In 1952, during the Campaign to Defy Unjust Laws, Matthews returned to the United States as the Henry Luce Lecturer in World Christianity at Union Theological Seminary. Luce

---

[40] Journal Article by Robert Edgar and Myra Houser, "'The Most Patient of Animals Next to the Ass': Jan Smuts, Howard University, and African American Leadership" (forthcoming). Presented at African Seminar at Duke University, Fall 2015.

[41] Matthews and Wilson, *Freedom for My People*, 97.

[42] Ibid.

[43] Eslanda and her son, Paul Jr., attended the wedding of Roseberry Bokwe in South Africa. While the Robesons visited the Matthews many Africans came by their house to meet Eslanda and to get the latest word on Paul Sr. Wilson, *Freedom For My People*, 122.

was the millionaire owner of *Life magazine* who believed the approaching age was the "American Century." The Defiance Campaign was a nonviolent protest against the South African pass laws. Pass books or Passes were identification documents that Africans were forced to carry. Designed to control the movement and labor of Africans, these documents were a constant source of frustration and humiliation that reified the inferior status of black South Africans. Matthews delivered important information about the campaign to the anticolonial activists in the United States who were organizing concurrent protest in solidarity with protestors in South Africa. This role of intermediary between the South African black community and the African American community was critical to the anticolonial campaign, which included the struggle to liberate South Africa. Matthews shared news with Paul Robeson, William Alphaeus Hunton, DuBois, and the other members of the Council on African Affairs in order for them to prepare literature and speeches supporting the Campaign. George Houser and members of Americans for South African Resistance (AFSAR), a spin-off group from the Congress of Racial Equality (CORE), had hesitated to join the fight, fearing that the nonviolent campaign might not remain peaceful if South African governmental authorities provoked the demonstrators. Matthews was able to give them reassurances that convinced the leaders of AFSAR to join the protest. AFSAR went on to hold parades and rallies, and even led a procession of cars with Defiance Campaign supporters to picket the South African consular office in New York.[44]

In 1952, when Matthew's returned, international and domestic events had precipitated a new willingness among many African Americans to openly identify with Africa. The Italian invasion of Ethiopia in 1935, the triumph of democracy over fascism and Nazism during World War II, the migration of rural black workers to sprawling urban industrial centers in the North, a better educated and expanding black middle class in the North, as well as the decade and a half old anticolonial campaign waged by the Council on African Affairs, all contributed to this new attitude. Matthews remarked that it was indeed "quite different."[45] On one occasion, he recalled strolling down 125th Street in Harlem and coming unexpectedly upon a big crowd of African Americans who turned out to be having a rally on African nationalism. He promptly joined them. On another occasion, he gave a speech to a group wherein he remarked that "Africa was for all who lived in it." After his speech, two African-American women accosted him and upbraided him for suggesting that Africa was big enough for whites too. It turned out that the women were Garveyites.[46] Militancy caught hold in South Africa during the 1950s as a new young generation of South African protest leaders came of age.

Mfanasekaya Gqobose was a leader of the Pan Africanist Congress (PAC) in South Africa. Robert Sobukwe launched the PAC, in 1959, after having broken away from the ANC a year earlier. Sobukwe was born in Cape Province in 1924. He became politically active while a student

---

[44] Matthews discusses planning for the Campaign in Z. K. Matthews to George Houser, March 13, 1952, Microfilm Reel 1, Records of the American Committee on Africa, Part 2: Correspondence and Subject Files on South Africa, 1952–1985, Library of Congress, Washington, DC. Also, George Houser, interview by author, May 1, 2003, interview transcript and recording in the possession of the author.

[45] "Drum Interviews Prof. Z. K. Matthews, April 1954 Issue," Foreign Service Dispatch 203, April 21, 1954, transcript in United States Embassy Pretoria, General Records, 1950–1954, Central Decimal File, General Records of the Department of State, Record Group 59, National Archives Building, College Park, MD.

[46] Ibid.

at the Native College at Fort Hare, joining the African National Congress Youth League in 1948. He was a teacher, excellent orator, and member of the ANC up until he split from the group in 1958. Sobukwe's decision to leave the ANC was based primarily on its policy of multiracialism—the idea that Africa was home for all who lived in it. Sobukwe was not a racist, but he believed that black South Africans needed to be at the head of their liberation struggle.[47]

The PAC from its inception was dedicated to the idea of Pan Africanism. Pan Africanism is a political ideology. Henry Sylvester Williams and W. E. B. DuBois are its earliest advocates although Marcus Garvey was probably its most successful practitioner. Pan Africanism is the idea that all people of African ancestry share a common heritage, a common oppressor, and a common destiny and therefore should work in solidarity to overcome their oppression. Gqobose was drawn to the PAC for the same reasons that Sobukwe had created the organization: he believed Africans needed to be the key decision makers in their fight for freedom. Sobukwe and Gqobose were not alone in sharing this concern about leadership.

Kwame Toure and Charles V. Hamilton raised the same concern during the Black Power Movement in the United States; it was the primary message of their book *Black Power*. Malcolm X explained the concern by saying that because white supremacy had conditioned blacks to think of whites as superior, whites who joined organizations working against colonialism and racial oppression had status and power that far exceeded their numerical representation in the group and that blacks out of respect to the white members often suppressed their anger. Black leaders often wanted to harness that anger to mobilize people and to advance the struggle, but found their efforts among interracial groups frustrated.

Gqobose's experiences are interesting because they highlight how transnational encounters between Africans and members of the African Diaspora breed a familiarity based on similar experiences of racial oppression that stimulated them to become politically active. During World War II, Gqobose was a member of the South African Defense Force (SADF). He served with other black troops from South Africa in Egypt, Libya, and Italy. It was customary for the troops to be racially segregated, especially during their non-work hours. Consequently, Gqobose spent much of his free time in an informal political laboratory comprised of black troops from virtually every corner of the African Diaspora: Great Britain, France, India, the West Indies, East Africa, West Africa, Australia, and the United States. Gqobose recalled that "the British Army [was] a cosmopolitan army" and that it had units with black soldiers from many of its colonies. His interaction with these black soldiers began what he called his "political understudy in the depths of politics." So it was that in the evenings, the black soldiers would meet for entertainment and casual discussion. Gqobose reminisced that, "We would have discussions about politics and . . . each one of us would regard his own experience from his own country and so on, it was a very good experience." African American soldiers were particularly strident in their remonstrations about the racial situation in the United States, according to Gqobose. After spending months wrestling over political ideas with his comrades in arms, he made the decision that when he returned to South Africa he would not be the pliable African he had been when he left for the war. He said, "I won't tolerate the old politics of this country

---

[47] Mfanasekaya Pearce Gqobose, interview by author, May 9, 2001, National Heritage and Cultural Studies Centre, University of Fort Hare, Alice, South Africa, tape recording in the possession of the author.

[South Africa], so I joined the ANC." He was a part of a new more militant generation of South African protestors.[48]

Gqobose joined the ANC Youth League in 1946 and became a follower of its leaders, Anton Lembede, Nana Mohomo, and Robert Sobukwe. Other Youth Leaguers included Oliver Tambo, Nelson Mandela, and Walter Sisulu, all of whom later became leaders of the ANC. Between 1953 and 1959, Gqobose was a part of the Africanist Movement in the ANC, and when the PAC was formed in 1959, he joined. He served as a regional chairman of the PAC in the Eastern Cape and was active in the PAC campaigns against the Pass Laws. In the early 1960s, he served as a member of the Planning Committee for Poqo, the military arm of the PAC. He was an armed South African freedom fighter. In 1967, Gqobose went to Kinshasa, Zaire presumably for military training. He had previously served three years in prison following his arrest in Lesotho in 1964 for subversive politic activity. Gqobose continued his commitment to the struggle until democracy was finally won for South Africa in 1994. After his "political education," he never again quietly suffered racial injustice.[49]

CONCLUSION

Ties between African Americans and black South Africans remained strong throughout the twentieth century. South Africans came to the United States looking for opportunities that did not exist for them in South Africa. Education was the biggest attraction, and the advances that African Americans had made were enough to convince them of its importance. HBCUs played a key role in offering education and hope to both African American and South African students. Many of the principal leaders of the South African liberation struggle were educated at black colleges in the United States. The same is true of the Civil Rights leaders. Because of segregation and white hostility, black South Africans often lived amongst African Americans during their stays in the United States. Propinquity breed familiarity between the groups and that led to the exchange of values and, in some cases, wedding vows.

By midcentury, Americans were becoming more familiar with the South African racial situation. World War II had presented challenges for African and Diaspora blacks and yet also created opportunities. It had been fought to end fascism, and men of every hue had died in the effort to beat back Nazism, but the comingling of colored soldiers provided a space for the free exchange of ideas, and through this interaction, the black soldiers came to know not only each other but also the communities and experiences of their fellow colored combatants. For blacks, implicit in national and international discussions of freedom and democracy were expectations and hopes of more rights and improved social standing. In the United States, an emergent Civil Rights movement was challenging Jim Crow, which in the shadow of the triumph of democracy was looking decidedly outmoded with each passing day. On the heels of the war, African Americans, like many Africans on the continent and blacks in the Diaspora, could sense the coming political changes though it is doubtful they knew the extent to which

---

[48] Ibid.

[49] Ibid. Gqobose could not recall how many times he traveled to the United States, but he did say that while he was in New York, he and other members of the PAC would receive assistance from the University of Rochester.

their yearnings for new rights and freedoms would be realized or over what period of time it would take for them to come to fruition, but nonetheless many had reason to have hope. South Africa was the exception. In 1948, the year India won its independence from Great Britain signaling the retreat of European colonialism, racial segregation in South Africa was given a name—apartheid. White nationalism in South Africa was climaxing, and apartheid became its trademark, a name that identified South Africa to the world as an enclave of white supremacy and racial injustice.[50]

Innovations in travel and communication during the World War II era, especially radio and television, made the world smaller, increasing the possibility for transnational and trans-subnational linkages. The exposure of African American and other black entertainers became global. World news reports raced around the globe at speeds that were inconceivable only a generation earlier. African American music, especially Jazz and Rhythm and Blues, beat a dulcet stream across the airwaves into the homes of blacks in the United States, Africa, and other parts of the African Diaspora. Thus, in the context of transnational encounters between African Americans and South Africans black entertainers gradually replaced the missionaries of the late 19th and early 20th centuries as the principle agents of African American Exceptionalism.

After the Sharpeville massacre in 1960 and the increase in political repression in South Africa that followed, the pace of out migration and the flow of South Africans seeking refuge expanded bringing wave after wave of young exiles to the shores of the United States and many other countries around the world. Many of the South African young people followed the path their predecessors had laid for them into institutions of higher learning in the United States and built on the Black Atlantic Communications Network that was now almost a century old.

KEY TERMS

Contemporary Hindsight	Native Land Act (1913)	Charlotte Manye
Ethiopian Church	John L. Dube	Pixley Ka Izaka Seme
Alfred Bitini Xuma	James Thaele	Defieance Campaign
Pass Books	Z. K. Matthews	

---

[50] "Announcement of the Nationalist Party's Policy of 'Apartheid'," Foreign Service Dispatch 158, March 31, 1948, American Consulate, Cape Town; General Records, 1946–1949, Decimal File, 848A.00/3-3148. General Records of the Department of State, Record Group 59, national Archives Building, College Park, MD.

CHAPTER 16

"THE TIES THAT BIND": AFRICAN AMERICAN CONSCIOUSNESS OF AFRICA THROUGH CULTURE AND SPORTS

Neo Lekgotla *laga* Ramoupi

ABSTRACT

Essay focuses on the cultural activisms of South African musicians, Miriam Makeba and Hugh Masekela; and explores the sporting activisms of African American Arthur Ashe and his South African protégé, Mark Mathabane, who in his 1986 autobiography, *Kaffir boy*, narrates life under apartheid. On his visit to South Africa, he plays and holds tennis clinics in Soweto where Mathabane follows every step of Ashe. Wherever Ashe went Mathabane followed because the young black boy from Soweto had never seen before a successful black man playing tennis, especially against white tennis players. After Ashe had returned to the United States, they continued to write to each other until Ashe brings Mathabane to the United States and the former writes a sequel *Kaffir Boy in America* (1989), which chronicles the life of Mathabane after the original *Kaffir Boy*.

Makeba and Masekela are well-known in the African American life; their cultural expressions speak to—and—about the ties that bind African people from the continent and the African Diaspora. Through their activism that is in their songs and music, culture awakens the plight of the black struggle across the Atlantic Ocean.

INTRODUCTION

The Ties that Bind: African-American Consciousness of Africa was the title of the doctoral dissertation of the late distinguished South African Professor, Bernard Makhosezwe Magubane. He completed the study at the University of California, Los Angeles (UCLA) in 1967. It was not published until two decades later in 1987. Being an African scholar from South Africa, myself and having studied for my doctorate in the USA, the focus of Magubane's research and subsequent book on the African American consciousness of Africa held immense meaning for me, just like it did for Magubane before me.

It is equally important, also, to understand why my countryman, Magubane, chose to research and write his doctoral dissertation on this subject. In his autobiography, *Bernard Magubane: My Life & Times* (2010), he explains:

At UCLA I had developed considerable interest, though, in African-American literature. I had read *The Souls of Black Folks* (1903) by W. E. B. Du Bois. I devoured everything I could get by Du Bois. A small book he had written, *The Negro* (1915), dealing with African-American civilizations from antiquity, was one of my favourite readings. I also became interested in Carter Woodson, a wonderful African-American historian teaching at the University of Virginia, and in John Hope Franklin. Alpheus Hinton was a member of the American Communist Party and had taught history at Howard University.[1]

I talked to John Horton and Leo Kuper and told them I wanted to do library dissertation on Africa and its meaning for African-Americans. That was a burning debate at the time. 'There is no way I can go back to South Africa,' I said, 'and I don't have the means to conduct empirical study. I have read African-American scholars and I want to interrogate their literature. They agreed. With the help of John Horton, I wrote my proposal and it was ultimately accepted. I settled on the question of African-American consciousness of Africa.[2]

When Professor Ben Magubane relocated back to his homeland, South Africa, in 1997, after more than thirty years of scholarship and teaching anthropology at the University of Connecticut (UConn), he was appointed in 2004 as the chief editor of *The South African Democracy Education Trust (SADET)*.[3]

When I returned from Howard University at the end of 2006, Sifiso M. Ndlovu, then Research Director of SADET, recommended to Professor Magubane that I should be appointed as researcher for the project. Magubane agreed that SADET was the nurturing space that would enable me to complete the write-up of my doctoral dissertation. My office was the first one as you enter our building at SADET, and every morning when "Prof"—our intimate name for Magubane—entered just after 9:00 a.m.; he would stand at my office door and greet me. Immediately, without fail, he would say, "Neo, you must finish writing your PhD! don't try to perfect it. A compete doctoral thesis is a finished one!" (and professor would walk away to his office, laughing). Daily, I got this fatherly and distinguished professorial encouragement from Magubane, and it really kept my spirits up towards completing my dissertation—and I am so grateful to Professor Magubane for his reassurance. I travelled to Washington, DC, to defend my dissertation at the end of March 2013, on Thursday, 28 March; and returned home with the title of "Dr" before my name, Neo lekgotla *laga* Ramoupi, PhD, the following Thursday April 4, 2013. The following week, on Friday April 12, 2013, Professor Magubane passed on peacefully in his home in Halfways, Johannesburg. My only regret is that I never got the chance to call professor and tell him "Prof, you were right! A complete Ph.D. is a finished one!" But I consoled myself that when he passed on, on April 12, 2013, I, his student, was two weeks into my postdoctoral days.

Amii Omara-Otunnu, executive director of the UConn-ANC Partnership, said in 1999 about Professor Magubane:

---

[1] Magubane (2010), 135–136. The author's copy was signed by Prof. Magubane at the SADET Project where he was our editor in chief of the project.

[2] See Footnote 1, 137.

[3] The South African Democracy Education Trust (SADET) http://www.sadet.co.za/about_us.html, accessed March 12, 2016.

What makes Ben Magubane a particularly interesting scholar is that his scholarship reflected his political commitment. He was not afraid to address the issues that he thought were critical in the South African context, even though many of his colleagues at the time were minimizing the role of race and racism in South African society.[4]

The objectives of this essay, "The Ties That Bind" are twofold; firstly, I want to bring into perspective the cultural activisms of South African black musicians, Miriam Makeba, Hugh Masekela, and few others, whose artistic careers came to fruition because of the benevolence of African Americans while they were in political exile in the United States of America. Secondly, I want to explore the sporting and political activism of African American, Arthur Ashe and his South African black youth protégé, Mark Mathabane. Mathabane's 1986 autobiography, *Kaffir Boy* (*Nigger boy*), narrates life as an African in South Africa under apartheid.

During Ashe's first visit to South Africa in the 1973, to play in the South African Open Tennis Tournament, he conducted clinics for the black children during the day and played in the tournament at night. In the process, he inspired young black men like Mathabane who were starved of respectful and dignified black role models. In future visits to South Africa, Ashe visited Soweto and taught tennis to aspiring black tennis players, and it was during such visits that Mathabane would follow Ashe everywhere he went. He had never seen before a successful black tennis player, especially one who played against white tennis players, something that was illegal according to apartheid legislation. A bond developed between Ashe and Mathabane, and the consequence is that after Ashe had returned to the United States, they continued to correspond by writing letters to each other until Ashe succeeded in bringing Mathabane to the United States. Mathabane wrote *Kaffir Boy in America*, his second autobiography, continuing from where *Kaffir Boy* ended in South Africa.

A HISTORICAL BACKGROUND

South Africa is an African country at the southern tip of the African continent with an estimated population of 55,276,654 people, as of January 1, 2016. This is an increase of 1.41% (766,993 people) compared to population of 54,512,661 the year before. In 2015, the natural increase was positive, as the number of births exceeded the number of deaths by 593,098. Due to external migration, the population increased by 173,895. The sex ratio of the total population was 0.982 (982 males per 1000 females), which is lower than global sex ratio. The global sex ratio in world was approximately 1016 males to 1000 females as of 2015;[5] and I would put the population at 60 million people because South Africa since 1994 has become the United States of Africa (USA) of Africa with whites and mostly our African brothers and sisters from all over the world, especially from the neighboring countries, migrating illegally into South Africa for a variety of reasons.

From as early as the 1600, the country that later came to be known as South Africa was colonized by various European countries. First, it was the Dutch through their Dutch East Indian Company (DEIC) with its Commander, Jan Van Riebeeck, who landed at the Cape of Good

---

[4] Omara-Otunnu (1999).
[5] South Africa Population, http://countrymeters.info/en/South_Africa, accessed March 7, 2016.

Hope in 1658. This period and date, 1658, became the starting point to teach, research, write, and speak about the history of South Africa. When the African and white children went to school and university in South African education system, this imperial, colonial, and apartheid history of South Africa is what they are fed and taught. Even in the postapartheid era, the South African education carries this baggage of the past.

It was the Dutch and during the 1600s that the place of banishment that famously came to be known as Robben Island was established and the Dutch banished to Robben Island all the African: Khoi and San land activists, such as Autshumato and Krotoa.[6] In the nineteenth century, South Africa was colonized by the British and they also used Robben Island to banish and imprison the African political activists and African Kings who fought the British during the long wars of land dispossession.[7] In the twentieth century, Robben Island first became a Navy Base for the South African Navy during the World War II; and secondly, it became the infamous Robben Island Maximum Security Prison—the Alcatraz of the Apartheid State—that incarcerated only black men, in particular the leadership of the African political movements or parties, such as Mangaliso Robert Sobukwe, founding president of the Pan Africanist Congress of Azania (PAC), and Rolihlahla Nelson Mandela of the African National Congress (ANC), and later became the President of both the ANC and the first African South African to be the President of the Republic of South Africa. Towards the end of the twentieth century, the prison Robben Island was turned by the Mandela Presidency into a National Monument and National Museum, and was renamed Museum, Robben Island Museum in 1997; and in 1999, it became a World Heritage Site.[8]

APARTHEID

In May 1910, the white settler and minority population that had from the time of the Dutch in the late 1600 settled in South Africa came together after the Anglo-Boer War of 1899–1902 and established the Union of South Africa, with English and Dutch as the official languages of the Union. Thus from this period, 1910, the African had lost the right to vote. Later on the language Dutch was replaced by Afrikaans language as the other official language of South Africa. Then in 1948, white South Africa went to the general elections and the Afrikaans-speaking whites won the elections and came to power and their official government policy came to be called in Afrikaans, "Apartheid." The term, apartheid means literally "apartness"; it was a policy or system of segregation or discrimination on the grounds of race.[9]

It is within this historical background and context that *The Ties That Bind: African-American Consciousness of Africa through Culture and Sports* should be understood.

---

[6] See Autshumato and Krotoa in Mandela (1994), Wells (2007), Bloem (1999), Malherbe (1990), Rankin (1990), Matthee (2000), and Samuelson (2007).
[7] Mbeki (1984).
[8] Neo Lekgotla *laga* Ramoupi, "Izingoma *zo Mzabalazo Esiqithini!* Role of Songs in the African Liberation Struggle of South Africa, 1960-1991. A Culture History of Robben Island," Unpublished PhD Dissertation, (May 2013) http://gradworks.umi.com/35/91/3591967.html. Ramoupi is currently rewriting this research for book manuscript.
[9] Hendrik Frensch Verwoerd | South African History Online, www.sahistory.org.za, accessed March 15, 2016.

MIRIAM MAKEBA: "MAMA AFRICA AND EMPRESS OF AFRICAN SONG"

> Music can do all sorts of things. It can make sad people happy. It can make dull people sit up and pay attention. I know what it does to me. Music gets deep inside me and starts to shake things up. I begin to squirm. My lips turn into a smile and my hands begin to clap against one another. My body moves. It is as if am possessed. The Bapedi [people in South Africa] stomp and sing out in the field, and there I am, on the edge, singing with them, apart from them but sharing their joy. Who can keep us down as long as we have our music?

> —*Makeba (1988), 15.*

Zenzile Miriam Makeba was born in Johannesburg on the 4th of March 1932 and died on November 9, 2008, at the age of 76 years old. Makeba's mother, Nomkomndelo Christina, was Swazi and her father, Mpambane Caswell, was Xhosa; and by African tradition, the child is the father's, making Makeba a South African of Xhosa descents, like Mandela. *Mama Afrika* was a South African most famous musician and she used her artistic power to highlight her home-land's struggle against apartheid in while in living in exile in the USA and in various African countries where she had lived during the course of her life; in the process, Makeba came to be a Pan-Africanist and an activist for human rights and civil rights.

In the first page of her autobiography, *Miriam Makeba: My Story* (1988), Mama Africa writes:

> I look at an ant and I see myself: a native South African, endowed by nature with a strength much greater than my size so I might cope with the weight of racism that crushes my spirit. I look at a bird and see myself: a native South African, soaring above the injustices of apartheid on wings of pride, the pride of a beautiful people, I look at a stream and I see myself: a native South African, flowing irresistibly over hard obstacles until they become smooth and, one day, disappear—flowing from an origin that has been forgotten toward an end that will never be.[10]

"The weight of racism," "the injustices of apartheid," "irresistibly over hard obstacles," and "an origin that has been forgotten": all these describe South Africa of Makeba then and even today; but it could easily be read to explain the African American—the black man and black woman's life in the United States of America then and now. Every black person in the world—be it in the Caribbean Islands or in the United Kingdom—can identify with Makeba's sentiments. These are "the ties that bind" people of African descents wherever they are in the world—consciously or unconsciously. That is why when Barack Obama became the *first* African American President of the Unites States of America; black people globally felt it was *our triumph!* I was at the late former President Mandela's Memorial in Soweto when President Obama delivered a rousing tribute to Mandela in a speech that had crowds at the FNB Stadium cheering. Obama was speaking for us and about "the ties that bind" us when he said in his tribute:

> It is a singular honor to be with you today, to celebrate a life unlike any other. To the people of South Africa – people of every race and walk of life – the world thanks you for

---

[10] Makeba (1988), 1.

sharing Nelson Mandela with us. His struggle was your struggle. His triumph was your triumph. Your dignity and hope found expression in his life, and your freedom, your democracy is his cherished legacy.[11]

In South Africa of the 1950s and 1960s, while the rest of Africa was gaining independence, the apartheid system was set up in South Africa, nipping the development of local and indigenous music in the bud and this pushing South Africa's best artists into exile abroad. At the top of that list was Miriam Makeba, Hugh Masekela, Jonas Gwangwa, and that famous and admirable musical couple, Caphuis Semenya and Letta Mbuli. Makeba's reputation abroad especially won her the much deserved title of "*Mama Africa*," which was accorded by her African Diasporic followers, as well by her South African compatriots, who Africanized the word which the word "Africa" in Mama Africa to "Afrika" replacing "c" with a "k," and called her *Mama Afrika*. According to *The New York Times* (May 5, 1961), Mama Africa was "*the first South African Negro to become an internationally popular performer.*" In another edition of the same newspaper, an article entitled "*Xhosa Songstress: A former housemaid from South Africa brings her exotic songs to New York*" (& February 28, 1960). Makeba was the ANC representative at the United Nations' Special Committee on Apartheid in July 16, 1963 (above). She spoke as the representative of the liberation movements in South Africa at the United Nations' Special Committee on Apartheid in the 1960s, which she said made people think she was political:

> I was never politically involved. People always think I'm political, but I'm not. I just speak the truth. When I say we have been oppressed, I'm not lying. It's the truth. I'm glad I've been vindicated, in a way. I could have been in Parliament, but I'm not a politician. I'm a singer. I love to sing. That's what makes me happy.[12]

The apartheid regime responded by banning her music records in South Africa. This gave her the courage to continue, and she addressed the United Nations' General Assembly for the second time in 1976 during the *International Year against Apartheid*. Harry Belafonte writes in his memoir, Song: A Memoir of Art, Race and Defiance (2011), how she met Makeba; I quote him lengthily because I think it is so fundamentally at the heart of "ties that bind":

> I spent the summer on my now-established concert circuit, from the Carter Barron Amphitheatre in Washington D.C., to the Greek Theatre in L.A., and up to the Riviera in Las Vegas. Summer was the season for large, outdoor amphitheaters where I could play to bigger audiences. Now, as part of that circuit, I flew to London for the first of several European concerts. And it was in London that I had a most unexpected—and—life-changing—encounter.[13]

Belafonte, returning at 1:00 a.m. to the Dorchester Hotel from one of his concerts, found Father Trevor Huddleston, a white English priest in a clerical collar, "flanked by three black students with skin so dark they were almost surely African."[14] "Mr Belafonte, I so apologize for

---

[11] Obama's tribute to Mandela: The full speech, http://mg.co.za/article/2013-12-10-obamas-tribute-to-mandela-the-full-speech, accessed March 10, 2016.

[12] Asmal et al. (2003), 278.

[13] Belafonte and Schnayerson (2011), 201.

[14] See Footnote 13.

encroaching on your privacy," said Huddleston, "but we are in truly desperate situation, and you're the only person I can think to ask for help."[15]

Belafonte sat down to listen to this priestly man; an Anglican that he quickly realized was the kind of priest he liked: a social activist. English born and educated who was sent to South Africa by his British church in England and the priest came to loathe the apartheid regime. Father Huddleston was the founder of the Anti-Apartheid Movement in Britain. He was meeting Belafonte because in his latest effort he as promoting the a searing documentary called *Come Back, Africa* that translated in an African South African language means *"Mayibuye iAfrika!"* that came to be famously known as the salutation of the ANC. This documentary was made by an American filmmaker, Lionel Rogosin; and it exposed the brutalities of the apartheid system. This film had caused a sensation at the Venice Film Festival and won the prestigious Italian Film Critics' Award. The South African government hearing this news was furious so the reason why Huddleston came to see Belafonte was that the apartheid leaders in South Africa did not hide the fact that all involved in the film will be punished—and in South Africa of that time, it could also mean death! Worse was that the three students who came with the priest were actors in that film and had come to Venice to promote it. Being African and black, they knew that they were in deep trouble with the regime back home; their visitor visas were about to expire and the British government were not prepared to extend them or provide them with political asylum, not surprising considering the economic relationship between the two countries based on the exploitation of African cheap labor in the mines and in farms. Father Huddleston thought if Belafonte can see Come Back, Africa, he might be moved by it and helps the cast of the film.

Belafonte says:

> I did watch the film the next day, and was riveted, not only by the atrocities it depicted but by an amazing young singer who appeared in a scene set in a *shebeen*—an illegal speakeasy. The singer, a young woman, was both gorgeous and gifted; her extraordinary voice seemed to capture all the hope and despair of black South Africa. when the film ended and the lights came on, a door opened and in walked the singer, along with the students and Father Huddleston. The singer's name was Miriam Makeba.[16]

In South Africa, we have a *Shebeen Queen* and a *shebeen*, which is a kind of outlawed pub or club in the townships where Africans and black people gather to drown their sorrows by consuming alcohol after being exploited by the whites in different forms; and the queen is the owner of the shebeen, who in most cases is a no-non-sense taker—and can beat the men who do not want to pay her or who misbehaves in her joint. But shebeen and the shebeen queen also are a symbol of the resilience of the black people, and both were used as a meeting place for political meetings. For example, in the film, *Cry Freedom* (1987)—and directed by the late Sir Richard Attenborough—where the African American Denzel Washington plays South African Black Consciousness activist, Bantu Steve Biko; Biko during his house arrests by the apartheid regime in the 1970s, uses the shebeen queen and her shebeen to meet at night with other activists to chat way-forward to liberate black people.

---

[15] See Footnote 13.
[16] See Footnote 13, 202.

Meeting between Belafonte and Makeba is one of the most important conventions in the cultural history of South Africa and the United States—and to be exact, of African Americans' consciousness of Africa imbued in the artistic and *Ubuntuful* (humaneness) of Miriam Makeba. The Makeba-Belafonte meeting is at the heart and soul of "the ties that bind."

After meeting Belafonte at the end of the screening of *Come Back, Africa*, which was arranged by Father Huddleston in London, in her autobiography, Makeba gives her impressions about Belafonte:

> Mr. Belafonte is a very great man. For years we have sung his songs, going back to the Cuban Brothers when they did "Day-O." We all saw him in Carmen Jones, and his hits have been translated into the tribal languages. I tell him all of this.
>
> This man is so handsome … His smile can light up a village. He introduces me to his wife, Julie. She is a very beautiful woman. I tell them that I will be going to the U.S. to do this Steve Allen Show and the Village Vanguard engagement when I get my visa. Mr. Belafonte gives me all his telephone numbers, and before he leaves he insists that I tell him if there is ever anything I need. We say good night. I see him go to Mr Rogosin. I believe they are talking about me and making plans…
>
> It does not surprise me to learn that Mr. Belafonte has all sorts of connections in the United States. I guess he really was impressed by my singing, because he want to be one of my sponsors in America. Somehow, he has arranged for my visa. I am to place myself completely in his hands, I am very glad to do so.[17]

When Makeba's airplane from London lands in Idlewild, New York, Belafonte has arranged a car to meet Makeba; and she driven straight to his offices on West Fifty-sixth Street. After they embrace, it's immediately straight to work because Makeba is to open at the Village Vanguard, New York, in five days.

Makeba was really impressed with Belafonte's generosity:

> His entire organization is mobilized to help me. A musical arranger begins his work after I choose the songs I will sing. He must send music to California right away for the one song I will do on the *Steve Allen Show*. And then he must prepare the Village Vanguard songs. Meanwhile Mr. Belafonte takes me to a designer named John Pratt. Mr Pratt is very talented and fast. He begins working at once on two dresses. The designer he creates is to become my trademark look for many years: a dress simple in style, strapless, with a cape over one shoulder. Mr Pratt uses beautiful material for me, Indian silk. One dress is gold and rust, and the other is blue and green. The colors fade into each other. Mr. Belafonte, off course, has to see the completed outfits and approve them. Sometime during the busy two days, I start using my name for him, and it sticks: Big Brother.[18]

The kindness of "Big Brother" Belafonte on one South African and up-and-coming artist, Makeba, helped to cement the consciousness of the African Americans in the United States about Africa, and in this case, about the South African antiapartheid struggle that *Mama Afrika* was, through her music on the superstardom journey to be South Africa's most outspoken musician.

---

[17] See Footnote 10, 81–82.
[18] See Footnote 10, 83.

I would like to illustrate with a personal story of that speaks to the outspokenness of Makeba about the South African struggle. When I arrived at Howard University to begin my doctoral studies in the fall 2003, I worked as a researcher for the South African Research Archival Project (SARAP, http://sarap.howard.edu), which researches the role of African Americans specifically, and Americans in general, in the antiapartheid struggle in South Africa and in the African liberation struggle in Southern Africa. It was headed by the distinguished professor of African Diaspora, Joseph E. Harris; and I worked with a research team consisting of Charles D. Johnson, who was the deputy to Harris—who were both African American; Tanzanian national, Azaria Mbughuni, and Erin Freas, a white American. When I introduced myself that "I am a South African from South Africa"; immediately Professor Harris's face brightened and he said "Ah! Miriam Makeba! Mama Africa! You know Neo, Miriam Makeba when she came to the United States, very few people, African-Americans, knew about the South African struggle against apartheid; and through her *Pata Pata* and click songs, Makeba introduced to the African American community the content and context of the struggle of the black people in South Africa. Through her music, Makeba conscientized the African American people about the antiapartheid struggle; she transported and brought that story to the people."[19] As a result, the SARAP website had this Makeba photograph with her "Big Brother" Belafonte in the background marvelling at the artistic talent of his protégé Miriam playing the drums the African way with her bare hands.

It is in this regard that I agree with Mark Gevisser, who wrote the biography of Thabo Mbeki, *The Dream Deferred: Thabo Mbeki*, when he asks:

> How many in the world would have even known about Nelson Mandela if Hugh Masekela hadn't written a song about him? Masekela, Miriam Makeba, Jonas Gwangwa,

---

[19] This SARAP Research Team of 2004-2006 when I relocated back home to South Africa: distinguished professor of African Diaspora, Joseph E. Harris is retired; Charles D. Johnson completed his PhD on African-Americans and South Africa and was the Assistant professor of History in the Department of History at Howard University, where he was such role-model teacher for many students in the department. "Abuti" (means "brother" in my mother-tongue, Setswana) is what I call Professor Johnson, he moved mountains to help me across the Atlantic Ocean to get my doctoral dissertation to Howard while I was writing it from South Africa and, without his Abuti-ship ('ties that bind') I do not know how I would have successfully defended my PhD dissertation at the end of March 2013, and him spending almost the entire night in his study formatting it to the specifications of the Howard Graduate School, while he allowed me to sleep, and I graduated in May 2013. Azaria Mbughuni completed his PhD on the role of Tanzania in the Southern African Liberation Struggles in Africa, and he is an Assistant Professor of History at Morehouse College in Atlanta, Georgia; and Erin Freas left Howard after her MA degree and went to do her PhD at Sussex University in England, and she recently completed; her dissertation is on Domestic Workers in KwaZulu-Natal, South Africa. The SARAP Project was for me a safe-and-reassuring space for me an African in an alienating individualistic American culture. So different from my South African culture of Botho/Ubuntu (humaneness) that Archbishop Desmond Tutu describes as "speaks of the very essence of being human. [We] say [. . .] "Hey, so-and-so has ubuntu." Then you are generous, you are hospitable, you are friendly and caring and compassionate. You share what you have. It is to say, "My humanity is caught up, is inextricably bound up, in yours." We belong in a bundle of life. We say, "A person is a person through other persons. A person with ubuntu is open and available to others, affirming of others, does not feel threatened that others are able and good, for he or she has a proper self-assurance that comes from knowing that he or she belongs in a greater whole and is diminished when others are humiliated or diminished, when others are tortured or oppressed, or treated as if they were less than who they are" http://www.goodreads.com/quotes/165597-ubuntu-speaks-of-the-very-essence-of-being-human Accessed 2016/03/15.

Caiphus Semenya and Letta Mbuli: these artists did more for the ANC's international profile than almost anyone else.[20]

Likewise, as I have argued in my doctoral dissertation on the role of songs in the African Liberation of South Africa that the body of songs and music of Bob Marley has done more to popularize the real issues of the African liberation movement than several decades of back-breaking work of Pan-Africanists and international revolutionaries.[21]

Mama Afrika lived in exile from 1959 when she left South Africa on the tour of *Come Back, Africa*, and she returned after the release of Nelson Mandela and other political prisoners in 1990; meaning she was in exile for almost thirty years.

When Mandela was elected as the President of the Republic of South Africa in May 1994, Mandela thought about making Makeba a Minister in his government—possibly of Culture—for a nonracial South Africa. Makeba remembers:

> Before the first democratic elections, I learned that I was advanced as a possible ANC candidate for Parliament. When they asked me, I said I was very honoured, of course, but I told them that if I did anything, it was to be in my own way, with my music. Mr. Mandela told me: 'You have been our ambassador, and you must continue to raise our voice in the world.' That meant more to me than any vote. Politicians come and go, you know, but music is forever.[22]

In his post-presidency years, Mandela continued to revere *Mama Afrika*; he requested her to write a piece on Culture titled "Homecoming" in his book, *Nelson Mandela, In His Own Words*, in which Makeba remarks about her exile and fame:

> Of course, I have had some remarkable experiences singing politically. Singing at the birth of the Organization of African Unity in 1963, meeting all the presidents, the men who led their countries to independence; that was, for me, something. Here I was, coming from nowhere, and singing to all these important people. And then there was the birthday salute to US President John F Kennedy in 1961, where I was the only foreign artist among the big giants of America paying tribute to him.[23]

Globally, Mama Afrika is perhaps only comparable to her longtime friend, Nina Simone, the African American diva of song who "When four black children were killed in the bombing of a church in Birmingham in 1963, Nina wrote *Mississippi Goddam*, a bitter and furious accusation of the situation of her people in the USA. The strong emotional approach of this song and the others on her first record ("Nina Simone In Concert"), would become another characteristic in her art. She uses her voice with its remarkable timbre and her careful piano playing as means to achieve her artistic aim: to express love, hate, sorrow, joy, loneliness—the whole range of human emotions—through music, in a direct way."[24]

In an August 2001 interview with *The Guardian* of London, Simone remembers:

---

[20] Gevisser (2007).

[21] Kwayana (1997), xii. Both Campbell and Kwayana came to "The Intellectual and Political Legacy of Walter Rodney, Twenty-Five Years After," at Howard University, Washington, DC, in September 29–30, 2005, when I was in the PhD Program there.

[22] See Footnote 12, 278–279.

[23] See Footnote 12, 278.

[24] Dr. Nina Simone Biography, http://www.ninasimone.com/nina.html, accessed November 10, 2008.

> I used to sing a song with Miriam Makeba, what was it... And Nina Simone starts to sing to me: "Bring back Nelson Mandela, bring him back home to Soweto, I wanna see him walking down the street with Winnie Mandela, tomorrow..." Wow. It's impossible to stop smiling.[25]

The friendship between Makeba and Simone was the other powerful example of "the ties that bind" African Americans and Africa. Nina, like Miriam, was one of the most focal and furious protest singers of the American Civil Rights Movement.

In his autobiography, *Ready for Revolution* (2003), Kwame Ture, formerly Stokely Carmichael, quotes from a letter by Gamal Nkrumah, Kwame Nkrumah's son, written in Cairo 1999:

> I was about fourteen years old when I travelled to Conakry for my father's funeral. There were a great many people and much too much ceremony and formalities for a fourteen-year-old boy to sort out. But one impression has remained clear—my utter fascination with Stokely Carmichael and Miriam Makeba. Why? I just thought they were the most strikingly attractive and intriguing-looking couple I'd ever laid eyes on . . . for some reason, I particularly remember them.[26]

Stokely Carmichael was a Caribbean by birth and studied at Howard University in Washington, DC, in the 1960s (see his chapter VI "Howard University: Everything and Its Opposite"), later changed his name in 1978 to Kwame Ture in honor of his mentors, the revolutionary African leaders Kwame Nkrumah of Ghana and Sekou Toure of Guinea Conakry, was married to Miriam Makeba. They were invited by various presidents of African countries to live in their countries after it became clear that the Federal Bureau of Investigation (FBI) in the United States had files on them for their role in the Black Power and Pan-Africanism movements in the Diaspora and in Africa.

"DAYS OF GRACE": ARTHUR ASHE AND SOUTH AFRICA

Arthur Robert Ashe, JR was an African American and was born on July 10, 1943, and died on February 6, 1993. He was an American World No.1 professional tennis player. He won three Grand Slam titles, ranking him among the best tennis players from the United States. Ashe was the first black player selected to the United States Davis Cup team and the only black man ever to win the singles title at Wimbledon, the US Open, or the Australian Open. He retired in 1980. He was ranked World No. 1 by Harry Hopman in 1968 and by Lance Tingay of *The Daily Telegraph* and *World Tennis Magazine* in 1975. In the ATP computer rankings, he peaked at No. 2 in May 1976.[27] In the early 1980s, Ashe is believed to have contracted HIV from a blood transfusion he received during heart bypass surgery. Ashe publicly announced his illness in April 1992 and began working to educate others about HIV and AIDS. He founded the Arthur

---

[25] Interview with Nina Simone, *Soul survivor:* Her voice is legendary. And so is her temper. Nina Simone's glorious, furious days as the protest singer of the American civil rights movement might be over, but she is still singing and snarling, *The Guardian,* Libby Brooks, August 6, 2001, http://www.theguardian.com/g2/story/0,3604,532415,00.html, accessed March 16, 2016.

[26] Carmichael (2003), 695.

[27] Arthur Ashe, https://en.wikipedia.org/wiki/Arthur_Ashe, accessed March 15, 2016.

Ashe Foundation for the Defeat of AIDS and the Arthur Ashe Institute for Urban Health before his death from AIDS-related pneumonia on February 6, 1993.

On December 3, 1994, while I was studying at the University of Natal in Durban (UND), South Africa, I bought *Days of Grace: A Memoir* by Arthur Ashe. I am certain that, like Mark Mathabane two decades earlier, I was attracted to Ashe because I have never seen before a successful black man playing tennis. By writing his memoir, Ashe hoped to express his views on certain issues of importance to him, such as race, education, politics, and sports, as well as to give an account of his experience as a patient with heart disease and AIDS.[28] But it was Chapters 4 and 5 of his memoir, "Protest and Politics" and "Burden of Race" that drew my attention to the extreme.

Ashe writes in "Protest and Politics":

> Even the most impressive record in tennis would not have stilled certain disquieting feelings that ran deeper in me than patriotism or sporting fame. I am African-American, one born in the iron grip of legal segregation. Aside from my feelings about religion and my family, my innermost stirrings inevitably have to do with trying to overcome racism and other forms of social injustice, with the search for dignity and power for blacks in a world so often hostile to us. Not the tennis court but the arena of protest and politics would be the single most significant testing ground for me in the middle years of my life. [29]

Ashe had just resigned from the Davis Cup captaincy when the sports editor of Jet magazine, a sister publication of the better known Ebony magazine, both devoted to the African American world, called him. He questioned him: "I mean your interests in human rights. For example, your ongoing support opposition to the practice of apartheid in South Africa?" replied Ashe, "I think so, I believe that my role in publicly protesting against apartheid probably had something to do with USTA deciding not to ask me back for next year. Some probably think I've gone too far." [30]

In the previous January, Ashe had been arrested in Washington, DC, while taking part in a demonstration against South Africa. "Quietly, innocently, South Africa had come into my life on an exquisite June afternoon in 1968[31], at the Queen's Club in London . . . I was sitting next to John Newcombe in a meeting with a group of top players, all bound for Wimbledon. Only two months after the first open tennis tournament, we were talking primarily about the possibility of forming an association of professional tennis players, a kind of trade union, and about the reception we could expect to receive from various governing bodies around the world. The first open Wimbledon was at hand. The first US Open would be held later in the summer.

One of the South African players, Cliff Drysdale, mentioned that the first South African Open would be held in the fall. He and his compatriots, top players like Frew McMillan and Ray Moore, were eagerly looking forward to the competition, which hoped to attract a stellar field to Johannesburg, South Africa.[32]

---

[28] Ashe (1993), ix.

[29] See Footnote 28, 106–107.

[30] See Footnote 28, 107.

[31] The author was 10 months old; he was born on August 24, 1967.

[32] See Footnote 28, 108-109.

Turning to Ashe, Drysdale said casually, "they'd never let you play." This startled Ashe, and he asked: "Is that bad?"

Drysdale continued, "Oh, the Lawn Tennis Association would let you play, I am pretty sure of that. In fact, they would love to have you come. But you would need a visa to enter South Africa, and the government would never let you have one."

Ashe asked again, "Are you serious?"

Drysdale replied, "Try them. You'll see."[33]

The following year, 1969, Ashe tested the waters. He mailed an application for a visa to allow him to play in the Open. His application was rejected. At the same time, South Africa was not a major political issue for American voters, white or black, or indeed for many people outside South Africa itself. The United Nations had not yet voted to impose social and cultural isolation on the nation of apartheid. Portugal still held the territories of Mozambique and Angola, which served as effective buffers between South Africa and independent Africa. South Africa still played in the Davis Cup. In fact, it would win the Cup in 1974, when India defaulted in the final rather than compete in sport with South Africa. Soweto students' uprising of June 16, 1976, had not happened.

Ashe tried again for a South Africa visa in 1970, and was rebuffed again. Finally, in 1973, Ashe was allowed in. It is important to be aware that it is not that South Africa had changed when it granted Ashe a visa, no, the apartheid government of South Africa was seeking to end their Olympic ban and wanted to use the Ashe granting visa a pretext that South Africa was no longer practicing apartheid, and so be readmitted to join the Olympic movement. Who was fooling who? As part of the Sporting Boycott of South Africa during the apartheid era, South Africa did not compete in the Olympic Games from 1964 to 1988. The South African National Olympic Committee (NOC) was expelled from the International Olympic Committee (IOC) in 1970. It was only after the release of Nelson Mandela and other political prisoners in 1991, as part of the transition to multiracial equality, a new NOC was formed and admitted to the IOC, and for the first time, South Africa competed at the 1992 Summer Olympics.

Ashe visited South Africa again in 1974, 1975, and 1977; and on each occasion (excerpt for 1977 when he was in South Africa on assignment for ABC Sports), he insisted that there be no segregated seating at his matches, and his request was granted. In 1973, Ashe created a sensation when he was playing so well in the court; and he explains:

> I looked apartheid straight in the face, saw the appalling 'whites only' and 'non-whites only' signs, the separate and drastically unequal facilities very much like those of my childhood in Virginia. I saw the sneer of superiority on the faces of many whites, and the look of obsequiousness, fatalism, cynicism, and despair on the faces of many blacks. I saw the rigid divisions between the black [African], and Coloured and Asian [Indian] and the Jewish and the English and Dutch [Afrikaner] peoples, with the Dutch [Afrikaner] holding the highest ground of apartheid. I met educated, kindly, but dedicated apologists for apartheid. I met liberal whites troubled by the system that sustained their privilege, and I even stayed in the home of one of them, a Jewish businessman. I was also befriended by Indians, Coloureds and blacks.*[34]

---

[33] See Footnote 28, 109.

[34] See Footnote 28, 110.

The term "Black" in South Africa encompasses three racial groupings: African, Colored, and Indian. See the definition of "black" by Bantu Steve Biko in his chapter on "Black Consciousness" in *I Write What I Like* (1978).

"The ties that bind" in the African American consciousness of Ashe with (South) Africa comes when he writes:

> I will never forget one black boy, about fourteen years old, who in 1974 seemed to follow me around in Johannesburg's Ellis Park, the most hallowed site in South African rugby, the national sport, and the site also of the South African Open. Every day, he was there when I arrived, and he seemed to be there when I left. He was watchful but shy as he shadowed me around the park. It was as if I exuded some precious, mysterious quality that he wanted to possess. Finally I confronted him, though gently. Tell me something, why are you following me around?[35]

Profound was the response from this black South African boy: "Because you are the first one I have ever seen." Ashe enquired, "The first what?"

This boy continued, "You are the first truly free black man I have ever seen."[36]

Ashe writes that

> When I heard these words, I felt a distinct chill. Nothing anyone else said or wrote during my stay captured as poignantly for me the abyss of inhumanity that was South African apartheid. The major aim of the system was to prepare, to programme, and to destine young blacks like this boy for a lifetime of servitude. He was obviously yearning for freedom, and I was touched to be a rallying point for him in his struggle.[37]

That black South African boy was Mark Mathabane, who through his correspondence with Ashe was able to come to the United States and wrote his autobiography *Kaffir Boy* (Nigger Boy) that narrates his life growing up in apartheid South Africa. During apartheid era in South Africa, white people called Africans and any black person a *Kaffir*, like a *Nigger* in the United States; and it is an insulting and contemptuous term that in postapartheid South Africa it is considered a crime to call someone a *Kaffir* and one could be arrested for doing so; but still some conservative and apartheid-loving Afrikaner and some whites in general continue to call black people *Kaffirs!*

In *Kaffir Boy* (1986), Mathabane wrote about what Ashe's example and his first to South Africa had meant to him:

> The more I read about the world of tennis, and Arthur Ashe's role in it, the more I began to dream of its possibilities. What if I too were someday to attain the same fame and fortune as Arthur Ashe? Would whites respect me as they did him? Would I be as free as he? The dreams were tantalizing, but I knew they were only dreams. Nevertheless, I kept dreaming; after all, what harm could that do me.'[38]

Finally, at Ellis Park Stadium, Mathabane saw Ashe play, and he remarks in *Kaffir Boy*: "How could a black man play such excellent tennis?" He wrote about Ashe's victory over a white

---

[35] See Footnote 28.
[36] See Footnote 28, 110–111.
[37] See Footnote 28, 111
[38] Mathabane (1986); see Footnote 28, 127.

opponent, "Ashe move about the court with such self-confidence, trash a white man and be cheered by white people?"[39]

Triumphing against apartheid and relocating to United States, Mathabane attended college and find expression for his literary talents that easily are not realized by the majority of black in South Africa and Africa in general. In his second autobiography, *Kaffir Boy in America* (1989), Mathabane offers his perspective on race relations that are personal and social in contemporary America.

HUGH MASEKELA: "BRING BACK NELSON MANDELA"

Hugh Ramopolo Masekela is a South African and was born on April 4, 1939, in Kwa-Guqa Township, Witbank, South Africa; and he is a world renowned trumpeter, flugelhornist, cornetist, composer, and singer. He began singing and playing piano as a child, and at the age of 14, after seeing the film *Young Man with a Horn*, in which Kirk Douglas plays a character modelled on American jazz cornetist Bix Biederbecke, Masekela took up playing the trumpet. His first trumpet was given to him by Father—and later to be—Archbishop Trevor Huddleston, the antiapartheid priest who founded the Anti-Apartheid Movement in England.

It was at the township of Kwa-Guqa, Witbank, a coal-mining area—*emalahleni*—where Hugh Masekela grew up, raised by his grandmother, Johanna. In his autobiography, *Still Grazing: The Musical Journey of Hugh Masekela* (2004), Masekela communicates how an environment like this—despite its appalling state—influenced him, musically.[40] In the mines often the unskilled labor force was Zulu men recruited in large numbers from KwaZulu-Natal province. Increasing numbers of other African laborers came also from Portuguese East Africa (Mozambique); Basotho and colored men went to the Kimberley diamond fields. It was not a surprise that most Zulu men hated underground work in mines and opted to leave to secure somewhat better paying jobs as domestic servants in the city itself and in the neighboring white suburbs. By the early 1920s, there were more than 200,000 migrant mine workers in the city and perhaps another 100,000 male domestic workers, laborers, laundrymen, and others.

Women and children did not exist officially. As a result, they were not counted. For all black people, the harshest living conditions prevailed, and even if working men had partners and children in the location, laws denying their right to be in town at all kept their wives out of formal economic activity.[41] The "illegal Johannesburg brewing liquor" gave many proud people who hated white employment the opportunity to go into business for themselves. Johanna, Masekela's grandmother, and her siblings, Martha and Jacob, established *shebeens* to serve the demands of the township's home-grown drinkers and the thousands who worked in the mines. *Shebeens*—which were illegal bars where millions of non-white South Africans—who were, until 1961, forbidden to drink alcohol, became a core township industry and in Witbank, Johanna was one of its most highly respected proprietors.[42]

---

[39] Footnote 28, 127.
[40] Masekela and Cheers (2004).
[41] Parsons (1993), 172.
[42] See Footnote 40.

Immediately following the Anglo-Boer War indentured Chinese mine workers were imported under conditions that resembled slavery. The consequence was that from its early days, the city of gold (Gauteng/Johannesburg) was a place full of Africans speaking many languages and carrying with them many cultural traditions, working with and for an equally mixed group of European migrants—Portuguese, Dutch, English, Italian, Irish, and Jews who fled Czarist regimes in Eastern Europe.

Other industrial and commercial centers saw similarly mixed communities developing. But because Gauteng grew at an alarming rate, so huge, so fast, on the basis of the mining boom, my forefathers/mothers—Setswana-speaking people—found their labor in demand either on their own farms or on surrounding farms to feed the hungry city and most of them did not seek work in town. The scale and impact of migration on the city of gold was probably the most dramatic in the region.

Around the city the African shantytowns and the racially mixed slums within it must have been terrifyingly crowded, foul, and noisy for those coming in from relatively thinly populated rural areas with free-running streams and clean air.

In particular, one sound made an impression: the steam train. It was the train that transported the many migrant workers from all over South and central Africa and brought them to the mines in Gauteng. In his autobiography, *Still Grazing: The Musical Journey of Hugh Masekela*, Masekela writing from his personal experience with this sound of the train, wrote a moving song titled *Setimela* (train) in which he communicates the history of the migrant laborers, their exploitation by the mines, as well as their drunkenness from the illegal liquor brewed by shebeen owners, including his own grandmother.[43] According to Masekela, the train has brought more suffering than happiness to the African people.[44]

Probably Masekela is famously known for a song that he titled, "Mandela: Bring Back Nelson Mandela."

Bring Back Nelson Mandela. ?
Bring him Back all to
Soweto.
I want to see him walking
down the street in South Africa - Tomorrow.
Bring Back Nelson Mandela. ?
Bring him Back all to
Soweto.
I won't to see him walking down the street
with Winnie Mandela.

This is an anthemic protest song that Masekela wrote and was released as the first track of his 1987 album *Tomorrow*. It was recorded in 1986 when Masekela was in exile in the United States, where, he, like Makeba, was helped by "the ties that bind" of Belafonte after he escaped the apartheid regime's police in South Africa that was looking for him for his political activism in the late 1950s. The melody of the song is buoyant, containing a number of powerful chords and trumpet riffs. The lyrics of the song demand the release of the ANC imprisoned leader, Mandela,

---

[43] See Footnote 40.
[44] See Footnote 40, 240; and Hugh Masekela Interview, in the film *Amandla! A Revolution in Four-Part Harmony*, 2003, by Lee Hirsch.

who had been imprisoned since 1964 by the white South African government on Robben Island Maximum Security Prison. The song became enormously popular, and turned into an unofficial anthem of the Anti-Apartheid Movement. It became one of Masekela's most performed live songs. It was later used as a part of the official soundtrack to the documentary film Amandla! A Revolution in Four-Part Harmony (2003), directed by American Lee Hirsch. In this documentary film, Masekela narrates how he came to write the lyrics of this song; while in exile in New York, he received a letter from the imprisoned Mandela, who was thanking him (Masekela) for keeping up the struggle with his music and songs. Masekela said he was overwhelmed by that letter, that, "here was a man who had been in prison for almost 30 years and took the time to sit down and write me a letter of appreciation for my songs"; and then there and there, Masekela sat down and composed the song, "Mandela: Bring Back Nelson Mandela."[45]

After more than thirty years in exile, Masekela returned home to South Africa in the early 1990s; and it was only in 2015 that Masekela's autobiography, *Still Grazing*, was published in South Africa by Jacana Media because in 2004 when it first became out in the United States it was never released in South Africa. When it was published last year, the jazz legend said:

> He believes South African society has become complacent since the time of Steve Biko and other young intellectuals of the apartheid era, and hopes that his book can stand as an example of the forthrightness needed to turn the country around.

> "In 1990, when all the apartheid laws were dropped, we were probably one of the most intelligent societies in the world," he said. "Since then, I think we have become dumbed down, not by freedom itself but by the hype that we are free now.[46]

Even before life in exile, while still in South Africa, Masekela, just like Makeba, informed about the influence of the music of Harry Belafonte in their musical careers.[47]

Masekela writes in his autobiography that

> In the spring of 1961 I finally met Harry Belafonte at his offices on 57th Street. He introduced me to his production manager, Bob Bollard, who immediately assumed development custody over my life. . . . In addition to my salary, Belafonte's foundation awarded me a stipend of $190 a month to supplement my living expenses.

> Belafonte was far better looking in person than the pictures of him on his countless album covers, or the movies I had seen him in, like *Carmen Jones*. Tall, athletic, and with golden porcelain skin and pearly white teeth, he also exuded the compassion and humility of the activist and philanthropist he was, with no pretentions of glamour or stardom. When he spoke t, he looked you straight in the eye and spoke with simple eloquence. He was very unaffected—and this was at the time when he was among the most famous entertainers in the world. Most of his staff addressed him as "Harry" or "Mr. B." Even though he joked around with everyone in the office, there was no doubt he was a very focused and serious person.[48]

---

[45] Hugh Masekela Interview, in the film *Amandla! A Revolution in Four-Part Harmony*, 2003, by Lee Hirsch.
[46] "I Don't Bite My Tongue in this Book"—Hugh Masekela Signs with Jacana for the Local Release of His "Lost" Memoir, http://bookslive.co.za/blog/2015/07/28/i-dont-bite-my-tongue-in-this-book-hugh-masekela-signs-with-jacana-for-the-local-release-of-his-lost-memoir/, accessed march 15, 2016.
[47] See Footnote 40, 90 and 138.
[48] See Footnote 40, 146.

Even before Makeba and Masekela left South Africa, while living and singing in Johannesburg, "a romance began to blossom between Miriam and me. She had a number of lovers, including, for a short time, my cousin Kappie, but we never hid our feelings for each other."[49] Eventually when Masekela got to the United States and New York, Masekela and Makeba married; and it was the most violent marriage, according to the former, and their marriage ended up in divorce.[50]

Makeba was the first to leave South Africa and when she was emerging into a successful singer through the benevolence of her "Big Brother" Belafonte in New York, she continued to write letters to Masekela in Johannesburg and continued to request for assistance within the African American community to bring Masekela out of apartheid South Africa.

> The success she was achieving filled us all with pride back home. Miriam also said she had talked to Belafonte, Louis Armstrong, Dizzy Gillespie, and John Mehegan about helping me get to New York for school.[51]

CONCLUSION

"The ties that bind" Africa and African Americans I am convinced is what made me to cross the Atlantic Ocean from South Africa, at the age of 35 years old, to study for a doctoral degree at Howard University, a historically Black University that was at the heart of the Civil Rights Movement struggle in the United States of America.

This chapter is a reflection, for me, of the ongoing ties that bind my generation of African and African American scholars—without the exclusion of the others, for example, the American and Diasporic colleagues that were part of our doctoral studies.

The reading and writing of this chapter was so overwhelming because all the books I used to carve its contents were part of my personal library. Take for example, *Miriam Makeba: My Story* (1988), is a book I purchased on April 13, 1988, at the Bantustan University of Bophuthatswana (UNIBO), where I had started my academic career in the previous year 1987. *Days of Grace: A Memoir* (1993) that I describe as a "Burden of Race" autobiography that had the greatest impact on me—second to Biko' *I Write What I Like*, (1978)—I had bought it in Durban on December 1994: the year that we had President Mandela as our president in South Africa! I say "my personal library" because this literature is not the collection of the literature of the University education of my tertiary academic training in the South African University that I attended in apartheid South Africa and in the postapartheid South Africa, between 1987 and 1998 when I completed my MA degree in the humanities in Durban. This symbolizes the social injustices of the education—at the Department of Basic Education (DBE) and Department of Higher Education and Training (DHET) of South Africa; and that has resulted in the current renewed social movements by universities' students whose protests in 2015 and ongoing into 2016 academic year in South Africa, i.e., #Rhodes Must Fall, #Fees Must Fall, #Open Stellenbosch, #Afrikaans Must Fall, and the other Must Falls in between, call for the decolonization of the African University

---

[49] See Footnote 40, 82.
[50] See Footnote 40.
[51] See Footnote 40, 105.

in their country, South Africa. It is a calling for a decolonized curriculum; these students, whose majority is black—and were not yet born when Mandela was released from prison in 1990, want to be taught by professors who look like themselves, and who can teach, research, and write from their own perspectives: viewpoints of their own struggles of enslavement, colonialism, and apartheid. The South African students demand to be taught and research their honors, masters and doctoral dissertations about the experiences of Bernard Makhosezwe Magubane, Archie Mafeje, Miriam Makeba, Hugh Masekela, Bantu Biko, Mangaliso Robert Sobukwe, Rolihlahla Mandela, Mark Mathabane, Harry Belafonte, Jonas Gwangwa, Caiphus Semenya and Letta Mbulu, Arthur Ashe, Father-and-Archbishop Trevor Huddleston, Stokely Carmichael/Kwame Ture, to name just a few.

In short, the formal and paid for education of the children of South Africa is an education that excludes the knowledge and culture of its majority citizens, who happen to be African and black. It is no wonder that South Africa's "ties that bind" them together are blurred, if not visible at all. These children are asking us: "Why is my curriculum white?"[52]—When we are in Africa; we mare Africans and we are "Black and Proud!"

Lastly, it is worth reiterating that "The ties that bind" Africa and the African Americans is a treasure trove that Magubane's generation valued, and that which my generation holds dear. It is the knowledge production that originates in the civilizations of Africa that we, the Africans in the African continent and the African Americans in the African Diaspora know little about; and is a wealth we must recover for ourselves, our children and for their children.

DEDICATION:

Professor Bernard Makhosezwe Magubane
    (August 26, 1930–April 12, 2013)

---

[52] "Why is my curriculum white?" https://www.youtube.com/watch?v=Dscx4h2l-Pk, accessed March 15, 2016.

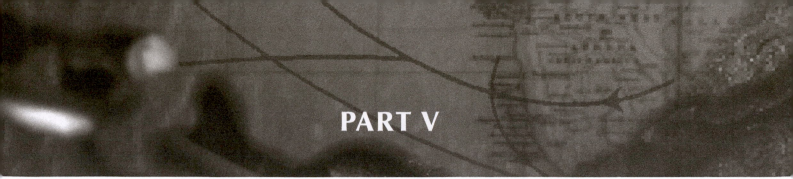

PART V

MIGRATION AND RESISTANCE MOVEMENTS: TWENTIETH CENTURY

CHAPTER 17

CARIBBEAN MIGRATION TO GREAT BRITAIN IN THE TWENTIETH CENTURY

Tony Frazier

The aim of this historiographic essay is to explore the literature concerning the history of Caribbean migration to Great Britain during the twentieth century. Black migration into Great Britain during the twentieth century changed the political, economic, and racial climate of the country. The migration streams under review began with World War I, and includes the inter-war years, World War II, and post-1945 West Indian migration. The essay also discusses recent scholarship that illuminates new dimensions posing questions about identity formation and return migration.

It is important for the reader to understand that migration to Great Britain was an experience for Asians, Africans, West Indians, and other minority groups who all come under the nomenclature of black in the social context of British racial classification. The large forces undergirding these groups were the legacy of the slavery, the slave trade, indentured servitude, imperialism, colonialism, the expansion of global capitalism, and decolonization. Two of the seminal events of the twentieth century were the world wars, which shaped the history of Britain and the West Indies as labor shortages and post-war recovery stimulated immigration from the colonies.

This essay focuses on migrants from the Caribbean. In addition, for purposes of this chapter, the terms Caribbean or West Indian will share the same meaning. The migrants who originated from the British Caribbean to the metropole were from the islands of Antigua, Anguilla, the Bahamas and Barbados, Belize, the British Virgin Islands, the Caymans, Dominica, Grenada, Guyana, Jamaica, Montserrat, St. Kitts and Nevis, St. Lucia, St. Vincent and the Grenadines, and Trinidad and Tobago.

PART I: OVERVIEW OF BLACK MIGRATION BEFORE AND AFTER WORLD WAR I

At the outset of the First World War, there were several thousands of blacks in Britain, who formed a burgeoning black community. Their occupations ranged from lawyers to doctors, nurses, laborers, domestics, and artisans, but the largest group was sailors from the West Indies, Africa, and Asia. Oftentimes sailors represented the most hard-pressed and destitute. These men and their (mainly white) wives, and their families, congregated in dockland areas of London and many other British ports, including Cardiff, Liverpool, Bristol, Hull, the Tyneside Ports, Exeter, and Glasgow. During World War I, thousands more blacks entered Britain to do work which would free whites for combat service. They replaced white British merchant seamen transferred to the Royal Navy, blacks worked in labor battalions and munitions and chemical factories. At the same time, a few black students continued to come to Britain; above all to London, reading for the bar or studying at London University; others studied at Cambridge, Liverpool, Glasgow, and Edinburgh.[1]

When the war ended, the black community numbered perhaps as many as 20,000 people. With the closing down of war factories and especially the contraction of the merchant-shipping industry after the war, a rapidly growing body of unemployed blacks became a feature of dockside areas, particularly in Cardiff and Liverpool. During the war, blacks had earned good money in the merchant navy. However, with the demobilization of white seamen from the Royal Navy, and contracting demand for seamen in the merchant service, they fell on hard times. Blacks faced displacement from jobs they had held for years just to make places for whites, and oftentimes these were foreign whites. As in the eighteenth century, the black community was predominantly male. According to Walvin, in all the places where there were concentrations of black workers, they married or consorted with white women. White workers resented lack men marrying or in any way associating with white women, which added to already smoldering issues towards the end of the war, dramatically exploded into wholesale riot in 1919. During the first half of the twentieth century, one-third of the British merchant fleet was black seamen. Race riots and violent affrays swept the port areas of such towns and cities as Liverpool, Cardiff, Barry, Newport Monmouthshire, Manchester, Hull, London, and Glasgow, and sporadic disturbances continued in some places until 1922.[2]

In assessing the causes of these disturbances, the British press stressed the issue of black men having white wives or friends, rather than blaming the white mobs who everywhere were the aggressors, or the police whose reactions were usually blatantly hostile to the victims. Sexual resentment has been a recurrent feature of the historical experience of blacks in British society. Reporting the Cardiff riots, and continuing the line by which implication justified the assault, murder, and attempted murder of blacks (and their families) by whites, *The London Times* of June 13, 1919 remarked that the black man's chief failing is his fondness for white women.[3] After the riots, the government sought to repatriate black men out of Great Britain.

INTER-WAR YEARS

The riots of 1919 represented one stage as the demand to restrict alien seamen during 1925 stood for another challenge to black immigration to Great Britain. The Special Restriction (Coloured Alien Seamen) Order of 1925 required that undocumented black seamen register as aliens in Britain. Black British subjects had to register as aliens, impairing their ability to get

---

[1] James Walvin, *Black and White: The Negro and English Society 1555–1945* (London: Allen Lane The Penguin Press, 1973), 202–04.

[2] Panikos Panayi, ed., *Racial Violence in Britain: 1840–1950* (Leicester: Leicester University Press, 1993), 97.

[3] Walvin, *Black and White*, 206.

work, and many lived under the threat of deportation. Black men found employment at colonial ports in Africa, Asia, the Middle East, and the Caribbean. They received special labor contracts and earned less pay than British seamen earn.[4]

Labor strife increased during the inter-war years amongst British seamen. The Seaman Union and the Home Office reacted to the concerns of white seamen who claimed alien workers were taking their jobs and replacing them on British ships. While the British government protected their white seaman's rights, they neglected the rights of black seamen who also were born in the British Empire. The British government held the view that black seamen were a threat to white labor. The Coloured Alien Seamen Order created a definition of British national hierarchy based on race, class, occupation, and gender. The question of who could claim citizenship became a contested space against the demands of the shipping industry, interwar economy, local and national politics, and state policy decisions.

The Coloured Alien Seamen Order of 1925 had wider and more specific powers than the earlier 1920 order. Although the main function of the 1925 order was to check the influx of alien seamen into the country, its effect was to put black alien seamen in the same category as other aliens and "obliged them to register in accordance with provisions made under the 1920 Order." Black seamen had no choice but to register with the police. There were no allowances for any nationality to establish residence. In some ports, not only aliens but also all black subjects who sought British residence had to register and carry registration cards to prove their nationality. This became a problem for many seamen who came from parts of Africa were no system of registration existed. Examination boards refused their applications for residence and classified them as aliens. The alien classification meant that they faced deportation at any time. Resistance to the order from black seamen included simple evasion to collective public protest. They used imperialist and nationalist rhetoric against the order by claiming their rights in the mother country. Black subjects argued that their war service was a price paid and granted them a right to work. Concerns that the order was affecting the loyalty of colonial elites and rousing anticolonial sentiments led to a decrease in implementing the order. Overall, the order failed because large numbers of seamen circumvented the order by exchanging passports before arrival in Britain.

Facing this discrimination, the black community in England began to form advocacy organizations such as the League of Coloured Peoples (LCP), founded in 1931 Dr. Harold Moody. The League of Coloured Peoples had four main goals: first, to promote and protect the social, educational, economic, and political interests. Second, to interest members in the welfare of colored peoples in all parts of the world. Third, to improve relations between the races. Lastly, to cooperate and affiliate with organizations sympathetic to people of color.[5] The League of Coloured Peoples (LCP admitted whites as members and advocated a legal and diplomatic approach to improving the welfare of Great Britain's blacks.

In the early twentieth century, London became a center of black intellectual activity and Pan-Africanism, a movement to unite people of African descent in a common struggle for independence. By the 1930s and 1940s, a generation of blacks born in Great Britain had come of

---

[4] Peter Fryer, *Staying Power: The History of Black People in Britain* (London: Pluto Press, 1984), 356.

[5] *The Keys*, 1933. The objectives of the League of Coloured Peoples. *The Keys* was the journal of the organization.

age. Much of this generation had grown up poor and suffered racism, including that of Oswald Mosley's Fascists. "Mosleyites" blamed black immigrants for the growing poverty of working class whites, spread anti-black propaganda, and advocated the repatriation of blacks to the West Indies. These blacks had seen Great Britain's racial policies progress somewhat, but had also witnessed the British tolerate and even accommodate American segregation and racism within the military during World War II.

Great Britain had a segregated racial order between the two world wars, which established an informal "colour bar" system. The bar represents the racism faced during and after both world wars. Blacks faced denial of lodging, no service at cafes, no admittance to dance halls, and could not ride trams and buses.[6] For instance, Learie Constantine, a Trinidadian cricketer hired by the British government, could not get a room at a London hotel because he was black. The court case that followed did much to expose the implicit racism of British policies.[7] The pan-African community was concerned with both the plight of blacks in Great Britain and the struggle for self-determination among peoples in Africa. For instance, the Fifth Pan-African Congress, held in Manchester in 1945, devoted much attention to planning strikes and boycotts against imperial rule in Africa as it was to fighting for racial equality in Great Britain.

WORLD WAR II

Mel Thompson's article "Forty-and-One Years On: An Overview of Afro-Caribbean Migration to the United Kingdom," in Ransford Palmer's *In Search of a Better Life: Perspectives on Migration* (1990) documents a different interpretation on World War II West Indian migration to the metropole. Rather than just accept blacks into the country, the Colonial Office worked behind the scenes to influence Colonial Governors to stop West Indian migrants in 1939.[8] Large-scale unemployment fueled by the worldwide Depression meant that the policy could never receive full implementation. Fearing mass labor unrest and political upheaval in the colonies and the repercussions that could engulf the homeland prompted British officials to retreat from their attempts to curtail blacks from entering Great Britain. Blacks came to work in the munitions industry in the North were other blacks also worked.[9]

The British Nationality Act of 1948 granted to all Commonwealth citizens the same legal rights accorded to all British citizens. This act allowed Great Britain to maintain its empire as self-determination grew amongst the former colonies after the Second World War. The idea was to circumvent citizenship policies of newly independent countries, thus rendering them meaningless in cases where former colonial citizens wished to claim British citizenship. Thompson claims that the real intent behind the act was an attempt to keep Canadians loyal and the consequence of West Indian colonists claim to citizenship could not suffer from dispute after the horror of Nazi Germany. He also added that the British did not wish to encourage the colonies to speed up independence. Thompson has concluded that any legislation the

---

[6] Fryer, *Staying Power*, 356.

[7] Ibid., 364–65.

[8] Ransford W. Palmer, *In Search of a Better Life: Perspectives on Migration From the Caribbean.* (New York: Greenwood, 1990), 40.

[9] Ibid., 41.

British government enacted could later face amendment and the British government would later change this liberal citizenship immigration policy.

The golden age of West Indian migration occurred after 1945. World War II brought another influx of colonial blacks-skilled labor to work in factories, and soldiers and sailors to fight the war. More than 4,000 West Africans enrolled in the Royal Air Force, as did more than 6,000 West Indians. These colonial subjects hoped that fighting for freedom in World War II would hasten the independence of the colonies form imperial rule. Their hopes tied to the fact that Great Britain faced a racist and fascist enemy, many blacks gained sympathy for their antiracist and anticolonialist efforts, and increased awareness had already elicited progressive actions from the government. The Colonial Development and Welfare Acts of 1940 and 1945 were an effort to distinguish Great Britain ethically from Nazi Germany. In addition, in 1941, England had signed the Atlantic Charter, which affirmed the right of all peoples to self-determination. After the war, Great Britain began decolonization in many of its territories. Although officials envisioned a slow route for African self-government, riots in Accra, Ghana, soon proved that this would not be the case. Many African and West Indian nationalists followed suit, and by the 1960s, most countries in Africa and the West Indies had gained independence.

The postcolonial era witnessed an influx of formerly colonized peoples into urban centers, such as London. The influx continued with the arrival of 492 Jamaicans onboard the *Empire Windrush* in 1948. That same year the Nationality Act offered colonial subjects British citizenship and the opportunity to stay in Great Britain as long as they wished. Most West Indians migrated to England for purely economic reasons, intending to return to their homelands as soon as possible. The arrival of the *Windrush* witnessed other migrants from other ships such as the *Orbita*, *Reina del Pacifico*, and *Georgic* carried more West Indians to Britain. Between 1948 and 1958, about 125,000 West Indians entered Great Britain. While in England, however, they generated a distinct culture, a tendency reinforced by discrimination in employment and housing. During the 1956 Suez crisis, Britain had an economic recession, and as racial tension mounted this resulted in white violence toward blacks, escalating into the 1958 Nottingham and Notting Hill Riots.[10] The government responded by threatening to close its borders. That year, the Commonwealth Immigrants Bill restricted entrance of colonial citizens with passports to those who also had employment vouchers; a clause permitted deportation if convicted of a crime within five years of their entrance.

This reaction to racial tensions, which essentially blamed the immigrants, repeated itself in 1965, when the number of employment vouchers available to immigrants was restricted. Although earlier immigration laws had treated aliens and commonwealth citizens differently, the Immigration Acts of 1968 and 1971 essentially lumped them together and stated only those who could trace their heritage to grandparents born in Great Britain were exempt from immigration controls. This meant that whites who had traveled to administer the British Empire could return freely to Great Britain and be secure in their citizenship, while nonwhites who had gained commonwealth citizenship as a result of their countries' domination by the expanding British Empire did not have such security. A 1981 Nationality Act later imposed a system of tiered citizenship, whereby those who lived in and traced their ancestors

---

[10] Fryer, *Staying Power*, 372–79.

to Great Britain gained primary citizenship rights, and commonwealth citizens remained in the second and third categories that offered limited rights to reside in Great Britain and gain citizenship. This concludes the summation of the black experience during the twentieth century.

PART II: POST-WAR RACE RELATIONS MODEL

The scholarship of the black presence in Great Britain began with anthropologists and sociologists in the 1950s. Their contributions as scholars provided a framework for social historians to construct black British history. In 1947, Kenneth Little provided a defining text concerning the black presence in Great Britain. His *Negroes in Britain* became the model of the race relations discourse in Great Britain between whites and blacks. Providing an overview of black history in British society from the sixteenth to the twentieth century, Little focuses on the conditions of black seamen in the ports of Cardiff and Bristol. Little's research concerned how black and whites dealt with each other in Great Britain. His work, despite later criticisms, started the inquiry into West Indian history in Great Britain. Little and other race relations experts became authoritative voices on matters of race in Britain at a moment when British policies toward immigrants became politically charged. Their emphasis on cultural differences came from their debt to the Chicago school of sociology, particularly that of Robert Park. Park emphasized thinking about racial differences in terms of the homogeneity of cultural groups. Although these scholars sought to diffuse race as the dominant factor in immigrant and host problems, their works remained preoccupied with race in the integration process. Leo Lucassen alludes to the criticism of race relations discourse as later scholars stressed that this approach reified "race" as an essentialist and biological concept and these race experts paid little attention to the power structures that support and uphold discrimination.[11]

In 1955, Michael Banton, a student of Kenneth Little continued the race relation scholarship model with his study, *The Coloured Quarter: Negro Immigrants in an English City*. Four years later, he published *White and Coloured: The Behaviour of British People towards Coloured Immigrants* (1959). Banton explored the concept of stranger in relationship to race relations between whites and blacks. This resulted in a line of thinking linked to blacks not being able to assimilate into British society. Banton links British limits on immigration to the Notting Hill riots in 1958. Sheila Patterson's *Dark Strangers: A Sociological Study of the Absorption of a Recent West Indian Migrant in Brixton, South London* (1963) continued the work of Little and Banton. Her anthropological study on Brixton reflected the general concern about the entry of West Indians into the English society.

Black Britons (1971) by Frank Field and Patricia Haikin continued to explore the impact of race relations in Britain. Their study dealt with the restrictions on immigration by the British government. The book does follow the groundwork set forth by Kenneth Little. Field and Haikin did not mention the Notting Hill riots in their study of race relations in Great Britain. The Commonwealth Immigrant Acts passed in 1962 and 1968 continued the impact of

---

[11] Leo Lucassen, *The Immigrant Threat: The Integration of Old and New Migrants in Western Europe since 1850* (Urbana and Chicago: University of Illinois, 2005), 116.

preventing more blacks from entering England. Caribbean immigration suffered considerably under these restrictive laws.

The departure from race relations discourse toward a more historical approach to the history of blacks in Britain began with Edward Scobie's influential text *Black Britannia* (1972). Like others before him Scobie owed much to Kenneth Little concerning the historical overview of blacks throughout British history. The book provides tidbits of information, personal opinions, and quotations. The value of the book is that Scobie provides a bibliography at the end of each chapter and he clearly provides a more detailed account of the black presence in England during the nineteenth and twentieth century than previous scholars. Earlier writings by Little and Banton did not include any lengthy discussions of the Coloured Seamen Act, Notting Hill Riots, black migration after World War II, and the Pan-African movement. Scobie's focus on these issues added detail for the reader to understand the lives of black people in Great Britain during the twentieth century.

James Walvin published a scholarly and objective history of the black presence in his work *Black and White: The Negro and English Society 1555–1945* (1973). Walvin, one of the leading historians concerning the black presence in England, provided an excellent overview of the history of blacks in Britain. His study is wide ranging, covering 400 years of British history. The parts of the book that pertain to this study are included in the chapter titled "Into the Twentieth Century: 1900–1945." Walvin covers the familiar terrain of Little and Banton with his information. He uses the newspapers to paint a portrayal that concludes that racism dominated the experience of blacks during the early part of the twentieth century. Two groups whom Walvin notes that Parliament sought to help were black sailors and West Indians who had migrated to Britain. The distressed condition of these two groups provoked remedies such as poor relief and repatriation. World War I witnessed a black population explosion, as Britain needed laborers. The result after the war resulted in the race riots in 1919.

Peter Fryer's *Staying Power: The History of Black People in Britain* (1984) provided great contributions to the history of blacks in Britain. Fryer traced a continuous black presence in Britain since the early sixteenth century. Much of his work is biographical with the stories of individual blacks dominating the main narrative. Fryer sets the black experience within the larger historical context of slavery, imperialism, and British racism. Fryer, like Scobie, traces the history of the Pan-African movement in the late nineteenth and twentieth centuries. Black Britons, West Indians, Americans, and Africans along with support from Asian nationalists participated in this movement. Fryer covers the daily lives of individual black leaders and activists within Britain, where an unofficial color bar discriminated against them in employment, housing, education, and public services. Riots in Cardiff and Liverpool in 1919 and again in 1948 connect the World War I and World War II generations of blacks and shows a continual British racism and the struggles of the black community. Fryer provides a wider context for blacks in British history.

In 1993, Winston James and Clive Harris coedited a volume of essays entitled *Inside Babylon: The Caribbean Diaspora in Britain*, which explored the conditions of West Indian migrants since 1945. The research in this volume pushes the scholarship to encompass gender, class, economics, as well as race. Before this publication, the historiography had been mostly silent on the question of gender. Harris's essay titled "Post-War Migration and the Industrial Reserve Army," addresses the labor surplus question that Great Britain used to employ immigrants. From a

Marxist viewpoint infused with race that covers the government policies during the 1940s and 1950s. Four chapters deal with black immigrant women and the issues of employment, abuse, relations with police, and organizing. Gail Lewis's essay "Black Women's Employment and the British Economy," delves into the subordination of black immigrant women not only in comparison to their male counterparts but also in relation to white women. Another chapter, "Women Abuse in London's Black Communities," by Amina Mama, contains twenty-one brief examples of Caribbean, African, and Asian immigrant women that illustrate how some aspects of immigrant settlement such as isolation, traditional enclaves, lack of housing, poor legal resources, and indifference by native professionals leave most immigrant women of color vulnerable to dangerous levels of abuse.

IDENTITY FORMATION

The theme of identity formation for the World War II immigrants from the Caribbean receives great treatment in *Inside Babylon* by Winston James. In a chapter entitled "Migration, Racism and Identity Formation: The Caribbean Experience in Britain," James constructs an innovative essay that examines the effects of racism on the development of West Indian identity and places this identity development into a wider community than one's own or parents' territory. Black migration to Great Britain followed similar patterns of other immigrations. The first foray is usually labor motivated, whereby single males leave their country to seek new opportunities and find places for their families. The second part involves the reunification of family, which could be months or years. The final stage of settlement involves the receding memory of the old country, as the first-generation black migrant began to no longer yearn for a return home. This longing to return is part of the collective psyche of some immigrants from the Caribbean who consider going home vital.

Slavery in the Caribbean had witnessed a social hierarchy based on skin color as the central characteristic of worth in society. Social mobility for many was higher if they had lighter skin. Darker skin meant one usually face subjugation. These castes like systems served to propel migration as well as labor shortages in Great Britain. In the Caribbean, a highly complex system determined race and had as its aim the limiting of privilege to blacks it deemed undesirable.[12]

Black migrants to Great Britain found in their journey to Great Britain a new chapter on how social hierarchy was to be determined. In Britain, they faced racism and not a class structure determined by race. To the British, regardless of skin color or place of origin, all West Indians were black. The migrants and their children who formed the second generation encountered employers, landlords, public officials, and police who found their presence in Great Britain unwanted and unnecessary. The treatment they received was one of being inferior and their social status in British society begin at the bottom. These conditions served to create a collective consciousness among a diverse group of people including Jamaicans, Barbadians, Grenadians, Kittians, Guyanese, and Trinidadians among others. The forces of British racism

---

[12] Winston James, "Migration, Racism and Identity Formation: The Caribbean Experience in Britain," in *Inside Babylon*, eds. Clive Harris and Winston James (London: Verso, 1993), 234.

had served to foster unity among these groups to combat the forces against them. Against this backdrop, the formation of a black identity took root among the people from the Caribbean.[13]

The experience of migration and the encounter with British racism forced a revaluation of what their role and place was in British society. Am I English? Am I a Jamaican if I have never been to Jamaica and never experienced life there? Migration had forced them to view themselves as black for the first time, as they confronted this idea of being invisible, a nonentity, a being who equaled nothing, absence of their humanity. As a bit of irony, blacks may have been too visible for others. Whites viewed blacks as a threat; it disrupted their own definition of self. The mere presence of blacks meant for them, who am I?

NEW DIMENSIONS IN SCHOLARSHIP

Laura Tabili's "*We Ask for British Justice*": *Workers and Racial Difference in Late Imperial Britain* (1994) illuminates the use of racial ideology in the interwar British shipping industry, and its impact on black and white seamen. She argues that British imperialism influenced the racial differences within Britain itself. Tabili places black workers within British labor history but unlike Scobie, and others she disputes the notion that the working class whites were naturally racist. She places the blame on ship-owners, union leaders, and the state who structured racial inequality to gain profit, power, and social control.

Kathleen Paul's *Whitewashing Britain: Race and Citizenship in the Postwar Era* (1997) locates the issue of post-World War II West Indian migration in Great Britain's dilemma to ensure their declining status as a global empire. The governments' first solution sought to combine its far-flung empire into a Commonwealth of 650 million people. They insisted that emigrants leave the mother country and go to the dominions, there they would constitute a segment of British population still loyal to the crown and increase the Commonwealth unity. The other issue was a declining birthrate when coupled with a need to rebuild war-ravaged export industries, which generated the cash for the welfare state. The British government encouraged overseas sources of labor to enter Great Britain. Paul's main themes were how formal citizenship matters less than the constructed national identity and the involvement of the government in immigration policies. Her questions revolve around the sense of Britishness as many different migrant groups entered the motherland after 1945. Some 345,000 displaced Europeans augmented Britain's domestic labor force in the later 1940s. These included 25,000 prisoners of war who were able to obtain permission to stay in Britain following the end of the Second World War, some 125,000 Poles who gained permanent residency status through their participation in the 1946 Polish Resettlement Corps, and another 78,500 workers recruited from Eastern Europe through the government's policy of western migration. After the war, Britain also displaced the United States as the primary destination of the emigrant Irish and by 1961, it was home to approximately one million Irish-born citizens.

Paul dissects the 1948 British Nationality Act and alludes to the fact that although all Commonwealth migrants were technically British subjects, all guaranteed the right to live and work in the mother country. In reality, however, most of them became second-class citizens,

---

[13] Ibid., 240.

largely because formal citizenship policies were on many occasions undermined by a series of informal beliefs about who rightly belonged to the national community. Between 1946 and the 1962, Commonwealth Immigration Act, Great Britain received about 400,000 people of color from the Commonwealth. Their color became an issue as one MP stated, "An influx of coloured people ... is likely to impair the harmony, strength and cohesion of our public and social life and to bring discord and unhappiness among all concerned."[14] The liberal immigration policies of the British government allowed West Indian migrants to believe that the motherland wanted them but Paul's research suggest the British government feared the new migrants of color. Their immigration policies contained race specific language after 1962.

Ian G. Spencer, author of *British Immigration Policy since 1939: The Making of Multiracial Britain* (1997), uses documents and papers of the British cabinet and related committees to re-examine immigration legislation concerning post-World War II migrants. According to Spencer, the cabinet was responsible for restricting migration from the former colonies, by means covert and overt in the post-1945 period. He dismisses the common interpretation that popular racism embodied in the 1958 Nottingham and Notting Hill riots created the new emphasis on limiting migration. Spencer suggests that the evidence dates from the 1940s as to the mechanisms utilized by Labour and Conservative cabinets that reacted to black migration with alarm and pursued restriction. Spencer did not put forth a new argument but his detailed and sustained investigation of the cabinet deliberations reveal that the British government wrestled with the contradictions of overt racial discrimination and attempting to preserve the harmony within the Commonwealth.

Spencer argues that the Asian migration created more problems for the cabinet due to fears of religious, linguistic, and cultural differences. He offers an interesting point about how black migrants were on average more educated and skilled than the indigenous population. He emphasizes their substantial contributions and achievements in education, economic mobility, and public life since the 1960s. Spencer did not include any voices from West Indian subjects only the official version from the documents and does not discuss race or racism, as he believes they do not exist. His analysis focuses only on the documents, which gives the official debate and not mention of other issues relating to West Indian migration. In comparison to Kathleen Paul's *Whitewashing Britain* (1997) published in the same year, offered much more context and analysis while also using government documents.

A 1997 article by Chris Waters entitled "Dark Strangers in Our Midst: Discourses of Race and Nation in Britain, 1947–1963," rebuts the race relations paradigm. Waters examines the history of race relations discourse began by Kenneth Little. The influx of black migrants into Britain gave rise to a new "science of race relations," pioneered by anthropologists and sociologists. Waters criticizes these race relations experts for their narration of the migrant as the 'stranger' as opposed to what it meant to be British. He disagrees with the views of earlier scholars like Little, Banton, Patterson because their model created an immigrant and host dichotomy that produced a homogeneous British society. The issues of adjustment and accommodation, individual prejudice and strangeness were the key variables in their accounts of what they saw

---

[14] As quote in Kathleen Paul, *Whitewashing Britain: Race and Citizenship in the Postwar Era* (Ithaca: Cornell University Press, 1997), 127.

as a new encounter between black migrants and white British people. Waters points out that Robert Park and the Chicago school heavily influenced the work of early pioneers of British race relations scholarship. This model underplayed social conflict and created the idea that the strangers (West Indians) in British society were not able to assimilate into British society.

The theme of identity formation continues through Mike Phillips and Trevor Phillips's *Windrush: The Irresistible Rise of Multi-Racial Britain* (1998). This book is about the nearly 500 West Indians who arrived in 1948. The book is a series of interviews with those passengers and their children. The sense of identity formation is evident throughout the book. The book is a social history of Great Britain in the last half of the twentieth century. Many of the migrants talked about returning to the Caribbean. Return, as a concept is very powerful in the formation of identity. The idea of somehow being unable to escape Britain made the migrants feel like they were in exile permeates some the stories in the book. Others found their conflicts with British society solved by the lifestyle that became accessible by living in England. Whether one remains or leaves, their notions of identity are still present in their minds. Most migrants initially planned to return after living abroad for a while. The realities of Great Britain meant greater struggles than imagined. The idea of return seemed far off.

One example of this idea is an interview of Oswald 'Columbus' Dennison. Dennison states "Well, as time went by, I get closer and closer to England because I started looking for family, because I started courting, and then getting married, married at Wandsworth, So, I never give any more thought of going once I started having a family here. And, as I say, I started having a family here. My sister still alive, but, it was quite alright for me to make a home here once I met my wife. Well, I don't know whether I was belonging to it or not, I felt I was here to stay."[15] Identity formation among migrants to Britain offers scholars a wealth of information to add more dimensions to the history of blacks in Britain.

Harry Goulbourne pushes the boundaries of West Indian migration with his volume *Caribbean Transnational Experience* (2002). He investigates what he calls today's transatlantic Caribbean community. He advances three central arguments, first, the problematic concept of Diaspora and the Caribbean Diaspora. Second, the African Diaspora and the different Caribbean Diasporas are part of the wider Atlantic world, which places them outside of the limiting confines of the West. Third, Goulbourne stipulates that to have any value discussions about diasporas must be empirically based and with sound theoretical insights. One of the main points in this work is the question of whether Caribbean migrants are another dimension of the earlier Indian, Asian, and African Diasporas.

The question about identity formations arises as Goulbourne maintains that some groups such as Barbadians, Antiguans, Jamaicans and others retain much of their distinctive culture within British cities. In terms of food, music, language, and other features, West Indian groups retain important aspects of their distinct national features. He establishes that some changes occur as each group lives in close proximity to others changes occur because of culture contacts.

---

[15] Mike Phillips and Trevor Phillips, *Windrush: The Irresistible Rise of Multi-Racial Britain* (London: HarperCollins Publishers, 1998) 138–39. Interview with Oswald 'Columbus' Dennison who sailed from Jamaica on the *Windrush*. He was the first of the *Windrush* passengers, according to the contemporary press, to get a job. After leaving the deep shelter at Clapham, Oswald Dennison settled in Brixton, where he worked as a street trader until his retirement.

The irony is that these groups confront one another in Britain for the first time because they do not meet in the Caribbean. Hence, the migrant groups develop bonds and commonalities in Britain that do not exist in their home regions. Goulbourne notes the Jamaican participation in the (originally Trinidadian) Notting Hill Carnival, the growth and popularity of reggae (originally from Jamaica), and the use of terms such as 'Afro-Caribbean' or 'African Caribbean' that possess little or no meaning within the Caribbean itself. The other factors include the inter-island marriages or partnership and households, children with common links to more than one country in the Caribbean. Goulbourne also explores questions of defining the transnational Caribbeans and theory, the common Atlantic heritage and fate, social and economic contexts of Caribbean transnationalism, Africa, the Unites States, and the Caribbean in popular discourses in Britain. Goulbourne also adds the new dimension of transnationality of families and the propensity of Caribbean-born and their offspring to return to the Caribbean from the mother country.

Goulbourne challenges the popular version of immigration to Britain. He cautions that Africans and Asians had a presence in Britain since the age of discovery and the *Windrush* generation from the Caribbean represents not the first but a new stream of migrants. He acknowledges the work of historians like James Walvin, Peter Fryer, and others who documented the black presence.

CONCLUSION

The scope of this historiographic essay was West Indian migration to Great Britain during the twentieth century. The evidence has shown that racism and discrimination represented a wall in front of West Indian migrants to metropole. The hidden history of British involvement in the slave trade, slavery, imperialism, and colonialism came home in the guise of West Indian migrants. The unique history of the Caribbean will continue to push our understanding of global migration. The strange twist of history that witnessed the Caribbean become populated with black bodies from the Atlantic Slave Trade witnessed the descendants of those black bodies return in a circular reversal of the triangle trade in a migratory pattern in the second half of the twentieth century. The question of identity formation and return migration among West Indian migrants will shed more light on an important segment of migration history. The reluctance of European nations to see themselves as immigrant nations will continue to be a challenge in the twenty-first century.

KEY TERMS

Special Restriction (Coloured Alien Seaman) Order of 1925
League of Colored Peoples (LCP)
Fifth Pan-African Congress (1945)
Empire *Windrush*
British Nationality Act of 1948

CHAPTER 18

EMPLOYMENT PATTERNS AMONG BLACK IMMIGRANT MOTHERS: IMPLICATIONS FOR CHILD WELL-BEING

Nina Smith

INTRODUCTION

Immigration—the movement of persons from one country to another with the purpose of permanently changing their place of residence—remains a popular topic of discourse in the United States, as the United States has long been a "nation of immigrants." In recent decades, immigration patterns in the United States have received renewed attention. The foreign-born population ages 18 and older increased from approximately 17.7 million to 37 million between 1990 and 2012. Immigrants currently make up 14 percent of the US population; compared to only 5 percent in 1965. Recent estimates suggest that in 50 years, almost 18 percent of the US population will be foreign-born. The significant shift in immigration patterns since 1965 has important implications for society.[1]

The current political landscape is filled with immigration-focused buzzwords such as "our nation's borders" and "immigration policies." Of particular interests are Latino immigrants who comprise the largest immigrant group and are projected to be the majority group in the United States by 2050.[1] While immigration to the United States continues to rise at rapid rates among Latino populations, the overall US immigration population is extremely diverse. As of 2013, Asians are the largest growing ethnic group in the United States. Similarly, groups of African descent have a long history of migrating to the United States. In fact, the role of Africa and the Caribbean in the African American experience has been oversimplified in many scholarly debates on diaspora traditions. For example, some scholars argue that present-day African American culture and traditions are highly influenced by customs that existed in Africa before the transatlantic slave trade. Others suggest that pretransatlantic slave trade African customs have not had a significant influence on African American values. Additionally, some scholars contend that other African diaspora patterns have been overlooked. While the transatlantic slave trade consisted primarily of West Africans, we know that later migration patterns among groups from many other regions of Africa and the Caribbean have also contributed to the African American population in the United States. Changes to US immigration laws in the 1960s triggered the most recent wave of black immigration. About half of black immigrants

---

[1] Dorman, "Pew: Immigrants." Also see, Anderson, "African Immigrant Population."

have Caribbean origins, but Africans make up a rapidly growing population of black immigrants in the United States. The increased pace of migration patterns among African and Caribbean groups accounted for one fourth of the black population growth between 2010 and 2013 in the United States.[2]

Changes in the native- and foreign-born populations have interacted to create varying family dynamics. US-born children of immigrants may encounter different experiences within the family context that could shape their later development. Migration patterns and familial well-being among Latino families have been extensively studied. Less is known, however, about black immigrant families and the factors that promote or inhibit family dynamics.[3] Additionally, research on the early childhood experiences of young children in black immigrant families is scarce. Using a nationally representative data set that follows a cohort of children from birth to kindergarten, the present essay attempts to address these gaps by providing information about the role of employment patterns of black immigrant mothers in shaping young children's well-being (i.e., cognitive, behavioral, and physical). Black immigrants refer to individuals who were born in Africa or the Caribbean but migrated to the United States and who identify as black or mixed-race black on measures of race regardless of Hispanic origins.

LABOR FORCE PARTICIPATION OF BLACK IMMIGRANTS

The composition of the US population has vital implications for economic productivity, taxation, and spending. Immigrant workers have become an important part of the US labor force over the past few decades, accounting for more than half of the net growth in labor participation between 1996 and 2003. Most immigrant workers who are parents demonstrate a strong commitment to paid employment to provide for their families. Although immigrants comprise roughly 13 percent of the United States' overall population, they are disproportionately represented in the labor force with a share of about 16 percent. Recent projections have determined that if present immigration trends and birth rates continue, by 2050 nearly all (93 percent) of the country's working age population growth will come from immigrants and their US-born children. The influx of immigrant workers in the United States coupled with the large number of working parents in this population highlights the importance of understanding how mothers' work experiences impact the dynamic of family life and child well-being in immigrant families. While the literature on work-family balance in immigrant families has progressed, it has typically focused on Latino immigrant families exclusively.[4]

In 2014, approximately 9 percent of the foreign-born labor force was black. A strong work ethic characterizes both black immigrant and native families. However, many children in immigrant families have fathers who do not consistently work full-time throughout the year. These fathers also tend to occupy jobs with low hourly wages. A number of immigrant children have

---

[2] Ibid.

[3] The term black immigrant(s) is used throughout to refer to African and Caribbean immigrants. The two groups will be discussed separately when analyses are presented.

[4] Bureau of Labor Statistics, "Foreign-Born Workers."

mothers who work for pay to assist the family. Moreover, many black immigrant families with children are likely to have another adult worker in the home.

As the United States continues to transition to a service economy, also known as the "24/7 economy," there arises a greater demand for service sector jobs which are likely to demand nonstandard work hours. Approximately 20 percent of workers in the United States occupy a nonstandard schedule, which is defined as instances in which at least half of a worker's hours fall outside of the 8 a.m. to 4 p.m. range. Many groups are overrepresented in nonstandard job occupancy—particularly second shifts that are low in complexity. For example, single parents, mothers with low levels of education, minorities, and immigrants are disproportionately over-represented in low-wage occupational sectors.[5]

DEVELOPMENTAL OUTCOMES OF CHILDREN OF BLACK IMMIGRANTS

Only a handful of studies have explored the developmental trajectories of young children in black immigrant families. Research on children of black immigrants generally focuses on later developmental periods, such as middle childhood and adolescence. While these studies have provided great insight, there are generational differences that may have implications for comparing findings across studies of varying developmental groups. For example, older children are more likely to be first generation—foreign-born children—rather than second generation—born in the United States with one or both foreign-born parents. As discussed below, the experiences of these two groups are influenced by various factors and may yield different outcomes.

On average, black immigrant youth outperform black children in native families on measures of achievement and are more likely to complete high school and pursue postsecondary education. These advantages are often referred to as the *immigrant paradox* and hold even after accounting for socioeconomic backgrounds. While children of black immigrants surpass certain groups, they lag behind others. For example, children of black immigrants academically perform better than children of Hispanic immigrants. Yet, they trail behind children of white and Asian immigrants. These findings warrant exploration of the potential importance of earlier academic experiences.[6]

The Role of Preschool

To better understand the immigrant paradox apparent among youth of black immigrants, many researchers have turned their attention to earlier developmental periods. Early childhood is particularly important as it has the potential to set the stage for later development. Young children of immigrants are the fastest growing group of children in the United States, making up approximately 20 percent of the country's total population of children. Immigrant families with children are often characterized by lower levels of income, education, and English proficiency. These factors have the potential to place children of

---

[5] Presser, *Working in a 24/7 economy*.
[6] Palacios, Guttmannova, and Chase-Landsdale, "Early Reading Achievement of Children." Also see, Fulgini, "Academic Achievement of Adolescents."

immigrants at risk for lower levels school readiness—the cognitive, behavioral, social, emotional, and physical capabilities of young children that will best promote their success in kindergarten and future schooling. Therefore, increased attention has been placed on the role of preschool in predicting children of immigrants' school readiness and later school success. Preschool is a heterogeneous term that encompasses many types of school- or center-based programs for young children who have not begun kindergarten. Such programs include daycare centers, nursery schools, home-based child care, prekindergarten in public schools, and the publicly funded Head Start. Although many children of immigrants begin kindergarten with the knowledge and skills expected of them, a significant share enter at a disadvantage. The few studies assessing indicators of school readiness among young immigrant children do not indicate a clear advantage. Recent studies have revealed weaker cognitive and language skills among children of black immigrants compared to black children of native parents. Other studies reveal higher scores on kindergarten math assessments among children of immigrants compared to their ethnic peers of native families. This advantage, however, appeared only after controlling for characteristics such as socioeconomic status and home language. Additionally, this advantage was not evident for children of Caribbean immigrants, who ranked among children of black native and American Indian families as one of the lowest scoring groups.[7]

Although this area of study is emerging, this small set of findings offers tentative evidence that children of black immigrants exhibit lower levels of school readiness compared to their peers in nonblack immigrant and native families. Therefore, the factors that explaining the positive outcomes for later schooling among children of black immigrants is unclear. For example, are differences attributed to generational status (i.e., first versus second generation) or other sociodemographic characteristics that have not yet been explored? Additionally, general comparisons of children in immigrant and native families oversimplify the noteworthy diversity that exists within these groups. Studies have demonstrated great variation in educational outcomes for immigrant populations. Outcomes varied by a host of factors such as generational status, country of origin, age at arrival, time in the United States, language, skin color, gender, and religion[8]. As emphasized previously, much of this research has focused on Latino and Asian children as the two largest sectors of the immigrant population, resulting in several unanswered questions about other immigrant groups. One potential explanatory factor worthy of exploration is parental employment; particularly maternal employment. In general, higher levels of maternal education and employment have been linked to more favorable developmental outcomes for children. However, we know little about the role of the *type* of schedule that working immigrant mothers occupy (i.e., shift and job conditions) and its implications for child well-being. Analyses below will build on this important body of work by examining the role of various maternal employment characteristics (namely nonstandard work schedules and job satisfaction) of black immigrant mothers in shaping young children's well-being.

---

[7] Crosby, and Dunbar, Patterns and Predictors of School Readiness.
[8] Lansford, Deater-Deckard, and Bornstein, Immigrant Families.

DATA AND MEASURES

Data from the Early Childhood Longitudinal Study, Birth Cohort (ECLS-B) were used to investigate the relationship between black immigrant mothers' employment patterns and young children's well-being. The ECLS-B is a prospective study of a large and diverse sample of approximately 14,000 children, followed from birth to school entry; this sample was drawn using birth certificate data to be representative of the full population of infants born in the United States in 2001. Some subpopulations were oversampled including Asian and Pacific Islander children, American Indian and Alaska Native children, Chinese children, twins, and low and very low birth weight children. Data were collected at four time points after the birth of the focal child: nine months (Wave 1), 2 years (Wave 2), approximately 4 years (Wave 3), and at kindergarten entry (Wave 4). The current analyses rely primarily on data from the third wave of the study, though some covariates used in analyses were assessed during the baseline interview at nine months.

As part of each data collection, home visits were conducted that involved administering direct assessments with children and interviews with parents. Parent data were collected using a computer-assisted personal interview (CAPI) and a parent self-administered questionnaire (SAQ). Primary caregivers/respondents were asked questions regarding household structure, parental education and employment, child care decisions, community characteristics, income, and other sources of support available. The interview also gathered detailed information about the focal child, the primary caregiver, the home environment, parenting beliefs and practices, and characteristics of the family. The respondent had to be familiar about the child's care and education, be 15 years of age or older at the time of the child's birth, and be living in the household with the child. Approximately 95 percent of parent interviews were completed by the child's biological mother. Most of the parent interviews were conducted in English; however, a Spanish version of the CAPI instrument was implemented when required. Special provisions were made for families who spoke languages other than English or Spanish (i.e., a household member or professional translator was used). The response rate for the preschool parent interview (i.e., Wave 3) based on the sample successfully recruited to participate at nine months was 88 percent (n = 8900).

Analysis Sample

The analysis for the current study includes a subsample of Wave 3 participants from the ECLS-B—namely children who had complete data on the outcome variables (i.e., direct assessments of school readiness characteristics). Like other researchers, children of immigrants are defined here as those whose mother was born outside of the United States. As highlighted previously, children of black immigrants, therefore, would be children whose mothers were born in Africa or the Caribbean. The immigrant population in the ECLS-B is very diverse and includes parents from more than hundred countries. Children of immigrants were categorized into eight groups based on mothers' region of origin (see Table 1). Analyses were not only conducted for children of black immigrants, but also between children of other immigrant groups and children of US-born mothers. The latter groups are also described in Table 1.

TABLE 1: Immigrant Status and Maternal Birthplace for Children Born in the United States in 2001

Immigrant Status Based on Mothers' Region of Origin	Countries Represented	Percentage of All Children
African immigrant	Algeria, Burkina, Cape Verde, Congo, Egypt, Eritrea, Ethiopia, **Ghana**, Guinea, Kenya, Liberia, Mauritania, Morocco, **Nigeria**, Rwanda, Senegal, **Somalia**, South Africa, Sudan, Toga, Uganda, Zaire, Zambia	0.8%
Caribbean immigrant	Antigua, Bahamas, **Cuba**, **Dominican Republic**, Guyana, **Haiti**, **Jamaica**, Trinidad and Tobago, West Indies	1.9%
Hispanic immigrant	Argentina, Bolivia, Brazil, Chile, Columbia, Costa Rica, Ecuador, El Salvador, Guatemala, Honduras, **Mexico**, Nicaragua, Panama, Peru, Venezuela, Uruguay	14.3%
East Asian immigrant	**China**, **Korea**, Japan, **Taiwan**	1.1%
Southeast Asian immigrant	Burma, Cambodia, Indonesia, Laos, Malaysia, Marshall Islands, Micronesia, New Guinea, Pacific Islands, **Philippines**, Singapore, Solomon Islands, Thailand, **Vietnam**	0.8%
Indian Asian immigrant	Bangladesh, **India**, Nepal, **Pakistan**, Sri Lanka	1.3%
Middle Eastern immigrant	Afghanistan, Armenia, Iraq, Iran, **Israel**, Jordan, Kuwait, Lebanon, Saudi Arabia, Syria, Yemen	0.8%
European immigrant	Australia, Belgium, **Canada**, Czech Republic, Denmark, Finland, France, **Germany**, Hungary, Ireland, Italy, Lithuania, the Netherlands, New Zealand, Poland, Portugal, Romania, Russia, Serbia, Spain, Switzerland, Ukraine, Uzbekistan, Yugoslavia	2.3%
Black native		11.9%
White native		50.1%
Hispanic native		10.0%
Asian/Pacific Islander native		0.3%
American Indian/Native Alaskan		0.5%
Multiracial native		3.4%

Notes: n = 10,600; all unweighted sample sizes are rounded to the nearest 50 per National Center for Education Statistics (NCES) restricted-use data regulations. Countries in bold account for at least 10 percent of the respondents in the respective region of origin category.

Source: Author calculations using the Early Childhood Longitudinal Study-Birth Cohort, nine month–kindergarten 2007 Restricted Use Data File, NCES, US Department of Education.

Demographic Characteristics of Sample

Mothers in this sample ranged in age from 19 to 69, with a mean age of 30.31 years (SD = 5.57). Approximately 44 percent of mothers indicated their child's race as non-Hispanic white, 16 percent as black, 17 percent as Hispanic, 11 percent as Asian, 3 percent as American Indian, and 8 percent as multiracial. Sixty-five percent (n = 3,150) of mothers were married, while 30 percent reported being separated, divorced, or never married. Seventy-seven percent (n = 3,350) of mothers reported working daytime shifts, 10 percent reported working evening shifts (n = 450), 4.5 percent reported working night shifts (n = 220), and 8.5 percent reported working rotating shifts

TABLE 2: Maternal and Family Characteristics for Children of Black Immigrant Mothers at Wave 3

	Children of Black Immigrants			Children of Other Immigrants					Children of US-Born Parents
	African	Caribbean	Hispanic	East Asian	Southeast Asian	Indian Asian	Middle Eastern	European	
Age									
	36	34	32	33	37	35	33	34	32
Marital Status									
Single[1]	13%	25%	31%	0%	12%	1%	0%	10%	25%
Married	79%	61%	65%	94%	81%	96%	89%	83%	72%
Divorced	2%	13%	2%	0%	3%	0%	3%	6%	6%
Education									
Less than high school degree	13%	13%	49%	3%	19%	6%	14%	3%	11%
High school degree/equivalent	25%	31%	26%	9%	21%	12%	25%	17%	27%
Postsecondary degree	62%	56%	25%	86%	59%	82%	58%	80%	61%
Work Shift									
Standard	55%	71%	57%	72%	61%	64%	47%	71%	53%
Nonstandard	45%	29%	43%	28%	39%	36%	53%	29%	47%
Poverty Status									
Below Poverty	26%	29%	46%	5%	16%	11%	22%	9%	24%
Above Poverty	74%	71%	54%	95%	84%	89%	78%	91%	76%
Food Security Status									
Secure Household	82%	84%	84%	96%	92%	97%	97%	95%	90%
Insecure Household	14%	14%	15%	3%	8%	2%	3%	4%	10%

Notes: n = 8,900; all unweighted sample sizes are rounded to the nearest 50 per NCES restricted-use data regulations. Not all percentages add up to 100 because some responses were not ascertained. [1]The single category encompasses mothers who reported being separated, widowed, or have never been married.
Source: Author calculations using the Early Childhood Longitudinal Study-Birth Cohort, nine month–kindergarten 2007 Restricted Use Data File, NCES, US Department of Education.

(n = 400). Approximately 39 percent of families report living below 185 percent of the poverty threshold. For each immigrant group, levels of food security are also presented. Detailed sociodemographic characteristics for immigrant and US-born mothers are presented in Table 2.

Measures

Maternal Employment Characteristics
Questions about the timing of work were asked of mothers who reported being employed at Wave 3. Mothers were asked, *"Which of the following best describes the hours you usually work at*

your main job?" Six mutually-exclusive choices were provided: daytime (6:00 a.m.–6:00 p.m.), evening (2:00 p.m.–12:00 a.m.), night (9:00 p.m.–8:00 a.m.), rotating (one that changes periodically from days to evenings or nights), split (one consisting of two distinct periods each day), and other (mothers were prompted to specify). A maternal nonstandard work schedule variable was created to indicate whether or not mothers worked a nonstandard schedule (coded as 1) or a standard schedule (coded as 0). Mothers were coded as having a nonstandard work schedule if they worked evenings, nights, rotating shifts, or split shifts; and were coded as having a standard working schedule if they reported working primarily a daytime shift.

Child Well-Being

- Early academic skills. During wave 3 (i.e., age 4), children's math and reading abilities were assessed by research staff in the child's home. Scores range from 1 to 100 and indicate how children compare to peers of the same age.
- Behavior. Children's behavior was assessed in the classroom and home settings. Teachers and mothers reported the frequency of positive and negative behaviors, such as sharing with others and exhibiting physical aggression. Values on the mother and teacher rating scale ranged from 1 ("never") to 5 ("very often").
- Health. During wave 3, children's Body Mass Index (BMI) was calculated using measures of height and weight. Higher BMI indicate overweight and obese status (i.e., above the eighty-fifth and ninety-fifth percentiles, respectively).

RESULTS

This section will provide a descriptive depiction of the important role that maternal employment plays in shaping the lives of children of immigrants. Given the scope of this chapter, findings for children of black immigrants are highlighted. Comparisons will also be made between children of all immigrants and children of US-born mothers. Results are also displayed in Tables 3 and 4.

Occupying a nonstandard work schedule was not significantly related to early math skills among children of both African and Caribbean immigrant mothers. These findings held even after controlling for a host of maternal demographic factors such as poverty status, education level, marital status, and age. However, nonstandard work schedules were significantly related to early reading skills for children of African immigrants only. Interestingly, working a nonstandard schedule appears to lead to more favorable scores on assessments of reading when controlling for maternal sociodemographic characteristics. When children of mothers from all immigrant groups were compared to children of native-born mothers, nonstandard work was not significantly related to early math and reading skills. Job satisfaction was significantly associated with young children's early math skills for children of African, but not Caribbean, immigrant mothers. These findings no longer remained significant when maternal sociodemographic factors were taken into account. Similarly, job satisfaction was significantly associated with young children's early reading skills for children of African *and* Caribbean immigrant mothers. Yet, the findings only remained significant for children of Caribbean immigrant mothers when maternal sociodemographic characteristics were controlled for. Nonstandard

TABLE 3: Linear Regressions Predicting Outcomes for Children of Black Immigrant Mothers from Employment Characteristics

| | Nonstandard Work Schedules | | | |
| | Children of Black Immigrants | | | |
	African	Caribbean	Children of Other Immigrants	Children of US-Born Parents
Early Academic Skills				
Reading	7.05*	−3.90	−1.91	−1.31*
Math	3.31	−0.93	−2.90	−1.48**
BMI				
	0.52	−0.59	−0.33	0.26
Behavior				
Positive	0.01	0.23	0.12	0.01
Negative	−0.06	−0.22	0.14	−0.08

Notes: * $p < .05$
** $p < .01$
Source: Author calculations using the Early Childhood Longitudinal

work schedules nor job satisfaction were significantly associated with BMI of young children of immigrant mothers. There was no significant relationship between employment characteristics (i.e., nonstandard work schedules and job satisfaction) and mother and teacher reports of child behavior.

Study-Birth Cohort, nine month–kindergarten 2007 Restricted Use Data File, NCES, US Department of Education.

DISCUSSION

The above analyses provide preliminary evidence that employment characteristics of black immigrant mothers have important implications for the well-being of their US-born children. Although studies on nonstandard work have typically unearthed negative associations with various child outcomes, the present analyses hint at the potential positive effects of nonstandard work. As illustrated earlier, nonstandard work was negatively associated with early reading and math skills among children of US-born mothers. Yet, it was positively related to early reading skills for children of African immigrant mothers. Working a nonstandard schedule may be a protective mechanism for children of African immigrant mothers. These schedules may offer mothers flexibility not offered with standard schedules. Job satisfaction also appears to be a vital component to child well-being in families with black immigrant mothers. Job satisfaction is an especially important factor, as black immigrants tend to occupy jobs of lower prestige compared to immigrant groups from other regions. Therefore, efforts to promote employee conditions for immigrants may serve as an investment in children's academic achievement. This may be particularly true for children of black immigrants.

Further research is warranted to better understand the role of parental employment in influencing the lives of children of immigrants. The analyses presented in this chapter provide

TABLE 4: Linear Regressions Predicting Outcomes for Children of Black Immigrant Mothers from Employment Characteristics

	Job Satisfaction			
	Children of Black Immigrants		Children of Other Immigrants	Children of US-Born Parents
	African	Caribbean		
Early Academic Skills				
Reading	0.83*	0.98**	0.78	0.05
Math	1.09*	−0.06	0.9	0.13*
BMI				
	0.1	0.01	0.05	0.04
Behavior				
Positive	0.56	0.78	3.4	−0.01
Negative	−1.10	−1.32	0.34	−0.01

Notes: * $p < .05$
** $p < .01$
Source: Author calculations using the Early Childhood Longitudinal
Study-Birth Cohort, nine month–kindergarten 2007 Restricted Use Data File, NCES,
US Department of Education.

no evidence for associations between employment characteristics (i.e., nonstandard schedule occupancy and job satisfaction) and children's health and behavior. There may be other elements of the labor force experience that influence such outcomes that were not tested here. Promoting favorable outcomes for children of immigrants requires understanding and effectively responding to migration trends of black populations.

KEY TERMS

Immigrants
Black immigrants
Nonstandard work schedules
School readiness
Immigrant paradox

CHAPTER 19

KENYAN NATIONALISM AND THE ARCHITECTS OF THE KENYAN STUDENT AIRLIFTS

Jim C. Harper II

During the nineteenth century, few Kenyans (men and women) had the opportunity to gain higher education in colleges and universities in the United States. Those students that did benefit from the liberalism by receiving financial assistance from philanthropic individuals and missionary organizations were expected to become pastors, evangelists, lawyers, doctors, and teachers. It must be noted that Kenyan women did not receive nearly as many opportunities to obtain college degrees as men during this time period. It was not until much later that they received a few more opportunities. To date, women in Kenya and across the continent of Africa are fighting for more educational opportunities for them. It was Kenyan nationalist and visionary, Tom Mboya, who made the connections with Americans to ensure that Kenyans were able to travel to the United States for higher education experiences.

As the Mau Mau rebellion ended, the ranks of the western-educated elites increased beginning in 1956. Kenyan students in growing numbers began to enter colleges and universities in the United States, England, the Soviet Union, India, the Middle East, Ethiopia, and even China. Leading the efforts for students to receive these opportunities for higher education abroad were Tom Mboya, Mbiyu Koinage, Kariuki Njiiri, Julius Kiano, African American Trade Unions, African American Civil Rights leaders, Congressmen, and the Department of State. Each of these actors sought to serve his particular agenda. The Kenyan participants admired the American education system and were politically attuned to western democracy. The African American Labor and Civil Rights leadership was inspired by the spirit of Pan-Africanism, the struggle against racial discrimination, the fight against European domination, rejection of communism, and the experience of the Mau Mae rebellion. The American government and politicians, caught up in the Cold War, were guided by the Eisenhower doctrine of combating the spread of Marxism around the globe, particularly in Africa, which was now moving steadily and surly toward independence. All of these factors provided the framework for American support of Kenyan students to come to the United States.[1]

Prior to Mboya's active networking with individuals and organizations in the United States, there were a few Kenyans who traveled abroad seeking education. As noted earlier, some of these students were sponsored by missionary organizations, philanthropists, or they were the

---

[1] Interview with Macharia Munene of the United States International University, Nairobi, Kenya, July 29, 1999.

children of wealthy Kenyan Chiefs. The first group of Kenyans to travel to the United States and to Europe were Molonket Ole Sempele, Muhammed Juma, Peter Mbiyu Koinange, Eliud Mathu, Kariuki Karanja Njiiri, Akiiki Nyambongo, Dr. Julius Gikonyo Kiano, Tom Mboya, Professor Reuel Mogu Gatheru, Dr. Njorogi Mungai, Dr. Mwai Kibaki, and Jomo Kenyatta. It must be noted that Molonket Ole Sempele, the Maasi graduate of Thogoto Missionary School was the first Kenyan to travel to the United States in 1908 with the assistance of the African Inland Mission. He studied at the Boydton Academic and Bible Institute in Boydton, Virginia. As a student, he heard of the atrocities (lynching) and witnessed the harsh treatment of whites toward blacks. He returned to Kenya, broke away for the mission and developed an Independent African Church. He established a network with another Maasai, Harry Thuku (Father of Kenyan Nationalism and founder of the East African Association). Ole Sempele remained a dominate figure in Kenyan nationalism throughout his life.

Another Kenyan, Muhammad Juma, arrived in the United States in 1915. His father, Juma Yohari, a *Swahili* man, had served President Theodore Roosevelt and his son Kermit as a porter as they traveled throughout Kenya big game hunting. President Roosevelt was so pleased with Juma Yohari's service that he (the president) promised to help his son, Mohammed, attend Tuskegee when Muhammad was able to travel to America. On October 24, 1915, Muhammad arrived at Cheechaw railway station in Alabama. His family and the community in Kenya provided the funding for his travels. He enrolled in Tuskegee and became the first student from East Africa to join its 1300 black students.[2] However, Mohammad soon realized that the strong emphasis on industrial courses at Tuskegee did not intrigue him. In Kenya, Mohammad had received his primary and secondary education at home with emphasis on jurisprudence, Arabic language and literature, mathematics, and history; therefore, Mohammad preferred liberal arts to vocational education. As a result, he did not attend his courses and instead, began to read books with great enthusiasm and determination, notwithstanding that he was nearly illiterate in English.[3] When President Roosevelt heard of Muhammad's obstinacy, he wrote to E. J. Scott, secretary of Tuskegee, to exhort the young Kenyan that industrial education was more important for him than literacy education. The letter reads:

> "Now will you read this to Muhammad Juma—What we are trying to make everybody in this country understand is that working with a man's hands, that is, industrial activity is even more important than a literacy education. Muhammad can never be a clerk in this country: he will never know enough; but he can be a very good man with his hands doing industrial work.[4]

Essentially, President Roosevelt's letter dismissed as irrelevant the Islamic education that Mohammad had received on the Swahili Coast in Kenya. Nevertheless, the exhortations of the president had no effect on Mohammad. He intended to receive the education he desired and therefore, he left Tuskegee a few months after President Roosevelt's letter was read to him.

---

[2] Tuskegee Registry. See also, Kenneth King, *Pan-Africanism and Education: A Study of Race Philanthropy and Education in the Southern States of America and East Africa* (Oxford, Clarendon Press, 1971), 1–2.

[3] Mohammad Jama, Tuskegee Registry, Memo to Mr. Scott regarding Mohammad Juma, October 10, 1916; Booker T. Washington Papers, Library of Congress, Washington, DC, Box 312.

[4] Kenneth King, *Pan-Africanism and Education: A Study of Race Philanthropy and Education in the Southern States of America and East Africa*, (Oxford, Clarendon Press, 1971).

He returned to Kenya. Later, another Kenyan, Peter Mbyiu Koinange, arrived in America and like Mohammad was seeking a liberal arts education. Koinange received the financial support required to travel to the United States from his wealthy father, Chief Koinange, chief of the Kikuyu. The Kikuyu are the largest ethnic group in Kenya. Mbiyu had the absolute freedom to choose whatever type of education he desired. At first, Mbiyu joined Hampton Institute, where he received vocational and technical training. However, he left Hampton to enter Ohio Wesleyan College, where in 1935 he obtained a Bachelor of Arts degree in Sociology and Political Science. Then he attended and graduated from Columbia University Teachers College with a Master of Arts degree in Education. Mbiyu became the first Kenyan to receive postgraduate education in any discipline.

Upon his return to Kenya, he strongly advocated for Kenyan students to seek higher educational opportunities in the United States. He encouraged Kenyans including Julius Gikonyo Kiano a 1945 graduate of Alliance High School. Mbiyu offered Kiano a teaching position, at his Kenya Teachers College where he worked for two years. In 1947, Kiano went to work at Makerere College in Kampala. Mbiyu was impressed with Kiano and in 1949, Mbiyu was instrumental in raising local funds that helped Kiano to travel and pay his tuition fees in the United States.[5] Kiano enrolled at the Pioneer Business Institute in Philadelphia. Thereafter, he attended Antioch College in Yellow Springs, Ohio. It was at Antioch that Dr. Kiano met and cultivated a close friendship with a classmate, Coretta Scott (later Coretta Scott-King), future wife of Reverend Martin Luther King Jr. This friendship proved its worth in later years when Kiano, together with two Kenyan leaders, Tom Mboya and Kariuki Karanja Njiiri, launched the successful drive to have Kenyan students study at American colleges and universities.

Upon graduation from Antioch College in 1952, Kiano received a fellowship from Stanford University that helped him obtain a Master of Arts degree in Public Administration. In 1956, he received a PhD degree in Political Science from the University of California at Berkeley, making Kiano the first Kenyan to receive a doctoral degree, and the second Kenyan to complete a nonvocational education in the United States. After graduation, Dr. Kiano returned to Kenya and began his career as the first Kenyan lecturer at the Royal Technical College (now the University of Nairobi) in Nairobi teaching constitutional law and economics. Like his mentor, Mbiyu, he advocated for Kenyan students to study in the United States. As a matter of fact, Dr. Kiano was so pro-America that Walter White, the Executive Secretary of the National Association for the Advancement of Colored People (NAACP), said of him that if the United States really wished to prevent the expansion of communism in Africa, then it must educate future African leaders such as Julius Gikonyo Kiano.[6]

Dr. Kiano and Kariuki Njiiri another graduate of a college in the United States set up the Cultural Society of New Africa (CSNA). The CSNA provided private financial support for Kenyan students to study in the United States. The money was collected at fund-raising events that were held in Nairobi, Muranga (Fort Hall), Nakuru, and Naivasha as well as in the Kikuyu villages. The Society succeeded in sending two male students to Smith College. One year after their arrival, Professor Gwendolyn Carter of Smith College and her students visited Kenya.

---

[5] Interview with Dr. Kiano, Nairobi, Kenya, June 29, 1999.
[6] Macharia Munene, "United States and Anti-Colonialism in Kenya, 1895–1963," vol. 12 of *African Review of Foreign Policy* (March 1999), 12.

Professor Carter offered the Society a scholarship for one student to study at the college. A young Kikuyu female student benefited from the scholarship; however, the sources do not mention her name nor do they give an account of her life.[7]

Kariuki Njiiri was the son of Chief Njiiri, of the Kikuyu. His father paid for his education in India. Njiiri attended along with Reul John Mugo Gatheru and George Mbugua Kimani, St. Joheph's Collegiate School, a Catholic institution in Allahabad, India in the late 1940s. Mugo Gatheru recalled that two years after his arrival in the United States, he successfully pleaded with Dr. Horace Mann Bond, the President of Lincoln University in Pennsylvania, to offer Njiiri and Kimani full scholarships to attend Lincoln University. He was successful and all three students were awarded scholarships in 1952. Njiiri majored in sociology while Gatheru majored in history and political science. Gatheru completed his undergraduate studies in 1954, while Njiiri remained at Lincoln University where he received his Master of Arts degree in 1954 making him one of the first Kenyans to receive higher education at a Historically Black College or University (HBCU) in the United States. Like Kiano, Njiiri entered the political arena as a member of the Legislative Council representing his home district, Muranga. However, it was not long before vacated his seat for Jomo Kenyatta to replace him. Njiiri went on to serve in several capacities in the National Parliament.

Dr. Kiano and Njiiri forged a friendship with Tom Mboya and their bond led to the establishment of the "Kenyan Student Airlifts" of 1959, 1960, and 1961. The three men worked in collaboration with private American organizations, particularly African American organizations, with private and some state colleges, as well as influential American figures to secure scholarships at American universities and colleges for hundreds of Kenyan students. These American educated Kenyan students would form the foundation of the highly educated workforce that Africanized or replaced the British elites that had dominated the country for decades before Kenya gaining independence. In an interview, Dr. Kiano stated that although Britain, the Soviet Union, France, India, and other countries offered scholarships to Kenyan students, the majority of the scholarships were extended by the United States.[8] This was the main reason that the American educated Kenyans occupied most of the top-level positions in independent Kenya. By 1958, Dr. Kiano left his teaching position at the Royal Technical College and became a representative of the Muranga District in the Legislative Council. He was now considered to be a nationalist politician. In 1959, he was selected as the Secretary of the parliamentary delegation that traveled to Britain seeking to persuade the British government to lift the State of Emergency and release the detained politicians during the Mau Mau insurrection. The Mau Mau insurrection is regarded in Kenya as one of the most significant steps toward a Kenya free of British rule. More than one million Kenyans fought during the rebellion, which lasted between 1952 and 1960. The Mau Mau rebellion in Kenya, coupled with the expansion of communism in Africa, caused the United States to focus on developing African leaders by providing educational opportunities to Africans. Mboya, Kiano, and Njiiri understood that these events created the right time for them to request financial assistance from the United States to send Kenyan students to American colleges and Universities. Therefore, Njiiri wrote to Senator John F. Kennedy asking for assistance of the American government. It was not long before he received a favorable response.

---

[7] Edmond J. Dorez to Department of State, August 22, 1957, Records of the Department of State, Decimal File 1955–1959, National Archives, MD, RG 59, Box 2141.
[8] Interview with Dr. Kiano, Nairobi, Kenya, June 29, 1999.

Political events in Kenya in the 1950s and other parts of the world that quickened the pace for the development of an American educated cadre of Kenyans, especially those who studied in black institutes of higher learning in the United States. It was due to the efforts of trade unionists like Tom Mboya, Asa Phillip Randolph, and George Houser to politicians like Congressman Charles Diggs Jr., Senator John F. Kennedy, and Reverend Martin Luther King Jr. to white wealthy activists like William X. Scheinman, to black entertainers and professional athletes such as Harry Belafonte, Sidney Poitier, and Jackie Robinson that provided the opportunity for hundreds of Kenyan students to attend black and white colleges and universities in the United States. It was Pan-Africanism, expansion of communism as well as the Mau Mau insurrection that were major catalysts that converged in a way that pushed the United States to work with Kenyan nationalists to create the "Kenyan Student Airlifts."

In the 1950s, Kenya was dominated by the Mau Mau revolution that erupted in October 1952. Kenyan nationalism, which began as early as the 1920s had reached its peak. It was in the 1920s that the mission-educated Kenyans began to form their own independent churches, schools, and young associations that challenged white rule, mission, and settler domination. These forces compelled the British colonials to make concessions to appease Kenyans. Consequently, in 1944 the colonial administration appointed Eliud Wambu Mathu, a Kikuyu former teacher who graduated from Fort Hare in South Africa and Oxford University in Britain, to the Legislative Council (Legco District). Later a former Luo teacher Beneah Apolo Obanga, was appointed to the Lego Legislative Council. Mathu and Obanga unsuccessfully fought for the expansion of education in Kenya.[9]

Kenyan nationalists immediately followed the appointment of Mathu to the Legislative Council with the establishment of the Kenya African Union (KAU) as an extra-parliamentary support group for him. In 1946, Jomo Kenyatta returned from Britain and the Soviet Union where he was advocating for an end to discriminatory policies enacted by the British government in Kenya and to press for self-government. Consequently, he was placed under constant surveillance as the British government was suspicious and fearful of his motives. Moreover, the inevitable confrontation between Kenyatta's organization, KAU, and the colonial administration ensued the rise of the Mau Mau and the declaration of the State of Emergency in October 1952 when the KAU sent a pro-Mau Mau statement to the Colonial Office. The statement read:

> Much of the present trouble is due to the fact that Africans are not adequately associated with the machinery of Government to make them feel that they are a real part or partners in the Government of their country. This has the two-fold effect of denying to the Government the benefit of considered African opinion in the making of Government policy, and on the other hand of creating an impression in the mind of the people that the Government because of its composition does not work in the interests of Africans. During the last thirty years. While the requests of the European community have been conceded, he requests of the African community has been consistently ignored. This has led the ordinary African to believe that only if he has a government of his own can he benefit and not otherwise.[10]

---

[9] Atieno Odhiambo, "The Formative Years: 1945–1955," in *Decolonization and Independence in Kenya*, 1940–1993, ed. Bethwell Ogot and William Ochieng. (London, James Currey, 1995), 27–31.

[10] Michael Twaddle, "The Struggle for Political Sovereignty in Eastern Africa," vol. VIII of *UNESCO General History of Africa*, ed. Ali Amamin Mazuri and Christophe Wondji, 235–236.

The British government believed that this statement was evidence that the KAU birth the Mau Mau rebellion and immediately proscribed the organization. The leadership of the KAU; Jomo Kenyatta, Paul Njai, Achieng Oneku, Bildad Kaggia, Fred Kubai, and Kung'u Karumba were arrested under Operation Jock Scot and placed in detention. A total of 128 leaders were incarcerated with Kenyatta receiving a sentence of seven years in prison with hard labor. The charge was complicity in helping to organize Mau Mau. From this point forward, Kenyatta was recognized as the embodiment of the aspirations of all Kenyans and the voice of discontent.

Mau Mau was the expression of the people's rejection of British rule and their dissatisfaction with the nonparticipation of Africans in the governance of the country, the expropriation of land by white settlers, white racism and discrimination, unemployment, forced labor, low wages, burdensome taxation, overcrowding, and miserable living conditions in the slums of urban centers. Mau Mau won the support of organized labor unions such as the East African Trade Union led by John Mungai and the Labor Trade Union, led by Bildad Kaggia. At this time, under the threat of being outlawed, Tom Mboya's Kenyan Federation of Labor along with the Kenya Federation of Registered Trade Unions led by Aggrey Minya, distanced themselves from Mau Mau.

Mau Mau was an alliance of peasants, workers, the unemployed, and Kenyan soldiers who returned from service in European armies abroad. The Mau Mau leaders Njunjiri, Washira Rugi, and Dedan Kimathi were not members of KAU. However, they were heroes to the Kenyan people. These courageous men found and died for the cause of independence and self-actualization for all Kenyans. There efforts let to international news coverage by the *New York Times* as well as other respected newspapers from London to India. Most importantly, Mau Mau caught the attention of black people around the globe, particularly African Americans, Afro-Caribbeans, and South Africans, all of whom were burdened by white racism and colonial domination. The Mau Mau insurrection succeeded in forcing the colonial authorities to reexamine their policies in Kenya in order to appease a highly disgruntled public. Nevertheless, Kenyans were never able to transform itself into an official African political party. It simply remained as an inspiration to Kenyan nationalists and black people throughout the world. The concessions did however, deepen ethnic divisions in the country as each ethnic group rushed to form a party that represented their particular interests.[11] Kenyans were able to secure more seats in Legislative Councils.

In 1956, one year after Mau Mau exited the political scene, Tom Mboya, Secretary-General of Kenya Federation of Labor, arrived in the United States at the invitation of the American Committee on Africa (ACOA). The ACOA was formed in 1953 by a group of African American leaders and white activists to publicize and lobby for African Independence and liberation movements. The ACOA was the largest and most effective private organization devoted to African American relations and American assistance to Africa. Importantly, it offered educational opportunities in America for future African leaders to have them prepared for the task of nation building, and at the same time to win them over to capitalism and democracy before

---

[11] The district parties that emerged were: The Mombasa African Democratic Union, the Abagusii Association of South Nyanza District, the Taita African Democratic Union, the District Association of East Nyanzathe, Nakuru African Progressive Party, the Abaluhya People's Association, the Nyanza North African Congress, and the Nakuru District Congress.

they fell "victim" to the dictatorship of communism. Noted members of ACOA included Asa Philip Randolph (founder of the Brotherhood of Sleeping Car Porters), George House (activist and a founder of the Congress of Racial Equality), William X. Scheinman (Philanthropist), Congressman Charles Diggs Jr. (founder of the Congressional Black Caucus), Hebert Humphrey, Revernend Dr. Martin Luther King Jr., Rayford Logan, Congressman Adam Clayton Powell, Jackie Robinson, Mrs. Franklin D. Roosevelt, Ms. Cora Weiss, Baynard Rustin, Roger Baldwin, Sidney Poitier, and Roy Wilkins. The voice of the ACOA was the journal *Africa Today*.

Mboya was invited to the United States by Rev. Michael Scott, a white minister who has been since the 1920s lobbying for Africans in South Africa and South West Africa. Rev. Scott lived and worked in South Africa for many years before he was sent back to the United States because of his activities in supporting the African liberation struggle. Upon leaving South Africa, he went to Britain where he set up the Africa Bureau to support the nationalist and liberation movements on the continent. George Houser, then president of ACOA, recalls that Rev. Scott wrote to them about Tom Mboya who was then (1956) attending a one year course at Ruskin College in Oxford, England, the foremost British trade union institution. Apparently, Mboya met with Rev. Scott in London and informed him of his interest in contacting trade unionists in the United States. Houser stated that the ACOA was reluctant to bring Mboya to the United States between August and September because those were not the best months for having speaking tours. At that time, the organization did not have the funding to support a nationwide tour. In addition, Mboya was not a known personality and the ACOA could not guarantee that he would be well-received at various labor unions, colleges, and churches. Nevertheless, strong recommendation by Rev. Scott convinced the ACOA that inviting Mboya would be worthwhile. To cover the expenses of the trip and engagements, ACOA raised the necessary funds by charging fee at the venues where Mboya spoke. Furthermore, Kenyan students in the United States including Mugo Gatheru, Julius Gikonyo Kiano, and Mungai Njorogi gathered in New York to support Mboya and help the ACOA with coordinating the tour. On August 8, 1956, Mboya arrived in New York. According to Houser, Mboya was the first African leader invited to the United States for a speaking tour.

His two-month speaking tour was a great success. He met with George Meany of the American Federation of Labor and Congress of Industrial Organization (AFL-CIO), Walter Reuther of the United Auto Workers, Asa Philip Randolph of the Brotherhood of Sleeping Car Porters, David Dubinsky of the International Ladies Garment Workers' Union, Philip Murray of the United Steelworkers, Sidney Hillman of the Amalgamated Clothing Workers, and Ralph Helstein of the United Packinghouse Workers, and so on in Detroit, Chicago, New York, Washington DC, Boston, Los Angeles, Atlanta, and Pittsburgh. Houser further acknowledged that it did not take long for Mboya to capture the attention of the rank and file of trade unionists in the United States. Mboya charmed and captivated his listeners by his charismatic personality and ability to speak without notes in front of him, and by his accent, which was more British than Luo. Above all, Mboya articulated the atrocities that were occurring to Kenyan workers at forums, on television, and at radio appearances.

Mboya requested that the AFL-CIO assist with training Kenyan trade union personnel in the United States, with the construction of a building in Nairobi to serve as headquarters for his Kenyan Federation of Labor and with scholarships for Kenyan students. As a result, the

AFL-CIO contributed $35,000 from its William Green Fund toward the construction of the building. Asa Philip Randolph presented the check to the Kenya Federation of Labor and the building was constructed. Both the AFl-CIO and the International Confederation of Free Trade Unions (ICFTU) were said to have continued to heavily subsidize the Kenyan Federation of Labor. It is further claimed that "the Central Intelligence Agency (CIA), through the ICTFU, gave the Kenya Federation of Labor $1000 per month, a huge sum of money those days."[12]

The AFL-CIO formed a committee of three—Asa Philip Randolph, George Meany, and Walter Ruther—to set up and administer training programs for the Kenyan trade unions. A sub-committee, the Workers Education Committee, composed of George Brown, John Connors, and Theodore Brown, was established to select schools and colleges that offered courses in workers' education. They also chose Maida Springer to oversee and dispense the scholarships. Once the institutions were identified, Kenyans were duly enrolled for three to four months and took courses in organization, administration, public relations, rules of engagement, rules of negotiation, operation of grievances, development and conduct of strikes, and observation of democratic trade unionism.[13] This trade union education program was established that since Africa was a primary target of communist ideology, African trade union leaders out not only learn the general history of organized labor and the mechanism of trade union organizations in America, but also gain a broad perspective of the difference between the forces of democracy and communism.[14] Vice President Richard Nixon (eventually became the thirty-seventh president of the United States), praised the collaboration of African American and Kenyan trade unions as an effective method of preventing the penetration of communism into Africa.[15] According to the *Sunday Nation*, a Kenyan newspaper, the United States considered Kenya the gateway to the landlocked East and Central African countries, "a strategic point in (its) push for capitalism in Africa—becoming communist was unsettling."[16]

The training program did not last long resulting from inadequate funding in its second year. Efforts to resurrect the program in East Africa with the collective efforts of the ICFTU and the AFL-CIO began. Mr. Hammerton, the ICFTU representative in Africa, managed the project. He decided on his own to construct the school in Kampala, Uganda. The trade school was called the African Labor College with George McCaray as its Principal was opened in 1959. Admission to the college was open to students who had a command of the English language, a minimum of five years of service in the unions, and some secondary school education. In that way, the College restricted admission to the top union officers not to the rank-and-file personnel.

In 1959, Mboya visited the United States for the second time. This time he came to secure funding for travel for seventy-five students that had already received scholarship to American colleges and universities. He also sought out scholarships and travel funding for more Kenyan

---

[12] "CIA Plotted Odinga's Removal From Office," in the Sunday Nation, July 2, 2000.

[13] C.H. Millard to George Many, August 23, 1957, letter, Papers of the Brotherhood of Sleeping Car Porters, Manuscript Division, Library of Congress, Box 97, Folder 1 Africa.

[14] Planning Document, the Papers of the Brotherhood of Sleeping Car Porters, Library of Congress, Manuscript Divison, September 4, 1957, Box 97, Folder 1 Africa.

[15] "The Emergence of Africa, Report to the President by Vice-President on his trip to Africa," White House Release, April 7, 1957.

[16] "CIA Plotted Odinga's Removal From Office," July 2, 2000.

students. To contribute to this educational fund-raising drive, Mboya, Scheinman, Frank Montero, and Dr. Julius Kiano established the African American Students Foundation (AASF) Inc. in New York. The Foundation inaugurated its services with organizing a fund-raising event. A host of powerful individuals with an interest in Africa attended. Among the speakers were Senator John F. Kennedy and Charles Diggs Jr.[17] Over the next couple of years, Senator Kennedy and Congressman Diggs would play a significant role in the "Kenyan Students Airlift." The AASF was responsible for seeking scholarships and funding as well as placing students, preferably in black colleges and universities in the United States. This organization, more than any other organization, was the major fund-raiser and scholarship seeker behind the "Kenyan Student Airlifts." They contacted the Department of State, lobbied Congress, and the White House, as well as philanthropic organizations and private companies for assistance.

Their efforts were a success by 1959 eighty-one Kenyan students arrived in New York prepared to attend American colleges and universities. Scholarships were received from schools such as Tuskegee, Columbia, Stanford, Howard, Cornell, Spelman, Lincoln, Clark Atlanta, Harvard, Hampton, Purdue, Fisk, and the University of California at Berkeley. By December 1959, the number of totaled four hundred and fifty-one compared to forty-five in Britain. In 1960, the scholarship opportunities had expanded to include students from Kenya and seven other regions of East and Central Africa and two hundred and twenty-two students came to America to attend colleges and universities. In 1961, one hundred and forty-eight students came to the United States. The "African Student Airlifts" were a tremendous success. The result of these efforts was the expansion of higher education opportunities not only Kenyan students but for African students across the continent who themselves became leaders in the independence movements of their countries.

Over a very short span of time, Mboya was able to extend his endeavor to secure scholarship opportunities for students seeking degrees from the United States. To do that, Mboya also appealed to the private and public sectors in the United States. He developed networks with black and white individuals, as well as universities and colleges who quickly furnished him with scholarships. Dr. Horace Mann Bond, president of Lincoln University, stepped forward and offered several scholarships and promised to admit any number of qualified students from Kenya. Throughout his tenure at Lincoln, Dr. Bond earned the reputation of never turning away a qualified African student. In fact, Lincoln University is the home of great African leaders including Nnamadi Azikiwe of Nigeria and Kwame Nkrumah of Ghana. Both of these men left Lincoln University and became presidents of their home countries. Mboya addressed the members of the Southern Christian Leadership Conference and developed a friendship with Rev. Dr. Martin Luther King Jr. It must be noted that Mboya met with and requested scholarships with many well-known African Americans including Sydney Portier, Jackie Robinson, Harry Belafonte, and others. All of which sponsored scholarships for Kenyan students under the umbrella of Pan-Africanism. Keep in mind this was during the time that the Civil Rights Movement was taking place in the United States. Black Nationalism in the United States and African Nationalism is worked on parallel planes to seek integration, equality, and independence.

---

[17] William X. Scheinman to Charles Diggs. June 29, 1959, letter, Papers of Charles Diggs, Box 194, Folder 15.

Williams Scheinman, a self-taught *Wall Street* analyst, the John F. Kennedy Foundation, and the Department of State all played a role supporting scholarship, transportation, and housing for Kenyan students to come to the United States to receive higher education. These students would later return to Kenya and many of them became leaders in the movement toward independence. They founded independent African churches, independent African schools, Young Associations, political organizations and upon independence in Kenya they served in the newly created Kenyan government. Meanwhile, Kenyans were fighting for their independence.

In 1957, eight Africans gained seats representing all eight districts. The majority of them were teachers. These eight western-educated elites presented programs that advocated nationalism and rejected the multiracial society that loyalists and settlers hoped to emerge in self-ruled Kenya. Tom Mboya raised the slogan "To Hell with European Domination." Mboya was elected in Nairobi. Oginga Odinga, graduate of Makerere former teacher, president of Lou Union, and founder of Luo Thrift and Trade Corporation, won in Central Nyanza; Daniel arap Moi, former teacher, won in Rift Valley; Ronald Gideon Ngala, graduate of Makerere and Reland College, Bristol, England won his Coast Constituency; Masinde Muliro, former teacher who graduated from St. Mary's Yala in Kenya, St. Peter's College in Uganda, and the University of Cape Town won in Nyanza North; L. G. Oguda, former teacher, won in Nyanza South; and Bernard Mati, former teacher who attended Alliance High School and Makerere then the University of Bangor in Wales and the University of Edinburgh won in Central Province.

Mboya, Oginga Odinga, Moi, Masinde, and Ngala formed a parliamentary pressure group that came to be known as the African Elected Members Organization (AMEO). This organization demanded that Africans be given fourteen seats equal to the seats assigned to the Europeans. The Colonial Office conceded to the demands and even gave them two ministerial posts. Dr. Julius Kiano and other Kenyans occupied seats in the Legislative Council. At the same time, events toward independence moved at a rapid pace. In January 1959, a delegation representing the elected Africans and Asians joined by one European formed a parliamentary pressure group, the Constituency Elected Members Organization (CEMO). They elected Julius Kiano, one of the first American-educated elites to serve as its Secretary, and dispatched him with a delegation to London to demand the lifting of the State of Emergency and the release of all political prisoners.

Independence was no longer just a notion. Prime Minister Harold Macmillan made his famous statement in South Africa in February 1960 that "the wind of change is blowing through the continent." The elected African members in the Legislative Council and the western-educated elites began to prepare themselves for the inevitable with the formation of countrywide political parties. In May 1060, the Kenyan African National Union (KANU) was formed with James Gicheru elected as president until Kenyatta was released from prison. Oginga Odinga became the vice president, while Mboya served as secretary general. The coastal representatives and those from smaller ethnic groups in the interior formed the Kenya African Democratic Union (KADU) with Moi as chairman, Ronald Gideon Ngala, as president, and Muliro, as vice president. The State of Emergency was lifted and Kenyatta was released in August 1961 to assume the presidency of KANU. The general elections of May 1963 witnessed the landslide triumph of KANU. Jomo Kenyatta became Prime Minister of independent Kenya. The victory of the western-educated elites was complete. June 1, 1963 marked *Madaraka* Day or Day of Responsibility/Self Rule/Independence. Western-educated and American educated elites were at the center of the struggle for independence for Kenya.

KEY TERMS

African American Students Foundation
American Committee on Africa
International Confederation of Free Trade Unions
Kenyan Student Airlifts or Africa Student Airlifts
Kenya African Democratic Union
Kenya African Union
Madaraka Day
Mau Mau
Young Associations

CHAPTER 20

FOLLOWING THEIR FOOTSTEPS: TRACING PUERTO RICANS' SOCIOPOLITICAL ACTIVISM IN NEW YORK CITY FROM AN AFROCENTRIC PERSPECTIVE*

Milagros Denis-Rosario

INTRODUCTION

In early December of 2010, I attended a town-hall style meeting at City College-CUNY, where a group consisting of academics, politicians, and grassroots leaders, among others, responded to the call of creating a task force to address issues of the **African Diaspora**. This group reports to the African Union (AU). Known as the AU Diaspora Task Team, it outlined its specific objectives to include the appointment of an **Afro-Latino** representative, who is a black Puerto Rican woman. This group proposes that despite the challenges confronting Africana and African Diaspora Studies departments/programs in the US higher education system, these departments should continue to receive attention from institutions promoting a better Africa. As stated by the AU ambassador to the United States in a Fall 2010 press release, "the African diaspora is an important component in the building of the African Union."[1] For this purpose, a better understanding of Africa's dispersed children must be documented, and the mechanism for accomplishing this task should be focused on renovating and reinforcing those "ties that bind" them to the motherland. The mother–child relationship is not simply a way of describing those who migrated or their descendants; instead, it must be a repatriation mechanism that many people follow as they try to recover what was left behind. When individuals rescue a relationship with their roots, we call it rediscovering one's "heritage." If it is a "country" that seeks to close such a historical gap, we can call it "home welcoming."

When the first generation of Puerto Ricans reached New York City in the late nineteenth century, they found themselves in the mid of a biracial discourse. They found that New York was unlike Puerto Rico. They had no choice but to articulate race within their historical and cultural background and to denounce racism in many instances, including during the interwar period and the era of the Civil Rights movement. In doing this, I use their example to examine aspects of Africana and African Diaspora Studies. However, first of all, as a historian, I revisit the life of Schomburg and review his perspective on the central role of Africa and its descendants in the history of the world giving voice to Afro-descendants' quest to preserve their culture

---

*A longer version of this article was published in the *Journal of Pan-African Studies* 5, no. 4 (June 2012): 112–28.
[1] *African Union* (2010).

wherever they are. Second, against this review, I trace the emergence of a cultural nationalist identity among the black Puerto Ricans of New York, specifically as that articulates with an Afrocentric identity or black consciousness, in accordance with the conceptualization of history propounded by the late South African historian C. Tsehloane Keto. In so doing, I follow the steps of those Puerto Ricans who arrived to New York City. Although they were confronted with issues of adaptation, racism, and persistent poverty, they embraced the city and forged an Afrocentric identity,[2] which became the driving force behind their sociopolitical activism.

COLONIALISM AND MIGRATION: THE MAKING OF THE PUERTO RICAN DIASPORA

The island of Puerto Rico was a Spanish colony from the early 1500s until 1898. The colonial situation of the island took a decisive turn when as a consequence of the Spanish American War (1898) the United States turned Cuba into a protectorate and made Puerto Rico a "colonial" possession. The presence of the United States influenced the island's politics, economy, and society. The island and its people became subjects of the US Congress, and in 1917 American citizenship was granted to the islanders. Puerto Rico became a model for the new sugar plantation economy that American companies were establishing in the Caribbean. This new economy affected the demand for labor and employment. By the time of the Great Depression of 1929, the Puerto Rican economy, which mainly depended on agricultural production, was suffering badly. The previous year hurricane San Felipe II had destroyed the crops. This economic crisis triggered an increase in the island's unemployment rate and a massive migration of Puerto Ricans to the United States.

The historiography of the Puerto Rican migration to the United States, which reaches its peak between the 1940 and the 1960s, focuses on their processes of arrival, issues of adaptation, and community building. However, even before becoming US citizens, many Puerto Ricans had migrated to the United States, most of them as political exiles who had fought for the island's independence from Spain. Many others were blacks. This is the case of Arturo Alfonso Schomburg (1874–1938). He moved to New York City in 1891 and embraced what would be considered a lifelong quest for Puerto Rican independence and for an affirmation of his African identity. This he did by documenting the history of the African diaspora. Interestingly, historian Jesse Hoffnung-Garskoff interpreted Schomburg's experience as one of many "migrations" that transformed him from a black Puerto Rican to an African American.[3] Schomburg fought

---

[2] This essay is informed by an Africa-centered approach as defined by Keto (1989). For Professor Keto, "The Africa centered perspective of history rests on the premise that it is valid to posit Africa as a geographical and cultural starting base in the study of peoples of African descent." Dr. Keto's conception is in harmony of what— Maulena Karenga articulated in the 1960s as Black Studies, which later changed to Africana and Molefi Kete Asante has most recently advanced what he calls "Africology." The conceptualization of the African Diaspora is an idea that people of African ancestry has articulated in many forms. It would be very difficult to frame Afrocentrism without recognizing the living experiences of people of African descents as a state of self-consciousness. I am greatly indebted to the transcendental work of Dr. Joseph Harris for expanding and conceptualizing the idea of a tangible community that promotes inclusiveness and solidarity.

[3] For a deeper understanding on Schomburg's identity journey see the work of Hoffnung-Garskof (2001).

racial oppression alongside other important figures of the black struggle, such as John Edward Bruce, Alain Locke, Marcus I. Garvey, and W. E. B. Du Bois. Schomburg's quest for affirming his black identity placed him at the forefront of the movement to develop Black Studies. His essay "The Negro Digs Up His Past," which was published in the *Survey Graphic* of Harlem in March 1925, influenced thousands of students and scholars, including the noted historian, John Henrik Clarke, who sought out Schomburg to guide him in his studies of African history.[4]

Schomburg was more than a bibliophile or a collector of books. A close look of his activities in the Negro Historical Society (which he cofounded in 1911) and the American Negro Academy illustrate his consistent Afrocentric endeavors. Elinor Des Verney Sinnette in her classic biography on Schomburg clearly asserts that Schomburg's ". . . motivation or inspiration was there, as were the need to educate himself, the need to find his personal identity, and the need to prove his ancestors' rightful place in world history."[5] For Schomburg, the accumulation of knowledge and material evidence on the role of black people in history was a serious undertaking. Every artifact or publication that Schomburg found was not only shared with his friends and colleagues in his intellectual group, but also became an object for dissemination to a broader public. An example of his zeal to propagate knowledge about Africa is the famous speech he gave entitled "Racial Integrity: A Plea for the Establishment of a Chair of Negro History in Our Schools and Colleges." Schomburg delivered this to a group of teachers at the Cheney Institute, Pennsylvania, in the summer of 1913. The speech denounced the neglect of Africa in history books and urged his listeners to get involved to change the situation and use the classroom to "improve" history:

> I am here with a sincere desire to awaken the sensibilities, to rekindle the dormant fibers of the soul, and to fire the racial patriotism by the study of Negro books. We often feel that so many things around us are warped and alienated. Let us see if we cannot agree to arrange a formula or create a basic construction, for the establishment of a substantial method of instruction for our young women and men . . . .[6]

Using Schomburg's concept of history as an example of an applied Afro-diasporic approach, literature Professor Adelaine Holton observes that, ". . . his interest lay in the contributions and experiences of people of African descent in the modern world . . ."[7] She continues, "in asserting the modernity of African people descent in the Americas, Schomburg did not challenge the Euro-American concept of civilization or its value structure, but instead worked to undermine arguments supporting cultural and racial hierarchies."[8] It can be argued therefore that in his speech of 1913, Schomburg was advocating the establishment of Africana Studies. His approach is analogous to what the South African historian C. T. Keto interpreted as a "non-hegemonic" perspective of history; meaning that Europe should not be seen as dominate and

---

[4] Clarke (1994).
[5] Sinnette (1989), 38.
[6] Schomburg (1913). Arthur A. Schomburg Papers, The Schomburg Center for Research and Black Culture, New York Public Library. This excerpt was also quoted in E. Sinnette, *Arthur Alfonso Schomburg*, 209 Footnote 22; see also the Spanish version in de Rivera (1989).
[7] Holton (2007).
[8] See Footnote 7, 235.

central but part of a diversity of civilizations that encompasses the global community.[9] In that context, Keto's analysis may be used to suggest that Schomburg is contributing to a "pluriversal" perspective of history approaching it from a nonhegemonic reference to Europe and positing Africa as an equal legitimate center of historical interpretation.

In addition to questioning white man's interpretation of history, Schomburg was urging black people/teachers/intellectuals to take control of their history by knowing their past. Schomburg stood for a broader interpretation of Africa and its descendants' history. His views would be articulated later in his essay "The Negro Digs up His Past." In this now famous piece, he confirmed what Alain Locke and other members of the American Negro Academy were advocating, that is, black people's history does not begin with slavery.

Schomburg's role in creating and advocacy for an Afrocentric perspective to history went beyond political or cultural borders. He exemplified the "African diasporic identity," denoting the conceptualization of the African Diaspora as a collective experience. In 1915, Schomburg addressed again the American Negro Academy. On that occasion, he lectured about the presence of Africans in Spain, Portugal, and in the colonial Latin America. He also emphasized that in all the circumstances in which blacks were oppressed, they rebelled. Here again, one can identify the Schomburg who is not only critical of forms of domination and oppression against the people of African descent; he is also acknowledging African people's agency in their resistance against colonialism and slavery. This aspect was a subject in which African American and Caribbean intellectuals were well versed in their own histories. However, Schomburg's contribution was that he expanded the discussion by including people of Central and South America. On this subject, his biographer, Elinor Sinnette, stated, "Schomburg brought the international dimensions of black history to the forefront of the American Negro Academy."[10] Schomburg in fact paved the way to Africana or African Diaspora Studies as a cross national/cross cultural field. I would argue that his thinking became the foundation for the Africa-centered theory defined by C. Tsehloane Keto, particularly in his book *The Africa Centered Perspective of History*. According to Keto, the Africa-centered approach positions Africa as the main focus of interpretation and seeks to "interpret" and "understand" global events by contextualizing the role of Africa and its diaspora within world events and activities.[11] Schomburg, along with his peers, not only had the courage to break the silence about Africa and its diaspora's past, but he also positioned himself as a leading figure in the struggle to eradicate racism. More importantly, in that process of researching, collecting material culture, participating in conferences, and traveling around the world, Schomburg pioneered Afrocentric Studies by positing Africa as a central source of his knowledge and experience. This paradigm or conception was the rationale behind his project to document the experience of the people of African descent globally. In this sense, Schomburg understood "the universality of the black man's history and that history has a common provenance: Africa.[12] For him, education was central to furthering this goal.

Schomburg continued his intellectual activism in support of the validation of people of African ancestry in world history until his passing on June 8, 1938. Hundreds of publications

---

[9] See Footnote 2, 11.
[10] See Footnote 5, 55.
[11] See Footnote 2, 19–20.
[12] See Footnote 5, 46.

deal with Schomburg's life and work, but more importantly, his papers and documents have become the foundation for the establishment of the *Schomburg Center for Research in Black Culture*. He is beyond any doubt a pioneer of the African Diaspora and Africana Studies.

Arturo Schomburg's personal experience has many resonances with those of Puerto Ricans migrating to New York in the United States. Until the 1930s, Puerto Ricans began to migrate in large numbers to the United States. Some settled in rural areas to work on farms; but the great majority moved to urban centers such as Philadelphia, Chicago, and New York City.

In the urban setting of New York City, Puerto Ricans crossed class and racial lines and integrated into communities, such as Harlem. Harlem is a historical section of the upper Manhattan and represents the cross-cultural interaction of peoples of African descent. There, African American and other Afro-Caribbean peoples created a site of intellectual exchange where black leaders, artists, writers, musicians, preachers, and workers established networks with Spanish speaking people, most of them Puerto Ricans.

In Harlem, Puerto Ricans also interacted with Italians, Irish Americans, and Jews, to mention a few. Since the 1950s, social scientists have begun to address issues pertaining to the Puerto Ricans' interactions in urban centers. Remarkably, in this scholarship, issues regarding Boricuas were tied in with other minorities, particularly with African Americans.[13] These studies established parallels and intersections between these groups and the competition for economic resources, political power and housing. They are important sources of validation of this essay. In their quest for social, political, and economic inclusion, both Puerto Ricans and African Americans intersected in different scenarios, sometimes combining strategies that included establishing social organizations. These addressed social issues, transforming, and affirming racial identity in the process.

ARTICULATING THE AFRO-BORICUA[14] IDENTITY DURING THE CIVIL RIGHTS ERA

Scholarship on Puerto Rican-based "social organizations" emphasizes how the community needed to organize itself on the basis of regional commonalities. This type of organization suggests that among Puerto Ricans race was not an issue. These assumptions contrast with Lorrin Thomas' study *Puerto Rican Citizen*, which reveals that Puerto Ricans' racial construction changed dramatically when they arrived in the United States. On the island, race had not

---

[13] A sample of this scholarship: Handlin (1959) and Glazer and Moynihan (1959). Studies comparing the collaboration between Puerto Ricans and African Americans include: Torres (1995); Jennings (1995), and Fernández (2003).

[14] According to the Puerto Rican Academy of the Spanish Language, "Boricua" refers to any person or object that comes from "Borikén," "Borikén," and "Borinquen" are the original names given to Puerto Rico by the Taíno Indians or native peoples of Puerto Rico. In the United States, people from Puerto Rican descent have widely adopted the word "Boricua" over "Puerto Rican." Editor Roberto Santiago states that "Boricua" could also be equivalent to what "brother" and "sister" mean for African Americans: "I imagined that *Boricua* was just affectionate slang for *Puerto Ricans*. I guessed that *Boricua* was just a word that proclaimed that you were down with your people and your culture—no different from *brother* and *sister*, the terms of endearment used by African Americans." In *Boricuas: Influential Puerto Rican Writings-An Anthology*. 1st edition. (New York: One World/Ballantine, 1995), xiii.

a binary concept for Puerto Ricans. It was based on a different color spectrum. The history of the island evolved from a "racially blind" society to racialized groups. Yet the US Puerto Ricans' nature and self-consciousness became to be built on a "conquered/oppressed" platform. After they settled in the United States, Puerto Ricans' reality changed for the worse, when discrimination, poverty, and all social disadvantages pushed them to an identity crisis. Furthermore, the contribution made by Puerto Ricans serving as soldiers in various US wars was not acknowledged upon their return. Issues of veteran inequality and discrimination were added to the injustices that the Puerto Rican community was already facing. In the case of New York City, community organizations, mostly labor and political groups, emerged to provide alternative services and support to Puerto Ricans. Documents testify to the existence of the activities of these institutions as early as the 1920s and 1930s.[15] However, Puerto Rican immigration reached a watershed in the post-world war era. And in addition to becoming an important period in the "making of the diaspora," as sociologist José Sánchez has observed, the postwar era was also the time when Puerto Rican "activism" and "radicalism" really took root. Yet it was not until the 1960s that discussion about racial identity became prevalent. At the height of the Civil Rights Movement, Puerto Ricans in New York City refocused on the racial issue and challenged preconceived notions by connecting it with the Afrocentric discourse, thereby problematizing the issue of Hispanic/Latino identity.[16]

In 1964, the Civil Rights Act was signed, prohibiting discrimination based on race in schools, public places, and places of employment. In 1965, the Voting Rights Act was passed, outlawing discriminatory practices used in the South to disenfranchise African American voters. In 1966, the Black Panther Party (BPP) was formed in Oakland, California. Motivated by these developments, Puerto Ricans also mobilized to demand their rights and formed coalitions with African Americans. These coalitions were documented in the black press.[17] African American and Boricuas students in the city of New York, who formed students' clubs, such as the Toussaint L'Overture and the Sociedad Eugenio María de Hostos, took the lead in the formation of alliances and the advancement of social causes.

GRASSROOTS/COMMUNITY ORGANIZATIONS

In the discussion of Puerto Rican advocacy and activism for their rights, one cannot overlook the role of grassroots organizations such as the United Bronx Parents, Inc. (UBP), founded by Dr. Evelina López-Antonetty (1922–1984) in 1965, years after she emigrated from Puerto Rico to the United States along with her mother and two sisters. The UBP was created as a result of "the lack of responsiveness of the public school system toward the needs of Puerto Rican and other minority children."[18] Under the dynamic directorship of López-Antonetty, the

---

[15] For more detailed information about this early period see the seminal study of historian Korrol (1983).

[16] Sánchez (2007).

[17] For the purpose of this research, I sampled *The Chicago Defender, New York Amsterdam News, Variety, The New York Times* and light publications such as *Jet* and *Ebony* magazines.

[18] Letter from Marilyn Amdur to Professor Beryl L. Bailey, November 17, 1969, Department of Black and Puerto Rican Studies, 1969–1978; letter from Charles Smith, April 29, 1970, box 2 folder 7, Hunter College Archives and Special Collections.

UBP became the stalwart in citywide struggles for quality education. At first, the organization consisted mostly of volunteer staff whose mission was to train parents and encourage their participation in decision making related to the schools. However, the UBP extended their offer of training programs and workshops to include educational workers, teachers, and students.

The UBP also embraced a pan-ethnic vision and was instrumental in furthering Afrocentric awareness. This happened as the organization broadened its mission beyond its Bronx headquarters. In addition to the community services offering technical assistance, bilingual counseling, educational, and summer lunch programs, it extended its range to the organization of events and distribution of literature that engaged both with pan-ethnic alliances and the Afrocentric discourse. Its programs included film screenings, plays and dance performances featuring Puerto Rican/Latino, and African American performers. The Hunt's Point Branch of the New York Library showed the film *No Vietnamese Ever Called Me Nigger* (released in 1969).[19] The UBP also organized events honoring African American civil rights leaders, such as Paul Robeson, and in 1981 they paid tribute to Dr. Martin Luther King Jr. Interestingly, many flyers were prepared and distributed informing the public that a discussion session would follow each activity.[20] What is captivating about those flyers is the Afrocentric language used in the announcements. Perhaps, this is a reflection of the times in which "Afro-identity" was a trend, but there was no need to implement publicity strategies using terms such as "black," or combining words such as "Latin-Soul," to rally people for an organization with a great majority of Puerto Ricans/Hispanic members. This "Afrocentered" language wouldn't have been adopted unless the UBP staff felt with the need to promote it. The response from the community—Latino and African American—and support for these activities were precisely the result of the efforts and pan-ethnic vision of the UBP members. It must be added that López-Antonetty became an adjunct professor at the Department of Africana and Puerto Rican/Latino Studies (Black and Puerto Rican Studies back then) at Hunter College. A closer look at her course syllabus and teaching materials emphasizes the struggle of black people.[21] In summary, the leadership of the UBP, represented by López-Antonetty, illustrates an important aspect of Puerto Rican activism that has played a key role in the implementation of the Afrocentric paradigm. In short, the UBP is the perfect illustration of a grass roots activist group, whose membership without knowing it was making "history from below."

For Puerto Ricans, sociopolitical activism means constant political participation and the creation of groups to empower the community. This was the case of *The National Association for the Advancement of Hispanic American People of African Origin* (NAAHAPAO). The legal incorporation of this nonprofit organization in 1989 was the task of Julio E. Sabater, who owned a consulting and development agency in downtown Manhattan.[22] The NAAHAPAO's name suggests that it was modeled after the NAACP. One might highlight the "ethnic reconciliatory

---

[19] Center for Puerto Rican Studies. Guide to the Records of United Bronx Parents Association Collection, 1. Accessed online November 19, 2011.

[20] The title of this film quotes from a statement that Muhammad Ali made when he refused to be drafted during the Vietnam War.

[21] The United Bronx Parents Association Papers (hereafter UBP), box 2, folders 1and 9 Center of Puerto Rican Studies.

[22] The Frank Torres Papers, box 19, folder 6, Center of Puerto Rican Studies, Hunter College.

dimension" of the group when they promote the advancement of "Hispanic American people of African origin." The naming of the association also suggests that by the late 1980s black Puerto Ricans had forged an Afro-Latino/Hispanic identity, a pattern that was already evident within the Young Lords, which was the Puerto Rican/Latino version of the Black Panthers in the 1970s. It is also important to note that their philosophy is parallel to that of African Americans in that it sought to reconnect with Africa. For example, documentation of the NAAHAPAO shows that some of the members adopted African names. In fact, in their memorandums and communications, Mr. Sabater signed his name as Oggunike. Moreover, an organizational chart shows that they adopted the Yoruba and Egyptian philosophical views of life.[23] This appears to have been an attempt to refocus the concept of Puerto Ricans' racial identity by adding a healthy dose of Africanity to them.

Moreover, the Afrocentric approach of the group is explicit in its constitution. Terminology such as "to create, promote, support activities designed to develop self-respect . . . racial pride," implies that Mr. Sabater and the other members of the group were deeply immersed in the Africa-centered/Black Pride movement. Another passage of the constitution describes one objective as being the dissemination of "historical facts about the greatness of ANCIENT BLACK CIVILIZATION (their emphasis) and their contributions to human development in the entire world." Unquestionably, this group aligned with the Afrocentric movement. There are links here to Professors John Henrik Clarke and Yosef ben-Jochannan, among others.

Dr. Clarke and Dr. ben-Jochannan (who were from Ethiopian and Puerto Rican heritage) had pioneered the intellectual movement for racial justice by writing, teaching and publicly lecturing about the history and culture of the African people. They remained active for more than four decades, and it is fair to state that they provided the foundation for what later became an Afrocentric movement. They planted many intellectual seeds among Black and Puerto Rican youth, and the grassroots leadership in Puerto Rican communities. They also played critical roles in the institutionalization of Africana and African American university programs. As stated earlier, the pledge of the NAAHAPAO members was a reaffirmation of the Afrocentric approach of the sociopolitical activism of Puerto Ricans in New York City. For example, in their pledge, the members confirmed their "conviction as GOD-GIVEN . . . to promote the well-being of all the descendants of our ANCIENT-AFRICAN-BLACK-ANCESTORS . . . ." They further added that "in order to promote the highest standards of brotherhood; social justice and human dignity . . ." they would fulfill the duties and responsibilities of the organization.

It seems that the organization and Mr. Sabater were very assertive in their strategy to promote their agenda. Correspondences of summer of 1989 and spring 1990 indicate that the group was engaged in a campaign of increasing public awareness by sending communications to the editor-in-chief of *The New York Amsterdam News*, Judge Frank Torres (the same person who notarized the paperwork of the organization), and even to the ambassador of Nigeria in the United Nations, among others. In these letters the NAAHAPAO demanded the "Restoration of Our Black Race" (sic). They had designed a "master plan geared to create among our people at large, economic and financial empowerment; and simultaneously to reprogram their minds

---

[23] See Footnote 22.

in order to free them from mental slavery . . ."[24] It is evident that in addition to joining the common cause of empowering the community and "restoring" ethnic pride, the NAAHAPAO broadened the ethnic definition in Puerto Ricans' and other Latinos' racial consciousness.

Mr. Sabater's efforts in promoting the citywide rights of "Latinos of African-American descent" are documented in a *New York Times* article in May of 1991.[25]. Following the results of a recent census showing that the white population in New York City was decreasing, an energetic Sabater advocated, "redistricting" the city. According to the *Times* story, the increasing number of the city's minorities had not been taken into consideration. At the hearings, Sabater represented "Latinos of African-American descent." That particular issue gave Sabatier the opportunity to demonstrate his litigation skills before an audience, for which he received "one of the loudest round of applause of the night." It seems that the early efforts of people such as Arthur Schomburg had left their mark throughout the city.

CALLING MOTHER AFRICA: SALSA MUSIC AS "RESISTANCE IN MOTION"

As an important additional note to this work, in the midst of all these historical developments, one cannot miss the fact that the popular music of Puerto Ricans has connected with Africa, particularly through *bomba*, *plena* and *salsa*. Salsa music testifies to the African influence in Puerto Rican/Latino culture, and New York City became the stage for this historic fusion. As many studies on salsa music suggest, this genre created a more inclusive venue for Puerto Ricans and Latinos' cultural expression.[26] These studies also point to the fact that the urban space of New York City serves as a scenario for Puerto Ricans and other ethnic groups to create an atmosphere of "ethnic camaraderie" and collaboration, not only in show business, but also in other spheres. Furthermore, just as Puerto Ricans have developed a kind of Afrocentric civic approach, a similar trait is discernible in their cultural activities, particularly in musical performance. And culture is a quintessential manifestation of any individual identity.[27] Observers in the field of Africana studies have seen that this has been used as a great resource to connect the diaspora to the motherland.

In 1974, Mohammad Ali defeated George Foreman in Kinshasa, then the Democratic Republic of Congo, now Zaire, to regain the world heavyweight championship. As part of the event, the production team organized a monumental cultural event that included top-rate African American performers such as James Brown, the Spinners, B. B. King, the Pointers Sisters and the most famous tropical-music band of the moment, the Fania All Stars, a musical ensemble established in the late 'sixties.[28] During the 1970s, the star-studded group became

---

[24] The Frank Torres Papers box 19, folder 2. "Letter to H. E. Joseph N. Garba" February 5, 1990.

[25] Lee (1991).

[26] These musical genres have been widely investigated. See for example, Washburne (2008); Flores (2000); Flores and Escobar (2008).

[27] On aspects of cultural manifestations in the diaspora see the work of Hall (2003).

[28] The Fania All Stars was a musical ensemble established in the late sixties by the composer Johnny Pacheco and the musician Jerri Massucci. The group ceased performing together in the 1980s when many members began solo careers and struggled with the emergence of other genres. Nonetheless, the Fania All Stars established a

renowned worldwide for their musical performances. The members were representative of a fair range of the ethnic background of New York City, since there were Puerto Ricans, Cubans and Dominicans.

Embracing Africa was part of the musical experience for those Puerto Rican musicians participating in the Kinshasa event. In a 2009 interview Cheo Feliciano, a black Puerto Rican singer and key member of the Fania group, reflected on that important moment: "When we arrived in Africa—and I think I can speak for everyone who was there—we returned to our roots, to the mother-land, to the origins . . ."[29] Feliciano's statement is a good example of the relationship between music and cultural identity. It is also a testimony to the fact that despite the external pressures that undermine the influence of Africa in the lives of its descendants, the wider universe conspires to revive such influences. For this Fania musician, the experience of traveling to the continent became a reaffirmation of his African identity. Here again, the city of New York, the point of departure for the long journey, became an important venue for Puerto Ricans to vindicate their culture, exhibit pride in their identity, view themselves as part of the African diaspora, recognize the contribution of their heritage, and rearticulate their connection with Africa: all processes that form part of the Afrocentric movement. The trip to the continent served as a vehicle for Puerto Ricans and African Americans to interact and reactivate the animus of those who felt ties to the continent. And for many of them, the trip turned out to be a homecoming.

CONCLUSION

The examples discussed in this article foreshadowed what the AU Diaspora Task Team in the anecdote at the beginning of this essay is seeking to do. Here, the author doesn't seek to reinvent the wheel, but to use her skills to review the work of Schomburg, who gave expression to Afro-descendants' who sought to preserve their culture and to refer to Keto who propounded the view of a central role for Africa and its descendants in world history. He suggested that from a nonhegemonic perspective of European history would emerge a "pluriversal" point of view in which Africa would seem equal to Europe and Asia. Inspired by this interpretation of history, I was able to trace the steps of individuals such as Arturo or grassroots leaders like Evelina López-Antonetty, and many others. Despite the societal pressure to ignore Africa, all of them, have succeeded in marking their distinct cultural and economic spaces, partly due to their embrace of the African World. This has partly enabled them to project a dynamic and progressive cultural existence in the city.

---

legacy for the new generation of salsa singers and validated the cultural contribution of Puerto Ricans and other Latinos in American pop culture. On the cultural and ethnic validation of salsa, see *Centro Journal* volume XVI No. 2 (Fall 2004). This is entirely dedicated to salsa and its influence. Also, Jerri Massucci/Leon Gast's 1970s documentaries *Our Latin Thing* and *Salsa* are key components of this scholarship. The multiethnic group's performance is chronicled in the video/documentary entitled *Fania All Stars Live in Africa* (1974), *When We Were Kings* (1996), and more recently in the film *Soul Power* (2009).

[29] Excerpt from documentary *Celia The Queen* (2009), directed by Joe Cardona and M. de Varona. Feliciano died in April 17, 2014 as a consequence of a car accident.

The leadership of the UBP illustrates the advantages of empowering students and teachers. Far from imposing limits on her organization, Mrs. López's mission and philosophy enabled her to communicate her "Afrocentric" views to the wider community through the different activities the institution organized. Then, the innovative strategy employed by the *National Association for the Advancement of Hispanic American People of African Origin* showed that by the late 1980s the definition and articulation of an Afro-Hispanic ethnic identity had perhaps become more complex. This is evident from the explicit appropriation of the Afrocentric philosophy within an Afro-Latino US context. This particular group needs to be further investigated and documented, and its trajectory located in the rich history of Afrocentric associations in New York City.

Symbolism associated with Africa is also manifest in the culture. African diasporic studies have a long trajectory of using cultural approaches to demonstrate how people of African descent resisted assimilation. This is demonstrated by the example concerning the participation of Puerto Ricans musicians in the event in Kinshasa, Zaire (today the Democratic Republic of Congo). The outcome of Puerto Rican/Latinos interacting with top-rated African American performers epitomizes Africa as the common denominator for the convergence of both communities. Furthermore, the testimonial of the Fania singer reminds us that there are many ways to understand the experience of people of African ancestry and that the coming together of different styles and approaches is conducive to this.

Similar to the initiative of the African Diaspora Task Team of the African Union, examples here of Puerto Ricans' Afrocentric views and approaches illustrate the efforts that have been made on one side (the Americas) and the other (Africa) in order to close the gap between those who seek to affirm their heritage, and the homeland that is willing to welcome them. I am quite sure that in a specific place in time both hands, that is, the continent and its Diaspora will embrace each other again.

KEY TERMS

Afrocenter
Afro-Latinos
Colonialism
Migration

CHAPTER 21

PROTESTING FOR SOUTH AFRICAN LIBERATION IN A NEGOTIATED SPACE: THE COLD WAR, AMERICAN ANTIAPARTHEID ACTIVISTS, AND THE VITAL CENTER, 1946–1954

Charles D. Johnson

INTRODUCTION

This essay is about how activists fighting for South African liberation in the United States adapted to the political climate of the post–World War II era, where Cold War reaction and repression threatened the viability of radical anticolonial protest. It contends that concerted efforts on the part of the United States government to contain communism meant that the anticolonial activists in the late 1940s and early 1950s were forced to operate in a diminishing and negotiated political space. Perhaps the best example of this is the former anticolonial radical and communist Max Yergan, who had helped to establish the Council on African Affairs (CAA) in 1937. Yergan had lived in South Africa for fifteen years before returning to the United States as an outspoken champion of liberation. By 1952, he had become an antitotalitarian liberal and apologist of apartheid. I argue this political retrenchment constituted a significant and near permanent break from the militancy of the decades before when, the CAA, the most militant anticolonial organization, often took an uncompromising stand in the struggle for South African liberation.

In South Africa and in the United States, 1946–54 was an important period in the struggle for South African liberation. In South Africa, the National Party defeated the United Party and introduced its program of strict racial segregation known as apartheid, a virulent and brutal form of racial segregation codified in legislation whose debilitating influence pervaded every aspect of the lives of black South Africans. Centuries old de facto racial segregation was amplified while being substantively and comprehensively written into law. There were numerous pieces of apartheid legislation that adversely affected blacks. These acts legalized the mistreatment of Africans, Indians, and Coloreds while privileging white South Africans. African Americans identified with their plight due to Jim Crow segregation in the United States. Together they forged a transnational alliance to topple apartheid. To break up the burgeoning internal antiapartheid movement and especially to prevent white South Africans from participating, the South African government skillfully played on ideas of national loyalty while treating challenges to its racist policies as a communist conspiracy directed against the sovereignty of the state. Thus, the aspirations of blacks in South Africa for the removal of racial impediments were folded into the putative communist plot and white South Africans were put on notice to tow the party line or else.[1]

This proved to be a significant challenge to African, Colored, and Indian protest groups who had not only to contend with the overwhelming oppressive apartheid forces but also to demonstrate to potential transnational allies that they were not communists. In response to increasing repression, the African National Congress (ANC), the South African Indian Congress (SAIC), and the Franchise Action Council (FAC), representing the Coloreds, joined forces in an impressive show of force to protest the racist and unjust laws of the apartheid government. This campaign to defy unjust laws or Defiance Campaign also resonated in the United States and became an important focal point for American antiapartheid activists to organize for South Africa's liberation.[2]

Cold War repression in the United States however created a political environment that was openly hostile to communists and that was suspicious of any form of political dissent that challenged the status quo. White supremacists hoping to slow social progress and to forestall economic competition from blacks were quick to label political nonconformists communists even if their "nonconformity" was in attempting to obtain basic civil rights at home and human rights abroad. Officials within the Truman administration cast a broad net in an attempt to root out organizations it deemed subversive. Consequently, the CAA came under such intense scrutiny and pressure that its membership fragmented along ideological lines into dichotomous factions, while the National Association for the Advancement of Colored People (NAACP) and other protest organizations attempted to avoid becoming entangled in the pervasive web of "red-baiting" by aligning its foreign policy agenda with that of the US government.

REVIEW OF LITERATURE

Intellectuals have debated the impact of the Cold War on the civil rights movement and how American race relations influenced its international relations including relations with South Africa, but not much has been written substantively about the impact of Cold War

---

[1] In Johnson (2013), I argue that African Americans such as Max Yergan who lived in South Africa during the early twentieth century were at the head of what would later become the antiapartheid movement in the United States exactly because they could identify with the African South Africans as cosuffers. Temporal elasticity in the meaning of "racial" designations makes them tedious and potentially anachronistic in works of history. In the spirit of clarity, I have chosen to be as specific as possible when making reference to members of different "racial" groups, for example, African, Indian, and Colored. Blacks most often refer to all three groups but should be understood in the context in which it is used.

[2] Matthews to Houser, March 13, 1952, Microfilm Reel 1, Records of the American Committee on Africa, Part 2: Correspondence and Subject Files on South Africa, 1952–1985, Library of Congress, Washington, DC. See also, Sisulu to Houser, March 26, 1952, Microfilm Reel 1, Records of the American Committee on Africa, Part 2: Correspondence and Subject Files on South Africa, 1952–1985, Library of Congress, Washington, DC. Lodge (1983), 40.

repression on the direction of the South African liberation struggle in the United States.[3] In 1974, E. S. Reddy, indicated the need for an examination of the impact of the Cold War on the antiapartheid movement.[4] Perhaps the first significant attempt came from Thomas Borstelmann who examined the foreign policy of the Truman administration in relation to the minority regimes in southern Africa during the Cold War.[5] Bortelsmann's emphasizes the strategies of the Truman administration to contain communism while advancing US interests with countries in southern Africa then vying for independence. The scope of his work is broader and with a different emphasis. This article places the anticolonial and antiapartheid activists in the United States in the foreground. Penny von Eschen gives perhaps the best rendering of the US government's persecution of anticolonial activists in the late 1940s and early 1950s. She rightly sees that the Truman administration began the assault on militant anticolonialism with the loyalty order of March 1947, by directing Attorney General Tom Clark to identify organizations deemed subversive, and by the vigorous and liberal use of the Smith Act to deport left-leaning opponents of the administration's foreign policy.[6] My contention is that this caused a major shift in transnational protest politics as former radicals were either cowed into the vital center or were condemned as part of a lunatic fringe of the liberation struggle.

Other works have looked more broadly at African American and US involvement in the struggle for South African liberation from a variety of perspectives. Francis Nujbi Nesbitt opens with a discussion of "Cold War and Apartheid" that touches on their impact on anticolonial radicals; he states for instance that "Robeson's leftist perspective and ties to the Soviet Union became a liability in his relations with the government, the media, and liberal African-American organizations such as the NAACP," but Nesbitt does not explain how this "liability" eventually forced protest toward a more moderate vital center such that when the antiapartheid movement in the United States becomes a popular movement it no longer has at its heart the radical elements that launched it. What emerges within the antiapartheid movement in the United States then is what David Hostetter calls "multicultural politics," a process that represents a political compromise between Pan Africanists and integrationists. I agree with Hostetter but contend that the shrinking space on the left essentially forced the Pan Africanists, who represented the radical element in the movement, to concede their position of militancy. More importantly, the birth of "multicultural politics" was located safely within the confines

---

[3] See, Dudziak (2000) and Borstelmann (2001). A work similar to but earlier then Borstelmann's is Noer (1985); students of US foreign policy might find Lynch (1977). Jackson's *From Congo to Soweto*, insightful. Jackson dedicates a chapter, "Afro-Americans and Africa: the Unbroken Link," to a discussion of their involvement in African liberation struggles including South Africa. Houser (1989) looks at the African liberation through an autobiographical lens. He dedicates three chapters to the South African liberation struggle. There are at least a few works that deal in depth with the Council of African Affairs including its entanglement with cold warriors, Lynch (1977) and the unpublished biography of Alphaeus Hunton by his wife Dorothy Hunton. See Footnote 1.
[4] Reddy (1974), 20.
[5] Borstelmann (1993)
[6] Von Eschen (1997), 114–21.

of the vital center, again with the radical element removed. The radicals had to either join the emerging consensus in the vital center or become political outliers.[7]

Shelly Leanne is a less well-known but important contributor to what we know about African American support of the antiapartheid movement. Her 1994 dissertation at the University of Oxford, "African American Initiatives Against Minority Rule in South Africa: A Politicized Diaspora in World Politics" intersects most directly with this work in the chapter "The Cold War and African Americans the Silencing of the NAACP the Demise of the CAA." Leanne argues convincingly, and I agree with her, that the Cold War totally deradicalized the already timid NAACP and that it crushed the CAA. Thus, pre-Cold War leadership of the movement shifted from a small group of unapologetic radicals—many of them communist sympathizers to a Cold War leadership that was more moderate and antitotalitarian.[8]

Nesbitt and Leanne also speak of the important contribution of the Nation of Islam (NOI) to the antiapartheid movement. It was perhaps one of the few protest groups that existed throughout the period of this study that maintained its radical inclinations. Later, the All-African Peoples Revolutionary Party (A-APRP), the African Liberation Support Committee (ALSC), and other radical groups would emerge as contributors to the South African liberation struggle. The NOI and the A-APRP were both highly radicalized, especially the A-APRP, but they both remained outside of the vital center of American protest politics, and I contend were thus not seen as legitimate by most American mainstream political activists.[9]

What remains to be told is how anticolonial activists adapted to the flood of political repression that distended the political center while collapsing the radical left, and, moreover, how on the other side of the initial wave of repression new leaders of the anticolonial movement emerged with different ideas than their militant predecessors about the form and method of protest that would shape the antiapartheid movement in the United States going forward.

THE VITAL CENTER

In the 1930s, the US intellectuals on the left were divided into three groups: communists, progressives, and liberals.[10] The advent of the Cold War at the conclusion of World War II and the reaction that followed caused many communists and progressives in the United States to shift toward the right of the political spectrum, to what historian Arthur M. Schlesinger, Jr. referred to as the vital center. Schlesinger argued that communism and democracy were mutually exclusive, that Americans must close ranks against communists, and that containing communism needed to be the cornerstone of American foreign policy. The vital center became an expression that was

---

[7] Nesbitt (2004), 2–3. Hostetter (2006), 3–4. Other works that follow a similar theme include Massie (1997) and Minter and Cobb (2008) Minter and Cobb include many historic photographs from the South African liberation struggle in the United States that makes this work unique.

[8] One of the better histories of African American involvement in the antiapartheid movement is Leanne's (1994) dissertation. Her treatment of US Foreign Policy is especially strong. Klotz (1995), 451–78.

[9] See Nesbitt (2004), 57 and a chapter by Leanne (1994), 271.

[10] Erhman (1995), 3.

synonymous with antitotalitarian liberalism or liberal anticommunism.[11] Thus, "centrist" organizations differed from their predecessors in several important ways: they were far less likely to rely on militant protest that decried American ideals; they were more closely aligned with the foreign policy of the US government; they were antitotalitarian and anticommunists; and liberal whites, increasingly, provided direction for these groups. The NAACP, Americans for South African Resistance (AFSAR), and its successor, the American Committee on Africa (ACOA), were examples of organizations that protested for liberation in South Africa from the vital center.

THE EMERGENCE OF COLD WAR POLITICS

In February 1946, George F. Kennan, a US Foreign Service Officer in Moscow, sent a "long telegram" to the State department warning that the Soviet Union was an expansionist state with intractable leaders who were hostile to capitalism. Within a matter of weeks, Winston Churchill, with President Truman by his side, made his famous "Iron Curtain" speech at Westminster College, in the President's home state of Missouri. That summer, presidential aides, Clark Clifford and George Elsey produced a report supporting the contentions of Kennan and Churchill. They avowed that the Kremlin was seeking to weaken and destroy US prestige in Europe, Asia, and South America. Therefore, the report concluded that because the war had left many countries with economies that were in shambles, the United States must assist all democratic nations menaced by the Soviet Union. This included segregationist South Africa.[12] On 12 March, 1947, fearing that "everywhere around the globe vulnerabilities grew and avenues for Soviet gains developed," President Truman set forth what became known as the Truman Doctrine, which declared the United States' intent to contain Soviet influence. This doctrine would guide the United States' policy for the next four decades.[13]

In South Africa, following the election defeat of the United Party in May 1948, the Department of State raised questions about the significance of the National Party victory. American diplomats responded with a confidential report appraising the policy trends of the new South African government. Initially, they mistakenly believed that the National Party's slim majority in Parliament would preclude them from introducing "radical or drastic changes in policy."[14] The report emphasized economic concerns and failed even to raise the pressing question of what the victory would mean

---

[11] Arthur Schlesinger's book *The Vital Center* became an important work to anticommunist and antitotalitarian liberals. See Schlesinger (1949); also see Footnote 10, 2.

[12] Leffler (1994), 52–53.

[13] The US government was particularly fearful of conditions in Western Europe. Reports were coming in from the US Embassies in Italy, France, and Germany that communists were gaining ground. Even more frightful was news that England was facing financial bankruptcy. Unable to maintain its hold on Greece and Turkey, British leaders informed Washington that they would have to pull out. See Footnote 12, 55.

[14] North Winship to Secretary of States, "Appraisal of Certain Probable Policy Trends of New South African Government," June 16, 1948, transcript in US Embassy Pretoria, General Records, 1945–1949, Decimal File, 848A.00/6-1648, General Records of the Department of State, Record Group 59, National Archives Building, College Park, MD. Borstelman concurs, see Footnote 5, 57.

for Africans and other people of color.[15] Containing communism remained at the top of the foreign policy agenda for the Truman administration and explains in part what appears to be its callous indifference toward the race question in South Africa. Concerns about race took on significance in the context of how it would influence Cold War politics.[16] As Borstelmann aptly points out, World War II demonstrated the importance of South Africa as a strategically. It was seen as a friendly port of call for its naval ships and other vessels making the long trek to the Middle East and south Asia around the Cape of Good Hope. More importantly, South Africa had large deposits of strategic materials such as platinum and, the all-important, uranium, which was used in the manufacture of nuclear weapons. With so much at stake strategically, the Truman administration accepted the idea of the permanency of the South African government and took aim at the most progressive organization pressing the anticolonial movement in the United States at that time, the Council on African Affairs. This position fit well with the agenda of segregationist in South Africa and the United States.[17]

YERGAN'S RETREAT FROM COMMUNISM

In 1922, Max Yergan arrived in South Africa an African American missionary for the Young Men's Christian Association. Because of his frustration with the racial situation in South Africa, he adopted communism as a means for bringing about a social revolution that would empower people living under colonialism. David Anthony and I examine Yergan's years in South Africa elsewhere, but I contend he returned to the United States in 1936 with the specific agenda of struggling for South Africa's liberation from racism and racial segregation. His political agenda underwent, a second reversal, as a consequence of the Cold War. This change propelled him into the forefront of the anticommunist forces in the United States.[18]

---

[15] See Footnote 14, 49.

[16] US diplomats followed the development and implementation of apartheid closely. See, Winship to Secretary of State, "The Racial Policy of 'apartheid' Implementation," September 13, 1948, transcript in American Consulate, Cape Town; General Records, 1945–1949, Decimal File, 848A.4016/9-1348, General Records of the Department of State, Record Group 59, National Archives Building, College Park, MD. See also, Winship to Secretary of State, "Constitutional Aspects of Apartheid," September 14, 1948, American Consulate, Cape Town; General Records, 1945–1949; Central Decimal File, 848A.4016/9-1448, General Records of the Department of State, Record Group 59, National Archives Building, College Park, MD. Recently, Giliomee (2003) has argued that apartheid evolved out of competition between the National Party and the United Party and that it was based in German missiology, as applied by Dutch Reformed Church missionary strategists in the Orange Free State.

[17] See Footnote 5, 50. Several authors discuss the work of the Council, see Footnote 6; Lynch (1997); see Footnote 1.

[18] Yergan's work in South Africa is outlined in Max Yergan to Jesse Moorland, May 15, 1922, transcript in YMCA—Max Yergan—Corr.—January–June 1922, Box 126–64, Jesse Moorland Papers, Moorland Spingarn Research Center, Howard University, Washington, DC. See also, Yergan to Moorland, June 1, 1925, YMCA—Max Yergan—Correspondence 1925, Box 126–65, Jesse Moorland Papers, Moorland Spingarn Research Center, Howard University, Washington, DC. Anthony (2006) has written a biography of Yergan. See Footnote 1.

Several key events occurred between 1945 and 1948 that had serious ramifications on the future viability of the Council. In the summer of 1945, with the war decided, the Soviet Union reversed its wartime ideological position of moderation and returned to a more traditional Marxist-Leninist dogma that called for class conflict and expansion. During World War II, liberals in the United States had vacillated between supporting the Soviet Union as a heroic bulwark against fascism and condemning it is a brutal utopian dictatorship.[19] In addition, in February 1945, Yergan divorced Susie Wiseman, his wife of more than two decades, and on 21 April, 1945, married Lena Halpern, a wealthy Jewish physician.[20] Oddly, Yergan's biographer David Anthony tells us very little about Halpern beyond mentioning her profession, that she was wealthy, had been a radical, and that she was a travel companion to her husband.[21] Yet, her background is inextricably linked to the turbulent Cold War era. Halpern's father Gustave was born in Warsaw Poland and her mother Annie F. Miller was born in Russia.[22] It is easy to imagine then with the Soviets repressing Jews during their occupation of Poland (1939–1945) that Halpern was alarmed and that she probably expressed her sentiments to her left-leaning husband. In all likelihood, this cruelty was personally visited upon her family, making her deliberate pleas for understanding that more poignant.

In November 1947, acting on the US government's policy of rooting out all communists as enemies of the state, Attorney General Tom Clark identified the highly visible Council as a communist front organization.[23] Shortly thereafter William F. Cochran, Jr. sought Yergan to clear up "one or two matters which have to do with the policy of the Council." Cochran was an affluent Baltimore businessman, a financial backer of the Council, and at one-time a socialist.[24] Cochran also impressed upon Yergan the need to sever ties to communists. Because of the correspondence between Cochran and Yergan, Cochran's influence on Yergan is much easier to trace. Cochran had spoken with Reinhold Niebuhr, a friend and prominent liberal theologian, who apparently convinced him the Soviet Union was a real threat to democracy and freedom.[25] Niebuhr had

---

[19] Discussion of the arguments between liberals and progressives concerning US foreign policy toward the Soviet Union can be found in Footnote 10, 5–7.

[20] Yergan divorced Susie Wiseman in Reno, Nevada on February 27, 1945. Legal discussion concerning Nevada found in Houston to Yergan, January 8, 1945, Yergan, Max, Box 163–14, Charles H. Houston Papers, Moorland Spingarn Research Center, Howard University, Washington, DC. Also see, Marriage Certificate, April 21, 1945, in Marriage Certificate to Lena Halpern, 1946, Box 206–1, Max Yergan Papers, Moorland Spingarn Research Center, Howard University, Washington, DC.

[21] Anthony spent three decades thoroughly researching Yergan, but oddly in his biography of Yergan, he does not delve into the background of his second wife Lena Halpern. His discussion of her can be found in Anthony (2006), 215, 269, 260–61, and 252–54.

[22] Bureau of the Census, United States of America (1900).

[23] Attorney General Clark's indictment found in Lynch (1977), 36.

[24] William Cochran's contributions to the Council can be found in William Cochran to Yergan, November 7, 1942, Cochran, William, Box 206–3, Max Yergan Papers, Moorland Spingarn Research Center, Howard University, Washington, DC. Cochran's biographical information can be found in *Obituary Record of Graduates* (1952), 110. Cochran was the owner and Chairman of Sherwood Forest Company (1910–1950). His parents were affluent, and his family was interested in YMCA work. This may have been how he became connected to Yergan.

[25] William F. Cochran to Reinhold Niebuhr, November 28, 1947. Transcript in Cochran, William, Box 206–3, Max Yergan Papers. Moorland Spingarn Research Center, Howard University, Washington, DC.

visited Europe in 1946 and returned an avowed antitotalitarian liberal. Within a week of Yergan's meeting with Cochran, Yergan informed Cochran that he had moderated the political tone of the *People's Voice*, a radical weekly newspaper, Reverend Adam Clayton Powell had established in 1942, and that he had resigned from the National Negro Congress, a depression era coalition of communists and noncommunist labor leaders who sought to ameliorate labor conditions for African Americans.[26] Powell was the pastor of the famous Abyssinia Baptist Church in Harlem, New York. Still not altogether persuaded by Yergan, Cochran responded that he was "a bit disappointed in what seems to be left out of the statements." Clearly, Cochran wanted Yergan to state explicitly his position relative to the Communists, and he wanted to know "how the Communists" within the Council on African Affairs had responded to his political retreat.[27]

In December, Yergan answered this request with news clippings that left no doubt he was moving away from radicalism. These clippings highlighted the huge fall out between Yergan and Doxey Wilkerson, the former executive editor and general manager of the *People's Voice*, over Yergan bowing to Cold War repression.[28] Wilkerson, Howard University professor and member of the Communist Party, quipped scornfully, "It is not surprising . . . to find during this period [of Cold War reaction] that certain individuals who gained prominence through profitable association with the labor—progressive movement are now finding it more convenient to make their peace with precisely those reactionary political forces they used to struggle against."[29] Several scholars, including myself, to varying degrees have chronicled the infighting that took place within the Council on African Affairs beginning in 1947 that led to its collapse. Yet, the initial influence from Halpern and Cochran that triggered Yergan's retreat was virtually unknown. Until it finally collapsed in 1955, Yergan opposed the Council on African Affairs.[30]

From outside the Council attacks came from liberals within the Vital Center. This was the case in 1949 when Walter White, Executive Director of the NAACP, wrote a newspaper column entitled, "A Reaction to Robeson: Walter White Cautions Denouncers to Think Twice Before Speaking." At the time, Paul Robeson was the leader of the Council and one of the foremost human rights advocates in the world. In the column, White responded to a declaration by Robeson at the Paris Peace Conference that Negroes would not fight the Soviets. White stated that he did not agree with Robeson, but he also explained that Robeson was reacting to racism in the United States. Nevertheless, White also believed that "The overwhelming majority of American Negroes think of themselves as Americans and will respond as other Americans to the call of their country

[26] Yergan to Cochran, November 13, 1947, transcript in Cochran, William, Box 206-3, Max Yergan Papers, Moorland Spingarn Research Center, Howard University, Washington, DC. Also see, Yergan to Cochran, November 25, 1947, transcript in Cochran, William, Box 206-3, Max Yergan Papers, Moorland Spingarn Research Center, Howard University, Washington, DC.

[27] Cochran to Yergan, November 28, 1947, Cochran, William, Box 206-3, Max Yergan Papers, Moorland Spingarn Research Center, Howard University, Washington, DC.

[28] Yergan to Cochran, December 30, 1947, transcript in Cochran, William, Box 206-3, Max Yergan Papers, Moorland Spingarn Research Center, Howard University, Washington, DC. Also see, "People's Voice Policy" (1948), 7.

[29] See Footnote 28.

[30] A good discussion of the collapse of Council can be found in Footnote 6, 141–44.

in time of war," a point that was supported by the fact that African Americans had served valiantly in every major war in which the United States had participated.[31]

Later White joined the government in an effort to undermine Robeson's influence on Africans. In 1951, Foreign Service personnel in the Gold Coast recommended that a prominent African American, who was sympathetic to the government's foreign policy but familiar with the race problem, write an article that would regretfully address Robeson's political views as a "spiritual alienation from his country and the bulk of his own people" and give the impression that Robeson suffered an "illness of the mind and heart" that could not be easily perceived but that was nonetheless dangerous.[32] In February 1951, Walter White wrote an article for *Ebony* with similar content entitled, "The Strange Case of Paul Robeson."[33] In the eighteen months that passed between White's two articles on Robeson, he and the leaders of the NAACP had become convinced that Robeson was going too far, and that he was threatening the push for civil rights at home with his concern for international protest politics. It is apparent that White was an anticommunist liberal who saw civil rights at home as a separate issue than the struggle of independence in Africa, a position that ran counter to that of the Council.[34]

MAX YERGAN: APOLOGIST FOR APARTHEID

Having entirely abandoned the radical anticolonial movement, in May 1952, Yergan appeared before the Senate Internal Security Committee and declared that he never was a member of the Communist Party. Portraying himself to the Senate committee as an unsuspecting victim that communists duped for ten years, he told the committee that he had "let the Communists use his name in some of their organizations in the belief that it would help the Negro people in this country."[35] Yergan also informed the committee that it was to his "everlasting shame" that he had allowed the Council to fall into the hands of communists.[36] Yergan's statements to the Senate committee were obvious attempts to distance himself from his previous associations

---

[31] Walter White, "A Reaction to Robeson: Walter White Cautions Denouncers to Think Twice Before Speaking," Robeson, Paul, General, 1945–53, Box A511, Group II, Library of Congress, Washington, DC. The clipping, dated May 1, 1949, did not contain the name of the newspaper from which it was taken.

[32] See Footnote 6, 127.

[33] In November, another article was published that attempted to discredit Robeson and portray him as a well-meaning but ill-fated traitor to his country and his people, this one appeared in *Crisis Magazine* under the title, "Paul Robeson—The Lost Shepherd." White (1951), 78–84. White also sent a letter and copy of his article to DeWitt Wallace at *Reader's Digest*, a conservative publication, a month before his article actually appeared in *Ebony*. See, Walter White to Wally, January 12, 1951, transcript in Robeson, Paul, General, 1945–1953, Box A511, Group II, NAACP Records, Library of Congress, Washington, DC.

[34] Eslanda Robeson to Walter White, October 16, 1947, transcript in Robeson, Paul, General, 1945–1953, Box A511, Group II, NAACP Records, Library of Congress, Washington, DC. Also, see White's reply, White to Eslanda, October 22, 1947, Robeson, Paul, General, 1945–1953, Box A511, Group II, Library of Congress, Washington, DC.

[35] "Reds Used Me" (1952); also found in Newspaper articles about Yergan, 1952–1958, Box 206–1, Max Yergan Papers, Moorland Spingarn Research Center, Howard University, Washington, DC.

[36] See Footnote 35.

with communists, affirm his patriotism, and at the same time further condemn the Council as being a communist-front organization.

In the summer and fall of 1952, Yergan would emerge as an anticommunist spokesperson who traveled to Ghana, Nigeria, and South Africa to warn Africans about the dangers of communism. Questions remain about who specifically, funded Yergan's trip. African newspapers reported that he was "a consultant to officials in America and to organizations of philanthropic character." He told audiences that he was concerned with issues regarding health, education, agriculture, and economic development. In light of his form radical associations, it seems more probable, however, that Yergan was somehow connected with the government, perhaps the State department, and that he was making a tour to spread American anticommunist propaganda and to shore up America's weak image in Africa on civil rights.[37]

Yergan's statements while he was in Africa lend credence to this argument. In Ghana, he was quoted as having said, "We [Negroes] are proud of America. We believe that we are now moving rapidly towards the solution of our problems." As a former anticolonial radical, his newly discovered optimism hinted at political opportunism, while his discussion of communism was even more telling. Yergan stated, "The desire of Negroes is to find the highest possible place in life of America, and we are approaching this problem through democratic means. The Negroes chose democracy as against totalitarianism." Yergan closed with a plea that sounded a lot like a warning, "the Negro population in America, and I believe all Africans too, should shun communism as they shun poison."[38] Yergan, who had become a poster child of antitotalitarian liberalism, was largely correct that African Americans preferred democracy to communism or any form of totalitarianism. However, African Americans living under the yoke of Jim Crow segregation in the Deep South were in communities that were essentially totalitarian, and his statement concerning how rapidly the United States was moving "towards the solution of our problems" was a huge overstatement of the then status of the nascent modern civil rights movement. It caught the attention of many Africans.

An editorialist in the *West African Pilot* pointed out that Africans "have heard this before." During the dark days of World War II when European overlords told them "to shun Nazism and Fascism as one shuns poison all because at the time we were—all lovers of freedom—engaged in a battle to guarantee freedom." The editorialist asserted that the outcome of the fight for freedom during the war had had a different meaning for Europeans than it did for the sons and daughters of Africa: "For the African, no less the Negro in the United States of America, two world wars have brought no dramatic changes in status." Turning to the not-so-ambiguous hypocrisy in Yergan's opinion that a social revolution in the United States was leading to a rapid solution to the race problem, the editorialist remarked mockingly, "When Dr. Max Yergan extols the jewels of democracy we peep across his shoulders and remind him of 'the folk down South.'"[39]

Yergan's return to South Africa gives a clear indication of how much he had changed from only a few years earlier. His change was in step with many left-leaning liberals who moved out

---

[37] For quotes about Yergan see, "American Negroes Hate Communism" (1952).
[38] See Footnote 38.
[39] "Dr. Yergan and Our Aspirations" (1952).

of the communists and progressive camps and took refuge in the vital center. Yergan would ultimately push through the vital center to the conservative right of the political spectrum becoming one of the first African American neoconservatives. With the Defiance Campaign in full swing and black South Africans being jailed by the hundreds, Yergan returned as a welcome guest of the apartheid government, and he made no attempt to meet with the leaders of the Defiance Campaign. Instead, through the media, he warned them to "beware of communism."[40]

Yergan's behavior in South Africa raised the suspicion of a surprised Nelson Mandela, President of the ANC Youth League and the Volunteer-in-Chief of the Campaign. Mandela stated, "I was struck with the fact that Mr. Yergan made no attempt to meet the Non-European leaders and discuss the defiance campaign with them directly." Ironically, the campaign was the reason Yergan had given for going to South Africa. As Mandela points out, not speaking to the leaders of the movement cast Yergan in a questionable light. His warnings about communism, Mandela lamented, "Sounded far more like the warnings of a United States government spokesman than from a Negro participating in any movement for Negro rights."[41]

It is clear that at this stage Yergan viewed apartheid as a buttress against the spread of communism. To him, the situation in South Africa was an explosive dilemma. Peering through the lens of antitotalitarian liberalism, he could see that apartheid created conditions among the Africans that communists would key on. "The [racist] policy and methods of the government" according to Yergan was to blame for creating an atmosphere among the Africans that the communist could exploit to their advantage. The conclusion was obvious: the South African government needed to reform its race policy.[42]

THE DEFIANCE CAMPAIGN AND THE EMERGENCE OF CENTRIST PROTEST IN THE UNITED STATES

In 1952, members of the civil rights organization Congress of Racial Equality (CORE) learned of the planned mass protest movement then being organized in South Africa. In response, they organized to lend their support.[43] American officials in South Africa received word about the

---

[40] "South African Leaders Blast Max Yergan" (1952).

[41] See Footnote 40. Yergan's papers at the Moorland Spingarn Research Center reveal that Yergan visited with Xuma. See Tentative Schedule, in Trip to Africa, itinerary, 1952, Box 206-1, Max Yergan Papers, Moorland Spingarn Research Center, Howard University, Washington, DC.

[42] Memorandum and Recommendations Based on Visits to Africa in 1952 by A. E. Jolis and Max Yergan, September 19, 1952, Max Yergan in South Africa, n.d., Box 206-5, Max Yergan Papers, Moorland Spingarn Research Center, Howard University, Washington, DC.

[43] Z. K. Matthews discusses planning for the campaign in Matthews to Houser, March 13, 1952, Microfilm Reel 1, Records of the American Committee on Africa, Part 2: Correspondence and Subject Files on South Africa, 1952–1985, Library of Congress, Washington, DC. In February 1951, The Franchise Action Council was formed at a meeting to discuss opposition to the removal of Coloreds from the common voter's roll. Lodge (1983), 40. Lodge refers to the Franchise Action Council as the Franchise Action Committee. However, correspondence announcing the NAC from Sisulu refers to the FAC as the Franchise Action Council. See,

planned protest in December of 1951.[44] A reliable reporter informed them that an "action committee" representing Africans, Indians, and Coloreds was going to recommend that the government be requested "to repeal discriminatory racial legislation" before a specific date in February. If the government did not comply, a demonstration would be held on April 6, the last day of the Van Riebeeck Festival, and on June 26, the campaign would begin in earnest; individuals and small groups would volunteer to violate apartheid legislation.[45] Of course, for its part, the South African government had no intention of changing its racial policies in a way that would weaken them.[46]

At the same time, William Sutherland, an African American peace activist, was visiting Birmingham, England to discuss the Peacemaker Project with British pacifists. While in England, he met Jacob Nhlapo, editor of the South African periodical *The Bantu World*. Nhlapo told Sutherland of the germinating plans for the Defiance Campaign and gave him a list of potential contacts inside South Africa.[47] When Sutherland returned to the United States, he informed George Houser and Bayard Rustin of his meeting in England. He and Rustin were both antitotalitarian liberals.[48] Sutherland, Houser, Rustin, and Farmer represented a new type of leadership in the struggle for South African liberation within the United States. Their backgrounds, not unlike the leaders of the Council on African Affairs, Paul Robeson, W. E. B. Du Bois, William Alphaeus Hunton, Jr., and even the African American missionary Max Yergan, were rooted in the anti-imperialism, antiwar, and peace movements. In addition, however, Sutherland, Houser, and Farmer were Christian ministers who diverged with the CAA leadership most notably, in two important ways: their pacifism and their antitotalitarian stance against communism. The Council was a radical organization similar to the ANC at that time in that it was not fearful of having members who were communists or working with communists.

Sisulu to Houser, March 26, 1952, Microfilm Reel 1, Records of the American Committee on Africa, Part 2: Correspondence and Subject Files on South Africa, 1952–1985, Library of Congress, Washington, DC.
[44] Lodge (1983), 41.
[45] 'JOINT WEEKA No. 50', Foreign Service Despatch 381, 14 December, 1951, transcript in United States Embassy Pretoria, General Records, 1950–1954, Decimals File, 745a.00(W)/12-1451, General Records of the Department of State, Record Group 59, National Archives Building, College Park, MD.
[46] "JOINT WEEKA No. 51," Foreign Service Despatch 393, December 21, 1951, transcript in United States Embassy Pretoria, General Records, 1950–1954, Decimals File, 745a.00(W)/12-2151, General Records of the Department of State, Record Group 59, National Archives Building, College Park, MD.
[47] Sutherland was a pacifist who was imprisoned in 1942 as a conscientious objector to World War II. List of African Contacts given to Sutherland by Nhlapo, n.d., [March 26, 1952], Microfilm Reel 1, Records of the American Committee on Africa, Part 2: Correspondence and Subject Files on South Africa, 1952–1985, Library of Congress, Washington, DC. The complete list included the following persons: Xuma, Moroka, Matthews, D. G. S. Timkulu, G. Pitje, H. G. Mpitso, S. M. Mokitimi, E. E. Mahabane, A. T. Habedi, J. M. Lekgotha, V. Sefora, and A. W. Blaxall. Also see, Biographical sketch of Sutherland found in Sutherland and Meyer (2000), 3, 148.
[48] George Houser, interview by author, May 1, 2003, interview transcript and recording in the possession of the author.

Houser and Rustin decided to form a committee to specifically work with the leaders of the Defiance Campaign. Americans for South African Resistance (AFSAR) initially was an ad-hoc committee within CORE, it eventually established its own identity. The initial inter-racial group consisted of Donald Harrington, Charles Y. Trigg, Roger Baldwin, Norman Thomas, A. Philip Randolph, Conrad Lynn, Rustin, and Houser. Harrington and Trigg served as cochairmen, Houser was secretary, and the others comprised the executive committee.[49] AFSAR had two aims: to bring word of the Campaign to the American public and to raise money for the growing resistance movement in South Africa.[50]

In February, Houser wrote to Manilal Gandhi, the son of Mahatma Gandhi, seeking information about the campaign in South Africa. Gandhi's response was less than encouraging as he felt that the participants lacked the discipline and know how to successfully carry out a passive resistance campaign.[51] In determining whether to enter the campaign, the group examined the ANC closely. Concerns were raised about its militancy, its discipline to carry out a nonviolent campaign, and whether communists had a predominant influence in the organization. It was decided that the Youth Leaguers were militant, but their official policy for the campaign was nonviolent protest. Ultimately, Patrick Duncan, a white South African political activist, sent a letter with a vote of confidence stating that communists did not dominate the ANC although there were communists in the organization. His reassurance satisfied the group.[52]

On April 6, in solidarity with the planned protests in South Africa, AFSAR held its first public meeting at Abyssinian Baptist Church in Harlem. About five hundred people attended the meeting and $200 was raised to send to South Africa. Canada Lee, an African American actor, was one of the keynote speakers. Earlier in the year, Lee had played the leading role in the movie "Cry My Beloved Country," which was filmed in South Africa. He later complained that the South Africans had treated him unfairly. After the meeting, participants formed a motorcade that stretched for several blocks and "circled on down to Park Avenue around 65th St. where at that time the South African

---

[49] George Houser, interview by Charles Johnson, May 1, 2003. In the interview, Houser also mentioned that the following persons participated in AFSAR: A. J. Muste, Walter Offutt, Bill Worthy, and Rayford Logan. Houser (1989, 12) does not mention them as being a part of AFSAR in his book. By March, Houser was already corresponding with Roy Wilkins about AFSAR. George Houser to Roy Wilkins, March 10, 1952, transcript in Africa South Africa General, 1950–1953, Box A7, Group II, NAACP Records, Library of Congress, Washington, DC.

[50] Discussion of Canada Lee can be found in Memoranda of Conversation, February 11, 1952, transcript in United States Department of State, General Records, 1950–1954, Press Reaction Union of South Africa, General Records of the Department of State, Record Group 59, National Archives Building, College Park, MD. Also see, Meeting Notice, Social Action Committee, Community Church of New York, March 24, 1952, Microfilm Reel 1, Records of the American Committee on Africa, Part 2: Correspondence and Subject Files on South Africa, 1952–1985, Library of Congress, Washington, DC.

[51] Houser to Gandhi, February 19, 1952, Microfilm Reel 1, Records of the American Committee on Africa, Part 2: Correspondence and Subject Files on South Africa, 1952–1985, Library of Congress, Washington, DC. Gandhi's response can be found in Gandhi to Houser, March 10, 1952, Microfilm Reel 1, Records of the American Committee on Africa, Part 2: Correspondence and Subject Files on South Africa, 1952–1985, Library of Congress, Washington, DC. Also see, "Press Statement by Mr. Manilal Gandhi," see Footnote 50.

[52] Houser (1989), 13–14.

Consulate was located." Houser acknowledged that having the demonstration on Sunday "was not necessarily the best day because the South African [Consulate] Office was closed." Nevertheless, he and the other members of AFSAR believed their first demonstration was a resounding success.[53]

On June 26, the Defiance Campaign commenced. US diplomats in South Africa reported that a total of 103 blacks had been arrested on the first day of the campaign; Nelson Mandela and Cachalia were among them. Police officials confided in American diplomats that "it was probable that they [black demonstrators] would be charged with more serious offences" than merely disturbing the peace. Press accounts suggested that the government might charge them with "conspiracy to commit public violence" even though, as an US Foreign Service Officers noted, "The violations so far have been conducted in a most orderly manner."[54]

According to estimates by US diplomats, the campaign came to a stop in December 1952. However, during its height from June through December, roughly 8,000 demonstrators were arrested for violating discriminatory laws, signifying a partial success for leaders of the ANC, SAIC, and FAC.[55] The size and duration of the protest, 160 days, garnered considerable attention from the international press, thus informing a larger audience about South Africa's race problems, and American foreign service officers noted that it caused "a measure of political awakening [that] became discernable in sections of the Native population previously lethargic."[56] South African leaders took note of the support it had received from groups in the United States. Walter Sisulu sent a message from the working committee of the ANC expressing "sincere appreciation for the moral and material support" that was being given to the Defiance Campaign.[57] In keeping with its primary foreign policy objective of containing communism, American Foreign Service Officers in South Africa were most concerned with how the "Natives" would choose to express this heightened sense of political awareness. This was evident in their reporting on the campaign.[58]

---

[53] Rev. Adam Clayton Powell was the Pastor of Abyssinia Baptist Church. George Houser, interview by Charles Denton Johnson, May 1, 2003. Also see, Houser to Sisulu, April 11, 1952, Microfilm Reel 1, Records of the American Committee on Africa, Part 2: Correspondence and Subject Files on South Africa, 1952–1985, Library of Congress, Washington, DC.

[54] "JOINT WEEKA NO. 79," Foreign Service Despatch 6, July 3, 1952, American Embassy Pretoria, General Records, 1950–1954; Central Decimal File, 754a.00/7-352, General Records of the Department of State, Record Group 59, National Archives Building, College Park, MD.

[55] NAC is discussed in Sisulu and Cachalia to Houser, June 18, 1952, Microfilm Reel 1, Records of the American Committee on Africa, Part 2: Correspondence and Subject Files on South Africa, 1952–1985, Library of Congress, Washington, DC.

[56] "Government versus Non-Europeans (A Recapitulation)," Foreign Service Despatch 550, June 5, 1953, transcript in United States Embassy Pretoria, General Records, 1950–1954, Decimals File, 745a.00/6-553, General Records of the Department of State, Record Group 59, National Archives Building, College Park, MD.

[57] "Message to the Negro People of the United States of America," September 1952, transcript in ANC Department—Deputy President—Personal Letters, 1952–1954, Box 6, Walter Sisulu Papers, African National Congress Archive, University of Fort Hare Library, Alice, South Africa.

[58] American Foreign Service officers wrote a large number of reports concerning the Defiance Campaign. Some reported that the South African government was using the threat of communism as a justification for repressing

George Houser and other members of AFSAR met with Z. K. Matthews and Reverend Michael Scott, an Anglican priest and pacifist who for many years advocated on behalf of the Africans in South West Africa, for advice concerning a permanent organization to support African liberation in the United States. A couple of weeks after the Defiance Campaign, an initial meeting was called on 16 December, 1952 that included Harrington, Houser, Jack, Rustin, and Scott.[59] At the December meeting, Scott discussed the Africa Bureau, an organization that he and others had organized in July 1952 as a vehicle of "support for lobbyists outside the left and pressure groups." A supporter of sanctions, boycotts, and constitutional redress for the legitimate aspiration of Africans living under colonialism, Scott believed the Africa Bureau could serve as a model for the new organization in the United States. In January, a second meeting was held at the Community Church in Harlem, New York, to continue discussions. Jack was particularly anxious to see the formation of an organization whose focus would be broader than that of AFSAR's. To prevent possible redundancy of effort, the group decided that a survey of the nongovernmental organizations working on African issues was needed. The group identified three key organizations: The International League for the Rights of Man (ILRM), the NAACP, and AFSAR.[60] The ILRM was giving assistance to the African delegations at the United Nations, including legal assistance. The NAACP was publicizing the aims of African student groups in the United States and giving assistance to Reverend Scott.[61] Notably missing from the list was the Council on African Affairs in spite of the fact that it was still actively engaged in the anticolonial movement. By this time, it had no doubt fallen out of favor with the Cold Warriors in the Truman administration and antitotalitarian peace and freedom activists. That it did not receive even a passing reference is a clear indication that the leaders of AFSAR did not view the Council as legitimate a view Houser intimated in our interview.[62]

Houser, Harrington, Rustin, and the other participants realized that AFSAR's base in the pacifist movement was too small to support the much larger effort they envisioned for the new

---

its opponents, the position the opposition held. See Footnote 57. Also see, "Suppression of Communism Act," Foreign Service Despatch 157, June 6, 1952, transcript in American Embassy Cape Town, General Records, 1950–1954, Decimals File, 745a.00/6-652, General Records of the Department of State, Record Group 59, National Archives Building, College Park, MD.

[59] Bayard Rustin to Henry Moon, December 13, 1952, transcript in Africa—Michael Scott, 1952, Box A6, Group II, NAACP Records, Library of Congress, Washington, DC.

[60] Africa Bureau and Michael Scott discussed in Gurney (2000), 129. See also, Rustin to Moon, December 13, 1952, Africa—Michael Scott, 1952, Box A6, Group II, NAACP Records, Library of Congress, Washington, DC.

[61] [Untitled Statement] discussing the group that formed ACOA; statement begins, "A group Meeting at the Community Church," n.d., manuscript in ACOA, 1955, Box A356, Group II, NAACP Records, Library of Congress, Washington, DC. Houser reported that AFSAR turned the money they collected over to Matthews and that he got it to South Africa through channels. He did not state specifically how Matthews was able to send the money back. George Houser, interview by Charles Denton Johnson, May 1, 2003. A report from US diplomats in South Africa indicated that money may have been going through the regular mail. See, "Communist Paper Features American Negro Support for Non-European Day of Protest, April 6," Foreign Service Despatch 69, March 21, 1952, transcript in American Consulate, Cape Town; General Records, 1950–1954, Decimal File, 848A.411/3-2152, General Records of the Department of State, Record Group 59, National Archives Building, College Park, MD.

[62] George Houser, interview by Charles Denton Johnson, May 1, 2003.

organization. Garnering such support in the United States, the group realized was a major challenge. Summary notes from the January meeting lamented that: "There is little indication of serious interest in Africa in the mainstream of America [sic] life, outside representative Negro groups." The group believed that there might be emergent interest in the labor movement in the United States, but the level of that interest was an unknown quantity.[63]

By February, Houser had delineated the types of work in which the new organization would participate and divided the program into four parts: education; service and relief; African students and visitors; and political action. The group believed that educating Americans about the problems in Africa was "a most important aspect of the program" because it would provide a means of growing their base of support, and foundations might be more inclined to contribute to efforts that were educational rather than strictly political. It was therefore necessary for the new organization to produce a bulletin that gave "up-to-the-minute news" concerning African developments. Other means of reaching the public included having national speaker's tours, making regular contributions to newspapers and periodicals, sponsoring workshops, and publishing literature on various aspects of Africa.[64] By service and relief, the group envisioned sending money and perhaps other forms of support to victims of political repression. Other potential services included recruiting technical experts to go to Africa to assist with development and to convince foundations to initiate more development projects in Africa.[65] Education for Africans in the United States was also included as part of the program.[66] Political action included the coordination of activities involving African affairs with Congress and various governmental agencies in Washington, DC, as well as the coordination of action on African issues brought before the UN. The group also envisioned supporting "unofficial African delegates" during their sojourn in New York or Washington as was the case with Matthews and Scott.[67]

In March, the group identified Rev. Dr. Homer Jack, minister of the First Unitarian Church in Evanston, IL, as the potential executive director of the new organization.[68] The group felt that his experience in race relations would be an asset going forward.[69] At the end of March, another meeting was held and a subcommittee including Harrington, Houser, Lynn, and Weiss was selected to draft a statement of purpose. The statement bore a close similarity to that conceived at the February meeting with the exception that three initial areas of program emphasis had dovetailed into two, leaving service and action as the two major areas of emphasis. Structurally,

---

[63] [Untitled Statement] discussing the group that formed ACOA, manuscript in ACOA, 1955, Box A356, Group II, NAACP Records, Library of Congress, Washington, DC.

[64] George Houser to Roger Baldwin, Homer Jack, A. J. Muste, and Walter Offutt, February 2, 1953, transcript in American Committee on Africa, 1953–1955, Box A356, Group II, NAACP Records, Library of Congress, Washington, DC.

[65] See Footnote 64.

[66] See Footnote 64.

[67] See Footnote 64.

[68] Meeting notes, March 10, 1953, transcript in American Committee on Africa, 1955, Box A356, Group II, NAACP Records, Library of Congress, Washington, DC. Houser noted that these minutes were not taken, only a summary of the meeting discussion.

[69] See Footnote 68.

it was to be a membership organization with an executive committee and a national sponsoring committee. The executive committee would set the policy of the organization and the national sponsoring committee would approve the executive committee members. Local groups could affiliate with the national organization and would have representation on the national sponsoring committee, thus giving them a voice in determining policy. The subcommittee also decided that the organization should be supported solely by contributions from "members and friends." Houser was adamant that the organization should not take money with strings attached for fear of losing the autonomy necessary to carry out an effective program.[70] By the time, the group met in mid-May, they had also decided on the American Committee on Africa (ACOA) as the name for the organization. The name reveals the undercurrent of concern Houser and the organizing group had with being associated with the radical left. ACOA was safe from any connection with "groups in bad public repute" because it did not contain the word council, which they believed was too closely identified with "the communist—front Council for African Affairs." Thus, from its inception the ACOA was a "centrist" organization because the organizers were antitotalitarian liberals and fervent anticommunists.[71]

In late June and early July, Houser began sending letters of invitation to perspective executive committee members, while Baldwin and Harrington sent letters seeking financial contributions for the association to individuals with an interest in African affairs.[72] Both letters discussed the nature of the organization's work and named some of the key individuals involved.[73] The group anticipated that the new organization would be officially launched in the fall. In addition to the internal correspondence, Houser mailed a prospectus of the association to activists with an interest in African affairs including the NAACP and the ILRM.[74] Walter White forwarded

[70] Houser to Friend, April 17, 1953, transcript in American Committee on Africa, 1953–1955, Box A356, Group II, NAACP Records, Library of Congress, Washington, DC. Draft of a Statement of Purpose, [April 17, 1953], manuscript in American Committee on Africa, 1953–1955, Box A356, Group II, NAACP Records, Library of Congress, Washington, DC. Statement attached to letter dated April 17, 1953. Also see, Meeting report, May 14, 1953, transcript in American Committee on Africa, 1953–1955, Box A356, Group II, NAACP Records, Library of Congress, Washington, DC.

[71] Memo XII: Choosing a Final Name, n.d., transcript in American Committee on Africa, 1953–1955, Box A356, Group II, NAACP Records, Library of Congress, Washington, DC.

[72] Homer Jack accepted the offer to help organize the ACOA. An interracial-steering committee was formed to assist him; Houser served as the chairman and the other members of the committee included George Carpenter, Maurice Dawkins, Walter Offutt, Fred Riggs, and Peter Weiss. Carpenter was associated with the Africa Committee of the National Council of Churches. Dawkins was a minister at the Community Church along with Harrington. Offutt, also a minister, was connected with the NAACP, and Weiss worked with the International Development Placement Association. See Footnote 71.

[73] See, Houser to Friend, June 26, 1953, transcript in American Committee on Africa, 1953–1954, Box A356, Group II, NAACP Records, Library of Congress, Washington, DC. Roger Baldwin and Donald Harrington to Friend, [July 6, 1953], transcript in American Committee on Africa, 1953–1954, Box A356, Group II, NAACP Records, Library of Congress, Washington, DC.

[74] Homer Jack to Sir, July 10, 1953, transcript in American Committee on Africa, 1953–1954, Box A356, Group II, NAACP Records, Library of Congress, Washington, DC. Also see, Preliminary Prospectus, July 3, 1953, manuscript in American Committee on Africa, 1953–1954, Box A356, Group II, NAACP Records, Library of Congress, Washington, DC.

his copy of the prospectus to a few of his trusted allies. Arthur Spingarn rebuffed the ACOA by responding pessimistically to their prospectus. "I am not favorably impressed with it [the prospectus]," announced Spingarn. The organizers, he admitted, were "largely 'persons of good will'," but he believed they lacked the necessary qualifications for work dealing with Africa. He also repeated the groups' own concern that they represented "too narrow a section of the public." Lastly, he noted that the operating budget they proposed, a minimum of $16,500, "seemed to indicate [they had] little appreciation of the magnitude of the work," which they were about to commence. He therefore recommended that the NAACP should proceed with caution.[75]

During an important meeting in early August, Carpenter submitted an outline of objectives and methods to arouse public interest in Africa and to garner support for the group's agenda. His methods were decidedly moderate, but he hoped they would nevertheless address the concerns that had been raised about the group's narrow base and "command the confidence and support of the largest possible number of people" but without alarming their friends and allies.[76] To avoid government or public reproach, Carpenter suggested that the ACOA be fair and accurate in reporting its findings, that it not identify with any one group or concern in Africa, and that it not commit its members to a specific course of action or to direct action in its own name. Racial tension in the colonial setting, he believed, was best resolved impartially, encouraging harmonious relations between Africans and Europeans. Finally, he felt that to "avoid irresponsible criticism," the association should attempt to understand the "problems" of the colonial powers.[77]

Houser believed Carpenter was beginning to conservative and was highly critical of Carpenter's suggestions. He agreed that the committee needed to be fair and accurate in its reporting, but he thought that it should focus on the victims of colonialism and not on the imperial powers. He also believed the committee should not feel ill at ease about being identified with any African group so long as it was not communist and nonviolent. He was particularly concerned about Carpenter's statement that the committee should "avoid irresponsible criticism." To him, the statement implied that the committee had to "take on the vested interests of other groups," which would directly undermine its ability to act independently. He felt the association's strength was in its autonomy. Finally, Houser stated that the committee should be action-oriented and willing to cooperate with other organizations but that it "shouldn't try to play down the nature of the situation in Africa."[78] Houser knew that Carpenter had gone too

---

[75] Walter White to Ralph Bunche, William Hastie, Rayford Logan, Arthur Spingarn, Channing Tobias, Thurgood Marshall, Henry Moon, and Roy Wilkins, August 5, 1953, transcript in American Committee on Africa, 1953–1954, Box A356, Group II, NAACP Records, Library of Congress, Washington, DC. Arthur Spingarn to Walter White, August 6, 1953, transcript in American Committee on Africa, 1953–1954, Box A356, Group II, NAACP Records, Library of Congress, Washington, DC. Houser's suggestion to contact other groups for their mailing list can be found in Houser to Friend, April 17, 1953, American Committee on Africa, 1953–1955, Box A356, Group II, NAACP Records, Library of Congress, Washington, DC.

[76] George W. Carpenter, A Note on the Function of the American Committee on Africa, August 5, 1953, transcript in American Committee on Africa, 1953–1954, Box A356, Group II, NAACP Records, Library of Congress, Washington, DC.

[77] See Footnote 76.

[78] Thoughts on the American Committee on Africa, n.d., transcript in American Committee on Africa, 1953–1955, Box A356, Group II, NAACP Records, Library of Congress, Washington, DC.

far in attempting to chart a course for the ACOA safe from any possible criticism of its program and had responded forcefully to prevent the committee's agenda from being pushed any further to the conservative right.[79] The membership resolved the issue at the August 13th meeting in Houser's favor by electing not to water down its orientation and voting to "carry on education and action within this context." This was the form and the direction that the American Committee on Africa would take when it began work in 1954 on its way to taking a leading role in the antiapartheid movement in the United States.[80] Nevertheless, the ACOA was positioned safely within the orbit of the Vital Center, which was a significant departure from the radical and uncompromising position of its predecessor the Council on African Affairs.

CONCLUSION

The Cold War diminished the ideological space on the liberal left and fragmented the anticolonial activists into camps. Where they stood with regard to communism was the major fault line between them. Civil rights leaders like Walter White were sympathetic to and even supportive of the international struggle against imperialism, but they privileged the struggle to obtain rights for blacks in the United States over the anticolonial movement. In unpacking White's thinking, it is clear that in an environment of shrinking ideological space—as it was in the United States at that time—where the policy of the government was aggressively hostile to communists and progressives, he believed he had to maneuver the NAACP in a manner that was least likely to bring it into serious conflict with the powerful forces of Cold War reaction.

Conversely, radicals and progressives like Robeson, Hunton, and Du Bois advanced a universal conception of freedom that was uncompromising. They saw apartheid in South Africa and Jim Crow in the United States as cousins, different forms of the same global economic system of exploitation based on race. They believed that the rights of African Americans were tied to the rights of Africans in South Africa, such that their freedom could not be separated. They also linked big capital to big government and openly derided the contradictions in the rhetoric and inaction of the Truman administration on both civil rights at home and human rights abroad.

The Truman administration saw South Africa as a powerful ally against the Soviet Union that gave the United States a strong partner in Africa in spite of its detestable race policies. Racism was the administration's Achilles heel. Jim Crow segregation in the south was an evident reminder to Africans and other people of color that the United States had not solved its own race problems and therefore called into question the legitimacy of its moral authority. Robeson and the Council saw the US strategic alliance with South Africa as an extension of Jim Crow into foreign affairs, a ploy to delay extending rights and freedoms to people of color in both countries, and therefore publicly attacked the government's foreign policy.

---

[79] Although revolutionary could be considered antithetical to nonviolent, Houser believed in the possibility of a nonviolent revolution, where political change could be achieved using nonviolence.

[80] Minutes, August 13, 1953, transcript in American Committee on Africa, 1955, Box A356, Group II, NAACP Records, Library of Congress, Washington, DC. Item misfiled.

In this atmosphere, the Truman administration treated groups and individuals that were not antitotalitarian as dangerous and potentially treasonous. Nonconformity became a justification to investigate, harass, and confine members of the radical left. Max Yergan shifted his allegiance to avoid the falling anvil of Cold War recrimination. Du Bois, Hunton, and Field were not so lucky. Each was arrested during this tumultuous period. Robeson would pay perhaps the greatest price for his courageous commitment to the anticolonial movement, which the antiapartheid movement was such a key component. An international celebrity in the 1930s and 1940s, he would all but vanish in the decades that followed the collapse of the radical left never to regain his former prominence. So great was the damage to his reputation that in the United States he continues to be widely viewed as a treasonous and out of touch malcontent who squandered talent, fame, and fortune. Few people know of the significance of his sacrifice and contribution to the struggle for human rights globally and the South African liberation specifically.

Cochran and Yergan were caught in a rising tide of Cold War reaction and recrimination that truly threatened them perhaps for the first time in their careers as a progressive. However, by 1947, the year Cochran instructs Yergan to tone down his radicalism and to severe ties with communists, Cochran was a septuagenarian and no longer the social romantic he was in his youth. As a young lad in Baltimore, he once sought through the newspaper public advice on how best to dispose of his substantial financial inheritance.[81] Yergan too was older and more pragmatic. He had divorced Susie Wiseman and married Lena Halpern, a wealthy physician with Eastern European ancestry. So Doxie Wilkerson was essentially correct: Yergan had come under the influence of wealthy whites, including his wife, who carried him with them as they exited the radical anticolonial movement. Had he not used this "escape hatch" his fate would have undoubtedly been the same tragic fate suffered by Robeson and other radicals who refused to cave to the government's immense political and social pressure and who consequently were ruined economically and publicly. Yet Yergan would not land in the consensus-seeking Vital Center, as many former radicals would. Instead, he pushed through the Vital Center and alongside George Schuyler became one of the first noted African American neoconservatives. Perhaps Yergan was attempting to compensate for having been radical in the past by becoming ultraconservative.

From his new position, he pursued conservative causes with a similar conviction as he had earlier pursued radical causes. It is tempting to believe that he was truly convinced of the communist threat and that caused him to create a new set of political and social priorities whereby African freedom and even civil rights had to give way to the more pressing issue of communist expansion. But though I argue this explains why he left the radical left and why others moved into the Vital Center, it does not fully explain why he chose to become a radical conservative. It is clear, as Anthony has shown, that he was able to live a lifestyle that afforded him material comfort and privileges not usually extended to blacks during segregation. Perhaps Yergan in his behavior began to reflect the repressed racial sentiments of his former progressive white benefactors who like Cochran had overcome their disillusionment with the status quo and come to terms with their internal contradictions.

---

[81] Cochran's social and political views can be found in, "Wants to Give Away Millions" (1915).

In time, many former progressives who moved into the Vital Center would eventually come to question the foreign policy of the United States, but radicals who called for revolution after the mid-1940s, and increasingly so over time, would be deemed outcasts by those who now found prominence as intellectuals and even as "radical" intellectuals from within the Vital Center. This was plainly evident at the organizing meeting of the ACOA when its leaders sought to distance themselves from the Council.

The ACOA emerged as a new protest organization on the shifting anticolonial landscape. Ironically, for all of the organizer's efforts to dissociate it from the radical left, the framework of its program bore a striking resemblance to that of the Council on African Affairs. Unlike the Council, however, the ACOA was firmly entrenched in the Vital Center and had no intentions of coddling communists. The formation of the ACOA was propitious for the cause of African freedom in the United States because it happened as the CAA was collapsing under tremendous pressure from the US government. When it commenced in 1954, its first initiative was to give financial assistance to Father Trevor Huddleston in South Africa for a school for Africans whose funding the South African government had taken away under the Bantu Education Act.[82]

During this period, the political tenor of protest in the United States shifted from a progressive mode that was willing to directly confront the foreign policy of the United States to a more moderate form that was reified in the formation the ACOA and the protest philosophy of its leaders, who viewed contestation that was left of the Vital Center as outside of the American mainstream and hence illegitimate. This would have serious implications for the future direction of the antiapartheid movement in the United States.

KEY TERMS

African Diaspora
African National Congress
American Committee on Africa
Americans for South African Resistance
Congress of Racial Equality
Council on African Affairs
Defiance Campaign
George Houser
Max Yergan
People's Voice
Paul Robeson
Vital Center
William Cochran

---

[82] Huddleston had sought outside support and the ACOA responded by raising $10,000 for his school in 1954. George Houser, interview by Charles Denton Johnson, May 1, 2003. Discussion of Bantu Education can be found in Lodge (1983), 116–17.